MODERNISM AND RELIGION

Edinburgh Critical Studies in Modernist Culture
Series Editors: Tim Armstrong and Rebecca Beasley

Available

Modernism and Magic: Experiments with Spiritualism, Theosophy and the Occult
Leigh Wilson

Sonic Modernity: Representing Sound in Literature, Culture and the Arts
Sam Halliday

Modernism and the Frankfurt School
Tyrus Miller

Lesbian Modernism: Censorship, Sexuality and Genre Fiction
Elizabeth English

Modern Print Artefacts: Textual Materiality and Literary Value in British Print Culture, 1890–1930s
Patrick Collier

Cheap Modernism: Expanding Markets, Publishers' Series and the Avant-Garde
Lise Jaillant

Portable Modernisms: The Art of Travelling Light
Emily Ridge

Hieroglyphic Modernisms: Writing and New Media in the Twentieth Century
Jesse Schotter

Modernism, Fiction and Mathematics
Nina Engelhardt

Modernist Life Histories: Biological Theory and the Experimental Bildungsroman
Daniel Aureliano Newman

Modernism, Space and the City: Outsiders and Affect in Paris, Vienna, Berlin, and London
Andrew Thacker

Modernism Edited: Marianne Moore and the Dial *Magazine*
Victoria Bazin

Modernism and Time Machines
Charles Tung

Primordial Modernism: Animals, Ideas, Transition (1927–1938)
Cathryn Setz

Modernism and Still Life: Artists, Writers, Dancers
Claudia Tobin

The Modernist Exoskeleton: Insects, War, Literary Form
Rachel Murray

Novel Sensations: Modernist Fiction and the Problem of Qualia
Jon Day

Hotel Modernity: Corporate Space in Literature and Film
Robbie Moore

The Modernist Anthropocene: Nonhuman Life and Planetary Change in James Joyce, Virginia Woolf and Djuna Barnes
Peter Adkins

Asbestos – The Last Modernist Object
Arthur Rose

Visionary Company: Hart Crane and Modernist Periodicals
Francesca Bratton

Modernist War Poetry: Combat Gnosticism and the Sympathetic Imagination, 1914–19
Jamie Wood

Abstraction in Modernism and Modernity: Human and Inhuman
Jeff Wallace

Modernism and Religion: Between Mysticism and Orthodoxy
Jamie Callison

Forthcoming

Modernism and the Idea of Everyday Life
Leena Kore-Schröder

Sexological Modernism: Queer Feminism and Sexual Science
Jana Funke

Modernism, Material Culture and the First World War
Cedric Van Dijck

Reading Modernism's Readers: Virginia Woolf, Psychoanalysis and the Bestseller
Helen Tyson

www.edinburghuniversitypress.com/series/ecsmc

MODERNISM AND RELIGION

Between Mysticism and Orthodoxy

Jamie Callison

EDINBURGH
University Press

Edinburgh University Press is one of the leading university presses in the UK. We publish academic books and journals in our selected subject areas across the humanities and social sciences, combining cutting-edge scholarship with high editorial and production values to produce academic works of lasting importance. For more information visit our website: edinburghuniversitypress.com

© Jamie Callison 2023, 2025 under a Creative Commons Attribution-NonCommercial licence

Edinburgh University Press Ltd
13 Infirmary Street,
Edinburgh, EH1 1LT

First published in hardback by Edinburgh University Press 2023

Typeset in 10/12.5 Adobe Sabon by
IDSUK (DataConnection) Ltd

A CIP record for this book is available from the British Library

ISBN 978 1 4744 5722 4 (hardback)
ISBN 978 1 4744 5723 1 (paperback)
ISBN 978 1 4744 5724 8 (webready PDF)
ISBN 978 1 4744 5725 5 (epub)

The right of Jamie Callison to be identified as the author of this work has been asserted in accordance with the Copyright, Designs and Patents Act 1988, and the Copyright and Related Rights Regulations 2003
(SI No. 2498).

CONTENTS

List of Figures vi
Acknowledgements vii
Series Editors' Preface ix

Introduction: Wavering Orthodoxy 1

1 Mass Distraction: Between Rites and Rights in David Jones 34

2 Spiritual Pathology: Diagnosing T. S. Eliot's Unconscious Christianity 76

3 Reversion Therapy: The Personalism of H.D.'s Return to Religion 122

4 Silent Protest: The Retreat Movement, 1920–45 169

Conclusion: The Distraction of Religious Poetry 196

Bibliography 204
Index 226

FIGURES

2.1	Paul Regnard, *Attitudes Passionnelles Extase*, 1878	80
2.2	Giovanni Lanfranco, *Ecstasy of St Margaret of Cortona*, 1622	81
2.3	Antonio del Pollaiuolo and Piero del Pollaiuolo, *The Martyrdom of Saint Sebastian*, 1475	83
3.1	Seal of the Moravian Church, c. 1870	129
3.2	Seal cast of the Temple, Bristol, c. 1200–1299, impression taken from original seal matrix in Bristol Museum, c. 1850–1915	130
3.3	H. B. Eggert, Central Moravian Church, Bethlehem, decorated for the one-hundredth anniversary of the Society for Propagating the Gospel, c. 1887	132
3.4	H. B. Eggert, sesquicentennial Christmas decorations, Moravian Church, c. 1891	132
3.5	H. B. Eggert, sesquicentennial Christmas celebration, Moravian Sunday schools, Bethlehem, PA, c. 1891	132
3.6	Gustave Doré, 'Moses in the Bulrushes', Exodus 2: 1–10	145
4.1	A suggested timetable for a weekend retreat for beginners	174
4.2	Chapel, House of Mercy, Horbury, Yorkshire	179
4.3	Leiston Abbey ruins, Suffolk, England	180

ACKNOWLEDGEMENTS

The present book began as a doctoral thesis undertaken at the University of Bergen, Norway and the University of Northampton, UK. Thanks to my supervisors: Richard Canning, Erik Tonning and Janet Wilson for their suggestions and encouragement. Over the course of my studies, Christopher Ricks hosted me at the Editorial Institute, Boston University and was very generous with his time. I also benefited from a Research Associateship at the Oxford Centre for Religion & Culture, Regent's Park College, University of Oxford. My doctoral examiners on both sides of the North Sea: Jakob Lothe, Steven Matthews, Bernard O'Donoghue and Rod Rosenquist challenged me in various ways and I have endeavoured to accommodate their insights in reworking the material for publication here. The book has been written in two English departments in Norway: the first at Nord University, Bodø Campus and, secondly, the University of Agder. I have benefited from the input of colleagues and students alike at both institutions.

Over the course of the project, library and archive staff at the Beinecke Rare Book & Manuscript Library, Yale University; the Bodleian Libraries, the University of Oxford; the Booth Family Center for Special Collections, Georgetown University; the British Library; the Houghton Library, Harvard University; the National Library of Wales; Marquette University Special Collections; Nord University Library; and the Cambridge University Libraries advised on, ordered or retrieved countless print volumes and numerous boxes of special collections material. My heartfelt thanks to the librarians for their assistance.

I am grateful, too, to Tim Armstrong and Rebecca Beasley, the series editors of Edinburgh Critical Studies in Modernist Culture for believing in this project and for their insightful comments on my manuscript. The editorial staff at Edinburgh University Press, especially Jackie Jones, Ersev Ersoy and Susannah Butler, guided this work through to publication with diligence and care. The comments from the Press's anonymous reviewers greatly improved this study.

My intellectual debts are too numerous to list, but I owe special thanks to: Thomas Goldpaugh, Suzanne Hobson, Andrew McKendry, Paul Robichaud and the participants and organisers of the London Modernism Seminar.

I thank the Trustees of the David Jones Estate, the Estate of T. S. Eliot and New Directions Publishing on behalf of the H.D. Estate for permitting me to consult or cite archival material.

Publication of *Modernism and Religion: Between Mysticism and Orthodoxy* under a Creative Commons license was made possible by a generous grant from the University of Agder.

Earlier versions of aspects of this book have appeared elsewhere. Elements of the Introduction, Chapter 2 and Chapter 4 appeared in 'Sacred Ground: Orthodoxy, Poetry and Religious Change', in the *Edinburgh Companion to Modernism, Myth and Religion*. They are reproduced here with the permission of Edinburgh University Press. Portions of an earlier version of Chapter 1 appeared in the *Modernist Cultures* article, 'David Jones's "Barbaric-fetish": Frazer and the "Aesthetic Value" of the Liturgy'. Further thanks to Edinburgh University Press for the additional permissions. Parts of an earlier version of Chapter 2 appeared in the *ELH* article 'Dissociating Psychology: Religion, Inspiration and T. S. Eliot's Subliminal Mind'. They are reproduced here with the permission of Johns Hopkins University Press. Preliminary aspects of Chapter 3 appeared in the chapter 'Redefining Marriage in Interwar Britain: Internal Transformation and Personal Sacrifice in the Poetry of H.D.', which was included in *Marriage Discourses: Historical and Literary Perspectives on Gender Inequality and Patriarchic Exploitation*. Thanks to De Gruyter for the permission to reproduce these elements.

I save a final expression of gratitude for my family, Dr Rashi Rohatgi and Jawahar Ignatius Callison, who have lived with this project alongside me – the latter for the whole of his life to this point. Thank you for the love, support and forbearance.

SERIES EDITORS' PREFACE

This series of monographs on selected topics in modernism is designed to reflect and extend the range of new work in modernist studies. The studies in the series aim for a breadth of scope and for an expanded sense of the canon of modernism, rather than focusing on individual authors. Literary texts will be considered in terms of contexts including recent cultural histories (modernism and magic; sonic modernity; media studies) and topics of theoretical interest (the everyday; postmodernism; the Frankfurt School); but the series will also re-consider more familiar routes into modernism (modernism and gender; sexuality; politics). The works published will be attentive to the various cultural, intellectual and historical contexts of British, American and European modernisms, and to inter-disciplinary possibilities within modernism, including performance and the visual and plastic arts.

Tim Armstrong and Rebecca Beasley

> *but my mind (yours)*
> *has its peculiar ego-centric*
>
> *personal approach*
> *to the eternal realities,*
>
> *and differs from every other*
> *in minute particulars.*
>
> H.D., *The Walls Do Not Fall*, 1944

That is the advantage of a coherent traditional system of dogma and morals like the Catholic: it stands apart, for understanding and assent even without belief, from the single individual who propounds it.

T. S. Eliot, *Dante*, 1929

INTRODUCTION: WAVERING ORTHODOXY

'I loathe the word mystic – it might mean anything', the modernist artist and poet David Jones, writing to a friend in 1927, opined.[1] He was clarifying his religious views and distancing his own work from the phenomenon. Coming from a practising Roman Catholic, Jones's statement might well appear odd, given that he had encountered the lives or writings of revered mystics such as Dionysius the Areopagite, Julian of Norwich and Catherine of Genoa. He worshipped in a church that counted numerous mystics among its saints and doctors and celebrated them in its liturgical calendar. Far from meaning 'anything', mysticism was – Jones might well have told himself – exemplified by such luminaries.

Jones's exasperation points to a shift in the term's usage. By the late nineteenth century, mysticism had decoupled from what Amy Hollywood calls the 'specifically Christian context' from which it initially arose.[2] Alex Owen has observed that 'the terms mysticism and mystical revival' referred to one of 'the most remarked trends' of the 1890s: the widespread emergence of a new esoteric spirituality and a proliferation of spiritual groups and identities that together constituted what contemporaries called the new 'spiritual movement of the age'.[3] Jones might well have worried that the label misrepresented his commitments. Yes, Catholics had their own mystics, but had they now been replaced by new figures who had little in common with those celebrated on feast days? More worrying still, had, as modernists such as Ezra Pound and H.D. claimed, this 'new esoteric spiritualty' always been a subterranean presence in Christianity, obscured by accumulated layers of tradition and the ongoing role of political suppression?[4] Was this 'spiritual movement' a hermeneutic lens through which aspects of the Christian tradition could be seen or seen again in ways more congenial to the modern age? Such questions informed Jones's disinclination to engage with mysticism, despite the willingness of commentators to designate him 'a visionary and a mystic'.[5]

Jones was an amateur commentator on the subject and perhaps unsurprisingly struggled with the term, but the word *mysticism* strained even bestselling authors on the subject. Evelyn Underhill's *Mysticism: A Study of the Nature and Development of Man's Spiritual Consciousness* was first published in 1911 and went through twelve editions between its initial publication and 1930.[6] A new preface to the twelfth edition, written nearly twenty years after the book first went to press, asserted that mysticism must be 'embodied' in 'history, dogma and institutions if it is to reach the sense-conditioned human mind'.[7] She went on to describe as 'false' the supposed 'antithesis' between the religions of 'authority' and 'spirit' or 'Church' and 'mystic' and to claim instead that each term required 'the other'.[8] A mysticism 'embodied' in 'history, dogma and institutions' jars with Owen's notion of a 'new esoteric spirituality'. Esoteric groups such as the Hermetic Order of the Golden Dawn had developed a rich and varied ritual life, so they did not resist embodiment altogether; they, too, had their own history and institutions. They nevertheless operated in defiance of, or in opposition to, the 'dogma' with which Underhill leads.[9] The apparent breadth and openness to which Underhill lays claim cuts across the field of mysticism, erecting borders and boundaries around what might be considered true mysticism. Underhill's understanding of the reciprocity between the institutional and the mystical came to her through her spiritual director, Friedrich von Hügel, whose study *The Mystical Element of Religion* situated his titular element alongside two more: the institutional and the rational.[10] A healthy personal religion, Hügel contended, required 'the harmonious blending of the three elements'.[11] In Underhill's mature thought, the accretion of religious tradition served as a bulwark against the fluid, free-flowing, unchurched mysticism that so unsettled Jones.

Making the matter more complex still, *Mysticism*, the study to which Underhill's preface was attached, in fact emphasises the antithesis between churches and the mystic. Her views changed between the first and the twelfth edition and the later preface misrepresents the study that it introduces. The volume reconstructs a mystic's progress through the stages of purgation, illumination and final union with God, using the psychological terminology Underhill discovered in William James's *The Varieties of Religious Experience*.[12] Underhill's *Mysticism* attends to the 'rearrangement of the psychic self' through the mystical journey and examines how the emergence of the 'spark of the soul', a term taken from the medieval mystic Meister Eckhart and which Underhill locates in the subconscious mind, reorientated a mystic's life.[13] In its focus on personal development and resistance to 'history, dogma and institutions', Underhill's study attended, as Grace Jantzen has noted, to 'themes that are standard in women's spirituality today: the interconnectedness of all things, the importance of looking for God within, the necessity of making the connections and allowing for spaciousness of thought and love'.[14] The Underhill of 1911 takes her place among the 'range of spiritual alternatives to religious orthodoxy that sprang up in the 1880s and 1890s and gained momentum and prominence as the old century gave way to the new'.[15]

While the differences between the two pieces of writing can be attributed to the twists and turns inevitable in any personal narrative, the present study contends that the clashes between church and mystic, authority and spirit, tradition and idiosyncrasy are more than a personal quirk. The tension animates, I argue, the poetry of Jones, T. S. Eliot, H.D. and much early twentieth-century religious culture, most clearly in the tensions evident in the transatlantic retreat movement investigated in the final chapter. The growing prominence of mysticism in modernist writing is reflected in shifts captured by the sociology of religion. Robert N. Bellah observed that the 'apprehension that faith is deeply embedded in man's existential situation and a part of the very structure of his experience' became 'an insistent note in twentieth-century religion'.[16] The emergence of a new mysticism marked one possible route to Bellah's endpoint; for modernism, given its long association with streams of consciousness, what Bellah calls the 'internalization' of religious authority resonates.[17]

The present study nevertheless argues that the aforementioned sociological process was incomplete during the first half of the twentieth century. The religious ideas of Jones, Eliot and H.D. often challenge what Charles Taylor describes in *A Secular Age* as the 'buffered self' and the political programme of liberal individualism to which it was tied.[18] The incomplete forms of sociological change outlined here provide a way of understanding hybrid works such as *The Anathemata*, *Four Quartets* and *Trilogy*. An awareness of the religious and social context that shaped forms of modernism enables readers to appreciate the shifts in tone and mechanical construction that characterise the aforementioned poems, where the various parts of a poetic sequence grind against each other. The concern with religious change at a societal level to which the present study attends replaces the emphasis upon biography in accounts of modernists and their religion, which have typically focused on authors' spiritual journeys as a matter of personal choice or individual circumstance. Before the present study attends to these poets in subsequent chapters, this introduction teases out, first, the forces that brought mysticism to cultural prominence in the age of modernism; and, secondly, to the influence the new mysticism exerted on the Christian churches as they reimagined themselves for the modern era.

Shaping the Secular

New Experiences: Redescribing Religion

The prominence of psychological models in both James's *The Varieties of Religious Experience* and Underhill's *Mysticism* reveals the outlines of the new mysticism about which Underhill would subsequently demur. In early twentieth-century Roman Catholicism of the kind Jones knew, mysticism often described a whole complex of visions and bodily manifestations that revealed the sufferer's special relationship with God.[19] Through their vicarious suffering, these mystics endured pain for the benefit of all.[20] The significance of feeling, touching and seeing God's presence in a mystic's body drew from, and gave support to, the sacramental concerns of Roman Catholic theology. Underhill and James, by contrast, offered a mysticism based upon the idiosyncratic insights of an individual subject. Summarising James's approach in 1912, the philosopher Josiah Royce explained that, for his Harvard colleague, mystical experience occurred when something 'wells up from the subliminal self, from the soundless depths of our own subconsciousness'.[21] In *The Varieties of Religious Experience*, mysticism is recognised by means of four distinctive marks: its ineffability insofar as the experience is difficult to describe; a noetic quality through which knowledge is communicated; its transience as evident in the short-lived nature of the experience; and the passivity of the subject to whom the experience happens.[22] A mystic, in James's reading, is one who enjoys these often unlooked for experiences. While they may confer insight, mystical encounters bearing these marks cannot be binding for anyone other than the mystic subjects themselves.

The early Underhill replaced James's emphasis on the disruptive, unexpected quality of religious experiences with the established topography of a religious journey.[23] While still making use of the subconscious and even exhibiting characteristics recognisable from James's schema, the mystical experience of purgation is, Underhill explains, different from that of union; one must have travelled through the former to reach the latter. Mystics are not merely subject to experiences of varying intensity, but rather develop at different rates through the requisite spiritual stages. William B. Parsons differentiates between the 'mystical *experience*' that interested James and the 'mystical *process*' that shaped Underhill's study.[24] The mystical process 'expands the episodic' mystical experience; it finds 'the latter's meaning in the context of the course of a religious life and in the cultivation of various dispositions, capacities, virtues, and levels of consciousness'.[25]

Psychological language works hard in both James and Underhill. Redescription of religion enables a focus on individuals, free from the dogmatic constraints, moral expectation or community standards of an institutional religion; it effects what Jeffrey J. Kripal calls the 'transit of the sacred out of a traditional religious register and into a new scientific one'.[26] Yes, Underhill makes use of the traditional triad of purgation, illumination and union in her reconstruction of the mystic life, but these stages are the means through which she describes the influence of the newly identified subliminal mind.[27] A new dimension of human consciousness – the channel through which James expected that God would act, should God choose to intervene in human life – becomes the staging ground for a confrontation with an otherworldly presence.[28] The subliminal mind staves off the threat posed by divine intervention depicted as an external authority that curtails freedom of thought. The power of what James calls 'uprushes' or 'irruptions' from a hidden part of the mind is nevertheless so overwhelming that it feels as if an external force has taken control, vital for the mark of passivity requisite for mysticism in *The Varieties of Religious Experience*.[29] A productive ambiguity thus informs James and Underhill's understanding of the source of mysticism; it comes simultaneously from within and without the subject.

The equilibrium between internal and external nevertheless remained difficult to maintain. Underhill's mysticism often sounds akin to a form of self-actualisation insofar as it assumes 'the existence of a discoverable "real", a spark of true being, within the seeking subject'.[30] Through a programme of psychic training, her mystic accesses otherwise hidden powers. The yearning for union with a transcendent God is obscured in her revision of the mystic's spiritual struggles. In James's understanding of religion as *'the feelings, acts, and experiences of individual men in their solitude, so far as they apprehend themselves to stand in relation to whatever they may consider the divine'* there is a danger, too, that the experiences to which he attends might well be construed as the proper site of religion, rather than merely a scientific redescription of what religious institutions had long articulated.[31] The possibility of a relationship with *'whatever'* one *'may consider divine'* fades into the background and a hunger for intense states takes its place. Comparable desires among would-be mystics for spiritual 'consolations' from God are often fiercely criticised in well-known mystical accounts.[32] James and Underhill thus relied upon a recent innovation in psychology to assure themselves of the noetic quality of their mystical experiences and to avoid an overemphasis on intense feeling. For those inattentive to, or unconvinced by, Myers's and James's psychological model that distinction falls away.

While enjoying a special place in James's thinking, mysticism was not his sole concern. A range of religious engagements was central to a science of religion where 'religious experience' would serve 'as an object of study' and function as 'a generic "something" that informed "religion-in-general" apart from any tradition in particular'.[33] Unlike spiritual seekers, James was uninterested in separating churches and mystics. He had no wish to create an alternative religion based on experience rather than dogma. He argued that a scientific study of religion should attend to the experiences of religious believers apart from what religious institutions might say about religion. By means of a redescription that even a thoroughgoing materialist could countenance, James aimed to ensure that religion could retain a place in public debate increasingly dominated by the sciences.[34] People of various religious commitments and none could ultimately discuss religion from the same starting point: the experience of individuals of and with what they consider divine, setting aside the status of the divine itself.

While he conceived of his scientific project as independent of the churches, James's work was facilitated by broader shifts in Protestant theology. In his intellectual history of experience, Martin Jay notes two lines of development going back to the late eighteenth century. First, Immanuel Kant 'turned to the power of what he called practical reason, the categorical imperatives of morality' to provide a 'viable ground of religion'.[35] Kant steered a course between forms of religion connected to speculative reason on the one hand and to irrational enthusiasm on the other. In doing so, he effected an 'elevation of moral obligation over other possible forms of religious experience', a move that, Jay notes, helped shape nineteenth-century Protestant theology.[36] Hastings Rashdall, an Anglican modernist thinker with whom Eliot grappled in an early highly critical review, continued to apply Kantian concerns in the twentieth century, challenging the emphasis placed on dogma and ritual by Anglo-Catholics and arguing that a focus on ethics best equipped Anglicanism to respond to the challenges of modernity.[37]

The prominence of moral obligation in religious thought is of particular interest to the study of religion and literature because it underwrites Matthew Arnold's famous contention that 'most of what now passes with us for religion and philosophy will be replaced by poetry'.[38] Arnold's prediction rested on an account of the origins of religion, which, he argued, could be traced to the personal satisfaction taken in righteous '*conduct*':

> As he had developed his idea of God from personal experience, Israel knew what we, who have developed our ideas from his words about it, so often are ignorant of: that his words were but *thrown out* at a vast object of consciousness, which he could not fully grasp, and which he apprehended clearly by one point alone, – that it made for the great concern of life, *conduct*.[39]

'God', for Arnold, expresses satisfaction at having acted well, serving the community rather than merely fulfilling one's own desires. Practising such behaviour at any scale requires social and emotional infrastructure outside the direct control of the individual subject. In time, the framework itself comes to be labelled 'God'. As religions aged, scripture, dogma and theology were produced to encourage such conduct. The intellectual system that reinforces the social code is what Arnold called *'extra-belief'* or *'Aberglaube'* (meaning 'superstition' in German).[40] Believing that traditional forms of extra-belief no longer offered such inspiration, Arnold looked to poetry to fill the gap in promoting right conduct.

Jay's other line of development was a reaction to, rather than a continuation of, Kant's thought. The German theologian and hermeneutician Friedrich Schleiermacher 'stressed the importance of something called *Leben*, or "life", against the mortifying implications of excessive ratiocination, impersonal legalism, and mechanical causality'.[41] Where Kant turned to moral obligation, Schleiermacher, inspired by romantic poetry, emphasised the insights afforded by intense emotion, famously defining Christian faith as neither intellectual assent to dogma nor adherence to ethical principles, but rather 'the feeling of absolute dependence' on God.[42] Schleiermacher's assertion could have been taken from *The Varieties of Religious Experience* and critics have speculated at length on James's knowledge of Schleiermacher's work.[43] Whether or not he read him directly, James encountered Schleiermacher's influence via his impact on, for example, liberal Protestant biblical scholarship through the nineteenth century. The influence of Schleiermacher led Adolf von Harnack and Auguste Sabatier, both figures cited in *The Varieties of Religious Experience*, to attend to the Bible's account of Christ's relationship with God the Father, his consciousness of the Kingdom of God, and to construe the subsequent development of Christian tradition as a corruption of the founding familial relationship.[44]

Figures like von Harnack and Sabatier also shared with James a conception of religious origins. In *The Varieties of Religious Experience*, James opined that most religious traditions owe their inception to a 'pattern-setter' who exhibited an active subliminal mind and an ability to awaken comparable impulses among acolytes.[45] Following the founder's death, the initial intensity of a movement faded as the cult became institutionalised, opening the door for subsequent movements of reform.[46] Such thinking informed not only the binaries of authority and spirit outlined by Underhill in her 1930 preface, but also what Pericles Lewis has described as the assumption among modernists that 'modern religious life resembles primitive (or pagan) feeling and that the twentieth century inaugurates a return to the essence of religion after the false refinements of the nineteenth century'.[47] Pablo Picasso's oil painting *The Young Ladies of Avignon*, completed in 1907, Igor Stravinsky's ballet *The Rite of Spring*, debuted in 1913, and Eliot's poem *The Waste Land*, published in 1922, not to mention a host of ancillary texts by figures including Jane Harrison and Lucien Lévy-Bruhl, reflect religious interests often associated with primitivism, but on the basis of the James-Schleiermacher connection they appear to owe as much to post-romantic theology. The 'return to the essence of religion' was a theme with which James himself grappled in his Gifford lectures.[48]

Spilt Mysticism: Challenging the Churches

The scientific redescription of religion in terms of experience could not be the neutral, value-free undertaking that James had hoped. The popularity of *The Varieties of Religious Experience* and the complications of the aforementioned intellectual history meant that James's specific intervention, the study of religious experience as a complement to what religious institutions said about their respective traditions, was often neglected. The potential of and for religious experience freed from the constraints of institutional religion enthralled.

Religious experience thus became a rival and not a complement to institutional religion. In *Myth and Miracle: An Essay on the Mystic Symbolism of Shakespeare*, published in 1929, G. Wilson Knight, a literary critic and committed spiritualist, identified a 'universal rhythm of the spirit of man' that elucidated William Shakespeare's *oeuvre*; it tracked the 'progress from spiritual pain and despairing thought through stoic acceptance to a serene and mystic joy'.[49] Knight's programme developed from reading James's lecture topics as sequential stages in a spiritual journey through the sick soul ('spiritual pain and despairing thought'), unification of the divided self and saintliness ('stoic acceptance') and into mysticism ('mystic joy').[50] Knight reorganised James's lectures into an overarching mystical process. *Sick soul, divided self, saintliness* and *mysticism* are no longer labels for different forms of religious experience; progression through these stages constitutes a spiritual vision otherwise obscured by the partiality of religious traditions. James intended to redescribe religion in terms acceptable to those engaged in secular debate. Writing from within a liberal arts tradition, he had no wish to replace the divinity school; both approaches, he felt, could discuss religions in their respective fora and with their own self-selecting audiences. Yet the separation did not hold. James's redescription undermined the self-understanding of institutional religions. Knight's 'universal rhythm' and related concepts become alternative religions, accessed through literature rather than ministry.

Mysticism was thus reshaped. Martin C. D'Arcy, a philosopher, Jesuit priest and Master of Campion Hall, Oxford, traced extensive confusion in contemporary uses of 'mysticism'. It seemed, he thought, 'to gather together under one heading the strongly-felt beliefs of the churchgoer, the emotions felt by sensitive souls in the presence of sublime natural beauty, vivid and passionate faith, and the mystic states of such diverse persons as St. Plotinus, Francis of Assisi, Shelley, Blake and St. John of the Cross'.[51] Within the Roman Catholic tradition, D'Arcy clarified, one was unlikely ever to meet a mystic; Jones, too, considered mysticism '*only the vocation of the few*'.[52] For D'Arcy, mystics were 'rare souls who have undergone a long religious discipline, a dark night of the soul, before they have emerged on the shining plateaux where they have experimental union with God'.[53]

In the wake of James, mysticism became a catch-all for every aspect of religion that was not neo-scholastic theology. Throughout the present study, this broadened and expanded sense of mysticism is termed 'spilt mysticism'. The phrase invokes T. E. Hulme's description of romanticism as a form of 'spilt religion':

> You don't believe in a God, so you begin to believe that man is a god. You don't believe in Heaven, so you begin to believe in a heaven on earth. [. . .] The concepts that are right and proper in their own sphere are spread over, and so mess up, falsify and blur the clear outlines of human experience.[54]

Belief in a transcendent God is far removed from the celebration of immanence associated with 'man is a god', but the revisionary concept uses the same term. Jones struggled with something similar in his complaint that the term *mysticism* 'might mean anything'.[55] For Hulme, strategic redescription of political projects in religious terms cloaked the liberal celebration of progress in messianism. 'Spilt mysticism' acknowledges that the confusion Hulme identified affected not only liberal intellectuals looking for alternatives to traditional religions but also practitioners of specific faiths. D'Arcy bemoaned the fact that any aspect of religious life invoking deep emotions could be labelled mystical, when mysticism once referred to a circumscribed and rare phenomenon. The Roman Catholic Church enjoyed a rich liturgical tradition, a powerful artistic legacy and a sacramental outlook, all of which provided the potential for emotional engagement with tradition that circumvented the language of mysticism. The redescription inherent in 'spilt mysticism' flattened hierarchies of value, so that a momentary intuition demanded equal or even greater attention than the entire body of Christian revelation. The apparent accessibility of experience dispensed with hermeneutics. D'Arcy, for his part, wanted to restore some nuance; he insisted that not all religion was mystical.

D'Arcy's Anglican contemporary, William Inge, the future Gloomy Dean of St Paul's, took a different approach. He urged his contemporaries to re-make institutional religion after the newfound emphasis on experience. He observed:

> The strongest wish of a vast number of earnest men and women today is for a basis of religious belief which shall rest, not upon tradition or external authority or historical evidence, but upon the ascertainable facts of human experience. The craving for *immediacy* which we have seen to be characteristic of all mysticism, now takes the form of a desire to establish the validity of the God-consciousness as a normal part of the healthy inner life.[56]

For Inge, figures such as Knight were not merely mistaken about mysticism. They surveyed instead a changed religious landscape. Anticipating later sociologists of religion, Inge described a shift in religious attention and practice. New forms of religious engagement are shaped by science. 'God-consciousness' and a 'healthy' inner life redescribe religious life once marked by prayer, upright living and love of God and the neighbour. *The Varieties of Religious Experience* does not provide a complement to the self-understanding of the mission of the churches; it transforms those understandings altogether. The Church of England, for example, is no longer, as described in *The Thirty-Nine Articles*, the 'visible Church of Christ', striving to preach the 'pure Word of God' and minister the sacraments 'according to Christ's Ordinance', so much as a setting where the subliminal minds of congregants can be nurtured and strengthened.[57]

The redescriptive aspects of 'spilt mysticism' are a prominent feature of the secular sphere. Contrary to popular assumptions, secularism does not confine itself to the neutrality in matters of religion to which it lays claim publicly. It 'entails', as Saba Mahmood explains, 'the reordering and remaking of religious life and interconfessional relations in accord with specific norms, themselves foreign to the life of the religions and peoples it organises'.[58] Taylor's *A Secular Age* shows at great length how the growth of the secular was characterised by not the 'subtraction story' of a withdrawal of religious voices from the public realm, so much as the replacement of one worldview with another.[59] In Taylor's account, the secular outlook is defined by the 'buffered self' whereby individuals are closed off from the world in their own interiority and non-porous in their relationships with the world outside themselves, and the 'immanent frame', through which goods and values that had once been arranged hierarchically become immediately accessible.[60] In concerning themselves with mysticism, Underhill, James, Knight, D'Arcy and Inge are not promoting the *secular* in the conventional sense of 'belonging to the present or visible world as distinguished from the eternal or spiritual world' (*OED* 3a). They saw themselves as concerned with quite the opposite. Yet their collected concerns witness to a redeployment of terminology at odds with conventional religious understandings. D'Arcy's frustration with the contemporary usage of mysticism registers a seismic shift in the religious landscape, shaken by the influence of secular thinking.

Literature was central to the development of what I have termed 'spilt mysticism' and the redescription of religious life. Among modernists, May Sinclair, Vita Sackville-West and Rebecca West all wrote studies of mystics or mysticism.[61] Shakespeare, in Knight's example, reveals what the churches obscure. Shelley and Blake likewise appear on D'Arcy's list of mystics. Inge would subsequently include essays on William Wordsworth and Robert Browning in his 1907 volume *Studies of English Mystics*.[62] Creative literature incorporates a broad range of experiences in a way that a catechism does not. Poets, exploring the emotional and ethical quandaries of the lyric 'I', speak to new spiritual concerns in ways that a minister expounding the Bible or warning about sin could not. The contrast between the adventurous lives of bohemian writers, on the one hand, and the conventionality or asceticism of those of the clergy, on the other, is striking. Great writing about experience is a product of a broad experience that a writer has a professional obligation to pursue. Ministers struggled to keep up.

Continuing a trend initiated by figures such as Inge, the modernist epiphany became a focal point for the religious transference associated with Hulme's 'spilt religion'.[63] Epiphanies are 'moments of imaginative or poetic intensity', one commentator observes, 'comparable in imaginative power to traditional theophanies or appearances of the divine'.[64] The epiphany is not merely a spur to ethical action as Arnold would have maintained; it represents instead a new form of revelation located in the heart of everyday experience. M. H. Abrams traced the antecedents of epiphany back to romantic poetry and the nexus of concerns that surrounded Schleiermacher. Abrams was particularly drawn to Wordsworth's early work, which, he argued, included 'encounters when a natural or human object unexpectedly shows forth a meaning beyond propositional statement'.[65] These moments, in Abrams's reading, were later reorientated by James Joyce, effecting a 'systematic translation of religious formulas into a comprehensive aesthetic theory, in which the artist, or artificer, undertakes to redeem both life and the world by recreating them into a new world'.[66] For Abrams, Wordsworth's poetry interrogates religious experience, recording not subliminal uprushes but rather a material spirituality whereby objects reveal non-propositional knowledge. Visionaries such as Wordsworth might enjoy these experiences while roaming the countryside, but it is in poetry that they are communicated and from which the reader, too, can learn. Modernism marks a falling away from Wordsworth's lofty concerns. Joyce attends to not the spiritual fullness of the everyday world, but rather the possibilities of his own art upon which he confers the ability to 'redeem both life and the world'.[67]

While Wordsworth made art out of religious experience, Joyce reworked aesthetics into religious experience, creating what Virginia Woolf termed his 'spiritual' style.[68] Abrams's reading of modernism is shaped by Clement Greenberg's influential understanding of the avant-garde as 'the imitation of imitating' where modernist poetry, for example, is 'centered on the effort to create poetry and on the "moments" themselves of poetic conversion, rather than on experience to be converted into poetry'.[69] Greenberg's recourse to a spiritual register in 'conversion' and 'converted' connects the self-referentially of the avant-garde to the secular relegation of religion to the private sphere. While for Abrams and Greenberg the shift from Wordsworth to Joyce is decisive, the modernist reworking of romantic insights within broader constructions of the secular is best understood as an act of fine tuning.[70] The most striking change associated with the epiphany is the turn away from the heavens, ministers and scripture in the search for religious insight along with a corresponding and newfound reliance upon literary texts.

Orthodox Moves: Christian Responses

The twentieth century's newfound fascination with mysticism coexisted with a self-consciously traditional version of what Eliot, G. K. Chesterton and, later, Mary Butts called Christian 'orthodoxy'.[71] Eliot insisted that *'personality becomes a thing of alarming importance'* when 'morals cease to be a matter of tradition and orthodoxy' and everyone is able to 'elaborate' their own.[72] Butts enthusiastically welcomed Eliot's orthodoxy.[73] Chesterton claimed that 'democracy and the self-renewing energies of the west' are found 'in the old theology'; if we want 'reform', he opined, 'we must adhere to orthodoxy'.[74] For these figures, orthodoxy incorporated a worldview that insisted on mediation rather than directness; the communal over the individualistic; and the traditional rather than the idiosyncratic. Orthodoxy becomes what Andrzej Gasiorek and Stephen Schloesser have termed a form antimodernism.[75]

Orthodoxy valorised Christian integralism or the idea that economic, political and social organisation should be shaped by religious principles. James Chappel explains that the 'central fact of Catholic intellectual life in the 1920s' throughout continental Europe was 'a sweeping rejection of the modern world of church-state separation, capitalist economies, liberal democracy and the nation-state'.[76] As a result, Catholic intellectuals 'idealized the Middle Ages as an era of political and economic virtue'.[77] In his 1927 Clark Lectures, Eliot concurred, presenting Dante's work as a perfect synthesis of thought and feeling, adding a psychological acuity to the virtues of medievalism.[78] At other times, social thinkers held up sixteenth-century England as a model to be imitated. For L. C. Knights, writing in *Scrutiny*, 'the economic organization from which the bulk of Elizabethan social morality derived was that of the small, local community *in which "human problems can be truly perceived"* – an organization, then, that was not merely "economic" – not merely determined by "economic" motives'.[79] By virtue of its systematic status, orthodoxy tames the dangerous forces of modernity. It integrates and orders other spheres of activity, standing in opposition to Taylor's non-hierarchical 'immanent frame'.

'Spilt mysticism' excludes the systemisation of orthodoxy, invoking the individualisation that religious antimodernism hoped to curtail. For the writers included in the present study, however, both mysticism and orthodoxy commanded attention. Eliot, Jones and H.D. were simultaneously captivated by new forms of spiritual practice and drawn to the reassertion of traditional Christianity. The frenetic oscillation between the religions of authority and of the spirit produces what I call a 'wavering orthodoxy'. This phenomenon informs the mixed register and uneven tone of the poetry discussed here. It is visible, too, in the rise of the retreat movement. Given its extolling of silence and withdrawal, retreat was often taken as a reappearance of medieval monasticism. Yet its focus on interior states also made it amenable to Inge, James and Underhill. The present study looks at how modernist poetry was pulled in these two opposing directions.

Variations on *Varieties*: Critiquing William James

So described, the religious sphere appears hopelessly divided: the new mysticism with its emphasis on the direct, the fragmentary and the individualistic on the one hand, and orthodoxy with its concern for the communal, mediatory and the systemic on the other. Scholarship on modernism and religion often identifies with one or the other; the former typically cast as a modernising force, while the latter is equated with the fringe views of a small number of reactionaries. Rachel Blau DuPlessis, for instance, considers Eliot's 'efforts as a Christian apologist' to be 'devoted to articulating and inspiring adhesion to a renewed "complex" under the aegis of Anglicanism', while Jason Harding speaks of Eliot's 'brand of reactionary Anglicanism'.[80] Elizabeth Anderson, too, sees Eliot subordinating his art to the 'demands of doctrine', contrasting his approach unfavourably with the 'religious syncretism' of H.D.[81] The present work, however, argues that the study of modernism and religion should be equated not with any one form of religion, but rather with the religious change reflected in 'spilt mysticism' and 'wavering orthodoxy'. The peculiarities of secular constructions of religion were identified by commentators in the age of modernism itself. The following section attends to two such critiques: one by the philosopher Royce, the other by Hügel, the Catholic modernist, that invoke aspects of orthodoxy to criticise the new mysticism, while nevertheless remaining broadly sympathetic to the newfound emphasis on experience. My aim is to bring together these apparently diametrically opposed approaches, the mystic and the orthodox, and to show how oscillation between the two animates the poetry discussed in the following chapters.

Beyond 'Personal Feeling': Religion as Shared Project in Josiah Royce

In *The Sources of Religious Insight*, Royce offers a two-fold critique of James's *The Varieties of Religious Experience*. First, he downgrades James's concern for 'intense and intimate personal feeling' to merely one, if neither the only nor the most important, of his sources of religious insight (p. 30). After considering personal feeling as a source of religious insight, Royce offers several local criticisms of James's formulations. Secondly, the phrase 'religious insight' reworks James's 'religious experience', retaining the 'closeness of personal touch' familiar from James's study (p. 6), while also addressing as James did not *'the postulate that man needs to be saved'* (pp. 8–9). Personal touch and postulate mix aspects of religion that James separated; 'religious experience' was a matter for the science of religion, whereas *'the postulate that man needs to be saved'* was for the churches and their theologians. Royce runs the two together.

Turning first to religious experiences, Royce argues that their power resides in not so much the feelings they generate as the perception of the limits of these feelings. Like one of James's sick souls, an individual may suffer from an intense sense of loss, an awareness of the brokenness of the present and a yearning for something more, but know, too, that these states of feeling are, to recall one of the mystical marks, transitory. They do not last. Feeling, Royce says, gives rise to a wish for something more than feeling; 'the value of one great spiritual ideal, the ideal of spiritual unity and self-possession' emerges in contrast with 'the reign of caprice' (p. 31). Royce's discussion of religious experience is promptly connected with the critique of feeling and the need for 'a Power or a Spirit that is in some true sense not-Ourselves' (p. 32). There is a need 'to transcend the boundaries of any *merely* individual experience', he adds, so that 'individual experience' can 'become some sort of intercourse with Another' (p. 32). For James, a tactful silence about the transcendent was foundational for a science of religion, which endeavoured to leave commentary on the 'not-Ourselves' to the religious traditions. Royce was nevertheless attentive to the unintended consequences of James's formulations, though he, too, ultimately avoids equating the 'not-Ourselves' with a transcendent God.

Royce's study thereafter moves beyond the individual's personal experience. He criticises his colleague for 'neglect' of 'the social roads that lead toward the experience of what one takes to be divine' (pp. 73–4). He argues that moving from the personal to the communal is necessary to correct 'the *narrowness* of view to which we are usually subject' (p. 48). 'A man corrects his own narrowness', Royce summarises, 'by trying to share his fellow's point of view' (p. 55). A communal organisation, or what Royce calls a church, affords the highest form of religious insight over and above the isolated, self-contained and inevitably narrow intuitions of the mystic. Church is not identified with specific authority structures, but rather characterises a community of people engaged in a shared project. It includes those who 'through the service of their common causes' are 'brought together in some form of spiritual brotherhood' (p. 272). 'The real unity of the life of such fellow-servants of the Spirit', Royce continues, 'is itself an instance of a superhuman conscious reality'; and its members are devoted to bringing themselves into harmony with the purposes of the universe (p. 272). The designation 'church' is not limited to communities bounded by denominational terms such as Episcopalian or Roman Catholic, but these forms of 'visible church' nevertheless remain 'unique' examples of religious community (pp. 277–78). By so defining church, Royce responds to tensions represented by Underhill's opposition of the religion of authority and the religion of the spirit. The church, as outlined in *The Sources of Religious Insight*, is an association of individuals, their personal narrowness expanded by a course of education that they themselves have chosen under the tutelage of the social world. Their identification with and commitment to an ideal beyond themselves, a 'not-Ourselves', confers upon the goals of the community, through the power of collective attention, 'a superhuman conscious reality' with which community members seek to bring the world into conformity. Royce refuses to equate religious community with the authority structures of institutional religion. The reframing of church and spiritual need is accompanied by a drastic redefinition of religion itself; like James, Royce shows little interest in the conventional markers of Christian religion: revelation, liturgy and ethics among them.

Royce nevertheless differs from his colleague in important ways. He emphasises the public character of religion as James did not. Mystical or spiritual religion is often construed as inward-turned, focused on the self or the self's relationship to God and little else. Franz Rosenzweig says that, for the mystic, the 'soul opens for God, but because it opens only for God, it is invisible to all the world and shut off from it', a position he considers 'thoroughly immoral'.[82] Demurrals about transcendence and attention to different emotional states further strengthens the wall between the modern mystic and the world outside. By contrast, Royce's invocation of the church, however strangely defined, challenges the relegation of religion to the private sphere. He speaks to the public purpose of the 'wavering orthodoxy' to which the present study attends.

Even inward-turned mysticism is necessarily public. 'Contrary to much academic and popular thought', Ann Taves explains, 'the idea of private experience, though still rhetorically powerful in many contexts, is not particularly relevant to the study of experiences people consider very special'.[83] The term 'private experience' is misleading because 'any experience for which anyone wants to make a claim (for example, that the experience is special, private and/or inaccessible) has to be represented publicly, if only by the sheer fact of making such a claim'.[84] The private experience of someone else is not something an observer would learn about; by definition, it could not be discussed or shared, at least beyond a narrowly defined group. It would remain forever inaccessible. Given that those remembered as mystics today often produced descriptions of their encounters for dissemination, such figures do not seem to have been much concerned with privacy. Even those figures in *The Varieties of Religious Experience* whose experiences led them to join a church, undertake a particular kind of action or even just to write to James to describe their experience in the first instance took a public stance. Jantzen has observed that the designation of mystical experience as private, or even as an experience, has long had gendered implications, effectively bracketing the insights of women writers of so-called mystical texts to distinguish their achievements from those of the men otherwise responsible for producing knowledge.[85] Royce's critique indicates that the revisionary characteristics of James's secular reframing of religion were recognised from the outset. *The Sources of Religious Insight* speaks to the public role accorded religion in the poetry discussed here.

Jones, Eliot and H.D. have all been charged with subjectivism or withdrawing from contemporary concerns. Critics from the political left had long challenged modernist literature in those terms and the religious views of the figures to which the present study attends ensured that such critiques were especially powerful. F. R. Leavis, too, considered the stylistic unevenness of *Four*

Quartets and its prosy protestations of helplessness to be evidence of Eliot's 'fear of life and contempt (which includes self-contempt) for humanity'.[86] The fear arose, Leavis thought, from an 'untenable conception of the spiritual'.[87] In recovering the public dimensions of religion in general and mysticism in particular, the present study re-reads these religiously informed works of modernism from an entirely new perspective.

Formative Experiences: Friedrich von Hügel's Elements of Personal Religion

Hügel took a different tack in his criticism of James. In a letter following the publication of *The Mystical Element*, Hügel wrote to James to offer commentary on *The Varieties of Religious Experience*:

> I continue to feel your taking of the religious experience as separable from its institutional-historical occasions and environment and from the analytic and speculative mind (which latter, not only ever more or less follow upon, but also ever more or less influence, that intuitive-emotional-volitional element which you attempt to take separately) – I feel this to be schematic, *a priori*, not what your method, so concrete and *a posteriori*, seems to demand.[88]

James takes 'intense and intimate personal feeling', what Hügel here calls the 'intuitive-emotional-volitional element' of religion, to be the whole of religious experience, which he isolates from dogmatic proclamation. For James, feeling and dogma are not merely distinct; the former precedes the latter in both time and significance insofar as religious experience 'spontaneously and inevitably engenders myths, superstitions, dogmas, creeds, and metaphysical theologies'.[89] For Hügel, by contrast, the 'institutional-historical' element of religion shapes and stimulates religious experiences. Christian teaching on the Incarnation, the existence of a range of intense devotions to Jesus, Mary and the saints and a rich and sensuous iconography are facets of religious tradition that facilitate the experiences that interest James, conferring upon them their distinct shape and nature. More broadly, Hügel defines religious experience as a relationship with a transcendent God fostered by the institutional-historical dimension of the visible church. Through such ministrations, the individual is awakened to, educated about and becomes desirous of the transcendent.[90]

Hügel's broader purpose is very different from James's. *The Varieties of Religious Experience* breaks down religion into distinct parts: the 'institutional-historical' element is a matter for the churches, while the science of religion concerns itself with the 'intuitive-emotional-volitional element'. Hügel, by contrast, offers a phenomenology of religious belief, outlining three elements that co-exist in a religious perception, with the 'analytic and speculative' added to the mystical and the institutional (1, pp. 50–82). As a Catholic modernist, Hügel hoped to overcome the emphasis on ratiocination so prominent in contemporary neo-scholastic thinking by showing that intellectual assent to dogma was not the sole feature of religious practice. His coordination of mystical and institutional elements endeavoured to alter a particular relationship with authority from within the Roman Catholic Church.

The insight represented more than an intervention into Vatican politics. The interplay between overwhelming events that may reorientate one's life on the one hand and prior mental schemas and worldviews on the other has proved important to the study of religious experience in general, which Taves has gone on to rename, recognising the importance of the factors Hügel describes, as the study of 'experiences deemed religious'.[91] Individuals attribute significance to particular experiences in line with their pre-existing worldviews, including, perhaps, the influence of the 'institutional-historical' element. Hügel's approach thus offers a sensuous, feeling-centred and imaginatively powerful version of religion, while nevertheless tying it to aspects of institutional religion that the new mystics wished to circumvent.

The three elements of personal religion often clashed with each other. Antagonism protected personal religion from becoming too staid, too irrational or too idiosyncratic. The multiplicity of Hügel's personal religion serves a similar function to that of the social world in relation to the mystic in Royce's work, though for Hügel the tension to which he attends is built into personal religion itself. In both Hügel and Royce, confrontation between mysticism on the one hand and institutional influence on the other broadens a religiously informed outlook otherwise liable to become blinkered. The relationship between 'spilt mysticism' and 'wavering orthodoxy' outlined over the course of the present monograph represents a comparable dialogue. Works such as *Four Quartets*, *The Anathemata* and *Helen in Egypt* are not orthodox in the antimodernist sense; they do not: oppose sceptical relativism with dogma, accentuate the benefits of medieval Europe or sixteenth-century England over the modern world or emphasise the institutional and systematic over the individualistic and fragmented. While fragments of antimodernist arguments bearing the imprimatur of orthodoxy appear in these texts, they clash with corresponding mystical impulses. The interplay is staged in insertions, juxtapositions and self-annotations, which often make the verse seem unwieldy or disjointed. These modernist stylisations are the means through which Jones, Eliot and H.D. dramatise the challenge of living out a version of orthodoxy in a period of unrivalled economic, cultural and religious change.

Searching for Modernism's Religion

Framing Religion

In his 2009 work *Anatheism: Returning to God After God*, Richard Kearney argues that works of imaginative fiction such as *In Search of Lost Time*, *Mrs Dalloway* and *Ulysses* train the religious imagination of readers and help 'recover the presence of holiness' in a world that, under the weight of the secular, has witnessed 'the disappearance of God'.[92] Kearney draws on both the association of modernist fiction with secularisation – he recovers God in texts that have apparently dispensed with God – and what Virginia Woolf called the 'spiritual' dimension of modernism.[93] Anatheism recognises the abuses committed in religion's name over the centuries and acknowledges as decisive the critique of the metaphysical dimension of religion, while also wagering on the continued possibility of God. Anatheistic moments are experiences of atheism, of the perception of the radical emptiness of the universe, followed by the affirmation of the creative possibility of divine presence; the former, in Kearney's reading, makes the latter possible. Kearney's interpretations of specific modernist texts uncover embedded quasi-metaphysical religious attitudes, which represent the persistence of a traditional religious outlook, and then go on to unpick the ways modernist texts undermine that view, ultimately embracing the spiritual potential of the everyday.[94] Anatheism functions as an 'antidote to dogmatic theism' and the modernist fusion of sacred and secular is the forge in which Kearney's concept is made.[95]

Kearney's work is situated in, and a major contribution to, the field of post-secular studies, which has sought to critique the Enlightenment assumptions underwriting much European and American intellectual life and social organisation and to rehabilitate religious insights.[96] The return to religion enables Kearney to re-inscribe the significance of an ethical prerogative, arguably neglected in constructs of the secular: the obligation of hospitality to the stranger. Such 'primal dramas of response serve as portals to faith, thresholds to new depths of divine recognition', Kearney writes; they imagine 'the other as other is what enables the self to become a host and the stranger a guest'.[97] Under the influence of post-secular studies, a number of recent works in intellectual history have endeavoured to recover the influence of twentieth-century religious institutions on among other things: the emergence of human rights, the process of decolonisation and responses to totalitarianism.[98] The energy released by the post-secular reorientation of the humanities and the social sciences has also been apparent in the growing literature addressing the relationship between modernism and religion.[99]

Kearney's treatment of religion bears traces of factors outlined in the present study. While his thought is shaped by Christian theological traditions, Kearney speaks of not Christianity, but rather religion more broadly. The nineteenth and twentieth centuries saw Christianity transformed by secular forces. In European and American universities, for example, academic knowledge was generated about world religions, which cast Christianity as merely one religion among many and issued in work on commonalities and differences between religions. Renewed attention to mysticism, whether as a common point of origin across world religions or as a phenomenon appearing in 'Eastern' and

'Western' guises, was one such outcome.[100] Anatheism responds to both the comparative pursuit of origins and the prominence in the wake of James's work conferred upon religious experience. In writing about reciprocal moments of doubt and affirmation experienced by individuals across religions, Kearney is inevitably forced to neglect the specificities of given traditions and their communal expressions. Anatheism is far removed from liturgies, communities and traditions, which are where most people typically encounter religion. James Wood, for instance, observes that Kearney avoids discussing 'prayer' in his writing because, from his perspective, 'there is no one to pray to'.[101] God after the death of God is a concept that cannot simply be inserted into the religious practices called into question by the concept itself. Post-secular religion resembles in the way it reshapes religious observance what I have termed 'spilt mysticism'.

The present study shares Kearney's interest in religion rather than Christianity or theology insofar as it argues that the religious changes of the twentieth century are as marked within institutional religions themselves as in the apparent retreat of institutional religion from the public sphere and in the rise of alternative religions. Unlike Kearney, however, the following chapters attend to religious change in the context of the cultural forms through which writers and readers encounter faith. The result is a study of modernism and religion that, rather than focusing on one element over another, attempts to connect the spiritual and the institutional, the mystical and the orthodox, the private and the public.[102] My negotiation of modernism's religion builds upon several recent studies in the field, and it is to these that I now turn.

Recent Accounts of Modernism and Religion

One prominent strand of work on modernism and religion has positioned modernist engagement with Christianity as a critique of modernity. For Erik Tonning in *Modernism and Christianity*, published in 2014, the critique was generated by the twentieth century's multiple social crises. Tonning writes:

> In a looming interwar crisis, Christianity could also plausibly be opposed to *ersatz* secular religions of all kinds. For some, it provided an independent critique and historical analysis of *all* political 'isms'; it could be seen as a bulwark against impending chaos and a vital source of values; and as offering its own regeneration cure for the ills of social atomism and injustice, a technocratic, despiritualised civilisation, and an impersonal and malfunctioning industrial capitalism.[103]

Christianity, in Tonning's account, is an immense and varied resource that modernists accented to meet what they understood as society's major challenges: the threat, for example, of political ideologies, social atomisation or unfettered capitalism. In Stephen Kern's 2017 study *Modernism After the Death of God*, Christianity's status as a hierarchic system proves particularly vital.[104] Christianity promises a sense of order alien to the modern world, representing an otherwise elusive cultural synthesis. Adam Schwartz's 2006 study *The Third Spring* characterises 'orthodox Christianity' as both a way of accounting for 'civilization's growing disenchantment' and 'a superior alternative way of life and thought'.[105] Christian counter-culturalism, for Schwartz, continues the romantic critique of industrial capitalism, enabling the flourishing of individuals in their depths and idiosyncrasies in response to the threat of economically induced homogeneity.

For other commentators, the invocation of traditional religion marks not so much a critique of the existing order as a failure to engage with its possibilities, being either 'reactionary', 'disciplinarian', or else functioning as 'a therapeutic abatement of the pressures of modernity'.[106] Given the assumed antithesis between modernism and Christianity, modernism's religion has typically been identified with the new religions. Helen Sword's *Ghostwriting Modernism*, published in 2002, Lara Vetter's *Modernist Writings and Religio-scientific Discourse* from 2010 and Elizabeth Anderson's 2013 monograph *H.D. and Modernist Religious Imagination* outline how new or alternative religions proved more responsive than their institutional counterparts to immediate personal needs.[107] They were free from the accumulated tradition that weighed so heavily upon the Christian churches. Spiritualism, for Sword, enabled women, under the auspices of mediumship, to become authors in ways not otherwise open to them and at a time when they were barred from clerical orders; the 'supposed thraldom', Sword writes of 'spirit mediums' to 'the voices of the dead is precisely what enables their individual autonomy, cultural authority, and literary productivity'.[108] Vetter's religio-scientific discourse enables female authors and writers of colour to voice concerns in and about 'an era in which the human body was increasingly seen as vulnerable to penetration – by everything from radio waves to medical instruments', making use of 'a language that merges science and religion'.[109] In Anderson, hermetic rituals serve as the basis for building communities across time and space and a means of developing a 'spiritual' and a 'creative' component in work towards peace.[110]

While the occult, theosophy and spiritualism appear to follow in matters of religion Pound's injunction to make it new, the present study argues that the close connection between 'make it new' and new religions is misleading. The prominence of new religions owed much to the broader redescription of the role of religion effected by secular thought. Michel de Certeau understood the process of redescription as a form of intellectual 'cleavage' that 'initiates a field of knowledge and an opposition between the scientific institution and the "phenomena" (historical, social, or psychological) henceforth under its jurisdiction'.[111] The newly redescribed intellectual field enables 'different types of "beliefs"' to be united in 'one general category (the "religious" or the "sacred")' and thereafter 'set in opposition to knowledge and thought of differently by it than they thought of themselves'.[112] As with James's recourse to experience, religions in the emergent secular order are redescribed in ways that adherents of these religions would not recognise. Institutional religions have enjoyed a long history of producing knowledge. They have contributed to the governance of societies, made statements about the world and articulated values. For Tonning, Kern and Schwartz, these capacities were what attracted modernists and intellectuals at a time of cultural crisis. In the secular order, however, the role of religion was drastically curtailed. Religions of various kinds, new and institutional, now offered merely different ways of accessing the sacred or forms of religious experience. New religions, largely unencumbered by pre-secular histories, were better adapted to the new moment and thus more in keeping with what Roger Luckhurst has called in his entry on religion for *The Oxford Handbook of Modernisms* 'the radicalism of modernisms'.[113] In the present study, however, spiritual seeking and churchgoing are viewed as not mutually exclusive versions of modernism's religion, but rather equally at the mercy of the forces that brought mysticism and religious experience to prominence.

Under the pressure of the secular, religion in the age of modernism becomes hybrid in nature. In his 1993 study *The Birth of Modernism*, Leon Surette argued that modernism was best understood as 'an accommodation of the mysticism and occultism of the late nineteenth century to the relativism of the twentieth'.[114] Modernism is defined by an uneasy mixture of revelation and rationalism. In *Angels of Modernism*, published in 2011, Suzanne Hobson situates Surette's fusion within the secular rewriting of religion. Focusing on depictions of angels in all their 'variety', Hobson argues that these figures 'register the complex and variegated pattern of belief and disbelief which more accurately characterizes modernism's "religion" than the old disenchanted version'.[115] For Hobson, the angel is already one of the 'slipways' by which orthodox religion slides towards the 'magical' and 'an everyday or secular register'.[116] Modernism, in Hobson's reading, is not straightforwardly religious or irreligious, enchanted or disenchanted. 'Belief' and 'disbelief' come together in a version of Surette's mixture of relativism and occultism. Angels were Janus-faced, offering opportunities for both devotion and dismissal. Doubleness was not a willed aesthetic strategy, 'not something that modernist writers *do*' Hobson reminds us, but rather an outcome of a process by which 'orthodox religion slides towards' the 'magical' and 'an everyday or secular register'.[117] My concepts of 'spilt mysticism' and 'wavering orthodoxy' function as parallel routes towards religious transformation, although the way pursued by the present study runs directly through, rather than merely circling around, institutional religion. The engagement with Christianity offered here thus differs from Tonning's, Kern's and Schwartz's versions because what it is at stake is not a reasserted traditionalism that speaks to the modernist crisis in surprising ways, but rather an institutional religion that is in a state of flux akin to Hobson's angels.

The process of change is, however, excluded from one of the most prominent approaches to modernism and religion, namely the 'secular sacred'.[118] In his 2010 study *Religious Experience and the Modernist Novel*, Pericles Lewis asserts:

> Something has certainly happened to religious experience during the first half of the twentieth century, and insofar as it involves an imagined emptying-out of the churches, it might plausibly be called secularization. Yet, the modernists did not accept secularization as inevitable or embrace a world emptied of the sacred. They sought instead to understand religious experience anew, in the light of their own experience of modernity and of the theories of their contemporaries. They sought to offer a new understanding of the sacred in their own texts, and in so doing they created a modern form of sacred text, charged with the meaning and power that seemed to them to have evacuated the church buildings.[119]

As Christianity loses its grip on institutions and alternative forms of knowledge gain prominence, the number of people sitting in church pews during weekly services falls.[120] Secularisation takes hold; traditional religious practice begins to disappear. Church buildings become not living places of worship, but rather museums dedicated to otherwise inaccessible religious observance. Yet Lewis is not content with what Taylor would call a 'subtraction story', which might see a basic humanism emerging from the ashes of institutional religion.[121] In Lewis's narrative, modernists take it upon themselves to write a new religion; the works of literature they produce become 'sacred text[s]', replacing the scriptures that formerly sat on the lectern. In an extension of the post-romantic epiphanic tradition, modernism becomes itself not merely a site of religious experience existing in tension with more traditional forms of religion, but rather in the manner of Sword, Vetter and Anderson a new religion.

When compared to the irresolution characteristic of Surette's and Hobson's understanding of religion, the striking feature of the 'secular sacred' is its confidence and self-direction. Matthew Mutter's 2018 study *Restless Secularism: Modernism and the Religious Inheritance* argues that modernist texts became a forum for working out secular versions of theological problems. Mutter attends to how the secular appropriated 'religion's capacity to model reality and establish normative valuations for moral (and other) experience'.[122] In a reading of *To the Lighthouse*, for instance, Mutter argues that the notion of 'the world as a work of art' outlined in the novel is best considered a 'secular theodicy' that 'subsumes the pain of the world into a higher, mystical pattern'.[123] Mutter's 'secular theodicy' fills the gap left by the withdrawal of its religious counterpart.

Mutter's reading is, I think, beset by the problems Abrams faced in his account of the transference from religion to literature. A Christian theodicy is embedded in a range of ritual practices, ethical principles and social structures that shape its interpretation; it is not a standalone framework for understanding suffering.[124] Literature, particularly that within the epiphanic tradition, is unable to call upon these broader social forms. Mutter argues that through Lily Briscoe's 'experience of distance as beautiful fullness rather than absence or sheer inaccessibility', Woolf offers a 'hint' that 'creation, as God's primordial act of self-distancing and "letting be", might have a creator'.[125] A secular theodicy facilitates a partial recovery of transcendence. The secular, through the work undertaken by modernist 'sacred text[s]', thus includes within itself a form of self-critique.

For a post-secular thinker such as Kearney, Mutter's argument advances in the wrong direction, travelling toward the metaphysical consolations that anatheism bypasses. The difference between Mutter and Kearney is attributable to matters of neither preference nor temperament alone. As with institutional religions in the pre-secular period and Arnold's understanding of extra-belief, Kearney's anatheism demands ethical commitment. Christianity's role as a system to which it was possible to commit was one of the factors that made it popular among modernists during a time of crisis. It is not, however, clear what is demanded of and by modernist 'sacred text[s]'. Mutter cannot explain what should be done with Woolf's glimpse of transcendence. His reading reveals, perhaps, the limits of what is possible in the field of religion for literary criticism. Aware of such limits, David Jasper suggests that creative literature might be best considered 'a prolegomenon to religion and theology' or a 'field or space into which religion might be called as appropriate'.[126] The tentativeness of 'prolegomenon to' and 'as appropriate' and the sense that creative literature and religion and/or theology are separate if nevertheless related endeavours attempt to contain the threat of post-romantic overreach implicit in the 'secular sacred'.

The present study dissents from the 'secular sacred' at least in part because the assured tone of Lewis's and Mutter's religious modernism jars with the hesitancies of the poems studied here. These works move from intense, epiphanic registers to prosy exasperation and back again. They reflect upon their own dividedness. The tonal palette owes something to the fact that institutional religion continued to exert influence upon these works. Churches were themselves transformed by the processes that produced the new religions of Sword, Vetter and Anderson, alongside the hybridity of Surette and Hobson. The 'wavering orthodoxy' to which the present study attends is thus far less sure of itself. The attention conferred upon a traditional body of knowledge in transformed intellectual and social circumstances not only produces a distinctive approach to religious poetry, but also provides further input into the question of what it is to be modern.

Beyond Epiphany: An Outline

In *The Treasure of the Humble*, published in 1898, the Belgian dramatist, essayist and Nobel laureate Maurice Maeterlinck describes the *fin de siècle* as a spiritual golden age, noting how 'in the work-a-day lives of the very humblest of men, spiritual phenomena manifest themselves – mysterious, direct workings, that bring soul nearer to soul; and of all this we can find no record in former times'.[127] Spiritual immediacy, Maeterlinck's 'mysterious, direct workings', was a central pillar of twentieth-century religion, ultimately informing anything from Bellah's 'internalization' of religious authority to the practice of being 'spiritual but not religious'. In the epiphanic tradition, literature becomes not only a repository of Maeterlinck's 'spiritual phenomena' but also a stimulant to new iterations of these phenomena. The aesthetic response to what Lewis calls the modernist 'sacred text' thus becomes a form of religious experience. The process of transference exemplifies what Eliot termed 'a weakling Mysticism' lying within 'the Maeterlinckian tradition'.[128] Each chapter of the present study, by contrast, offers an alternative to the new mystical religion of direct access.

Chapter 1 presents David Jones's work as a challenge to epiphanic aesthetics. Far from looking to art as a replacement for religion, Jones allows his thinking about art to shape his relationship with his religious tradition. Within scholarship on Jones, the emphasis on the influence of his creative work on his religion challenges overly reverential interpretations, which typically see him responding to traditional themes. Jones was, of course, an observant Roman Catholic from his time at Ditchling until his death, but his artistic thinking often pushed Catholic convention to daring lengths. In his hands, for instance, the Christian liturgy becomes a beacon for a wider population than Christians alone insofar as it celebrates what Jones took to be the gratuitous, non-utilitarian and ultimately creative element of human nature. In Jones's recently recovered long poem, *The Grail Mass*, his insight into the role of creativity in human nature can be understood within the broader contexts of the political project that produced in 1948 the Universal Declaration of Human Rights and shapes a critique of imperialism in its contemporary British and historically Roman guises from a distinctly religious vantage point.

Sustaining Jones's emphasis on the public role of religion, Chapter 2 repositions critical portrayals of T. S. Eliot's religion, resisting attempts to unite certain biographical events and the religious intensities of his poetry into a form of spiritual journey. Instead, the chapter situates Eliot in the broader context of religious change, charting the lifelong influence of the psychology of religion on his understanding of the relationship between the religious subject and society. Eliot's early martyr poems are deeply influenced by the French neurologist Jean-Martin Charcot's attempts to diagnose the mystics of the Christian church as hysterics. Charcot's interpretative move had far-reaching consequences for both psychology and religion more broadly and went on to shape everything from Eliot's understanding of the creative process to his sociological work and even the way he imagined *Four Quartets* interacting with the wartime public. Going beyond a description of the tensions between mysticism and orthodoxy, Chapter 2 finds in Eliot's work a renegotiation of the borders between the secular and the sacred that reflect developments in contemporary theology and which have far-reaching consequences for our understanding of religion in the age of modernism.

Chapter 3 uses H.D.'s return to Moravian Christianity to provide another vantage point on the reimagination of the role of religion. H.D.'s re-engagement with her past was spurred by a surprising description of Moravian history discovered in the personalist Denis de Rougemont's study *Passion and Society*. Rougemont's understanding of the Moravians led H.D. to reimagine her childhood religion and to describe visionary scenes across works such as *The Gift*, *The Mystery* and *Trilogy* that were shaped simultaneously by the excitement of new discovery and scepticism stemming from the realisation that her experience of the Moravians as a child had been different to that proffered by Rougemont. The chapter uses the idea of a return to position H.D.'s midlife re-engagement with religion as a creative revisioning of the tradition, rather than the act of recovery it is often construed as in the critical literature; there, the benign influence of Moravians is often contrasted with what are taken to be more restrictive examples of institutional religion, while here H.D.'s redeployment of Moravian ideas parallels developments in Jones and Eliot. In turn, H.D.'s reassessment of religion was mobilised to challenge the most strikingly misogynistic elements of psychoanalysis, enabling H.D. to circumvent reductionist and mechanistic aspects of Freud's thought. In her epic poem *Helen in Egypt*, H.D. also turned to the personalism of Rougemont and Emmanuel Mounier to formulate a religiously informed response to twentieth-century militarism. The presentation of H.D.'s epic as not only an anti-war poem but also a text that sought to reimagine the social and political organisation of society more broadly is a revealing instance of the radical, public-minded work that re-engagement with Christian thought often facilitated in the age of modernism.

Building on the mixture of tradition and innovation in the religion of Jones, Eliot and H.D., the retreat movement, as Chapter 4 shows, was an attempt on the part of religious authorities to confront the pervasiveness of unchurched spirituality. The apparently traditional character of the response obscured its experimental design and purpose. The retreat movement, as seen through the lens of both the Association for Promoting Retreats' in-house journal *The Vision* and selected published and archival materials connected to the Catholic Worker's retreat, unites orthodoxy and mysticism. As an emergent and contested cultural form, the retreat complicates Lewis's trajectory for modernism and religion, where religious attention moves from church buildings to modernist texts. The retreat house, itself a construction that was not entirely new and not entirely old, complicates matters. Attending to Dorothy Day's yoking of social justice and retreat, Chapter 4 outlines a new way of engaging with society from a religious perspective, which ultimately eschewed the labels of liberal and traditional or left and right.

Aspects of retreat inform the poetry discussed here. Jones's imaginative musings find sanction in retreat's emphasis on silent reflection. Eliot's concern with the psychology of religion meets its counterpart in retreat's emphasis on psychic health. The new life rhythms established by retreat are paralleled by the distinct patterning H.D. brings to the idea of conversion. More broadly, the public role conferred by retreat upon what would otherwise be a personal act – joining a community that occupies a specially constituted space to undertake what is essentially a private act of reflection – functions as an analogy for the hybrid form of works such as *The Anathemata*, *Four Quartets* and *Helen in Egypt*, which all mix visionary and worldly registers.

The poetry of retreat serves as a counterpart to what the renaissance scholar and the future editor of H.D.'s work, Louis L. Martz, called *The Poetry of Meditation*. The meditation in question derived from Ignatius of Loyola's *Spiritual Exercises* and united 'the senses, the emotions, and the intellectual faculties' in 'a moment of dramatic, creative experience'.[129] Ignatian meditation, in Martz's estimation, illuminated modernist verse as much as it did the seventeenth-century poets he studied. *The Poetry of Meditation* broaches the idea of religion-to-literature transference; what began as a Christian devotion shortly became an artistic method independent of religious concerns. Martz wanted literature or the interpretation of literature to occupy a cultural space once reserved for religion.

The present study moves in the opposite direction. Jones, Eliot and H.D. turn to religion to think through the challenges occasioned by modernity. These poets and their poems are situated alongside representatives of Catholic modernism, Christian sociology and personalism, drawing on their ideas in startling and surprising ways. The field of modernist studies has been slow to reckon with the broader sociological and theoretical implications and consequences of the secular to which the present study attends. These concerns would not, however, have surprised modernists themselves. In assuming a difference in the religious outlook of, for example, John Donne and Eliot, the present study has recourse to the acts of intellectual cleavage undertaken in the name of the secular, redescribing religion in terms that previous generations of believers might have struggled to recognise. The recent theoretical language of the post-secular is prefigured in Jones's own talk of 'The Break' or Eliot's much-discussed notion of the 'dissociation of sensibility'; the sense, that is, that modernism must be understood as a form of rupture with the past.[130] The tension between 'spilt mysticism' and 'wavering orthodoxy' not only construes modernism's concern with the new as a product of the secular transformation of religion, but also reveals other ways of being modern.

Notes

1. David Jones to Jim Ede, 4 November 1927, in *Dai Greatcoat: A Self-Portrait of David Jones in His Letters*, ed. by René Hague (London: Faber & Faber, 1980), pp. 44–45 (p. 45).
2. Amy Hollywood, *Sensible Ecstasy: Mysticism, Sexual Difference, and the Demands of History* (Chicago: University of Chicago Press, 2002), p. 148.
3. Alex Owen, *The Place of Enchantment: British Occultism and the Culture of the Modern* (Chicago: University of Chicago Press, 2004), p. xviii.
4. See Ezra Pound, 'Psychology and Troubadours', in *The Spirit of Romance*, rev. edn (New York: New Directions, 1952), pp. 87–100 (p. 95). H.D., *The Gift by H.D.: The Complete Text*, ed. by Jane Augustine (Gainesville: University Press of Florida, 1998), p. 265n; further references are to this edition and are given after quotations in the text. See also Leon Surette, *The Birth of Modernism: Ezra Pound, T. S. Eliot, W. B. Yeats, and the Occult* (Montreal: McGill-Queen's University Press, 1993), p. 104.
5. David Jones in conversation with Thomas Dilworth, 4 June 1971. Quoted in Thomas Dilworth, 'David Jones and the Chelsea Group', in *David Jones: A Christian Modernist?*, ed. by Jamie Callison and others (Leiden: Brill, 2018), pp. 107–22 (p. 116).
6. For an extended discussion of *Mysticism*, see Jamie Callison, 'Directing Modernist Spirituality: Evelyn Underhill, the Subliminal Consciousness and Spiritual Direction', in *Modernist Women Writers and Spirituality: A Piercing Darkness*, ed. by Elizabeth Anderson and others (Basingstoke: Palgrave Macmillan, 2016), pp. 39–54.
7. Evelyn Underhill, preface to *Mysticism: A Study in the Nature and Development of Man's Spiritual Consciousness*, 12th edn (New York: Dutton, 1930), pp. vii–xi (p. ix).
8. Underhill, preface to *Mysticism*, 1930, p. x.
9. Owen, pp. 56–68.
10. Friedrich von Hügel, *The Mystical Element of Religion as Studied in Saint Catherine of Genoa and Her Friends*, 2 vols (London: Dent, 1909), 1, pp. 50–82. Further references to this work are given after quotations in the text.
11. Cuthbert Butler, 'Religions of Authority and the Religion of the Spirit', in *'Religions of Authority and the Religion of the Spirit' with Other Essays* (London: Sheed & Ward, 1930), pp. 16–46 (p. 44n).
12. See Jamie Callison, 'Dissociating Psychology: Religion, Inspiration and T. S. Eliot's Subliminal Mind', *ELH*, 84 (2017), 1029–59 (pp. 1040–44).
13. Callison, 'Directing Modernist Spirituality', p. 47.
14. Grace M. Jantzen, 'The Legacy of Evelyn Underhill', *Feminist Theology*, 4 (1993), 79–100 (p. 94).
15. Owen, p. 12.
16. Robert N. Bellah, 'Religion and Belief', in *Beyond Belief: Essays on Religion in a Post-Traditionalist World* (Berkeley: University of California Press, 1991), pp. 216–29 (pp. 221–22).
17. Bellah, 'Religion and Belief', p. 224.
18. Charles Taylor, *A Secular Age* (Cambridge, MA: Harvard University Press, 2007), pp. 38–39.

19. Paula M. Kane, *Sister Thorn and Catholic Mysticism in Modern America* (Chapel Hill: University of North Carolina Press, 2013), p. 53, p. 121.
20. Kane, p. 53.
21. Josiah Royce, *The Sources of Religious Insight* (Edinburgh: T & T Clark, 1912), p. 47. Further references to this work are given after quotations in the text.
22. William James, *The Varieties of Religious Experience: A Study in Human Nature* (London: Longmans Green, 1902), pp. 380–81.
23. Underhill's *Mysticism* uses the triad of purgation-illumination-union familiar from much mystical writing. See Underhill, 1911, pp. 198–231, pp. 232–65, pp. 413–43.
24. William B. Parsons, *Freud and Augustine in Dialogue: Psychoanalysis, Mysticism, and the Culture of Modern Spirituality* (Charlottesville: University of Virginia Press, 2013), p. 15.
25. Parsons, *Freud and Augustine*, p. 16.
26. Jeffrey J. Kripal, *Authors of the Impossible: The Paranormal and the Sacred* (Chicago: University of Chicago Press, 2010), p. 40.
27. See Underhill, 1911, pp. 200–1.
28. See Ann Taves, *Fits, Trances, and Visions: Experiencing Religion and Explaining Experience from Wesley to James* (Princeton: Princeton University Press, 1999), p. 279.
29. See James, pp. 234–35.
30. Underhill, 1911, p. 24.
31. James, p. 31.
32. See Denys Turner, *The Darkness of God: Negativity in Christian Mysticism* (Cambridge: Cambridge University Press, 1995), pp. 1–10, pp. 186–210.
33. Taves, *Fits, Trances, and Visions*, p. 271.
34. See Leigh Eric Schmidt, 'The Making of Modern "Mysticism"', *Journal of the American Academy of Religion*, 71 (2003), 273–302 (pp. 288–89).
35. Martin Jay, *Songs of Experience: Modern American and European Variations on a Universal Theme* (Berkeley: University of California Press, 2005), p. 84.
36. Jay, p. 86.
37. See Hastings Rashdall, *Conscience and Christ: Six Lectures on Christian Ethics* (London: Duckworth, 1916), pp. 286–7; T. S. Eliot, 'A review of *Conscience and Christ: Six Lectures on Christian Ethics*, by Hastings Rashdall', in *The Complete Prose of T. S. Eliot: The Critical Edition*, ed. by Ronald Schuchard, 8 vols, Project MUSE, https://about.muse.jhu.edu/muse/eliot-prose/, 1: *The Apprentice Years, 1905–1918*, ed. by Jewel Spears Brooker and Ronald Schuchard, pp. 428–29 (p. 428).
38. Matthew Arnold, 'The Study of Poetry', in *Essays in Criticism: Second Series* (London: Macmillan, 1888), pp. 1–55 (p. 3).
39. Matthew Arnold, *Literature and Dogma: An Essay Towards a Better Apprehension of the Bible*, 2nd edn (London: Smith Elder, 1873), pp. 38–39.
40. Arnold, *Literature and Dogma*, p. 77.
41. Jay, p. 95.
42. Cited in Jay, p. 98.
43. See Hans Joas, *The Power of the Sacred: An Alternative to the Narrative of Disenchantment*, trans. by Alex Skinner (Oxford: Oxford University Press, 2021), pp. 35–44.

44. For an account of Harnack, see Alfred Loisy, *The Gospel and the Church*, trans. by Christopher Home (London: Isbister, 1903), p. 3; For Sabatier, see Butler, p. 22.
45. James, p. 6.
46. James, p. 433.
47. Pericles Lewis, *Religious Experience and the Modernist Novel* (Cambridge: Cambridge University Press, 2010), p. 25.
48. See James, pp. 1–25; Taves, *Fits, Trances, and Visions*, pp. 278–79.
49. G. Wilson Knight, *Myth and Miracle: An Essay on the Mystic Symbolism of Shakespeare* (London: Burrow, 1929), p. 29. For Eliot and *Myth and Miracle*, see Paul Murray, *T. S. Eliot and Mysticism: The Secret History of* Four Quartets (New York: St Martin's Press, 1991), pp. 205–14.
50. James, pp. 127–65, pp. 166–88, pp. 379–429.
51. Martin C. D'Arcy, *The Nature of Belief* (New York: Longmans Green, 1931), p. 232.
52. Jones to Ede, 4 November 1927, in *Dai Greatcoat*, p. 44.
53. D'Arcy, *Nature of Belief*, p. 232.
54. T. E. Hulme, 'Romanticism and Classicism', in *The Collected Writings of T. E. Hulme*, ed. by Karen Csengeri (Oxford: Clarendon Press, 1994), pp. 59–73 (p. 62).
55. Jones to Ede, 4 November 1927, in *Dai Greatcoat*, p. 45.
56. William R. Inge, introduction to *Light, Life and Love: Selections from the German Mystics of the Middle Ages* (London: Methuen, 1904), pp. ix–lxiv (p. lviii).
57. *The Book of Common Prayer: The Texts of 1549, 1559, and 1662*, ed. by Brian Cummings (Oxford: Oxford University Press, 2011), p. 679.
58. Saba Mahmood, *Religious Difference in a Secular Age: A Minority Report* (Princeton: Princeton University Press, 2015), p. 21.
59. Taylor, *Secular Age*, p. 22.
60. Taylor, *Secular Age*, pp. 38–39, pp. 539–93.
61. May Sinclair, *A Defence of Idealism: Some Questions and Conclusions* (London: Macmillan, 1917), pp. 240–89; Vita Sackville-West, *The Eagle and The Dove – A Study in Contrasts: St Teresa of Avila, St Thérèse of Lisieux* (Garden City, NJ: Doubleday Doran, 1944); Rebecca West, *A Letter to a Grandfather* (London: Hogarth, 1933).
62. W. R. Inge, 'The Mysticism of Wordsworth' and 'The Mysticism of Browning', in *Studies of English Mystics: St Margaret's Lectures, 1905* (London: John Murray, 1907), pp. 173–206, pp. 207–39.
63. Hulme, p. 62. Monographs on the modernist epiphany include: Morris Beja, *Epiphany in the Modern Novel* (Seattle: University of Washington Press, 1971); Ashton Nichols, *The Poetics of Epiphany: Nineteenth-Century Origins of the Modern Literary Moment* (Tuscaloosa, AL: University of Alabama Press, 1987); Sharon Kim, *Literary Epiphany in the Novel, 1850–1950: Constellations of the Soul* (Basingstoke: Palgrave Macmillan, 2012). Modernist epiphany is central to Kearney's work. See Richard Kearney, *Anatheism: Returning to God After God* (New York: Columbia University Press, 2010), pp. 101–32.
64. Martin Bidney, *Patterns of Epiphany: From Wordsworth to Tolstoy, Pater, and Barrett Browning* (Carbondale: Southern Illinois University Press, 1997), p. 1.
65. M. H. Abrams, *Natural Supernaturalism: Tradition and Revolution in Romantic Literature* (New York: Norton, 1971), p. 390.

66. Abrams, p. 422.
67. For an alternative view of epiphany and Joyce's development, see Richard Kearney, 'Epiphanies in Joyce', in *Global Ireland: Irish Literatures for the New Millennium*, ed. by Ondřej Pilný and Clare Wallace (Prague: Litteraria Pragensia, 2005), pp. 147–82.
68. Virginia Woolf, 'Modern Fiction', in *Selected Essays*, ed. by David Bradshaw (Oxford: Oxford University Press, 2009), pp. 6–12 (p. 10).
69. Clement Greenberg, 'Avant-Garde and Kitsch', in *Art and Culture: Critical Essays* (Boston, MA: Beacon Press, 1961), pp. 3–21 (p. 8, p. 7).
70. Greenberg, p. 7.
71. The present and the following paragraph draw on Jamie Callison, 'Sacred Ground: Orthodoxy, Poetry and Religious Change', in *Edinburgh Companion to Modernism, Myth and Religion*, ed. by Suzanne Hobson and Andrew Radford (Edinburgh: Edinburgh University Press, 2023), pp. 375–88.
72. T. S. Eliot, '*After Strange Gods: A Primer of Modern Heresy*', in *Complete Prose, 5: Tradition and Orthodoxy, 1934–1939*, ed. by Iman Javadi, Ronald Schuchard and Jayme Stayer, pp. 15–55 (p. 40).
73. Mary Butts, 'The Heresy Game', *The Spectator*, 12 March 1937, pp. 466–67 (p. 466).
74. G. K. Chesterton, *Orthodoxy* (London: Bodley Head, 1908), p. 230.
75. See Andrzej Gasiorek, *A History of Modernist Literature* (Oxford: Wiley-Blackwell, 2015), pp. 444–45. Schloesser is similarly attentive to the 'anti-modernist aspect of modernism'; Stephen Schloesser, *Jazz Age Catholicism: Mystic Modernism in Postwar Paris, 1919–1933* (Toronto: University of Toronto Press, 2005), p. 12, see also pp. 141–72.
76. James Chappel, *Catholic Modern: The Challenge of Totalitarianism and the Remaking of the Church* (Cambridge, MA: Harvard University Press, 2018), p. 23.
77. Chappel, p. 27.
78. See T. S. Eliot, 'The Clark Lectures. Lectures on the Metaphysical Poetry of the Seventeenth Century with Special Reference to Donne, Crashaw and Cowley', in *Complete Prose, 2: The Perfect Critic, 1919–1926*, ed. by Anthony Cuda and Ronald Schuchard, pp. 609–761 (p. 653).
79. L. C. Knights, 'Shakespeare and Profit Inflations', *Scrutiny*, 5 (1936), 48–60 (p. 54). Quoted in Stefan Collini, 'Where Did it All Go Wrong? Cultural Critics and "Modernity" in Inter-War Britain', in *The Strange Survival of Liberal England: Political Leaders, Moral Values and the Reception of Economic Debate*, ed. by E. H. H. Green and D. M. Tanner (Cambridge: Cambridge University Press, 2011), pp. 247–74 (p. 265).
80. Rachel Blau DuPlessis, *Genders, Races, and Religious Cultures in Modern American Poetry, 1908–1934* (Cambridge: Cambridge University Press, 2001), p. 156; Jason Harding, *The Criterion: Cultural Politics and Periodical Networks in Inter-War Britain* (Oxford: Oxford University Press, 2002), p. 184.
81. Elizabeth Anderson, *H.D. and Modernist Religious Imagination: Mysticism and Writing* (London: Bloomsbury Academic, 2013), p. 21.
82. Franz Rosenzweig, *The Star of Redemption*, trans. by William W. Hallo (New York: Holt, Rinehart and Winston, 1970), p. 207, p. 208.
83. Taves, *Religious Experience Reconsidered*, p. 86.
84. Taves, *Religious Experience Reconsidered*, p. 86.

85. See Grace M. Jantzen, *Power, Gender, and Christian Mysticism* (Cambridge: Cambridge University Press, 1995), p. 21, p. 169.
86. F. R. Leavis, *The Living Principle: 'English' as a Discipline of Thought* (London: Chatto & Windus, 1975), p. 205.
87. Leavis, p. 205.
88. Friedrich von Hügel to William James, 10 May 1909, in James Luther Adams, 'Letter from Friedrich von Hügel to William James', *The Downside Review*, 98 (1980), pp. 214–36 (p. 230).
89. James, p. 433.
90. For Hügel and transcendence, see Gabriel Daly, *Transcendence and Immanence: A Study in Catholic Modernism and Integralism* (Oxford: Oxford University Press, 1980), pp. 119–29.
91. Taves, *Religious Experience Reconsidered*, pp. 8–9.
92. Kearney, *Anatheism*, p. 5, p. 40.
93. Woolf, 'Modern Fiction', p. 10.
94. Kearney, *Anatheism*, pp. 101–32; see also Kearney, 'Epiphanies in Joyce', pp. 147–82; and Richard Kearney, 'Epiphanies of the Everyday: Toward a Micro-Eschatology', in *After God: Richard Kearney and the Religious Turn in Continental Philosophy*, ed. by John Panteleimon Manoussakis (New York: Fordham University Press, 2006), pp. 3–20.
95. Kearney, *Anatheism*, p. 6.
96. For an introduction to the return to religion, see John D. Caputo, *Hermeneutics: Facts and Interpretation in the Age of Information* (London: Pelican Books, 2018), pp. 273–304 and Lori Branch, 'Postsecular Studies', in *The Routledge Companion to Literature and Religion*, ed. by Mark Knight (Oxford: Routledge, 2016), pp. 91–101.
97. Kearney, *Anatheism*, p. 8, p. 41; David Tracy notes Kearney's unusual ability to unite the mystical and ethical strands of contemporary theory. See David Tracy, 'God: The Possible/ Impossible', in *After God*, pp. 340–54 (pp. 345–46).
98. See, for example, Samuel Moyn, *Christian Human Rights* (Philadelphia: University of Pennsylvania Press, 2015); Giuliana Chamedes, *A Twentieth-Century Crusade: The Vatican's Battle to Remake Christian Europe* (Cambridge, MA: Harvard University Press, 2019); Edward Baring, *Converts to the Real: Catholicism and the Making of Continental Philosophy* (Cambridge, MA: Harvard University Press, 2019); Elizabeth A. Foster, *African Catholic: Decolonization and the Transformation of the Church* (Cambridge, MA: Harvard University Press, 2019); Sarah Shortall, *Soldiers of God in a Secular World: Catholic Theology and Twentieth-Century French Politics* (Cambridge, MA: Harvard University Press, 2021).
99. See, for example, Roger Luckhurst, 'Religion, Psychical Research, Spiritualism, and the Occult', in *The Oxford Handbook of Modernisms*, ed. by Peter Brooker and others (Oxford: Oxford University Press, 2010), pp. 429–44; Finn Fordham, 'Between Theological and Cultural Modernism: The Vatican's Oath against Modernism, September 1910', *Literature and History*, 22 (2013), 8–24; Anthony Domestico, *Poetry and Theology in the Modernist Period* (Baltimore: Johns Hopkins University Press, 2017); W. David Soud, *Divine Cartographies: God, History, and Poiesis in W. B. Yeats, David Jones, and T. S. Eliot* (Oxford: Oxford University Press, 2016);

Chrissie Van Mierlo, *James Joyce and Catholicism: The Apostate's Wake* (London: Bloomsbury Academic, 2017); Joanna Rzepa, *Modernism and Theology: Rainer Maria Rilke, T. S. Eliot, Czesław Miłosz* (Basingstoke: Palgrave Macmillan, 2021). For a survey of the field, see Suzanne Hobson and Andrew Radford, introduction to *Edinburgh Companion to Modernism, Myth and Religion*, pp. 1–18.
100. See Parsons, *Freud and Augustine*, pp. 143–44; Taves, *Religious Experience Reconsidered*, pp. 17–22; Underhill, 1911, pp. 40–41, p. 87.
101. James Wood and Richard Kearney, 'Imagination, Anatheism, and the Sacred, Dialogue with James Wood', in *Reimagining the Sacred: Richard Kearney Debates God with James Wood and Others*, ed. by Richard Kearney and Jens Zimmermann (New York: Columbia University Press, 2015), pp. 19–45 (p. 25).
102. Luckhurst contrasts the 'conservative trajectory' of Eliot's Christianity with the 'radicalism' of the new religions. Luckhurst, p. 444.
103. Erik Tonning, 'Old Dogmas for a New Crisis: Hell and Incarnation in T. S. Eliot and W. H. Auden', in *Modernism, Christianity and Apocalypse*, ed. by Erik Tonning and others (Leiden: Brill, 2015), pp. 236–59 (p. 237). See also Erik Tonning, *Modernism and Christianity* (Basingstoke: Palgrave Macmillan, 2014), p. 60.
104. Stephen Kern, *Modernism After the Death of God: Christianity, Fragmentation, and Unification* (Oxford: Routledge, 2017), pp. 1–21.
105. Adam Schwartz, *The Third Spring: G. K. Chesterton, Graham Greene, Christopher Dawson, and David Jones* (Washington, D. C.: Catholic University of America Press, 2005), p. 6.
106. Harding, *Criterion*, p. 184; Luckhurst, p. 444; Tim Armstrong, *Modernism: A Cultural History* (Cambridge: Polity Press, 2005), p. 4.
107. See Helen Sword, *Ghostwriting Modernism* (Ithaca, NY: Cornell University Press, 2002); Lara Vetter, *Modernist Writings and Religio-scientific Discourse: H.D., Loy, and Toomer* (Basingstoke: Palgrave Macmillan, 2010), p. 9; Anderson, p. 4.
108. Sword, p. 86.
109. Vetter, p. 2.
110. Anderson, pp. 53–54.
111. Michel de Certeau, *The Mystic Fable: The Sixteenth and Seventeenth Centuries*, ed. by Luce Giard, trans. by Michael B. Smith, 2 vols (Chicago: University of Chicago Press, 1995–2015), 2, p. 10.
112. Certeau, 2, p. 10.
113. Luckhurst, p. 444.
114. Surette, p. 94.
115. Suzanne Hobson, *Angels of Modernism: Religion, Culture, Aesthetics 1910–1960* (Basingstoke: Palgrave Macmillan, 2011), p. 5.
116. Hobson, *Angels of Modernism*, p. 7.
117. Hobson, *Angels of Modernism*, p. 7.
118. Lewis, p. 21.
119. Lewis, p. 19.
120. The classic account is Peter L. Berger, *The Sacred Canopy: Elements of a Sociological Theory of Religion* (Garden City, NY: Doubleday, 1967). For a recent restatement, see Steve Bruce, *Secularization: In Defence of an Unfashionable Theory* (Oxford: Oxford University Press, 2011).

121. Taylor, *Secular Age*, p. 22.
122. Matthew Mutter, *Restless Secularism: Modernism and the Religious Inheritance* (New Haven, CT: Yale University Press, 2017), p. 27.
123. Mutter, p. 77.
124. See, for instance, the relationship between the Reformation's reforms to ritual and social change in Edward Muir, *Ritual in Early Modern Europe* (Cambridge: Cambridge University Press, 2005), pp. 202–51.
125. Mutter, p. 113.
126. David Jasper, *Heaven in Ordinary: Poetry and Religion in a Secular Age* (Cambridge: Lutterworth Press, 2018), p. 6.
127. Maurice Maeterlinck, 'The Awakening of the Soul', in *The Treasure of the Humble*, trans. by Alfred Sutro (London: George Allen, 1898), pp. 23–42 (p. 33).
128. T. S. Eliot, '[Inconsistencies in Bergson's Idealism]', in *Apprentice Years*, pp. 67–89 (p. 79).
129. Louis L. Martz, *The Poetry of Meditation: A Study in English Religious Literature of the Seventeenth Century* (New Haven, CT: Yale University Press, 1954), p. 1.
130. T. S. Eliot, 'The Metaphysical Poets', in *Perfect Critic*, pp. 375–385 (p. 380); David Jones, preface to *The Anathemata: Fragments of an Attempted Writing*, 2nd edn (London: Faber & Faber, 1955), pp. 9–43 (pp. 15–16).

I

MASS DISTRACTION: BETWEEN RITES AND RIGHTS IN DAVID JONES

David Jones's reverence for the Roman Catholic Mass was unshakeable. Half his life was spent on a never to be completed poem reflecting on the rite, much of it excerpted or expanded upon in his major published poetic writings: *The Anathemata*, *The Sleeping Lord and Other Fragments* and the recently recovered long poem *The Grail Mass*. Jones not only attended Mass regularly, but also annotated liturgical texts, turning them through his painted inscriptions into visual artworks. When the liturgy was revised following the Second Vatican Council, he responded with outraged letters to the Catholic papers.[1] Jones's behaviour hints at a temperamental piousness around which his personal, aesthetic and theological concerns coalesced. For Adam Schwartz, such piety was central to Jones's early religious and artistic development. Although he was an adult convert to Roman Catholicism, Jones never underwent 'a single galvanising crisis of faith', Schwartz contends, but rather 'believed from an early age in the importance of sacramental action and grew progressively disenchanted with what seemed staunch hostility to such practices in his received Protestantism'.[2] He recounts various anecdotes of Jones as a child embarrassing his low church parents: from kneeling at the creed's mention of the incarnation to marching with a handmade crucifix on Good Friday.[3] Jones, from these reports at least, was drawn from his earliest days to orthodoxy.

Jones also wanted, from an equally young age, to be an artist. His subsequent interest in the liturgy illuminated his vocation. A personal anecdote, outlined in his 1955 essay 'Art and Sacrament', connects his artistic vocation and his religious commitments:

> The question of analogy seemed not to occur until certain Post-Impressionist theories began to bulk larger in our student conversations. Then, with relative suddenness, the analogy between what we called 'the Arts' and the things that Christians called the eucharistic signs became (if still but vaguely) apparent. It became increasingly evident that this analogy applied to the whole gamut of 'making'.[4]

The host and the chalice, Jones's 'eucharistic signs', facilitate the transformation at the heart of the Mass. By the ministrations of the Holy Spirit and the cultic actions of the priest, the natural forms of bread and wine are as the *Catechism of the Catholic Church* explains changed at the core of their being, even as their outward appearance remains the same, in order to welcome the 'real presence' of Christ into the world.[5] Transubstantiation, the transformation enacted during the Mass, illuminates the post-Impressionist idea of 'significant form'. A painting of a mountain is to be understood not as an imitation of a natural form, so much as a new reality created by an arrangement of shapes and colours.[6] 'Significant' here invokes what Raymond Williams identified as an older sense of the terms 'real' or 'realism', which was connected to the idea of Platonic forms and contrasted 'not with *imaginary* but with *apparent*', denoting 'the true or fundamental quality of some thing or situation'.[7] The older sense co-exists with the more common usage of realism today to describe a form of art that is attentive to the concrete. The older usage, as Williams notes, stretches back to the medieval philosophers who formulated the ideas inherent in Jones's 'eucharistic signs'.[8] Thus, in connecting 'significant form' and 'real presence', Jones articulated a version of realism that both responded to the work of Roger Fry and Clive Bell and supplemented what he found lacking there.

The anecdote provides an alternative autobiographical trajectory. Here, Jones is not a Catholic-in-waiting drawn to art through his sacramental sensibility, but rather an artist who found in sacramental teachings an extension of his 'student conversations'. Jones-the-artist needed Roman Catholicism. His religion presented possibilities for his work and shed light on recent critical developments. While the mere fact of chronology – artist earlier, Catholic later – reveals little about the relative value ascribed to each aspect, the anecdote is nevertheless suggestive of an idiosyncratic outlook often obscured in accounts of Jones's art and religion. Kathleen Henderson Staudt, for instance, argues that across his work Jones exploits 'a carefully developed analogy between the act of sign-making performed by the poet and the acts performed by Christ (i.e., in Jones' orthodox Roman Catholic belief, by a fully human God) at the Last Supper and on the cross, actions that are effectively "re-called" at every celebration of the sacrament of the Eucharist'.[9] W. David Soud has described the poet in Jones's imaginings as 'a kind of lay priest' with artistic practice functioning as an analogy for the cultic actions undertaken at the altar.[10] Thomas Goldpaugh has even suggested that Jones's art itself is a subspecies of the Eucharist.[11] In all these readings, the features of what Staudt calls 'Jones's orthodox Roman Catholic belief' are assumed; they are part of the overarching Christian system to which Jones assents. Jones daringly unites modernist artistic expression and an orthodox outlook to produce a hybrid of the new and the traditional. Part of the burden of these accounts is to demonstrate the conviction with which Jones engaged with church teaching. He was an artist and a Catholic, but his was no aesthetic religion. Jones fused the otherwise non-religious concerns of modern art and the religious tropes of real presence, priestly intercession and the Eucharist in a unique form of modernism.

Even among intellectual converts, however, Jones's journey from post-Impressionism to Roman Catholicism was atypical. Fry and Bell, Jones's favoured theorists, were not known for their missionary fervour.[12] Jones's point of entry led him to view the Roman Catholicism he professed through the lens of his artistic commitments. Art informs his religion as his religion informs his art. The shift from a one-sided to a reciprocal understanding of the relationship between these terms reflects recent scholarship on lived religion. Given that the 'concepts of religion and religious commitment developed out of the European crucible of religious contests', our 'conceptual apparatus', Meredith B. McGuire observes, 'has simply failed to question the image of religious membership and individual religious practice built on mutually exclusive, indeed antagonistic, categories'.[13] Jones's post-Impressionist Roman Catholicism exemplifies the idea that lay or popular 'individual religious practice' is often far more idiosyncratic and creative than clerics and theologians have appreciated and provides a point of departure for a broader revaluation of modernism and antimodernist orthodoxy. Far from being a rigid, timeless, unbending system demanding only assent from adherents, orthodoxy is, Jones's example suggests, endlessly reimagined by its practitioners. Orthodoxy in its disciplinary guise is, itself, a product of the broader rewriting of religion effected by the secular. What Patrick Allitt has called the 'ostentatious orthodoxy' of converts, Robert Hugh Benson, G. K. Chesterton and Ronald Knox among them, is a measured response to features of twentieth-century religion and culture, including the developments outlined here under the heading of 'spilt mysticism'.[14]

The present chapter ranges over Jones's writings to describe a reimagined orthodoxy. First, it examines Jones's conception of sacrament across his aesthetics and cultural criticism, and then attends to Jones's unique understanding of participation in the Mass. The line of argument associated with the latter draws upon the relationship between the institutional and mystical elements of religion central to Friedrich von Hügel's work. While the connections Jones made between art and religion may well seem inward-turned or of merely denominational interest, the third section of the chapter presents Jones's 'wavering orthodoxy', exemplified by the recently recovered long poem *The Grail Mass*, as the basis for a religious critique of European imperialism. My survey of Jones's religious thought reveals neglected aspects of Jones's poetry. Following Thomas Dilworth's groundbreaking study *The Shape of Meaning in the Poetry of David Jones*, published in 1988, critical work on Jones has often emphasised what Dilworth sees as Jones's Coleridgean equation of form and sense, given Dilworth's attention to the macrostructure of *The Anathemata* and his discussions of local detail in relation to an overarching whole.[15] In attending to the poet's daring reformulations, the present chapter uncovers the dissonances, mismatches and divisions of Jones's 'wavering orthodoxy', revealing a different Jones and a new form of religious poetry.

BEYOND FRAZER: CHRISTIAN RITUAL IN THE AGE OF MODERNISM

Memory and Presence: Art in the Liturgy

Reading the study shortly after its publication in 1945, Jones was fascinated by Dom Gregory Dix's monumental work of liturgical scholarship, *The Shape of the Liturgy*, and the controversy it occasioned. Dix argued that revisions to the Anglican *Book of Common Prayer* challenged, or at least profoundly altered, the status of the Eucharist as a sacrament.[16] Setting aside understandings of the Eucharist as a re-enactment of Christ's sacrifice, the Prayer Book offered, as Jones put it, 'a quite un-Catholic interpretation of the Eucharistic Sacrifice' in the form of a memorial of a historical act now long since passed.[17] In the service outlined in the *Book of Common Prayer*, congregants did not, or so Dix claimed, participate in a sacrifice made possible by the ministrations of the priest; they merely memorialised Christ's actions, '*reminding* us of something no longer present'.[18] Dix was what John G. Maiden calls an Anglo-Papalist, a member of the Church of England desirous of reconciliation with Rome, and a vowed religious in an Anglican Benedictine community.[19] His argument thus resists the idea of the Anglican Church as a *via media* between the corrupt pomp of Roman Catholicism and reductive iconoclasm of Protestantism. For Dix, the Anglican liturgy was as Protestant as it came, representing a break with the Christian heritage that the Church of England was obligated to protect.

While rooted in sixteenth-century polemics, Dix's concerns with the status of the Eucharist enjoyed, somewhat surprisingly, considerable prominence in the age of modernism. A decade and a half before he published his study, Dix's interests were debated, albeit in slightly different terms, in the House of Commons and the House of Lords in 1927 and then again in 1928, after the Church of England sought and ultimately failed to obtain parliamentary approval for a revised *Book of Common Prayer*.[20] The 1927 Prayer Book, which given the outcome of the vote was never officially adopted, endeavoured to incorporate Catholic language and practices to mitigate what the committee charged with the revisions considered the excesses of Anglo-Catholic worship.[21] The parliamentary debate, however, was mobilised around the perceived challenge various concessions to Catholic practices posed to the Protestant identity of the Church of England, even if the intent behind the revisions had been to limit the influence of Roman Catholic liturgical practice on Anglican worship.[22] Dix's book reflects a political reality as much as his own religious affiliations.

Discussion of national Protestant identity was also bound up with questions about the relationship between religion and modernity. Incorporation of Catholic practices represented, in the eyes of some of the loudest voices in the Prayer Book debate, a falling away from the Protestant impulses that had, in ways that recall Max Weber's famous analysis, laid the basis for an emergent capitalist economy and propelled Britain forward as an industrial and imperial power.[23] Through the 1920s, Anglican liberals, otherwise known as modernists, grew increasingly concerned by the prominence Anglo-Catholics conferred upon what the modernists considered outdated ritualism.[24] A 1926 essay entitled 'Primitive Sacramentalism' published in the *Churchman's Union*, the organ of Anglican theological modernism, and written by the amateur anthropologist and canon H. J. D. Astley, drew on J. G. Frazer's *The Golden Bough* for the historical and theoretical justification to his argument that Protestant styles of worship represented a superior stage of religious development. Astley accepted Frazer's contention that Christian sacramental practice had its roots in an ancient, pre-Christian worldview. He drew on the processes of substitution and sublimation that Frazer outlined across his work to understand the Eucharist. *The Golden Bough* registers shifts in ritual practice: from the violence of the sacred murders at Nemi to later animal and vegetable sacrifices bearing only a faint resemblance to their founding violence. Such ritual 'cannibalism' anticipates the Eucharist, which later developed through animal and plant substitutions into the Christian unbloody sacrifice.

Astley's essay appeared as a committee was busily adding Catholic elements to the Prayer Book. His genealogy carried a none-too-subtle barb:

> Ideas as old as man, and still endowed with a living power among savages, are sublimated to the uses of the world's highest religion; while superstition, the surviving relics of these ideas of the antique world, still endows the Bread and Wine in the Eucharist with the actual Body and Blood of the Crucified, Risen, and Glorified Christ.[25]

For Astley, the paths of sublimation and substitution which led away from the founding violence of the rite were not, as they were for Frazer, processes of ossification leaving extant rites obscure, their original meanings and justifications lost in the process of change, but rather stages in a process of teleological evolution.[26] Belief in the real presence was regressive. Eucharist-as-memorial, by contrast, was the fruit of an ongoing civilising process and exemplified ethical progress in Christian history. Hastings Rashdall, a leading Anglican modernist himself, argued that the 'performance of ritual ordinances, sacrifices, acts of worship' are only 'valuable in so far as they stimulate to the doing of God's will in the service of man'.[27] Rashdall's concern was not sacrifice or memorial but rather ritual or no ritual. In a modern, forward-looking, socially useful church, ritual should yield to ethics, functioning as what Matthew Arnold termed '*extra-belief*, belief beyond what is certain and verifiable' that existed only to encourage upright conduct.[28]

Jones challenged apologists who often ascribed educational purposes to the Mass.[29] The Eucharist, as far he was concerned, effected change in and of itself. He found an ally in Dix. Jones drew on the scholar's description of the Greek term 'anamnesis', the word Christ uses in the gospels to institute the Eucharist, to understand how art works; *The Anathemata* says 'DO THIS | for my Anamnesis'.[30] Anamnesis is usually translated into English as 'in remembrance' (Luke 22: 19), but *remembrance* and *memorial*, Jones explains, connote 'something *absent* which is only mentally recollected'.[31] The Greek term, however, has, as Dix notes, 'the sense of "recalling" or "representing" before God an event in the past, so that it becomes *here or now operative by its effects*'.[32] Dix thus uses anamnesis to describe the re-presenting of Christ's sacrifice in the Mass in ways that undermine Protestant emphasis on the Eucharist as memorial.[33]

Jones was not driven solely by denominational antagonism. Anamnesis resonated further. In an undated letter draft most likely from the mid-1960s, Jones described his responses to the Mass, displaying an intense, almost connoisseur-like interest in every part of the rite. He outlined the significance of priestly vestments:

> And here at High Mass, in addition to the audible and immemorial chant, there was visible before one's eyes not only the chasuble & act of the celebrant, but the laticlaved tunicles of deacon & subdeacon, and one was thus taken back across the recent centuries, back over the middle-ages, beyond the barbarian invasions, back to the late-Roman world when these garments we have now were the paenula, tunica & linea worn by all respectable citizens of either sex, but by the 6th and 7th century conserved only by the Church and hence have become saturated with sacral associations.[34]

Here the Mass summons the Roman world of the Latin church. The historical dimension strikes the onlooker with force; priestly vestments, through their preservation of classical fashions, are responsible for a movement whereby one is violently transposed from the here and now and 'taken back' to that time. The past becomes part of the present, the present invaded by the past.

A similar manifestation turns on the movement between liturgical languages in an Easter week service. In the preface of *The Anathemata*, Jones writes:

> When in the Good Friday Office, the Latin, without any warning, is suddenly pierced by the Greek cry *Agios o Theos*, the Greek-speaking Roman church of the third century becomes almost visibly present to us. So to juxtapose and condition the English words 'O Holy God' as to make them do what this change from Latin to Greek effects within this particular setting, would not be at all easy.[35]

The moment is disorientating. Coming face-to-face with these Greek communities appears to be an essential part of the experience of the Mass and one that is obliterated by translation. Jones's 'present' recalls not only the re-presentation of anamnesis but also the real 'presence' of Christ. The Mass functions in anamnesis of not only Christ's sacrifice, but also a wealth of Christian history that floods a Mass-goer's attention at every given moment.

Jones and Dix were both unhappy with the term 'memorial' given its place in Reformation polemic. Yet, cultural memory is as important to Jones's appreciation of the liturgy as to his artistic work. The Roman and the Greek communities who shaped the aforementioned rites have long since disappeared; their significance is nevertheless recalled, recollected and honoured in the Mass. An act of memorial is an element but not the entirety of anamnesis, which requires for its completion a further addition. The re-presented past becomes manifest in tactile form. 'Real presence' is inevitably bound up with the actions of a priest. By means of intoning the prescribed prayers and in cooperation with the Holy Spirit that which is recollected is made present. Cultic prayers are less prominent in Jones's clothing- and language-related examples because anamnesis is generated by various forms within the Mass itself: the intricate drapery of priestly dress and the hybridity of the liturgical poetry, both distinct from the priest's utterances. Jones's examples highlight human craft: the rich embroidery of the 'laticlaved tunicles' and the careful work of the liturgists who juxtaposed rites in two different languages. Anamnesis requires memorial and creativity; the tactility or sensation of the latter exceeds what might otherwise be 'mentally recollected'. Jones's peculiar use of *The Shape of the Liturgy* could not have been anticipated by its author. Dix attended to the underlying structure of the liturgy, outlining how it made real the drama of the passion. Over the centuries, multiple editors had kept the outlines of the liturgy crisp and clear. Jones, alongside other cultural modernists such as Evelyn Underhill, maintained that the *Roman Missal* was an 'incomparable art-form'.[36] Jones's assessment reflected more than the quality of the liturgical poetry or illuminating organisation of the texts. Art was the means through which the Mass worked and that which it was ultimately about. The artistic dimension of religious practice, for Jones, shaped his entire engagement with Catholic dogma.

An encounter early in his career with Jacques Maritain's study *Art and Scholasticism* helped Jones make these connections. Jones read Maritain with Eric Gill in the Roman Catholic artistic community at Ditchling, Sussex in the early 1920s.[37] He did so under the guidance of Fr John O'Connor, who was both responsible for the first English translation of Maritain's work – itself printed at Ditchling – and the priest who received Jones into the Roman Catholic Church.[38] Contrary to what Maritain's title suggests, scholasticism, as Stephen Schloesser has noted, lacked an overt aesthetics.[39] Maritain revelled in the creative opportunity afforded by the absence, bringing together the scattered sayings of the schoolmen on the arts and reinterpreting other teachings through the lens of aesthetics. He also introduced modern sources into his discussion of medieval thought, reading Henri Bergson and Thomas Aquinas side-by-side. His idiosyncratic approach paired accounts of the scholastic position on art in the body of the text with footnotes from contemporary proponents of non-representational art. Maritain argued that scholastics and modern artists alike pursued 'a deeper sense of "form"' or an 'internal *entelechy* (and not "outward shape")' in their work; a version, that is, of the 'real' as opposed to the 'apparent'.[40] They both accepted 'the "deformation" of surface representations' in opposition to 'imitation as understood by nineteenth-century naturalism' in ways that resonated with Jones's attention to 'significant form'.[41]

The Catholic dogma Jones learned at Ditchling was thus already shaped by his artistic concerns. In a biographical sketch written in 1935, fifteen years after his conversion, Jones explained that 'certain ideas implicit or explicit in Catholic Dogma' had liberated his work.[42] First, 'the reality of matter and spirit that both are real and both good' was a principle, Jones explained, that united 'form and content and demands that in each particular the general should shine out, and that without the particular there can be no general for us men'.[43] Secondly, he learnt that 'God made and sustains the whole show <u>gratuitously</u>'; 'this gratuitous quality', he claimed, 'makes a painting good or bad'.[44] Jones's emphasis on the gratuitous speaks to Maritain's account of art as a habit or virtue, built up from the consistent exercise of a skill developed under expert tutelage.[45] Art is judged 'good or bad' not against preconceived standards, but rather according to whether or not it represents the discharge of an intrinsic skill. 'Art' is also a practical matter or, as Maritain writes, 'a *habitus* of the practical understanding'.[46] It deals, in Jones's words, with the 'reality of matter and spirit' and the 'particular'; it is not an effort to implement a theory or to put ideas into paint or words. The Roman Catholic Church sustained a spiritual 'order' tied to God's creativity, invoking the real beyond or behind the concrete details of realism. Jones's own art never embraced abstraction. The combined influence of the real on the one hand and 'significant form' on the other prevented his still-life paintings from becoming, through their attention to exquisite detail, merely faithful replicas of the world to which they attended.[47] He always hoped that his art gestured beyond itself towards Maritain's 'deeper sense of "form"'.

The conjunction of post-Impressionism and Catholic dogma responds to the religious transference of the epiphanic tradition. The post-Impressionist allusion to the older sense of 'real' appropriated the deeper values with which religions had once concerned themselves. In a painting by El Greco, for instance, a critic informed by post-Impressionism would insist that it is 'significant form' rather than the interplay between artistic vision and Christian subject matter that opens out on to the deeper emotions once associated with the divine mysteries. The role of art in relation to religion exhibits a curious doubleness. On the one hand, it preserves emotions and experiences typically deemed important to religion and which a purely rational world order might disregard. On the other, it insists that art itself is the conduit for those emotions and experiences and one need not gesture towards a metaphysical or spiritual component of reality. Charles Taylor describes the resulting tension in relation to the rise of total music:

> A love song evokes our being moved profoundly by some love story which seems to express a human archetype: Romeo and Juliet, say. The love song, play, opera gives us both the response expressed, and the intentional object of this response. Now with the new absolute music, we have the response in some way captured, made real, there unfolding before us; but the object isn't there. The music moves us very strongly, because it is moved, as it were; it captures, expresses, incarnates being profoundly moved. (Think of Beethoven quartets.) But what at? What is the object? Is there an object?[48]

The deep emotions once channelled by religious worship are here stoked by an art disconnected from dogma or theological definition. We are left instead with powerful, epiphanic experience. The new art, so moving and unexpected, subsequently becomes the object of theorisation. Attention shifts away from dogmatic or theological debate; the aesthetic experience itself, tinged with its religious emotions, replaces Christian revelation as the object of attention.

Post-Impressionism was itself a response to the declining status of representation. Bell's 'significant form' described how an onlooker might relate to a work of art without reference to anything outside the picture. The 'ontic commitments' of art become in the process 'very unclear'. Art may, Taylor continues, 'disclose very deep truths which in the nature of things can never be obvious, nor available to everyone, regardless of spiritual condition', but at the same time, 'combine with a denial of the deep ontic realities out there'.[49] The new art channels the emotions that once ran through religious traditions and – by at once challenging religion's exclusivity and presenting such exclusivity as outmoded – critiques the intellectual and organisational scaffolding upon which such responses had been erected. In her essay on 'Modern Fiction' from 1919, Virginia Woolf described James Joyce's *A Portrait of an Artist as a Young Man* as 'spiritual' in contrast to the work of Edwardian 'materialists'.[50] Joyce's lyrical interiority has more in common, she argued, with the intensity of pious self-examination than reform-minded realist fictions. Modern fiction captures an aspect of human experience neglected by the Edwardians. Woolf's 'spiritual' commitments nevertheless circumvent the emotional, intellectual and organisational framework in which pious self-examination had once been undertaken. Woolf's attention to the inner journey made possible by modern fiction draws, as Jane de Gay has argued, on her familial connection with the evangelical Clapham Sect, but it also takes the place of the institutional religious practice around which the Sect built their lives.[51] 'Spiritual' here is at once religious in its anti-materialism and antagonistic toward the practice of religion insofar as it assumes epiphanic transference.

Jones supplements Bell and Fry with the idea of real presence. The experience of looking at a painting through the post-Impressionist lens is flat, triggered by the surface of the canvas. While the painting might engage with the real rather than the apparent in its preference for deeper form over concrete detail, the status of that real risks circularity. The real becomes that towards which the juxtaposition of form gestures; the real is assured of its realness because it is that to which the juxtaposition of form gestures.[52] Unsatisfied by these ambiguities, Gill, during the lengthy colloquies he held while chiselling stone in his workshop at Ditchling, responded to Jones's enthusiasm for 'significant form' with a question 'significant of what'?[53] Jones met Gill's objections. He yoked post-Impressionism and the Eucharist to develop an analogy between the real presence of Christ in the communion wafer and the mountain under the forms of paint. Real presence invokes a gradient of value that supplies what was found otherwise wanting.

Jones also extended what he considered art in ways that reflect his fascination with priestly vestments and liturgical craft. Fiona MacCarthy suggests that Ditchling is best understood as a continuation of the Arts and Crafts movement.[54] Like William Morris, Jones found beauty in everyday objects. His greatest wish was to reintegrate the gratuitous and utilitarian, so that the excellence of, say, the chair-maker's skill might shine out in the beauty of his product.[55] Yet what Jones considered beautiful about such a chair was not its usefulness, but rather that it was made in line with the excellences of the relevant craft. It was produced neither in response to a market niche for a well-made chair nor because one design was more practical than another. The chair-maker had been trained to feel in a tactile sense the principles undergirding a well-made chair. The piece of furniture was the product of habituated knowledge. Jones understood the exercise of an artist's skill in an accordance with the values of a specific art as the gratuitous.

The process was ultimately understood as analogous to the creation story: 'And God said, Let there be light: and there was light. And God saw the light, that it was good: and God divided the light from the darkness' (Genesis 1: 1). True artists do not merely create – the equivalent of God's 'Let there be light' – they also share God's confidence in the excellence of their production; God saw that what he had created 'was good' (Genesis 1: 1). The artist recalls, shares in and makes present again and again divine creative power.

Going beyond even the Arts and Craft movement, Jones came to understand art in the broadest possible terms. Every exemplification of a habituated skill undertaken for non-utilitarian purposes became an art: from the decoration of a birthday cake to the development of military strategy; 'likeness derives from the fact that the art implicit in strategy is, like all other art, a sign of the form-making activities universally predicated of the Logos'.[56] Like painting or chair-making, cake decoration and strategising require the exercise of a particular skill in accordance with the good of a given discipline. The same might be said of the editors of the Christian liturgy as Jones found them discussed in Dix. These figures maintained the *Missal* with great skill not because they were aesthetes with a fine poetical or dramaturgical sense, but rather because they kept the aims of the liturgy as instituted by Christ at the forefront of their minds. They steered clear of any educative or polemical purposes, seeking instead to preserve, throughout periods of renewal and revision, an act of anamnesis.

Jones's expanded sense of art challenges the Mass-goer. The edited Mass has been organised with care by liturgists. Yet the liturgy is an amalgam of various arts: the poetic, the dramatological, the musical, even the textile, to name but a few. Jones understands these arts by means of analogy with the anamnesis at the centre of the Eucharist service. Analogy emphasises the difference between two terms while also underlining connections; human activity shares in God's work, even as the gulf between the two remains insurmountable. As with figurative language, there is similarity and difference. Jones nevertheless runs together the human and the divine. In his essay 'Art and Sacrament', for instance, artists

> partake in some sense, however difficult to posit, of that juxtaposing by which what was *inanis et vacua* became radiant with form and abhorrent of vacua by the action of the Artifex, the Logos, who is known to our tradition as the Pontifex who formed a bridge 'from nothing' and who then, like Brân in the *Mabinogion*, himself became the bridge by the Incarnation and the Passion and subsequent Apotheoses.[57]

The phrase 'partake in some sense, however difficult to posit' at once elucidates and circumvents analogy, hinting at a closer relationship between God and the artist even as it invokes official distance. More significant still, acts of artistic anamnesis within the liturgy, the presence of priestly vestments and the juxtaposition of liturgical languages, appear in close temporal proximity to the real presence at the heart of the Mass. Seen through Jones's eyes, the Mass represents multiple, varied acts of anamnesis. It dazzles. The other arts embedded in the liturgy are purposefully disruptive, breaking in on the consciousness of the assembled worshippers in epiphanic fashion. 'Spilt mysticism' pervades even traditional worship.

Celebration Rites: Eucharistic Theology and In Parenthesis

In staging these moments of distraction, Jones took his lead from a work of eucharistic theology produced by the Jesuit theologian, Maurice de la Taille, a man whom he once labelled 'my theologian'.[58] Over the course of his three-volume work, *Mysterium Fidei* – an opus that was helpfully summarised for the English lay reader by both the priest himself and Jones's friend, the Jesuit priest Martin C. D'Arcy – Taille argued that traditional views of the Mass underemphasised the role of Christ's self-offering in the passion.[59] Christ is, Taille argued, not merely a victim, but rather a *willing* victim; 'having put himself SYMBOLICALLY in the state of Victim', Taille writes, Christ 'hands himself over and dedicates himself to the Passion itself'.[60] Jones summarised Taille's words as follows: Christ made 'oblation of himself' and placed 'himself in the state of a Victim'.[61] Self-donation meant that Christ's sacrifice began not with his legal condemnation, his bitter journey along the Via Dolorosa or his subsequent crucifixion, but rather the 'oblative words & manual acts' of the Last Supper:

> He, on the day before he suffered death, took bread into his holy and worshipful hands, and lifting up his eyes to thee, God, his almighty Father in heaven, and giving thanks to thee, he blessed it, broke it, and gave it to his disciples, saying: Take, all of you, and eat of this:
>
> FOR THIS IS MY BODY.[62]

Christ was an artist. The 'incomparable art-form' of the 'Western Liturgy' did not form around him by accident or as a pseudo-scientific incantation designed to facilitate his reappearance. Sign-making was sanctioned by Christ through the bequest of the rite.[63]

Just as the Father created the universe, the Son creates in the Eucharist. Michon M. Mattheison notes how Taille resisted an 'essentially immolationist' understanding of sacrifice, which demanded 'destruction or change in the victim' via the communion wafers consumed by priest and congregation.[64] Taille instead separated the oblative-symbolic and immolative-physical acts; Jones made use of the differences between these terms. The Mass is at once performed poetry and sanctification of poetic vision. The act of making is itself part of the religious event, forever conjoined with the sacrifice on the cross.

Taille's new understanding of ritual informs a central scene from Jones's first book-length creative work, *In Parenthesis*, where art, eucharistic theology and comparative anthropology come together in an act of bricolage. Private John Ball, gazing out at Mametz Wood at stand-to, catches sight of a damaged branch. The sight is rendered in visionary terms:

> His eyes turned again to where the wood thinned to separate broken trees; to where great strippings-off hanged from tenuous fibres swaying, whitened to decay – as swung
> immolations
> for the northern Cybele.
> The hanged, the offerant:
> > himself to himself
> > on the tree.
> Whose own,
> whose grey war-band, beyond the stapled war-net –
> [. . .]
> Come from outlandish places,
> from beyond the world,
> from the Hercynian –
> they were at breakfast and were cold as he, they too made their dole.[65]

The passage resounds with religious violence. The sacrificial overtones of the damaged tree follow from the pun on 'strippings-off', which recalls across linguistic boundaries one of Jones's favourite texts, 'The Dream of the Rood'. In the Old English poem, the figure of Christ, described here as 'the young hero', is said 'to strip' before mounting 'the tree'.[66] In the Anglo-Saxon text, the hero's embarkation occurs after the tree had been uprooted and relocated to Golgotha. These acts are described as a violent assault. There is dramatic impart in associating the sacrifice with the German troops. Jones alludes to the common ancestry of Odin's Swedish worshippers and the German soldiers to underscore the savagery of the enemy in ways that reflect British propaganda or the trench-talk of Ball's company: 'these | barbarians, | them | bastard square-heads'.[67] The Germans on the other side of Mametz wood are the 'grey war-band' from the 'Hercynian wood' whose ancestors sacrificed to Odin, the 'northern Cybele'.

In describing a vision of crucifixion, Jones switched from Christian history to *The Golden Bough* to shine new light on the Christian mysteries. Jones was drawn to the correspondence between the Odin story and the Christian gospel. He invoked the older tale, he later explained, to enable readers to 'feel the amazing nature of what our theology proposes'; the 'primitive, stark realism' of the Uppsala scene 'jolts one into some apperception of the total mysterium'.[68] The influence of Frazer is felt in the lines 'The hanged, the offerant: | himself to himself | on the tree'. These lines adapt an Icelandic poem recalling a ritual murder. The source is quoted in Jones's endnotes to *In Parenthesis*:

> I know that I hung on the windy tree
> For nine whole nights,
> Wounded with the spear, dedicated to Odin,
> Myself to myself.[69]

The Icelandic poem recounts an act of substitution for the ritual murder of the divine king in which the King of Sweden, Od, sacrificed 'nine of his sons to Odin at Uppsala in order that his own life might be spared'.[70] Jones's 'hanged' recalls both the painful posture of the crucified Christ and Odin's role as 'Lord of the Gallows'. The relationship with the Christian saviour invoked by the allusion to *The Golden Bough* serves as a connection between British and German troops, but the hints of barbaric violence cannot be expunged.

How should the relationship between the Christian message and the primal violence found in Frazer be understood? For an answer, Jones turned to Taille. The Jesuit's eucharistic theology was built on terminology never previously expounded systematically in church documents, namely the terms 'immolation' and 'oblation'. While the terms had often been used interchangeably, Taille teased out the differences. He explained:

> the Supper and the Passion answer each other. They complete and compenetrate each other. The one presents to our eyes the sacerdotal, sensible, ritual oblation, wherein consists the mystic immolation; the other adds to it the real, bloody, all-sufficient immolation, of which the first was the figure.[71]

The crucifixion, like the sacrifice of Odin's sons, was an act of immolation; it involved the destruction of a physical body and was thus in keeping with contemporary neo-scholastic understandings of the Eucharist. Christ was immolated on the cross and he is immolated again in every celebration of the Mass. In addition to immolation, Taille continued, every sacrifice included oblation or a formal liturgical offering made from an inward disposition.[72] The Last Supper and the Passion, while not separate, are not one and the same; to treat them otherwise would be to present the trappings of the Christian liturgical tradition as nothing more than the staging of a technical, cultic act. The congregation attending the Mass partakes in Christ's immolation, but also enters what Taille called 'the order of signs'.[73] The creative, tactile element of anamnesis draws its life from Taille.

The connection between immolation and oblation runs through *In Parenthesis*. Following the vision of the Christ-Uppsala sacrifices in the wood, German carollers disrupt Ball's reverie:

> And one played on an accordion:
> > *Es ist ein' Ros' entsprungen*
> > *Aus einer Wurzel zart.*
>
> Since Boniface once walked in Odin's Wood.
> Two men in the traverse mouth-organ'd;
> four men took up that song.
> > *Casey Jones mounted on his engine*
> > *Casey Jones with his orders in his hand.*
>
> Which nearer,
> which so rarely insular,
> unmade his harmonies,
> honouring
> this rare and indivisible
> New Light
> for us,
> over the still morning honouring.[74]

The previous gesture towards Germanic violence is shrugged off as oblation answers immolation. The German soldiers strike up a carol on the accordion. Their volley is returned by two British mouth-organists and four singers, the sound of whom echoes through the passage, working its way into the poem itself in snatches of song. The voices of the opposing armies modulate against each other. The English-language musical retort sounds out as an antiphon to the German carol – the scene takes place on Christmas Day – and the narrative reflects in a lyrical tone upon the event, signified by the move into a spiritual register and changing typography. Strikingly, the narrative elements of the Passion story are reordered. While Christ's symbol-infused self-offering at the Last Supper prefigures his suffering on the cross, the visionary representation of immolation in *In Parenthesis* receives an answer in the oblative music the soldiers, even in the face of wartime privations, continue to offer. Reworking Frazer's comparative ritualist approach, Jones connects ancient rites and Christian tradition via not the violence in which they engaged, but rather their creative dimension.

For Jones, the creative dimension of human history revealed an essential truth. To treat oblation as merely ornament obscuring the violence inherent in ritual practice is to misinterpret not only the rites but also human identity and motivation. Elsewhere, as the final section of this chapter demonstrates, Jones invoked such terms to criticise imperialism. A human being 'is *essentially* a creature of sign and *signa*-making, a "sacramentalist" to the core', he maintained; an article of faith revealed to him through the creation story and Christ's institution of the Eucharist.[75] Empire, as Jones understood it, stifled the creative impulse. The administrators of empire dismissed sign-making, making it impossible for all but a few to live out their true human nature.

Jones's insight came to him via his recast religion. Not only did he transpose Catholic dogma onto aspects of modern art, but also reworked the Catholic doctrine of real presence. Jones's remodelled doctrine demanded the attention of even non-Catholics or non-artists (in the narrow sense). Everyone was a sign-maker, Jones contended, able to look to the Roman Catholic Church for guidance. In pursuing a set of interrelated artistic questions, Jones came to see the problems faced by an idiosyncratic painter and poet like himself as foundational for modern society. His Roman Catholicism not only helped him universalise, but also provided a means of effecting change.

CHURCHGOING, MIND-WANDERING: VARIETIES OF
RELIGIOUS PARTICIPATION

The Art of Bricolage: Describing Personal Religion

While he remains the committed Catholic familiar from earlier accounts, the Jones who emerges from the present chapter remakes and reimagines central elements of his tradition. Censorship has obscured Jones's idiosyncrasy. In editing Jones's manuscripts for *The Roman Quarry*, Harman Grisewood and René Hague, for instance, suppressed a passage in which Jones described Christ as 'both the sign and thing signified'; the material was 'dauntingly theological', they explained, and the phrase in question, at the outset of the 1980s when the valences of 'sign' and 'signified' were being debated in poststructuralist theory, was 'picked up and mis-used by expounders of D. J.'.[76] Treating Christ as a 'sign' questioned his status as a historical personage. In context, the passage refers to the Last Supper, where Christ is at once the historical personage who instituted the Eucharist ('thing signified') and the real presence in the communion wafers offered thereafter ('sign'). The suppressed passage testifies to the significance Jones conferred upon 'the order of signs', an emphasis that jars with pre-conciliar understandings of the Mass.

Grisewood and Hague's account of Jones's Catholicism was inhibited by the limited critical language available for the discussion of personal religion. Making a similar point, T. S. Eliot criticised Irving Babbitt for contrasting a version of Buddhism Babbitt himself had developed from the careful study of scripture and philosophy with a form of Christianity equated with the decayed religiosity of a childhood Sunday school.[77] The comparison was illegitimate, Eliot thought. Buddhist scripture and philosophy should be paired with Christian scripture and philosophy; if Babbitt wanted to look at popular religion he would have to turn to sociology. The mismatch served Babbitt's rhetorical aims, his argument for the superiority of Buddhism to Christianity, but also finds him treating the mixing of religious registers as unproblematic.[78] Grisewood and Hague knew their friend to be a Catholic and equated his religious commitment with acquiescence to traditional pieties, underestimating the degree to which Jones reworked his tradition. While Eliot's manifesto 'Tradition and the Individual Talent' is a literary-critical document, the 'great labour' of reordering literary monuments might well provide a means of understanding the relationship between personal religion and a religious tradition.[79]

Recent scholarship on lived religion has turned its attention to lay belief. Scholars have emphasised the degree to which lay believers mix ideas and concerns otherwise kept carefully separate by religious leaders, creating a form of bricolage. McGuire describes bricolage as 'a social practice by which an individual constructs a creative assembly by eclectically pasting together seemingly disparate, preexisting bits and pieces of meaning and practice'.[80] 'The pieces may appear disparate to the outside observer', McGuire continues, 'but they are not nonsensical to the person engaging in such creative syntheses, which make sense and are effective in his or her world of meaning and experience'.[81] For some groups of spiritual seekers, a 'creative synthesis' might constitute a new religious movement. Blending doctrines and practices from the occult and a variety of non-Western religions, theosophy is a prominent large-scale example, but one might also look to, say, the fusion of Protestant Christianity with either bodily healing in Christian Science or Pan-African ideas in Rastafarianism. Comparable acts of bricolage occur on a smaller scale within orthodoxy, too. Individuals and groups draw on traditional and non-traditional sources alike to develop a religious practice that makes 'sense' of various strands of religious tradition and becomes 'effective' in 'meaning and experience'.

Jones's marrying of Frazer, Taille and post-Impressionism renders him a bricoleur. Looking back on his career in 1961 in a letter to a friend, Jones described the central influences on his art, poetry and cultural criticism. He explained that the influence of the Roman Catholic Church, of his friends the historian Christopher Dawson and publisher Tom Burns, the literary innovations of James Joyce and Eliot, combined with the religious and culture insights of Oswald Spengler, Taille and Hügel provided 'a kind of "unity of indirect reference" which seemed to tie-up with what little artistic perceptions one had by nature oneself, and gave edge and certainty and conviction to one's work'.[82] The named figures answered questions Jones himself had posed and their answers seemed to respond to each other such that their insights conferred a particular shape upon his work. Jones's art served as a lens through which he viewed his own religion and the resulting bricolage weighed upon his approach to the sacraments.

Friedrich von Hügel's Religious Tensions

Hügel, a name included in Jones's pantheon of inspirations, offered a nuanced account of personal religion helpful for understanding Jones's work. Hügel was an Austrian-born Roman Catholic philosopher of religion and a naturalised British citizen, well-known to Catholics in England and across Europe. He was a friend and an associate of two prominent priests: the polemicist and spiritual writer George Tyrrell and the biblical scholar Alfred Loisy, figures excommunicated from the Roman Catholic Church in the wake of the antimodernist bull *Pascendi Dominici Gregis* (1907).[83] Hügel, himself a prominent modernist, avoided Tyrrell's and Loisy's fate due to his status as a layman. Jones considered him an influence on *The Anathemata* and elsewhere admitted to having been 'quite addicted' to his work in the late 1920s and early 1930s.[84] The philosopher of religion shaped Jones's attitude to the liturgy as seen in the poet's attention to the Mass-goer during Mass. Jones's poetic work from the late 1930s onwards attends to the Mass-goer's experience. Hügel helped Jones understand how, during a religious service, he could be at once an artist and a Catholic.

Hügel's advocacy for mysticism served as a counterweight to a particular kind of Catholic mindset. Jones discussed the issue at length with friends, including the aforementioned Dawson. Writing in 1942, Jones recalled that Dawson told him Catholics were 'getting far more, not less, "institutional" (in the bad sense) and mechanical'.[85] To Dawson, 'the age of von Hugel [*sic*], the "belief" in the Holy Ghost, in the subtlety of where truth resides' appeared 'far away' and had been replaced by a 'belief in effecting things by organization and formulas'.[86] Dawson's and Jones's understanding of '"institutional" (in the bad sense)' came from Spengler, a figure whom Jones praised for his 'very special insight into the cyclic character' of 'periods of decline'.[87] Jones noted the oscillation in Spengler between phases of ascendant 'culture', which develop new symbolic, creative forms of expression, and periods of descending or degenerating 'civilisation', which reuse the now-mummified forms of the previous period of cultural growth.[88] The cultural phase births religions, Christianity included, and encourages creativity, while the prominence of a critical attitude marks civilisational epochs, which typically concentrate their intellectual labour on imperial expansion. Contemporary religious practice was shaped by civilisational concerns, leading Catholics to mimic bureaucratic procedures rather than to engage creatively with their tradition. In a 1941 article for a Catholic paper, Jones criticised proposals for a Catholic Art Guild, which would have endeavoured to ensure that Catholic artists produced art reflective of the Roman Catholic Church's principles. Jones insisted: 'The Church cannot by making rules or by any other direct means hope for an art congenial to her liturgical forms from a civilisation that does not, and cannot, by its very nature, produce such art'.[89] While the reference to a 'civilisation' failing to produce art is drawn directly from *The Decline of the West*, Jones's distaste for a contemporary church obsessed with 'rules' reflects a distinctive application of Spengler's theory.

The term 'institutional' played a different role in Hügel's critical vocabulary. *The Mystical Element of Religion* attends to personal religion, rather than ecclesiological organisation or theological consideration, offering a phenomenology of religious belief. Personal religion is constituted by various elements: the institutional, the rational and the mystical (1, pp. 50–82). The institutional element encompasses the degree to which the individual adopts or internalises the teaching of dogma and tradition. Hügel explained:

> We have seen how all religiousness is ever called into life by some already existing religion. And this religion will consist in the continuous commemoration of some great religious facts of the past. It will teach and represent some divine revelation as having been made, in and through such and such a particular person, in such and such a particular place, at such and such a particular time; and such a revelation will claim acceptance and submission as divine and redemptive in and through the very form and manner in which it was originally made (1, p. 70).

Institutional religion is a repository of 'divine revelation' and its ministers exercise a teaching role. Churches communicate historical revelation, delivered initially in a particular time and place, to subsequent generations of adherents, always adapting the received teaching to meet new circumstances. The institutional element registers an individual's engagement with public and historical facets of organised religion. Yet Hügel remains open to different forms of response. The truths communicated 'claim acceptance and submission' from adherents. Orthodoxy frequently portrays the churches as formulating, and the laity as assenting to, 'the demands of doctrine'.[90] Scholars have traced the emergence of such attitudes to the pressures that eighteenth-century natural sciences exerted on the idea of religion.[91] Religious dogmas came to enjoy an equivalence to first principles in matters of science; acceptance of precepts was required both to participate in religious life and to understand subsequent natural processes. In early twentieth-century Roman Catholicism, the dominant neo-scholastic theological tradition typically understood itself, too, as an objective, holistic rational system, largely distinct from the assumptions of modernity. Neo-scholastic orthodoxy, according to Gabriel Daly, was conceptualised as 'devotion to an alleged "whole" which had to be defended against the modification of any of its parts'.[92] As a modernist who criticised the prevailing tradition, Hügel argued that the acceptance of 'religious facts' was merely one facet of personal religion; he goes on to add rational and mystical elements to the institutional. Yet elsewhere the institutional element requires more than mere assent. Hügel highlights how religion is 'called into life' by the churches in ways that hint at something deeper than 'acceptance and submission': a sense of awe that overpowers the individual, even if subsequent work involves the 'commemoration' of 'religious facts of the past'.

Hügel used a developmental analogy to depict the relationship between his elements. He explained that for a child, religion is 'a Fact and Thing' with a solidity that tends towards the institutional (1, p. 51); for an adolescent, it is 'Thought, System, a Philosophy' (1, p. 52); and for a mature adult, it becomes that which is 'felt' rather 'than seen or reasoned about' (1, p. 53). The dangerous transition between institutional and rational religion presents the three elements as successive stages in a process of spiritual development. Hügel highlights what he terms the 'necessary' and 'perilous' transition from the 'child's religion' to the 'right and normal type of a young man's religion' (1, p. 54). Transition meant leaving behind the former, which was 'so simply naïve and unselfconscious, so tied to time and place and particular persons and things, so predominantly traditional and historical, institutional and external' (1, p. 54). Later, Hügel highlights the moment of transition from the rational religion of youth that is 'incomplete and semi-operative' to the adult incorporation of what is 'deepest and nearest to his will' (1, p. 55). To rely too greatly upon pre-formulated doctrines or to be forever arguing about their legitimacy is to stunt one's own religious development. Religious maturity assumes passage through all three stages and an ability to think broadly, deeply and creatively about one's own religious tradition and the world in relation to that tradition. Moving from childhood to adolescence remains 'perilous'. The elements of religion do not tesselate but rather grind together, wearing each other down or even pulling apart.[93] The refusal of harmony had political significance. Hügel was a modernist who challenged the prevailing neo-scholastic outlook which had, in the words of Lawrence F. Barmann, equated modern Roman Catholicism with 'the narrowest of scholastic orthodoxies' that 'left no room in the Roman church for any efforts towards a theological synthesis which would take seriously the intellectual advances made since the thirteenth century'.[94] The developmental analogy encodes a critique of the intellectual system it challenged, finding it immature and limited. Hügel casts the mystical element of religion as a counterpart to neo-scholasticism. Tyrrell shared Hügel's concerns. He used, for instance, his reading of the mystical writer Julian of Norwich with her visionary, emotionally engaged, creatively astute meditations on sin and evil to challenge the received formulation of the doctrine of hell.[95] Unimpressed by such musings, the Vatican labelled the modernists 'pseudo-mystics' and condemned their work.[96] Tyrrell and Hügel both worried that the emphasis neo-scholastic theology placed on rationalism undermined the status of Roman Catholicism as a living tradition.

Hügel's sensitivity to the tension between elements of religion informed his work as a spiritual director. His letters of spiritual guidance to Gwendolen

Greene (then Parry), collected as *Letters from Baron Friedrich von Hügel to a Niece*, became a spiritual classic upon its publication in 1928, and often touched on the inverse of Dawson and Jones's complaints. One such letter read:

> You know, dear, how much and often I insist with you on the visible, the historical, the social, the institutional. But this is done without even the temptation to doubt, or to treat lightly, moments of formless prayer. Such formless prayer, where genuine, is, on the contrary, a deep grace, a darling force and still joy for the soul.[97]

Greene had written about a moment of 'formless prayer' experienced in her parish church. While neo-scholastic Roman Catholics might be accused of over-emphasising 'the visible, the historical, the social, the institutional' or the role of ratiocination, Greene's problem was the opposite: she was prone to these mystical explorations.

For Hügel, his niece's spiritual preferences were characteristically modern. He began *The Mystical Element* with the observation that religious people today 'want a strong and interior, a lasting yet voluntary bond of union between our own successive states of mind, and between what is abiding in ourselves and what is permanent within our fellow-men' (1, p. 3). In the twentieth century, religion is shaped by an attraction to the 'strong and interior'. The communal and ethical facets of religion can no longer be promulgated, so the argument runs, via administrative or dogmatic fiat; they must appeal to what is 'abiding in ourselves and what is permanent within our fellow-men'. The pervasiveness of secular mysticism helped reshape religious practice, although Hügel's example highlights how the cultivation of inner depths might co-exist with respect for the institutional element of religion.

The system outlined in *The Mystical Element* contextualises the spiritual diagnosis Hügel afforded Greene. He warned that over encouraging the mystical element in some spiritual constitutions risked cultivating an 'impoverishing oneness': a concentrated monomania in which all worldly concerns are neglected as the individual retreats inwards (1, p. 73). The soul becomes 'weak or feverish' through refusal to bend 'under the yoke' of institutional religious practice (1, p. 74). He concludes:

> And hence the soul of a Mystical habit will escape the danger of emptiness and inflation if it keeps up some [. . .] of that outgoing, social, co-operative action and spirit, which, in the more ordinary Christian life, has to form the all but exclusive occupation of the soul, and which here, indeed, runs the risk of degenerating into mere feverish, distracted 'activity' (2, p. 356).

Given her preference for the formless, Greene needs, he thinks, the spiritual friction consequent on 'outgoing, social, co-operative' pursuits, while for others these activities would be harmful distractions. In those in whom the mystical element is underdeveloped, there is a risk of *'simultaneous* exclusiveness' (1, p. 71), where religion becomes a mere 'thing' to be protected from all other things: 'Science and Literature, Art and Politics must all be starved or cramped. Religion can safely reign, apparently, in a desert alone' (1, p. 71). There is a danger, too, of *'temporal, successive* exclusiveness' in which religion stands in need of defence 'against any kind of modification' that rational consideration or emotional intuition might suggest (1, p. 71). Thinking of modern resistance to religious authority, the sociologist Robert N. Bellah has reminded us that the 'intellectual has always needed to find a religious form that genuinely expressed his own individuality'.[98] Far from a marker of elite religion, Hügel depicts the search for 'a religious form' expressive of 'individuality' as a feature of the mature religion of all believers. Mysticism counters childish attachments to religious facts and arguments.

Forms of Formlessness: Individualistic Worship in The Anathemata

The developmental account of the elements of religion receives extensive annotation in Jones's copy of *The Mystical Element of Religion*. Likewise, the tension between the institutional and the mystical shapes the poem to which Jones returned throughout the second half of his life: one attending to the daydreams of a Mass-goer during the Mass. The roots of Jones's attempt to make a work of art by recording the perception of a Mass-goer lie in his 'Absalom, Mass', a piece that Jones drafted around 1939.[99] The draft incorporated the following passage:

> The eyes of the testy
> man in cloth of Reims gilt-edged seems to
> be regarding intently No. 6 switch — that's
> for the onion stone in the South Aisle.
> *General Gandolf late of this parish*
> *And all his men drowned at*
> *Passchendaele in a very dark sea.*
> He hunches free of wrist with tetchy twist the Gothic folds,
> (O give us a fiddle back any day).
> You can hear a penny stop, or
> beads dropt, or cat-call from pleasure-go-round other side
> Tiber, or bat-wing brush in sanctus-pent
> high up and over the table spread. [. . .] The lumpish man
> clears his throat; Brother Ass must belch for all

> his May Day hat; the belly mumbles though
> it serve Melchisedec. He makes bold with the
> initial vowels. Thumbs a page or so. Smooths the
> violet marker out. Swift on professionally to mind his
> Roman step. Seems to search for what
> mislaid, tilts this ever so little with curious deliberation,
> backhands Mrs. Naylor's leaning lily clear of the instruments.
> His recollected fingers now. The supports close in.
> Each to his proper station. He stands upright
> now in the midst of the traverse, his cuisses on
> his thighs, his feet shod. Girt about the paps
> the Cyrenian deacons lean inward to
> relieve the weight.
> (You can hear the whine now in the south
> porch where Mrs. Fipps has chained Argos the dog
> for a thousand quarantines).[100]

The excerpt follows the speaker's roving eye as he tracks back and forth between a priest's cultic actions and the goings-on in a parish church: the worries of a parishioner, a war monument, the strange silence, some bodily noises, the flowers on the altar and a barking dog. Even the rite itself becomes a form of distraction. The minute weighing of the priest's actions: his pronunciation of the Latin, his gait, his thumbing of his Mass book, borders on the bathetic. The effect is exacerbated by the religious register in which bodily functions are recorded: the rumbling of the priest's stomach and his bloated state on the one hand and his role as servant of Melchisedec and St Francis's description of the body as 'Brother Ass' on the other. The passage attends to the spiritual connotations of the everyday or rather the mundane context for much religious practice.

Jones nevertheless struggles to confer order and purpose on his account of distraction. Robert Browning's lines from 'The Bishop Orders his Tomb at St. Praxed's Church' – 'Old Gandolf with his paltry onion-stone, | Put me where I may look at him!'[101] – confer the name on the general remembered in the memorial as Jones's text trips from 'onion stone' to 'General Gandolf'. Jones's dramatic personage rehearses what he sees. The allusion to Browning, however, is made by the author and directed to the reader over the head of the character. Such verbal gesticulating is the stock-in-trade of the dramatic monologue; the repetitive sputtering about 'Gandolf' in Browning's own dramatic monologue, for instance, underlines the petty rivalries that drove the bishop in life. Jones's allusion reveals an unresolved tension between the dramatic personage's roving eye and the associative mind of his creator.[102] It is unclear whether we are exploring what the speaker sees or using his stray thoughts as a springboard to further meditation.

In the Mass that frames *The Anathemata*, Jones depicts a similar moment of distraction, but excises altogether the dramatic personage. He follows instead the shifting foci of what Dilworth calls 'a meditative daydreamer', increasing the emphasis on the material associated with the mystical element and minimising the dramatic situation itself.[103] Jones's experimental text oscillates between 'the visible, the historical, the social, the institutional' represented by the rite and his own creative thoughts that lead off in various directions from Arthurian legend to Roman Britain and the shipyards of Bermondsey. In dropping the dramatic personage, *The Anathemata* – with its mixture of Roman Catholic culture, artistic concerns and fascination with English and Welsh history – became more personal: the poem shares these interests with its author, and simultaneously more general insofar as Jones is freed from the limited perception of a given character. The mystical aspect of *The Anathemata* is best understood as not so much a retreat inward to be alone with God as a branching out that connects past and present, the gratuitous and the utile, the sacred and the secular.

Unsurprisingly, perhaps, for a man for whom Roman civic life and early Greek-speaking Christians were summoned up in the liturgy, Jones's mystical response to the Mass was idiosyncratic. He lived through a protracted campaign for, and ultimately the achievement of, a vernacular Roman Catholic liturgy; the shift reflected worries about the limited participation afforded the congregation in the Tridentine Latin rite. According to Donald Attwater, a monk Jones met on Caldey Island while on retreat and who eventually became a vocal proponent of a vernacular Mass, the 'text-book answer' to the question of lay participation was that the Mass was 'an action in which we amply co-operate by interior union and a general knowledge of what is being done, and that we need not bother about anything else'.[104] The imaginative engagement that drove Jones does not feature. Religious assent is pictured as compliance or even the mere absence of dissent, amounting to little more than showing up and not complaining too much. By being physically present at the Mass, the laity participated in a rite undertaken on their behalf by the priest. Attwater observed that such participation meant that 'most of the worshippers are not using their voices at all, their bodies very little and that not ritually and understandingly; and their inward worship is individualistic, their minds confined within the limits of their own resources instead of being enlarged by the words and actions of the Church's rite'.[105] For Jones, the opportunity for 'individualistic' worship amidst the bustle of communal prayer was precisely what attracted him.

Not everyone concerned with the liturgy was content to leave the congregation to their own devices. The liturgical movement, of which Attwater was a key British exponent, was an international network led by the American Benedictine monk Virgil Michel and the journal *Orate fratres*, which sought to achieve social reform through increased attention to the liturgy.[106] Dismissing concerns like Jones's, Romano Guardini, a German liturgical scholar and author of the seminal study *The Spirit of the Liturgy*, insisted that, in coming to the Mass, a member of the congregation must 'shake off the narrow trammels of his own thought, and make his own a far more comprehensive world of ideas' and 'go beyond his little personal aims and adopt the educative purpose of the great fellowship of the liturgy'.[107] Guardini asked Mass-goers to lose themselves in the ritual; they were to favour dignified ordonnance over emotive despair, leaving 'personal aims' at the door of a 'great fellowship'. In demanding the congregation's attention, the liturgical movement elevated lay involvement in the Mass, turning those in the pews from spectators into participants. The project was linked to the theological idea of the Roman Catholic Church as the mystical body of Christ, composed of members, lay and clerical, all of whom made distinct contributions: 'Through the sacraments of Christian initiation, men and women are incorporated into Jesus Christ. Such incorporation unites them not only to Christ, but also to one another through shared membership in that same body. All members share in Christ's life and in his priesthood'.[108] For Jones, by contrast, incorporation was centred on art and making, epitomised by the Eucharist but undertaken outside as much as inside church services and ultimately open to Christians and non-Christians alike.

These theological reflections are at a far remove from Hügel's *The Mystical Element*. While it became a central motif at the Second Vatican Council, the mystical body exemplified the contentious ideas from which Hügel shied away through his attention to personal religion. Jones, too, revelled in the space *The Mystical Element* created. While Attwater and Guardini's interest in liturgical reform was driven by their theological commitments, Jones's attachment to the Mass owed much to its place in the 'unity of indirect reference' sanctioned by Hügel's understanding of mature religion as incorporating what was 'deepest and nearest to his will'. Rather than seeking systematic exposition, the poet-artist probed the connections between his various interests, forever straining the supposed unity. Jones took inspiration from Hügel's fascination with the tensions between the elements of religion. Friction strengthened religion by chastening any potential triumphalism (2, pp. 378–79). Christian engagement with the sciences, for example, was to be understood as a necessary asceticism that hurt and troubled, but ultimately transformed a religious tradition into a more coherent whole.

Jones's dramatisation of the divided mind during the Mass played out in the daring 'Mass within the Mass' scene in the 'Mabinog's Liturgy' section of *The Anathemata*. The daydreaming so central to Jones's text is captured in the poem's misdirection of the reader. The passage begins with a celebration of Queen Gwenhwyfar's dress, prior to her entry into her chapel, before shifting its focus to the altar. The passage continues:

So, wholly super-pellissed of British wild-woods, the chryselephantine column (native the warm blood in the blue veins that vein the hidden marbles, the lifted abacus of native gold) leaned, and toward the Stone.

And on and over the stone the spread board-cloths and on this three-fold linen the central rectangle of finest linen and on the spread-out part of this linen the up-standing calix that the drawn-over laundered folds drape white.[109]

Jones works hard to suggest a continuity between the two paragraphs. The presentation of the respective last and first lines as a single, albeit broken, line insists upon a connection that is further emphasised by the repetition of 'stone' across the paragraphs. Likewise, the coordination of 'And on and over' maintains a section-long pattern in which the narrator directs the reader's gaze over Gwenhwyfar's clothing.[110] As the narrative shifts its attention from the queen's drapery to the dressed altar, these features work to obscure the switch between referents of the nouns: Gwenhwyfar (the 'column', 'the hidden marbles' and 'the Stone') and the altar ('the stone'). The distractions of the 'Absalom, Mass' (the whining dog outside, the whispers in the pews, new hats) become a puzzle for the reader: proper and improper objects of devotion mingle and do so as part of Jones's expanded sacramentalism. The Mass and Gwenhwyfar's dress are both celebrations of gratuitous sign-making.

Hague worried about the implications of the interplay between sacred and secular. He wonders whether Jones thought 'he could carry off successfully so fantastic an exaggeration of praise' but concludes the poet's 'sense of worship and the obliquity with which the praise is offered' ultimately facilitated his success.[111] Jones's supposed self-doubt tells against the radicalism of juxtaposing the Eucharist and human craft. Jones's decision, however, was no mere accidental association, but rather the driving force behind his creative and critical work and a structuring principle of the poem. Hague's attempt to enforce the boundaries of orthodoxy rubs up against the creative freedoms Jones found in Hügel's mystical element.

While the demotic language of the earlier Mass text is not retained, *The Anathemata* scene nevertheless ends with an earthy joke that gestures towards the everyday concerns of the 'Absalom, Mass'. After the queen arrives, the narrative voice observes:

It was fortunate for the innate *boneddigion* of Britain that when at the prayer *Qui pridie* she was bound as they to raise her face, she as they, faced the one way, or else when the lifted Signa shone they had mistaken the object of their Latria.[112]

The eyes of the assembled gentlemen (*'boneddigion'*) are drawn to the brilliantly dressed queen when convention demands that they look to the elevated host. The assiduous politeness of 'mistaken the object of their Latria' is mismatched with what is reported, namely the laddish joke about the attention the queen's looks command: the assembled men could not take their eyes off her. The confusion between the human craftsmanship evident in the queen's vestments and the proper 'object of their Latria' enables Jones to cultivate an equivalence between the two. In his reading of *The Anathemata*, Soud hints at a similar process at work elsewhere by which Jones endeavours to 'conflate' the roles of priest and artist and thus to break down rigorous theological distinctions.[113] Moments of distracted worship cast art and religion alike as sacramental pursuits.

The adoption of a disembodied lyrical voice not only allows the poem to capture distraction without risking banality, but also empowers Jones to refine his account of distraction. In *The Anathemata*, the verse is not concerned with stray coughs and stifled giggles; what distracts from the Mass is the intricacy of human craftsmanship. Jones saw ritual emanating in evolutionary terms from the human capacity for dream and creativity.[114] He commended *The Golden Bough* not for its central thesis, the link between the king and the health of the land as a connecting thread between multiple rites, but rather the creative capacities revealed by the rites themselves. The Christian gospel provided a hermeneutic, revealing the special value accorded human sign-making; via the exercise of creativity, we share in divine action.

'A Great Robbery is Empire': Politics and Religious Critique
Rituals and Rights: Catholic Thought and the Dignity of the Human Person

Jones's celebration of distraction conflicted with other aspects of his aesthetics. From Maritain, Gill and his own experience at Ditchling, Jones learned the importance of a workshop tradition that recalled medieval artistic guilds. In describing his expansive understanding of art in 'Art and Sacrament', Jones talked about bakers and strategists who were just as much as the painter or the sculptor engaged in the gratuitous activity of sign-making. He invoked not outstandingly talented bakers and strategists, but rather those who trained with other bakers and strategists and learned the excellences of their art before themselves implementing these excellences.[115] Art is a group undertaking that has little in common with the isolated daydreamer of *The Anathemata*.

The high valuation of medieval guilds reflects a Catholic corporatist outlook. Most broadly, corporatism represents a way of looking at society that stands opposed to liberalism's concern with the rights of the individual. It concerns itself instead with the good of the group. More specifically, as James Chappel has noted, it represented 'a belief that the state should be empowered to assist in the mediation of worker and employer interests, normally by creating employers' and workers' syndicates'.[116] Corporatist ideas were set out in Pius XI's encyclical *Quadragesimo anno* (1931), itself developing the Catholic social teaching outlined in Leo XIII's encyclical *Rerum Novarum* (1891), and received political expression in the Portuguese Constitution of 1933 and the Austrian Ständestaat constitution of 1934.[117] A comparable outlook informs Gill's distaste for an art market that relied on 'exceptionally gifted' artists and 'similarly exceptional buyers' who together produced 'a more or less eccentric art and craft'.[118] A guild of Catholic artisans, such as the community Gill cultivated at Ditchling, offered an alternative to an art market constructed by producers and consumers who were in their own ways exceptional.

The Anathemata's more individualistic approach is also represented in Jones's critical thought. His central insight was that to be human was to be '*essentially* a creature of sign and *signa*-making, a "sacramentalist" to the core'.[119] Human beings are 'not only capable of gratuitous acts'; these acts are their 'hall-mark and sign-manual'.[120] Human beings are sign-makers not insofar as they are members of a guild of similar sign-makers, but rather by virtue of their human nature as revealed by the Last Supper. Writing at the end of 1942, Jones expanded upon the rights and powers inherent in the individual in an essay entitled 'Art and Democracy', where he argued that human beings are distinguished from animals by their ability to create signs. He continued:

> This digression about animals, which the question of their being or not being 'makers' inveigled us into [. . .] leads us on to the whole question of 'equality' and 'equalities' and to the different 'rights' of the different 'equalities', and all these resolve themselves into a question of dignities due and to human dignity and so, inevitably, to the basic conception of 'democracy' [. . .] Art is the distinguishing dignity of man and that it is by art he becomes dignified, and 'democracy' means nothing, or means only something bad, if it misconceives the right of man to exercise his distinctive function as man, i.e. as artist – as culture-making animal.[121]

Jones depicts democracy as little more than a confusion between different kinds of equalities and rights. As Tom Villis has shown, the anti-democratic tenor of the passage reflected widespread sympathy among British Catholics for fascist causes.[122] Jones nevertheless went on to link, however grudgingly, 'human dignity', 'art' and political representation. To be truly humane, a society must promote the symbolic, sign-making and creative dimension of human life. Only in a society committed to such goals can democracy truly flourish. State suppression of artistic endeavour or religious practice (also, to Jones's mind, a sign-making endeavour) restricted the expression of human dignity. Democracy became either impossible or else a representation of 'something bad'. *Quadragesimo anno* insisted that 'Labor' is 'not a mere commodity'; 'the worker's human dignity in it', the document continues, 'must be recognized'.[123] Dignity is identified with a group such as workers. One shares in that dignity so far as one is a member of that group. Jones, however, strikingly connects 'dignity' and the person.

Jones's multiple entanglements reflect broader tensions in Catholic thought in the 1930s. Chappel highlights, for instance, the conflict between corporatist approaches drawing on Catholic social teaching and 'fraternal' Catholics more attuned to individuals (or more properly, persons) and rights.[124] By the early 1940s, fraternal Catholicism was in the ascendency. It received expression in Pope Pius XII's 1942 Christmas address, where he outlined the 'Dignity of the Human Person'. The speech included the following exhortation:

> He who would have the Star of Peace shine out and stand over society should cooperate, for his part, in giving back to the human person the dignity given to it by God from the very beginning [. . .] He should uphold respect for and the practical realization of the following fundamental personal rights; the right to maintain and develop one's corporal, intellectual and moral life and especially the right to religious formation and education; the right to worship God in private and public and to carry on religious works of charity.[125]

For Samuel Moyn, Pius XII's speech set the tenor for the emergence of human rights as a conservative Cold War discourse.[126] By connecting human dignity and specific legal rights, the Pope hoped to counter Soviet totalitarianism. Attempting to engage with modernity rather than expressing antimodernism, Pius presented the Roman Catholic Church as not merely the custodian of Christian concerns, but rather a beacon of free-world values. Like Jones's essay, which the Vatican radio broadcast may well have inspired, Pius XII's speech evinced a cautious embrace of democracy, marking a break with the Roman Catholic Church's previously favoured political form: the European imperialism of the Habsburg Empire.[127] In *The Grail Mass*, Jones went even further. He called out empire, particularly in its contemporary British guise, for deforming both coloniser and colonised. Imperialism suppressed the creativity necessary for human dignity.

Right to Create: Types of Religious Syncretism in The Grail Mass

The close of Jones's book-length poem *The Grail Mass* crystallises his anti-imperial directive. The poem ends with a monologue that Jones excerpted and published as 'The Tribune's Visitation'. The piece takes place in Roman-occupied Jerusalem at the time of the crucifixion. The speaker, a military tribune, visits the Roman soldiers patrolling Jerusalem's walls. In the speech, the tribune dismisses the local rites and practices of the communities swallowed up by the

Roman Empire and attempts to rally the troops behind the Roman cause. The character explains:

> Suchlike bumpkin sacraments
> are for the young-time
> for the dream-watches
> now we serve contemporary fact.[128]

The stated commitment to 'contemporary fact' reveals the tribune as one of Spengler's fact-men, a recognisable type in the civilisational stage of history and one committed to the imperial project. Spengler explained:

> Men of this sort do not broadcast their millions to dreamers, 'artists', weaklings and 'down-and-outs' to satisfy a boundless benevolence; they employ them for those who like themselves count as material for the Future. They pursue a purpose with them. They make a centre of force for the existence of generations which outlives [. . .] single lives.[129]

The symbolic life of religion is marginalised as Rome embarks upon the serious business of world rule. The tribune dismisses 'bumpkin sacraments' like a fact-man wary of 'dreamers, "artists," weaklings and "down-and-outs"' and commits to the higher 'purpose' of transforming the world in Rome's image. The verse nevertheless resists these plans. The character's unsentimental dismissal of local rites jars with the poem's lingering attraction to denigrated cultural heritage in the yearning appositional phrases 'for the young time' and 'for the dream watches', the elegiac lyricism contrasting with the plainspokenness of 'contemporary fact'. The delineation and the repetition render the lament for a lost world in slow motion; the lines linger over what once was and could have been still, were it not for empire.

Depicted as a standalone poem, 'The Tribune's Visitation' is difficult to place. The tendency of a poem's verbal texture to question a dramatic personage's speech by gesturing to the reader over the head of the speaking character is the stock-in-trade of the dramatic monologue. The delineation depicts the shift from culture to civilisation, from symbol to fact, as loss, even if the character throws his lot in with the demands of Rome. The poem includes reference to the '*sacramentum*' or the oath the soldiers must swear upon joining the army; a term that would take on new life in Christian theology and liturgy and, as we have seen, was foundational for Jones.[130] Like the delineated nostalgia 'for the young time', '*sacramentum*' is rich in value of which the character is unaware. By working for Roman expansion, the tribune believes himself to be destroying 'bumpkin sacraments' when, as the reader recognises, he ultimately disseminates similar forms. The poem oscillates between continuity and critique.

When the episode is situated in *The Grail Mass*, the critical intent underwriting the passage comes to the fore. It picks up, for instance, on the earlier treatment of Roman syncretism in a conversation between the patrolling soldiers. One soldier notes:

> These, if the cult
> grows strong, need hope and hope is only given
> by the men of rule for their purpose, and so
> it will be with your sibyls, baals, the lord
> of the gibbet who would free the world.
> Let them plant his signum where they choose—
> let the empire acclaim him Rex, let Caesar
> be the vicar of a Syrian mathematici, let
> Roman Jove go hang, call the Great Mother
> by some other name—what's the odds?
> The men of rule know all about such
> trifles and how to accommodate, if needs
> must.[131]

Roman syncretism is coercive. In allowing the growth of local cults with an eye to appropriating them once they reached a certain scale, Rome discovered a new vector of power that helped contain the potential for dissent. The shrug of 'call the Great Mother | by some other name—what's the odds?' illustrates the disdain in which non-Roman traditions are unofficially held. In their nonchalance, the 'men of rule' are contemptuous of even their own culture. In the civilisational phase of history, symbolic life of all stripes is dismissed out of hand. Any cult that grows sizable enough is shunted into the state religion. Distinctive features of weaker traditions are disregarded to present the 'sibyls, baals, the lord | of the gibbet who would free the world' as a type of the appropriate Roman deity. The policy of official tolerance merely gives the cult enough rope to hang itself.

Jones's poem began with a vision during his visit to Jerusalem in the mid-1930s.[132] Catching a glimpse of British mandate soldiers in Palestine, Jones found himself transported into the presence of the ordinary Roman soldiers who guarded Jerusalem at the time of the crucifixion. He thereafter set out to render his experience in verse. The imaginative transformation of British imperial presence might function as a sleight of hand through which contemporary politics are obscured by an allusive and ultimately elusive evocation of religious history.[133] Yet reflections on the British colonial project seep into Jones's historical narrative. In 'The Roman Dinner Conversation', a piece attached to *The Grail Mass* project, the character Jones refers to merely as 'the girl' in the company of an 'old Roman blimp' and a 'subaltern' alludes to the 'organized deception whereby we make an emporium | and call it a Commonwealth', before going on to reflect on the regions incorporated into the empire: '(I can't believe they all believe the bunk about Dominion status – honestly)'.[134] 'The girl' herself is undeceived about empire's mode and purpose. 'Commonwealth' is merely an attempt to make palatable an otherwise unpleasant reality. The idea of a Commonwealth of either Dominions or decolonised states with a stature equal to that of the metropole is, in the speaker's opinion, complete 'bunk'.

The critique is continued in *The Grail Mass* itself. One soldier complains:

> That's the cost
> of empire, Oenomaus, that is. You can't stretch
> the navel string indefinitely and empire is
> a great stretcher of navel strings and a snapper
> of 'em, a great uprooter is empire – it's
> a great robbery is empire, it robs the
> pieties, you can't have the pieties to my way
> of thinking, unless you're rooted.[135]

Imperial expansion must be funded. Dominions are forced to become more economically productive, subjugating the artistic and the gratuitous to the utilitarian needs of the present. People, too, are often required to move unwillingly around the empire to meet economic and military demands; the speakers of the poem are, for example, conscripted Celts. Destruction is visited upon regional symbolic rites, the 'pieties' connected to rootedness, through simplification. Displaced, economically precarious people have little time for the rites of their forbears from whom they have in any case been cut off. Empire deforms everything it touches. While the consequences are extreme for those on its periphery bearing the brunt of its demands, the culture of the metropole is also buffeted by the demands of empire.

Jones himself, as Thomas Goldpaugh has argued, was dissatisfied with the tone and style of the Roman elements of *The Grail Mass*.[136] The Roman episodes suffer from limitations like those of the 'Absalom, Mass', which in its commitment to both a dramatic personage and an exploration of distraction found it difficult to impose order on the verse. Likewise, Jones's demotic musings on the 'great robbery' of empire struggle with his contradictory aims of tracing commitment to sign-making through history, evident in his interest in the Roman use of '*sacramentum*' that prefigures Christian theological practice, and challenging imperial assumptions. In response, Jones split the Roman material in two and inserted between the two sections several reflections on Celtic culture written in not a dramatic voice but rather the disembodied, highly wrought meditative voice familiar from *The Anathemata*.

Thinking about continuities across different phases of history and the significance of the link between pieties and rootedness, Jones describes forms of syncretism different to the manipulative Roman version. At one point during a Celtic meditation, he reflects on the religious history of Anglesey, an island off the north coast of Wales. One passage reads:

> Is he seas-high over
> Sarn Badrig, his back streamers
> lavering Gwaelod — five fathoms
> high-over the drowned caerau
> (where Lyr has multiplied his holdings)
> and speaking of Lear, where's Nuada
>   where's the Roarer, or was he
> the Strider, or what, by his
> shape-shifting name, is he properly
> called?
>   They're all shape-shifters — all a
> changeling bunch of amphibious hierarchs
> refracted in a misted prism
> — there's none stays put in their
>   changing phantom sphere.[137]

The verse is awash with gods and heroes from different cultures: Lear, like Shakespeare's king, is associated with Wales; Nuada is an Irish hero; the Roarer or Beli is drawn from Norse mythology; and the Strider is an alternative name for the Roman god of war, Mars. The passage underlines the rich heritage of Anglesey, where various groups have fought, settled and left behind cultural deposits. As a result of the similarities between the many strands of mythology that have marked the intellectual, emotional and physical geography of the area, a form of composite ghost haunts the region: 'they're all shape-shifters — all a | changeling bunch of amphibious hierarchs'. Like the related 'Angle-Land' section of *The Anathemata*, the region is freighted with cultural associations, nearly buckling under the pressure. An abiding richness of reference arises from the past and is, perhaps, best understood in geological terms as the build-up of various layers of sediment. These layers nevertheless interpenetrate. The confusion as to the identity of the deity ('where's the Roarer or was he | the Strider') underlines the mixed, commensurable religious heritage of the area in a warmhearted, jocular fashion, far removed from the cynicism of 'what's the odds?' in the Roman passage.

Rootedness does not correspond in any simple way with the 'local'. Thinking of *Finnegans Wake*, Jones described Joyce as the artist 'who, more than any other, for all the universality of his theme, depended upon a given locality, for no man could have adhered with more absolute fidelity to a specified site, and the complex historic strata special to that site, to express a universal concept'.[138] Attention to the local, for Jones, is not parochial; it makes universality possible. Anglesey is simultaneously a single place and legion. Jones's imagination was drawn to areas with a complex cultural heritage. By focusing on the richness of a given place he makes, for all the apparent partiality of his glare, something general and wide-ranging. Such places resist empire's attempts to manipulate culture for its own ends. The various peoples who inhabited Anglesey had time and space to practice their pieties in ways that the frenetic pace of imperialist designs attempted to forestall.

Jones was not drawn to Anglesey for its history alone. The act of making, the presence of human craft, was also a prominent consideration, represented here by the power of the meditative poetic voice itself. Strategic deployment of non-translation is one means by which Jones gestures towards historical strata; he uses the untranslated Welsh for castle in 'drowned caerau', the phrase referring to the myth of *Cantre'r Gwaelod* or the sunken kingdom. The mixed registers of lines such as 'changeling bunch of amphibious hierarchs' pitch the Anglo-Norman and Middle English etymology of 'changeling bunch' against the Latinity of 'amphibious hierarchs'. The interlinear shift from the folksy to the scientific alerts the reader to the discordant elements within the crowd of regional deities. Macaronic strategies are part of what Paul Robichaud has called Jones's attempt to make 'the remote past alive for the present by using equally remote diction'.[139] What is striking here, though, is not so much the identity of historical groups with a particular lexicon but rather the clashes between registers. They function as a microcosm of the discordance in intent, style and theme in the move between the Roman and the Celtic material.

The poetic language of the Anglesey passage is markedly different to the voice of the Roman section. The contrast in the soldiers' discussion of syncretism between the repeated imperatives of 'Let the empire acclaim him Rex, let Caesar | be the vicar of a Syrian mathematici, let | Roman Jove go hang' and the informal shrug of 'what's the odds?' is merely oratorical. It presents a critique of empire dressed up in Roman garb, while the startling shifts in vocabulary in the Celtic material seek to make visible an alternative to empire, even in a political situation where other possibilities remain difficult to imagine. While the aims and needs of empire are simple and focused such that all activity is subordinated to them, the verbal variety of Jones's Celtic poetry makes sensuously present another form of life. In Jones's understanding, the form of modernism that he, Joyce and Eliot practised, is at once religious and anti-imperial in nature. Its willingness to mine and to make from the cultural memory otherwise dismissed by imperialists represents what he understands as the fulfilment of a sacramental vocation. Through his dual focus on both the presence of the sign-maker within all people and the right to express the creative dimension of human nature,

Jones's poem serves as a distinct application of the Roman Catholic Cold War yoking of human dignity and individual rights.

Jones's attention to the syncretic also touches on a prominent strand of critical writing on modernism and religion. Wide reading, religious experiment and a propensity to combine various strands of learning into new wholes is often considered characteristic of modernist religion more broadly. John Bramble finds modernism 'open to syncretism – especially East-West syncretism'.[140] H.D.'s *Trilogy*, Scott Freer insists, exemplifies a 'syncretic mode of modernist mythopoeia'.[141] For Elizabeth Anderson, 'religious syncretism' allows H.D. 'to engage with spiritual concerns in her writing without subordinating it to the demands of doctrine'; this sets H.D. apart from writers such as Eliot 'who ultimately viewed art as subservient to religion'.[142] Unhappy with the religious options available, modernists traversed multiple traditions, picking out striking themes, ideas and practices. They created new amalgamations of religious ideas that spoke to their needs better than what was on offer elsewhere. Modernist religion, in these accounts, is that of the spiritual seeker and resembles a modernist poem: an orchestration of various voices plucked from diverse circumstances.

In place of the prominence of *syncretism* in accounts of modernism, scholarship on lived religion prefers the term 'bricolage'.[143] *Syncretism* once designated a heresy and thus reflects a fascination with borders and boundaries about which lay religion proves unconcerned. Syncretism, church authorities alleged, ultimately amounted to a rival religious system, otherwise opposed to orthodoxy (*OED* 1). Drawn from twentieth-century aesthetics and invoking artwork produced from found objects, *bricolage* shifts attention from syncretism as an overarching system to the making of connections, of bringing texts and ideas from different parts of life together, to create a new whole. In McGuire's words, bricolage 'highlights the degree of agency ordinary people exercise in the construction of their lived religions'.[144] Jones's Roman Catholicism was neither a syncretic heresy nor a mere restatement of the catechism; it marshalled the resources of a religious tradition to respond in imaginative ways to contemporary concerns.

Public Religion: Reimagining the Churches

Jones's critique of empire arose from sources different to those that shaped the contemporary discourse of decolonisation. He expressed neither a belief in the importance of national self-determination nor an understanding of empire as a form of enslavement, but rather challenged it from the perspective of his religious-aesthetic insights into human nature.[145] He was informed by not only sacramental theology, but also the ritual life of the Roman Catholic Church. Jones's work stands as a particularly rich account of lay participation in the liturgy. *The Anathemata*, a significant swathe of the critical writings and

The Grail Mass offer a way of being that marries a deep respect for the rites they recount and the creative, emotive responses that Hügel termed the mystical element of personal religion. Orthodoxy is not merely a system to which one conforms, but rather a form of life one cultivates, develops and inhabits: made anew in each life it shapes. Jones left a more substantial record than most of his lived religion.

While his journey was a personal one, Jones's musings were not inward-turned. Franz Rosenzweig characterised the mystic as a self-indulgent figure who immorally turned his back on all that is not God.[146] For Jones, mysticism worked quite differently. His readings of Taille and Fry were not fodder for his own world, closed off from all around him; they fed a sustained critique of contemporary international politics. We are at a far remove from the secular presentation of mysticism as a private undertaking. Jones engaged in a public debate about empire from a distinctly, albeit idiosyncratic, Roman Catholic perspective, which aligned him with broader post-war shifts in Vatican attitudes towards modernity.

Jones was acutely aware that his audience did not necessarily share his religious background. Dilworth advises Jones's would-be readers of the 'suspension of religious disbelief' necessary to engage with the poet.[147] No doubt reading Jones through the eyes of militant New Atheism would pose a challenge, but Dilworth's critical stricture obscures the degree to which Jones presented the Eucharist as a rite of significance to more than Christians alone. It revealed something about, and provided the means of worshipping, God and exposed a truth about humankind; we are all sign-makers at the deepest level of our being. The Roman Catholic Church had an ongoing role in everyone's lives, limited to neither Roman Catholics nor Christians more widely, because it had been tasked with celebrating, protecting and recalling an otherwise easily neglected aspect of human endeavour. Over the next chapter, too, we will see how and why Eliot, like Jones, used mystical language to address not merely an insular Christian community, but rather a largely secular public on the cusp of an overwhelming loss.

NOTES

1. David Jones to Harman Grisewood, 6 July 1964, and David Jones to René Hague, 8–16 June 1966, in *Dai Greatcoat*, pp. 205–9, pp. 221–25.
2. Schwartz, *The Third Spring*, p. 289.
3. See Schwartz, *The Third Spring*, pp. 291–92.
4. David Jones, 'Art and Sacrament', in *Epoch and Artist: Selected Writings*, ed. by Harman Grisewood (London: Faber & Faber, 1959), pp. 143–79 (p. 171).
5. *Catechism of the Catholic Church*, 2nd edn (Vatican City: Vatican Press, 1997), p. 347 (para. 1378 of 2865).
6. See David Jones, 'Art in Relation to War', in *The Dying Gaul and Other Writings*, ed. by Harman Grisewood (London: Faber & Faber, 1978), pp. 123–66 (p. 136).

7. Raymond Williams, *Keywords: A Vocabulary of Culture and Society,* rev. edn (Oxford: Oxford University Press, 1985), p. 258.
8. Williams, pp. 257–58.
9. Kathleen Henderson Staudt, 'Incarnation Reconsidered: The Poem as Sacramental Act in *The Anathemata* of David Jones', *Contemporary Literature,* 26 (1985), 1–25 (p. 5).
10. Soud, p. 110.
11. Thomas Goldpaugh, '"A Heap of All That I Could Find": David Jones' Fragmented Sacrament', in *David Jones: A Christian Modernist?,* ed. by Jamie Callison and others (Leiden: Brill, 2017), pp. 17–36 (p. 25).
12. For Bloomsbury attitudes to Roman Catholicism, see Lytton Strachey, 'Cardinal Wiseman', in *Eminent Victorians: Cardinal Manning, Florence Nightingale, Dr. Arnold, General Gordon* (London: Chatto & Windus, 1918), pp. 1–114.
13. Meredith B. McGuire, *Lived Religion: Faith and Practice in Everyday Life* (Oxford: Oxford University Press, 2008), p. 12.
14. Patrick Allitt, *Catholic Converts: British and American Intellectuals Turn to Rome* (Ithaca, NY: Cornell University Press, 1997), p. 11.
15. See Thomas Dilworth, *The Shape of Meaning in the Poetry of David Jones* (Toronto: University of Toronto Press, 1988), pp. 168–74.
16. Dom Gregory Dix, *The Shape of the Liturgy,* 2nd edn (London: Dacre Press, 1947), pp. 613–734. Jones's edition is held at the National Library of Wales. See Huw Ceiriog Jones, *The Library of David Jones: A Catalogue* (Aberystwyth: National Library of Wales, 1995), p. 88.
17. David Jones to Harman Grisewood, 6 July 1964, in *Dai Greatcoat,* pp. 205–9 (p. 208).
18. Dix, p. 263.
19. See John G. Maiden, *National Religion and the Prayer Book Controversy, 1927–1928* (London: Boydell & Brewer, 2009), p. 51.
20. Maiden, p. 134.
21. Maiden, pp. 39–40.
22. Maiden, pp. 90–104.
23. Maiden, p. 175; see Max Weber, *The Protestant Ethic and the Spirit of Capitalism,* trans. by Talcott Parsons (London: Routledge, 1930), pp. 155–84.
24. See H. D. A. Major, 'Sign of the Times', *The Modern Churchman,* 11 (1921), 148–64. For the growth of Anglo-Catholicism, see Barry Spurr, *'Anglo-Catholic in Religion': T. S. Eliot and Christianity* (Cambridge: Lutterworth Press, 2010), pp. 64–110.
25. H. J. D. Astley, 'Primitive Sacramentalism', *The Modern Churchman,* 16 (1926), 282–95 (p. 294).
26. See Timothy Larsen, *The Slain God: Anthropologists and the Christian Faith* (Oxford: Oxford University Press, 2014), p. 22.
27. Rashdall, pp. 286–87.
28. Arnold, *Literature and Dogma,* p. 77.
29. Jones to Hague, 8–16 June 1966, p. 222.
30. Jones, *The Anathemata,* p. 205.
31. Jones, *The Anathemata,* p. 205n.
32. Dix, p. 161.
33. Dix, pp. 613–734.
34. David Jones, 'Letters about Religion', CF2/9, David Jones Papers, National Library of Wales, Aberystwyth.

35. Jones, preface to *The Anathemata*, p. 13.
36. David Jones, 'Letters to *The Tablet*', CF2/8, David Jones Papers. See Evelyn Underhill to Marjorie Robinson, 12 May 1907, in *The Making of a Mystic: New and Selected Letters of Evelyn Underhill*, ed. by Carol Poston (Champaign: University of Illinois Press, 2010), pp. 102–3 (p. 103).
37. See Thomas Dilworth, *David Jones: Engraver, Soldier, Painter, Poet* (London: Jonathan Cape, 2017), p. 67; Paul Robichaud, 'Avant-garde and Orthodoxy at Ditchling', *Renascence*, 69 (2017), 186–97.
38. *The Kensington Mass* carries the inscription 'in affectionate recalling of J. O'C. sacerdos' on its title page. David Jones, *The Kensington Mass* (London: Agenda Editions, 1975), p. 7.
39. Schloesser, p. 148.
40. Schloesser, p. 148.
41. Schloesser, p. 148.
42. David Jones to Jim Ede, 5 September 1935, letter 22, Letters to Jim Ede, Kettle's Yard Archive, University of Cambridge.
43. Jones to Ede, 5 September 1935, letter 22.
44. Jones to Ede, 5 September 1935, letter 22.
45. See Jacques Maritain, '*Art and Scholasticism*', in '*Art and Scholasticism*' *and* '*The Frontiers of Poetry*', trans. by Joseph W. Evans (Notre Dame, IN: University of Notre Dame Press, 1974), 3–115 (p. 46).
46. Maritain, p. 12.
47. See Jonathan Miles and Derek Shiel, *David Jones: The Maker Unmade* (Bridgend, Wales: Seren, 203), p. 242, p. 290.
48. Taylor, *Secular Age*, p. 355.
49. Taylor, *Secular Age*, p. 355.
50. Woolf, 'Modern Fiction', p. 10.
51. See Jane de Gay, *Virginia Woolf and Christian Culture* (Edinburgh: Edinburgh University Press, 2019), pp. 196–99.
52. See Roger Fry, '"A New Theory of Art", *Nation* (7 March 1914)', in *A Roger Fry Reader*, ed. and with an introduction by Christopher Reid (Chicago: University of Chicago Press, 1996), pp. 158–62 (p. 159).
53. David Jones to René Hague, 19 January 1973, quoted in Miles and Shiel, p. 306n.
54. See Fiona MacCarthy, *Eric Gill* (London: Faber & Faber, 1989), p. 62.
55. See Dilworth, *Engraver, Soldier, Painter, Poet*, p. 67.
56. Jones, 'Art and Sacrament', p. 160.
57. Jones, 'Art and Sacrament', p. 160.
58. Quoted in Thomas Dilworth, *Reading David Jones* (Cardiff: University of Wales Press, 2008), p. 170. The present section adapts Jamie Callison, 'David Jones's "Barbaric-fetish": Frazer and the "Aesthetic Value" of the Liturgy', *Modernist Cultures*, 12 (2017), 439–62.
59. See Maurice de la Taille, 'An Outline of *The Mystery of Faith*', in *The Mystery of Faith and Human Opinion Contrasted and Defined* (London: Sheed & Ward, 1934), pp. 5–37. These ideas are summarised in Martin C. D'Arcy, *The Mass and the Redemption* (London: Burns, Oates & Washbourne, 1926).
60. Taille, 'Outline', pp. 10–11.
61. David Jones to René Hague, 28 May 1974, CD2/6, David Jones Papers.

62. *The Missal in Latin and English, Being the Text of the Missale Romanum with English Rubrics and a New Translation* (London: Burns, Oates & Washbourne, 1950), p. 729.
63. David Jones, 'Letters to *The Tablet*', CF2/8, David Jones Papers.
64. Michon M. Matthiesen, 'De la Taille's *Mysterium Fidei*: Eucharistic Sacrifice and Nouvelle Théologie', *New Blackfriars*, 94 (2013), 518–39 (p. 530). Vincent McNabb, for instance, called Taille's theory a 'denial of the mind of the Church'. Vincent McNabb, O. P., 'A New Theory of the Eucharistic Sacrifice', *Blackfriars*, 4 (1923), 1086–1100 (p. 1095).
65. David Jones, *In Parenthesis* (London: Faber & Faber, 1937), p. 67.
66. The Old English verb is 'ongyrede' or 'ongyrwan'. 'The Dream of the Rood', in *The Cambridge Old English Reader*, ed. by Richard Marsden (Cambridge: Cambridge University Press, 2005), pp. 192–203 (p. 197).
67. Jones, *In Parenthesis*, p. 68.
68. Jones to Hague, 28 May 1974.
69. Jones, *In Parenthesis*, p. 204n.
70. J. G. Frazer, *The Golden Bough: A Study in Magic and Religion*, 3rd edn, 12 vols (London: Macmillan, 1906–15), 6: *Adonis, Attis, Osiris: Studies in the History of Oriental Religion (Part 2)*, p. 220.
71. Taille, 'Outline', p. 13.
72. Taille, 'Outline', p. 10.
73. Jones, *Epoch and Artist*, frontispiece.
74. Jones, *In Parenthesis*, pp. 67–68.
75. Jones to Hague, 8–16 June 1966, p. 222.
76. Harman Grisewood and René Hague, notes to David Jones, *The Roman Quarry and Other Sequences*, ed. by Harman Grisewood and René Hague (London: Agenda Editions, 1981), p. 218n.
77. See T. S. Eliot, 'Introduction to *Revelation*, eds. John Baillie and Hugh Martin', in *Tradition and Orthodoxy*, pp. 472–96 (p. 485).
78. See Irving Babbitt, 'Buddha and the Occident' (1936), in *On Literature, Culture, and Religion: Irving Babbitt*, ed. by George A. Panichas (Oxford: Routledge, 2017), pp. 224–70.
79. T. S. Eliot, 'Tradition and the Individual Talent', in *Perfect Critic*, pp. 105–14 (p. 106).
80. McGuire, p. 195.
81. McGuire, p. 195.
82. David Jones to Harman Grisewood, 9 October 1961, in *Dai Greatcoat*, pp. 184–85 (p. 185).
83. For the modernist crisis, see Fordham, 'Between Theological and Cultural Modernism', 8–24.
84. David Jones to Desmond Chute, 17 November 1956, in *Inner Necessities: The Letters of David Jones to Desmond Chute*, ed. by Thomas Dilworth (Toronto: Anson–Cartwright, 1984), pp. 88–91 (p. 90).
85. David Jones to Harman Grisewood, 1 June 1942, in *Dai Greatcoat*, pp. 119–120 (p. 120).
86. Jones to Grisewood, 1 June 1942, p. 120.

87. David Jones, 'The Myth of Arthur', in *Epoch and Artist*, pp. 212–259 (p. 242).
88. Jonathan Miles, *Backgrounds to David Jones: A Study in Sources and Drafts* (Cardiff: University of Wales Press, 1990), pp. 39–41.
89. David Jones, 'Religion and the Muses', in *Epoch and Artist*, pp. 97–106 (p. 103).
90. Anderson, p. 2.
91. See Peter Harrison, *The Territories of Science and Religion* (Chicago: University of Chicago Press, 2015), pp. 83–115.
92. Daly, p. 187, p. 188.
93. My emphasis on tension contrasts with the immediate reception of Hügel's work, which assumed him to be making the case that a 'fully developed, properly balanced, personal religion must be made up of the harmonious blending of the three elements'. Butler, p. 44n.
94. Lawrence F. Barmann, *Baron Friedrich von Hügel and the Modernist Crisis in England* (Cambridge: Cambridge University Press, 1972), p. 198.
95. See George Tyrrell, preface to *XVI Revelations of Divine Love Shewed to Mother Juliana of Norwich* (London: Kegan Paul, Trench, Trübner, 1902), pp. v–xvii.
96. See Pius X, *Pascendi Dominici Gregis: Encyclical of Pope Pius X on the Doctrines of the Modernists* (8 September 1907), Vatican website <http://www.vatican.va/content/pius-x/en/encyclicals/documents/hf_p-x_enc_19070908_pascendi-dominici-gregis.html> [accessed 1 March 2022] (para. 14 of 58).
97. Friedrich von Hügel to Gwendolen Parry, 12 June 1919, in *Letters from Baron Friedrich von Hügel to a Niece*, ed. by Gwendolen Greene (London: Dent, 1928), pp. 35–44 (p. 44).
98. Bellah, 'Religion and Belief', p. 219.
99. Thomas Goldpaugh and Jamie Callison, 'The Chronology of *The Grail Mass* Manuscripts', in David Jones, *The Grail Mass and Other Works*, ed. by Thomas Goldpaugh and Jamie Callison (London: Bloomsbury Academic, 2019), 273–76 (p. 273).
100. David Jones, 'Absalom, Mass', in *The Grail Mass and Other Works*, pp. 209–12 (p. 210).
101. Robert Browning, 'The Bishop Orders his Tomb at St. Praxed's Church', in *Robert Browning: Selected Poems*, ed. by John Woolford and others (Harlow: Pearson Longman, 2010), pp. 232–45 (p. 239).
102. See Eric Griffiths, *The Printed Voice of Victorian Poetry* (Oxford: Oxford University Press, 1988), pp. 1–97.
103. Dilworth, *Reading David Jones*, p. 119.
104. Donald Attwater, *'In the Beginning was the Word': A Plea for English Words in the Worship of the Roman Church* (London: R. D. Dickinson, 1944), p. 11.
105. Attwater, p. 12.
106. See Keith F. Pecklers, *The Unread Vision: The Liturgical Movement in the United States of America, 1926–1955* (Collegeville, MN: Liturgical Press, 1998), pp. 25–80.
107. Romano Guardini, 'The Spirit of the Liturgy', in *'The Church and the Catholic' and 'The Spirit of the Liturgy'*, trans. by Ada Lane (London: Sheed & Ward, 1935), pp. 119–211 (p. 144).
108. Pecklers, pp. 32–33.
109. Jones, *The Anathemata*, p. 203.

110. 'Below', 'here', 'together', 'within', 'And from where', 'Downward from', 'down over', 'Downward then' and 'Over other than all this'. Jones, *The Anathemata*, pp. 196–201.
111. René Hague, *A Commentary on* The Anathemata *of David Jones* (Toronto: University of Toronto Press, 1977), p. 222.
112. Jones, *The Anathemata*, p. 205.
113. Soud, p. 131.
114. See Robert N. Bellah, *Religion in Human Evolution: From the Paleolithic to the Axial Age* (Cambridge, MA: Harvard University Press, 2011), pp. 1–43.
115. Jones, 'Art and Sacrament', pp. 159–61, pp. 163–64.
116. Chappel, p. 79.
117. See Moyn, p. 34.
118. Eric Gill, 'Christianity and Art (1927)', in *Art-Nonsense and Other Essays* (London: Cassell, 1929), pp. 216–249 (p. 221).
119. Jones to Hague, 8–16 June 1966, p. 222.
120. Jones, 'Art and Sacrament', p. 148.
121. David Jones, 'Art and Democracy', in *Epoch and Artist*, pp. 85–96 (p. 89).
122. See Tom Villis, *British Catholics and Fascism: Religious Identity and Political Extremism* (Basingstoke: Palgrave Macmillan, 2013), pp. 9–26.
123. Pius XI, *Quadragesimo Anno: On Reconstruction of the Social Order* (15 May 1931), Vatican website <https://www.vatican.va/content/pius-xi/en/encyclicals/documents/hf_p-xi_enc_19310515_quadragesimo-anno.html> [accessed 1 March 2022] (para. 83 of 148).
124. Chappel, pp. 111–14; Moyn, pp. 33–39.
125. Pius XII, 'The Internal Order of States and People (Christmas Message for 1942)', in *The Major Addresses of Pius XII*, ed. by Vincent Yzermans, 2 vols (St Paul, MN: North Central Publishing, 1961), 2, pp. 53–64 (p. 60).
126. See Moyn, pp. 65–100.
127. See Chappel, p. 27, p. 32.
128. David Jones, 'The Tribune's Visitation', in *The Sleeping Lord and Other Fragments* (London: Faber & Faber, 1974), pp. 42–58 (p. 50).
129. Oswald Spengler, *Decline of the West*, trans. by Charles Francis Atkinson, 2 vols (London: Allen & Unwin, 1918–22), 1: *Form and Actuality*, p. 350.
130. Jones, 'The Tribune's Visitation', p. 56.
131. David Jones, 'The Grail Mass', in *The Grail Mass and Other Works*, pp. 25–152 (p. 72).
132. Thomas Goldpaugh and Jamie Callison, introduction to *The Grail Mass and Other Works*, pp. 1–24 (p. 3).
133. See Fredric Jameson, 'Modernism and Imperialism', in *Nationalism, Colonialism, and Literature*, intro. by Seamus Deane (Minneapolis: University of Minnesota Press, 1990), pp. 43–68.
134. Jones, '*The Grail Mass*', p. 168, p. 163; See Adam Schwartz, 'These Global Days: [Review of] *The Grail Mass and Other Works* by David Jones, ed. by Thomas Goldpaugh and Jamie Callison. Bloomsbury Academic, 2019. Hardcover, xi + 279 pp., $176.', Russell Kirk Center Website, 6 October 2019 <https://kirkcenter.org/reviews/these-global-days/> [accessed 1 March 2022] (para. 3 of 9).

135. Jones, 'The Grail Mass', p. 79.
136. Goldpaugh, '"A Heap of All That I Could Find": David Jones' Fragmented Sacrament', pp. 17–36.
137. Jones, 'The Grail Mass', p. 115.
138. David Jones, 'Notes on the 1930s', in *Dying Gaul*, pp. 41–50 (p. 46).
139. Paul Robichaud, *Making the Past Present: David Jones, the Middle Ages and Modernism* (Washington, D. C.: Catholic University of America Press, 2007), p. 162.
140. John Bramble, *Modernism and the Occult* (Basingstoke: Palgrave Macmillan, 2015), p. 2.
141. Scott Freer, *Modernist Mythopoeia: The Twilight of the Gods* (Basingstoke: Palgrave Macmillan, 2015), p. 8.
142. Anderson, p. 2.
143. McGuire, pp. 188–90.
144. McGuire, p. 196.
145. See Adom Getachew, *Worldmaking After Empire: The Rise and Fall of Self-Determination* (Princeton: Princeton University Press, 2019), pp. 71–106.
146. See Rosenzweig, p. 207.
147. Dilworth, *Shape of Meaning*, p. 5.

2

SPIRITUAL PATHOLOGY: DIAGNOSING T. S. ELIOT'S UNCONSCIOUS CHRISTIANITY

T. S. Eliot did not want *Ash-Wednesday* described as '"religious" verse'.[1] Following the sequence's publication in 1930, Eliot urged Martin C. D'Arcy, a Jesuit priest and Master of Campion Hall, University of Oxford, to avoid such a categorisation when speaking about the sequence at a Catholic Poetry Society meeting.[2] By way of explanation, Eliot added:

> I don't consider it any more 'religious' verse than anything else I have written: I mean that it attempts to state a particular phase of the progress of one person. If that progress is in the direction of 'religion', I can't help that; it is I suppose the only direction in which progress is possible.[3]

Whether or not D'Arcy heeded Eliot's request, the *New York Times Book Review* carried Eda Lou Walton's review of *Ash-Wednesday* that same month, which was titled 'T. S. Eliot Turns to Religious Verse'.[4] Barry Spurr justifies his own designation of *Ash-Wednesday* as 'an Anglo-Catholic poem' on the basis of its allusions to 'devotion to the Blessed Virgin', 'the rite of Mass in *The English Missal*', 'the formula for auricular confession' and 'the intercession of the saints', which serve as 'key reference-points in the meaning of the poem'.[5]

In his letter to D'Arcy, Eliot passed off Spurr's 'several elements' as window dressing, indicative of 'a particular phase of the progress of one person'. Writing the sequence as a new member of the Church of England, Eliot was immersed in Anglo-Catholic religious culture and the exposure informed his artistic palette. Eliot worried that the combination of Anglo-Catholic elements, membership of the Church of England and the ascription of the word 'religious' to the verse would position the sequence as a form of self-limiting minor poetry, which was produced by a member of a religious community for the enjoyment of that particular community.[6] Religious poetry excluded the 'major passions' and thereby confessed its 'ignorance of them', Eliot thought.[7] Devoid of the alchemy of great art, religious poetry merely traded on the emotions generated by religious worship. Absent, too, in this form of verse was a reckoning with the changes the secular context of society had wrought on the nature and role of religion, even for those who laid claim to a faith.

The circumstances of *Ash-Wednesday*'s composition also told against its status as a religious poem. In a letter to the Bishop of Chichester, George Bell, outlining the genesis of the poem's imagery, Eliot surmised that Bell would be 'shocked' to 'learn how much' of *Ash-Wednesday* the author himself 'can't explain'.[8] The poet joked that the 'imagery' of the sequence: 'the yew trees, the nun, the garden god', should be abandoned to 'the ghoulish activities of some prowling analyst' because the figures emerged from 'recurrent dreams'.[9] Christian symbolism provides a ready context for their interpretation: an Edenic garden, a virginal figure such as Mary or Beatrice and the temptations of pagan sensuality. Eliot, however, insisted that the images presented themselves to him involuntarily, rather than following an overt wish to write about religious themes. Their appearance is explicable in scientific terms as the product of either the mind's defence mechanisms or previously uncharted layers of the psyche, depending on the chosen psychological model. They are neither reflective of the devotional poet's accomplished craft nor evidence of a mystical vision from God. They are something else altogether.

The argument invokes a pillar of psychological engagement with religion. Since the late nineteenth century, psychologists had tried to reinterpret extreme religious phenomena, from levitation through stigmata and visions, as symptoms of previously undiagnosed pathology.[10] These origins, newly explicable via modern medicine, were rehearsed by psychologists of religion to challenge the claims made by the Roman Catholic Church based on the extraordinary lives of mystics and saints.[11] Supernatural significance was undermined through recourse to natural origins and the therapist sought to replace the priest as expositor of the unknown.[12] *Ash-Wednesday* is not religious verse, Eliot claimed, because its Anglo-Catholic elements are the product of neither conscious devotion nor divine revelation. Imagery explicable in terms of the Christian tradition is present, yes, but its manifestation is idiosyncratic. Eliot nevertheless declines to use psychological insight to explain away his verse's religious elements. In the letter to Bishop Bell, for instance, Eliot complained that the religious illiteracy of his critics led them to miss the liturgical allusions scattered throughout the sequence.[13] Their readings were the poorer for it.

Strikingly, the definition of the poem as a non-religious work involves an extremely narrow understanding of what constitutes the 'religious'. To count as such, the poem's inspiration must come from God like a mystical vision or else be directed at a religious community. To argue otherwise, Eliot assumes, is to produce a version of T. E. Hulme's 'spilt religion'.[14] Eliot's own thinking about the relationship between religion and society was shaped by not only Hulme but also Charles Maurras, the leader of Action Française, whose career he had followed since his own time in Paris.[15] Maurras's resistance to the aims of the French Republic, and particularly his support for the hierarchical form of the institutional church as a guarantee of social order, received widespread support from priests and Catholic intellectuals notwithstanding Maurras's own atheism.[16] The Catholic establishment accepted Maurras, for a time at least, on the basis of a belief that 'the natural order' of the world 'exhibits a rational structure that is intelligible to human reason without the aid of revelation'.[17] The existence of a 'rational structure' enabled, as Sarah Shortall observes, 'nonbelievers' and 'Catholics' to 'discern the same set of truths about the social order that were prescribed by natural law, even if they disagreed on the origin of that law'.[18] In the case of *Ash-Wednesday*, Eliot worried that its idiosyncratic psychological genesis risked infecting with merely human '*personality*' the 'coherent traditional system of dogma and morals' that stood apart 'from the single individual who propounds it'.[19] His solution was to deny, however counter-intuitively, that a poem entitled *Ash-Wednesday* and structured by the Catholic liturgy should be understood as a religious poem.

From the 1930s onwards, the boundaries in Catholic thought between natural and supernatural orders became increasingly porous. The increased recognition of the interplay between sacred and secular worlds was manifest in new Vatican policies, such as the development of the Catholic Action programme, which sponsored faith-based organisations to engage in secular affairs, and in the development of rival theological approaches, including personalism and the *Nouvelle théologie*.[20] The present chapter, too, argues that Eliot's letter to Bishop Bell did not sunder sacred and secular matters permanently. In refusing to elide religion and literature, Eliot ultimately allowed for a greater degree of interplay between the two. His early poetry was driven by an engagement with the psychology of religion, not only in the pathological saint-like figures of his martyr poems but also in the reserved, diagnostic tone of his quatrain poems. Eliot was, as the first section of the present chapter argues, by turns attracted to and repulsed by the new approach to revelation represented by the psychology of religion. His fascination continued long after his entry into the Church of England. The chapter's second half tracks the continued influence of 'spilt mysticism' on Eliot's later works. His fascination with mysticism diluted the hierarchical structures outlined in *The Idea of a Christian Society* by conferring attention upon the psychological effects of the reforms it envisioned.

Four Quartets, too, drew on Christian thinking to console a range of audiences in the face of an impending wartime defeat. A Christian Eliot emerges who is surprisingly close to the sceptical philosopher of his youth. The present chapter's account of Eliot's religion is defined by not so much the antithesis between, as the interpenetration of, the sacred and the secular. The renegotiation of long-established boundaries ultimately helps shift our understanding of the relationship between modernism and institutional religion.

Between Dissociation and Irruption: Poetry and the Psychology of Religion

Martyrs, Murders and Mental Illness in the Early Poetry

In his Clark lectures, delivered at Trinity College, Cambridge in 1926, Eliot went beyond his stated topic, metaphysical poetry, and began to delineate different types of mysticism.[21] He justified the digression through reference to the close relationship between mysticism and poetry. Three years later, in correspondence about *Ash-Wednesday*, he would instead emphasise the differences between the two. Over the academic year 1932–33, the relationship between mysticism and poetry was considered at greater length in his Charles Eliot Norton lectures, delivered at Harvard and later published as *The Use of Poetry and the Use of Criticism*. In the earlier lectures, Eliot contrasted the Latinate, monastic mysticism of Richard of St Victor with the vernacular mysticism of St Teresa of Ávila. He argued that the former facilitated 'the development and subsumption of emotion and feeling through intellect into the vision of God', while the latter sought 'to substitute divine love for human love'.[22] As with the relationship between the major poetry that Eliot pursued and the minor religious verse he devalued, the transformation of 'emotion and feeling' is central to the distinction between these modes. In Latinate mysticism, an alchemical process comparable to that outlined in 'Tradition and the Individual Talent' takes place. Subsequent 'development and subsumption' of 'emotion and feeling' through 'intellect' facilitates access to the 'vision of God'. By contrast, the 'vision of God' in St Teresa is more of a fantasy. Love and sexual passion are redirected from a human to a divine object via an act of substitution. A given subject's personality, their yearning and desires, is entertained and stimulated to the detriment of the pursuit of God.

The distinction between mysticisms invokes aspects of Eliot's earlier work. Donald J. Childs has identified antecedents in Eliot and John Middleton Murry's debate over the respective merits of classicism and romanticism.[23] The two terms neatly map on to Latin and vernacular mysticism. Eliot's understanding of mysticism also reflects a far broader cultural discourse concerning the relationship between psychology and religion. In her *Defence of Idealism*, published in 1917, May Sinclair mined the same seam. She contrasted her favoured form of mysticism, one that fused Indian religious texts, idealist philosophy and Jungian psychology, with Christian mysticism, whose practitioners, she claimed, 'had not learned how to "sublimate their libidos"' and were thus left at the mercy of sexual urges.[24] While Sinclair's observation pre-empts his interpretation of vernacular mysticism, Eliot, a trained philosopher whose thesis concerned itself with idealism, is unlikely to have turned directly to a popular work on the subject produced ten years earlier in preparing his Clark lectures.

Instead, Eliot and Sinclair's analysis bears witness to the influence of the French neurologist, Jean-Martin Charcot. Charcot is best known for the diagnostic criteria he developed for hysteria, which he used to identify both contemporary and historical cases of the disease. In the photographic plate from *Iconographie photographique de la Salpêtrière* [Figure 2.1], the woman's raised hands, her eyes turned heavenward and her tilted head bathed in an unseen light – all features of the ecstatic stage of hysteria – are offered up as symptoms of pathology. The volume from which the photograph was taken was prepared by Charcot's students. It lies at the intersection of medicine and technology.

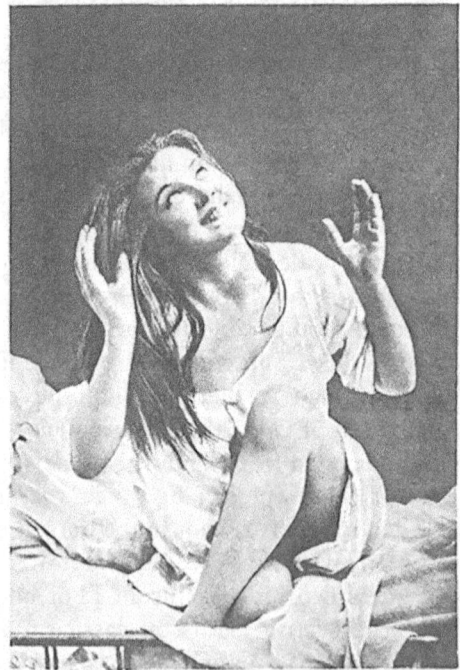

Figure 2.1 Paul Regnard, *Attitudes Passionnelles Extase*, 1878, Photograph, 10.3 × 7.1 cm, J. Paul Getty Museum, Los Angeles. Digital image courtesy of J. Paul Getty Museum Open Content Program.

SPIRITUAL PATHOLOGY

The elusive stages of a shadowy disorder were fixed on photographic plates, then developed, collected and published in a reference work that medical professionals and enlightened members of the public could consult.[25]

The pose struck by the patient was familiar from religious paintings. In *L'hystérie dans l'art*, a document compiled by one of Charcot's associates, reference is made to the *Ecstasy of St Margaret of Cortona* by Giovanni Lanfranco [Figure 2.2], where the central character raises her hands and eyes while tilting her head towards Christ descending from the heavens.[26] Margaret was a reformed sinner in the tradition of Mary Magdalene. These sexual overtones are carried over from the painted canvas to the photographed patient insofar as the anonymous young woman is as undressed as she is distressed.[27] Her thin nightgown rides up to expose her naked thighs and slips down, too, at the shoulder. A male photographer coaxes and captures her performance for the perusal of his peers. Ecstasy, the stage of hysteria captured in the image, is more familiar from religious or sexual contexts than medical ones. The connection was not lost on Charcot and his followers. The similarity between the hospital photographs and religious iconography provided warrant for Charcot's retrospective diagnoses of mystics and saints, a key pillar of the medical profession's struggle with the Roman Catholic Church for power and status.[28] Charcot re-read Christian

Figure 2.2 Giovanni Lanfranco, *Ecstasy of St Margaret of Cortona*, 1622, oil on canvas, 230 × 185 cm, Galleria Palatina (Palazzo Pitti), Florence. Digital image courtesy of Wikimedia Commons, Creative Commons.

iconography, arguing that mystics and saints were driven by not faith but rather a disease of the nerves. He portrayed the Roman Catholic Church's claims to truth as at best naïve.[29]

Many found Charcot's interpretative schema crude. In *The Varieties of Religious Experience*, for instance, William James established a methodological distinction between origins and value, separating the scientific study of religion on the one hand and anti-religious polemic on the other.[30] He expressed a wish 'that the bugaboo of morbid origin' would no longer 'scandalize' religious observance.[31] The Catholic layman and philosopher of religion Friedrich von Hügel also recognised that the mystical tradition rested on commentaries that stressed the 'directly miraculous character' of 'certain psycho-physical states' that would today be considered 'neural abnormalities' (2, p. 3). He worried that to approach 'these psycho-physical peculiarities and states' from a 'temperamental and psychological standpoint' was to treat them as 'self-explanatory' (2, p. 8). It ensured 'our preliminary conclusions about such neural phenomena' became 'the measure, type, and explanation of and for all such other facts and apprehensions as our further study of the religious mind and experience may bring before us' (2, p. 8). Modern psychology boasted advanced tools for understanding such phenomena, but its diagnostic criteria risked becoming blinkers. Commentators identified criteria, offered a diagnosis and moved on. To break the cycle, Hügel compared the teachings of St Catherine of Siena with more established and less problematic thinkers. Even if pathology were present, Hügel found much in the saint's work worthy of continued attention (2, pp. 62–110).

The efforts of Hügel and James ensured that paintings such as the *Ecstasy of St Margaret of Cortona* would never be viewed entirely through Charcot's revisionary lens. The prominence of Charcot's hermeneutic nevertheless shifted understandings of the picture, regardless of whether one agreed with the schema. The pathological interpretation of religious phenomena lingered. Eliot betrayed similar concerns when standing before Antonio and Piero del Pollaiuolo's *The Martyrdom of Saint Sebastian* (1475) in the National Gallery in London [Figure 2.3]. In 1909, Eliot had described the work as part of a Harvard course on Florentine painting; upon relocating to England, he was able to see it in person.[32] Recollections of *The Martyrdom of Saint Sebastian* prompted Eliot to consider the mind of painters like the Pollaiuolos: 'why should anyone paint a beautiful youth and stick him full of pins (or arrows) unless he felt a little as the hero of my verse', he wrote in 1914 to Conrad Aiken.[33]

The 'verse' in question, 'The Love Song of St. Sebastian', is spoken not by the titular character but rather by a figure who, Eliot conjectures, shares a worldview with the Pollaiuolos. The reader of the dramatic monologue overhears the speaker working himself up into a pitch of excitement and murdering his lover. The homicidal excitement is generated by an extended period of self-flagellation that sits somewhere between elaborate ritual and self-induced trance. The speaker

SPIRITUAL PATHOLOGY

Figure 2.3 Antonio del Pollaiuolo and Piero del Pollaiuolo, *The Martyrdom of Saint Sebastian*, 1475, oil on canvas, 291.5 cm x 202.6 cm, National Gallery, London. Digital image courtesy of the National Gallery, London.

finds himself transfixed before a 'lamp in the night' at 'the foot of your stair' for 'hour on hour'.[34] The staging draws upon Charcot's own performances. Through public demonstrations with current patients, Charcot showed hysterics to be particularly susceptible to hypnosis and argued for an equivalency between hypnotic and hysteric states.[35] In 'The Love Song of St. Sebastian', the speaker puts himself into what is essentially a hypnotic-hysteric trance through his waiting and watching. In describing the 'shirt of hair' and the accompanying ritual flogging (p. 265), Eliot mixes modern medicine with the 'fee-fi-fo-fum *décor* of medievalism' of the French novelist J. K. Huysmans.[36] The trance forms the prelude to the speaker's murder of his lover. The poem closes with the admission:

> You would love me because I should have strangled you
> And because of my infamy;
> And I should love you the more because I had mangled you
> And because you were no longer beautiful
> To anyone but me (p. 266).

The narcissism of the speaker's rationale and his projection of an extreme masochism onto his sleeping victim is sounded out by the full, polysyllabic rhyme 'strangled you' and 'mangled you', which jangles out of tune with his

83

protestations. Given its comic overtones, the speaker's reveal of motive and rationale merely exposes the delusions at work. Rhyme proffers a diagnosis.

The poem is complicit in the speaker's actions. Only in the final lines does the verse offer some resistance. The poem's willingness to tolerate the murderer's antics speaks to the unassimilated influence of Huysmans. Eliot read the French novelist at Harvard and positioned him as a major figure out of whose shadow the modern writer needed to move.[37] Huysmans, as Ellis Hanson has argued, was a keen reader of Charcot; he used the language of hysteria to capture religious enlightenment and to break out from the routines of everyday life. Hanson notes:

> The three great converts of his fiction – Des Esseintes, Gilles de Rais, and Durtal – all have in common a histrionic longing to embrace the faith, a longing that they articulate through choking, fainting, convulsions, and other symptomatic maladies generally attributed to hysteria.[38]

The delayed resistance of Eliot's poem owes something to the writer's own lack of clarity over his attitude towards the poem's speaker. If the speaker's trance-inducing, pre-murder ritual is not quite the same as a 'histrionic longing to embrace the faith', there is nevertheless a fascination with what Manju Jain describes as 'the tenuous dividing line between sanity and insanity' in Eliot's work, which results in a 'realization that what is considered to be madness by ordinary social standards may often be the prelude to the perception of a significance beyond the ordinary frontiers of experience'.[39] The jangling of the poem's finale is a merely dutiful – if ultimately uncommitted – attempt to cast his hero as a version of Robert Browning's 'Porphyria's Lover' when in fact he has more in common with Des Esseintes, Gilles de Rais and Durtal.

The mixture of the theological and the medical runs through another early poem, 'The Death of Saint Narcissus'. Eliot searches for transformative revelation in unusual places and betrays a simultaneous willingness to pathologise the search. As a narrative lyric, the poem surveys the religious journey of the titular martyr, including transformations into various animals and a final martyrdom achieved while dancing to God as arrows rain down. Narcissus – the very name hinting at a psychological disorder – is marked by a pathological self-sensuousness, with the character registering 'his limbs smoothly passing each other | And of his arms crossed over his breast' (p. 270). The character's journey recalls, too, critical writing on mysticism. The lines 'If he walked in city streets | He seemed to tread on faces, convulsive thighs and knees' (p. 270) remember a passage from the *Life of St Teresa of Ávila* quoted by Henri Delacroix and noted down by Eliot in 1912 in what the catalogue by the Houghton Library, Harvard University describes as his 'notes on religion and mysticism': 'I was not yet twenty years old and I trod, it seems, underfoot the vanquished world'.⁴⁰ Delacroix disagreed with Charcot's view that mysticism was merely undiagnosed hysteria. He undertook a psychological analysis of St Teresa to underscore her personal strength and the social good her visions facilitated. In Delacroix's narrative, the words so important to Eliot's poem follow the saint's first, brief taste of union with God in prayer, serving as a summary of her spiritual journey to date. She thereafter goes on to pursue her visions and to prove herself a capable and energetic social reformer.⁴¹

Like St Teresa, Eliot's character makes a break for a new life. Burdened by his knowledge of 'something different', the young man turns his back on the world. The break for the spiritual nevertheless has darker undertones. Teresa's 'the vanquished world' – invoking the Christian opposition between this world and the next – becomes Narcissus's 'faces, convulsive thighs and knees'. 'I trod [. . .] underfoot' becomes a violent act that reprises the mindset in which one would 'paint a beautiful youth and stick him full of pins'. These 'pins' reappear in the protagonist's martyrdom: 'He danced on the hot sand | Until the arrows came' (p. 271). Narcissus's rebirth is marked not by so much a new spiritual direction as the unbearable physical reality of city life. The impulse hints at the psycho-sexual issues of the Charcot tradition or even the 'nervous sexual attacks' to which the young Eliot was prone when 'alone in a city'.⁴²

The frisson the poem's psychological intertexture introduces helps Eliot talk about revelation and even offer up Narcissus as a spiritual model for his reader. The quality of the poetry is nevertheless questionable. It is unclear why Narcissus commands attention or how he develops over the course of the poem. The character's kinetic energy (he walks, dances and shapeshifts) notwithstanding, the poem is remarkably static; emphasis, for instance, is placed on minor verbal shifts from 'a dancer *before* God' to a 'a dancer *to* God' (p. 270, p. 271, my italics), marking a shift from worshipper to sacrifice without foregrounding the significance of the change. 'Gerontion' and *The Waste Land* and even the earlier 'The Love Song of J. Alfred Prufrock', contain similar hints at mysterious transformations in unlikely settings, but are more willing than the martyr poems to undermine such possibilities. Their volatility of tone, the fast-paced oscillation between spiritual yearning and cynical dismissal, is how Eliot's verse breaks free from the self-dramatising heroes of Huysmans's fiction.

Poetry as Therapy: Eliot's Metaphysical Verse

Eliot reflected on the stylistic shifts of his poetry. Both his pieces on sainthood post-dated Prufrock. Far from functioning as a new beginning, they represent a direction in which the poet chose not to travel. The religious psychology of the earlier pieces nevertheless haunts Eliot's account of the 'dissociation of sensibility', outlined in his 1921 essay 'The Metaphysical Poets'.⁴³ In the later critical context, the resulting complications do not confer a frisson of excitement, so much as incur displeasure. While, in service of his art, he had once entertained overlapping religious and medical explanations of mystical phenomena, Eliot went on to adopt Charcot's diagnostic attitude.

The psychological dimension of the 'dissociation of sensibility' has been documented. As Nancy Gish has recognised, the phrase drew, 'on a widely held and pervasive theory of consciousness' that was 'well known in the Boston of his college years'.[44] Murray McArthur has also noted that one of the central figures in the generation of psychologists that succeeded Charcot, Pierre Janet, lectured at Harvard in 1906, when Eliot was a college freshman, and has outlined some of the continuities between the lectures and Eliot's subsequent work.[45] Gish and McArthur focus on Janet's theory of mind and its implications for Eliot's thought and poetry. They neglect the cultural rather than the clinical application of Janet's theories to religion. For a figure such as Eliot who once remarked that psychology leads 'either to glands or to theology', the connection between psychology and religion was inescapable.[46] Eliot's worry that he would shock Bishop Bell by discussing *Ash-Wednesday* and psychology side-by-side follows from the weaponisation of psychology against religion in the late nineteenth and early twentieth centuries.

The psychological associations of the 'dissociation of sensibility' ensure that the phrase runs counter to Eliot's typical usage of *dissociate* or *dissociation*. In Eliot's lexicon, *to dissociate* typically denotes the judicial separation of ideas in critical analysis. In a review of Bertrand Russell's *Mysticism and Logic* from 1918, for example, Eliot writes, 'literary standards' help us 'dissociate the social and the histrionic from the unique'.[47] Likewise, in a commentary published in *The Criterion* in 1928, he adds, '*The Criterion* is interested, so far as politics can be dissociated from party politics, from the passions or fantasies of the moment, and from problems of local and temporary importance'.[48] *Dissociation* was the word that Ezra Pound chose, too, to praise the French critic Remy de Gourmont's writing in 1920: 'we find in it typical dissociation'.[49] Criticism, in the views of Eliot and Pound alike, involves the breakup of complex ideas into their constituent parts. *Dissociate* and *dissociation* function as synonyms for *distinguish* and *distinction* respectively.

Eliot's usage in 'The Metaphysical Poets' also turns the tables on its source text. As Louis Menand has noted, Eliot discovered a version of the 'dissociation of sensibility' in Gourmont's essay on the poet Jules Laforgue.[50] Gourmont considered Laforgue's 'intelligence' to be 'very keen, but closely linked to his sensibility'.[51] Gourmont's praise was double-edged. As one 'grows older', Gourmont observed, 'one acquires the ability to separate intelligence from sensibility', which is achieved 'through the acquisition of scepticism'.[52] Laforgue, however, 'died before reaching that stage'.[53] The poet's youth marred his work. Its strength was simultaneously its weakness. Gourmont was fascinated by the tensions between the mind and the senses. His argument itself is a model of critical dissociation insofar as he differentiates between 'intelligence and sensibility' even while stressing that Laforgue died before separating the two. Eliot shared Gourmont's fascination. Yet, where the French critic considered the distinction between intelligence and sensibility desirable, Eliot rued the fact that the distinction had become necessary: 'something [...] happened', Eliot wrote, 'to the mind of England between the time of Donne or Lord Herbert of Cherbury and the time of Tennyson and Browning'.[54] The shift from France to England is not the only difference between the respective essays. No longer regarded as evidence of maturity, dissociation has, for Eliot, become pathological. Gourmont's understanding of the creative process is entwined with Janet's medical outlook.

The damage inflicted upon the 'mind of England' recalls Janet's argument about the existence of multiple layers of consciousness.[55] Janet understood consciousness as a continuous chain of fields of attention or what James, a figure central to not only the psychology of religion but also psychology itself, termed 'the ordinary field, with its usual centre and margin'.[56] A 'dissociated' personality was created by a traumatic rupture of the continuous chain of memory. Thereafter, the patient's consciousness became divided with two or more distinct, discrete chains of attention running parallel to each other. Psychological disorders were produced by interference between these chains.[57] Therapeutically, Janet used hypnosis to return the patient to the site of the initial trauma to create an opening for the traumatised self to find resolution.[58]

As a graduate student, Eliot learnt about trauma-induced dissociation from Janet's *Névroses et idées fixes*, published in 1898. His notes to the volume include phrases from the following text:

> Observation 51: cerebral dissociation [...] it was evident that he was performing many absurd actions. He took excessive care of his personal cleanliness, taking two baths a day and changing his socks every two hours. [...] It was the Spirit who had been kind enough to direct his hygiene regime and which had accused him of being dirty and forced him to wash constantly. [...] The Spirit avenged disobedience: the Spirit tore his clothes, broke his furniture and muddled his papers. [...] Recently, this poor man had to be removed from the water after throwing himself into the Seine; he returned to his house soaking wet and in a pitiful state.[59]

'The spirit' here in Janet's diagnosis is the result of 'cerebral dissociation'. The man's dissociated consciousness, split off from the mainline of his personality, interferes with his primary consciousness. The secondary self thereafter makes exaggerated demands for and about the patient's personal cleanliness.

Janet's suffering souls stand at a far-remove from the urbane literary distinctions of Gourmont. By breaking with his own habitual use of dissociation,

Eliot distances himself from the French critic. For Eliot, *dissociation* relates to critical practice; the man of letters makes revealing distinctions. The poet's task, however, involves 'fusion'.[60] There is an implicit criticism of Gourmont's willingness to address poetic practice, too, in terms of distinctions. Eliot's 'mind of England' identifies a historical rupture. He turns back to a pre-modern paradisiacal moment when poets were, he claims, able to 'feel their thought as immediately as the odour of a rose'.[61] The very fact that critics dissociate intelligence and sensibility reveals an underlying social and historical trauma. In a healthy society, thought and feeling combine in a single activity. The critical function is itself a symptom of a more virulent pathology. Like Janet's primary and dissociated consciousnesses, sensibility and the intelligence become, in Eliot's essay, two distinct states with the dissociated sensibility liable to interfere with the work of the intelligence.

Eliot's diagnosis unites therapeutic and poetic concerns. Psychology, Eliot insisted, is 'justified, if at all, by its therapeutic value'.[62] The 'dissociation of sensibility' outlined a dilemma facing a practising poet. Eliot's *Poems*, collecting his terse, metaphysical quatrain poems, had been published in 1920, the year before 'The Metaphysical Poets'. The 'dissociation of sensibility' also alluded to a historical phenomenon that had far-reaching and extra-literary consequences. His invocation of *sensibility* walks the line between the claims of perception and those of history insofar as it denotes not only the 'power of sensation or perception' (*OED* 2a) but also the 'capacity for refined emotion; delicate sensitiveness of taste' (*OED* 6). The first citation for the latter definition dates from 1756, which makes it more or less contemporary with Jean-Jacques Rousseau's *Julie, or the New Heloise*, published in 1761, and *Emile, or On Education*, published in 1762.[63] As Christos Hadjiyiannis has observed, Irving Babbitt, Eliot's tutor at Harvard and a formative influence upon the poet, described Rousseau as the 'great modern romancer' and 'linked Rousseau's belief in the fundamental goodness of human nature to the "evils" of sentimentalism, individualism, and sensationalism'.[64] Eliot's word choice thus identifies both the local problem of two distinct faculties in the personal or collective mind and the social consequences that follow from such a divide. A faulty poetic consciousness overflows into the cult of sensibility and testifies to the burgeoning romanticism that Eliot, Hulme and other conservative modernists despised.[65]

The possibility of a cure remains. Symptoms of disorder are evident in the slippage between Eliot's 'feel' ('feel their thought') – where tactility is at the forefront of a poet's mind – and the emphasis on 'emotions' in the cult of sensibility. The issue at stake is not only the proportion of intellect and sensation in each perception, but also a change in how one encounters the world. One does not 'feel', but rather has the 'capacity for refined emotions'. Eliot's diagnosis implies that the new modernist aesthetic – the self-consciously '*difficult*' poetry he mentions elsewhere in the essay – could serve as a course of treatment: a means through which one could, if not exactly feel one's own thought, then at least bypass the cult of sensibility.[66]

Eliot distanced himself from the drift of both 'The Love Song of St. Sebastian' and 'The Death of Saint Narcissus'. Where those earlier works invoked psychological illness to rewrite religious experience, the poems collected in Eliot's 1920 volume refuse to be sucked in. 'The Hippopotamus' (pp. 43–44) and 'Mr. Eliot's Sunday Morning Service' (pp. 49–50), for instance, coolly satirise the imperfections of institutional religion. 'Sweeney Erect' (pp. 36–7) closes off the revelatory possibilities Huysmans found in hysteria. The poem details a sexual encounter in a house resembling one of Prufrock's 'one-night cheap hotels' and finds connections between desire, disease and violence (p. 5). During his encounter with the prostitute Doris, Sweeney:

> Tests the razor on his leg
>   Waiting until the shriek subsides.
> The epileptic on the bed
>   Curves backward, clutching at her sides.
> (p. 37).

Doris's 'curving backward, clutching at her sides' is at once a symptom of a neurological disorder, a representation of an 'epileptic' fit, and a continuation of the vigorous sex invoked in the 'Gesture of orang-outang' and 'Jackknifes upward at the knees' (p. 36). In claiming dispassionate distance while nevertheless revelling in the salacious, the poem is akin to one of Charcot's photographs. The yoking of 'razor' and 'shriek' suggests, too, that orgasmic cries can all too easily become the death throes of a 'mangled' lover (p. 265).

Eliot distances 'Sweeney Erect' from his earlier work by virtue of his handling of viewpoint. Where the earlier poems linger over a combination of sex and violence, the quatrain poem swiftly cuts away:

> The ladies of the corridor
>   Find themselves involved, disgraced,
> Call witness to their principles
>   And deprecate the lack of taste
>
> Observing that hysteria
>   Might easily be misunderstood;
> Mrs. Turner intimates
>   It does the house no sort of good.
> (p. 37)

The breathless appositional syntax of Eliot's prose poem 'Hysteria' from the 1917 collection *Prufrock and Other Observations* had attempted to register the speaker's growing loss of self-control in literary form (p. 26). Here, though, 'hysteria' functions as a magnet for social disdain. Martha Noel Evans notes that in France the majority of 'hysterical patients' were 'working-class women'.[67] Elsewhere in Europe, the distribution of hysteria amongst social class differed, but it was in the context of Eliot's time in Paris that his interest in the phenomenon took hold. The ladies' fear that 'hysteria | Might easily be misunderstood' thus carries with it notions of seediness alongside concerns about status. It captures the social conventionality of these faintly ridiculous figures rehearsing social pieties ('Call witness to their principles | And deprecate the lack of taste') in hackneyed language ('Might easily be misunderstood' and 'no sort of good'). The poem has turned its lens from the woman of Charcot's 'Extase' to the middle-class figures looking on at her photographic image with a mixture of titillation and prurience. The ladies' valuation of 'hysteria' is worlds away from that of the author of the martyr poems. Wary of those mixed achievements, Eliot moves from probing the religious potential of a hysterical scene to a refusal to confer value upon it. The social satirist replaces the spiritual seeker.

The tonal shift of the quatrain poems meets the challenge of 'The Metaphysical Poets'. Eliot began to write poetry that traded on terse juxtapositions. The abrupt shift from Sweeney's room to the corridor corresponds with an even starker change of focus at the outset from the world of ancient Greek myth ('the unstilled Cyclades', 'Aeolus | [. . .] Reviewing the insurgent gales' and 'Ariadne's hair') to the sexual exertions of Sweeney and Doris (p. 36). The shepherding of the reader's viewpoint – the first line instructs in the imperative mood: 'Paint me a cavernous waste shore' – counters the unstructured uncertainty of the earlier works (p. 36). The commanding opening invokes the studied control, direction and hardness that Ann L. Ardis considers characteristic of the high modernist programme of 'reconstituting the literary sphere as a "masculine" domain'.[68] Such a programme found an ally in Charcot's diagnostics. The metaphysical lyric is offered up as a salve for the dissociation Eliot traced in his critical prose. In contrast to the looser ambiguity of the martyr poems, the firmness of 'Sweeney Erect' offers at once a diagnosis of the earlier mode and, in leading the reader away from an unhealthy obsession, a form of therapy.

Beyond the Frontiers of Consciousness in Ash-Wednesday

For Janet, dissociation was always pathological. Given his disagreement with Gourmont on the desirability of a dissociation of intelligence and sensibility, Eliot appeared to concur with the medical assessment. Other psychologists, however, took Janet's theory in a different direction. James, for instance, believed that Janet's work on multiple forms of consciousness represented a paradigm shift for psychology. He explained:

the discovery, first made in 1886, that, in certain subjects at least, there is not only the consciousness of the ordinary field, with its usual centre and margin, but an addition thereto in the shape of a set of memories, thoughts, and feelings which are extra-marginal and outside of the primary consciousness altogether, but yet must be classed as conscious facts of some sort, able to reveal their presence by unmistakable signs.[69]

These levels of consciousness in 'addition' to 'the consciousness of the ordinary field' recall Janet's description of dissociated selves. Consciousness here is multiple as it was for Janet's patient whose secondary self was forever making unpleasant comments about his personal hygiene. James's language, however, is very different to Janet's: 'memories, thoughts, and feelings' existing 'outside of the primary consciousness altogether' and revealing 'their presence by unmistakable signs' are worlds away from Janet's belief that secondary selves undermine the pursuit of a fulfilling life. To James's mind, Janet had not merely described the symptoms of a psychological disorder, but rather uncovered an otherwise hidden dimension of human existence.

The reworking of Janet's thought came to James via his friend and colleague in the Society for Psychical Research (SPR), Frederic W. H. Myers. In addition to being a classicist and an inspector of schools, Myers had coined the term and identified the phenomenon known as telepathy. Eliot counted him among 'the more eminent critical names' of the late Victorian era.[70] Myers's two-volume work, *Human Personality and Its Survival of Bodily Death*, was published, fittingly for a book so titled, posthumously in 1903. He worked closely with James through the 1890s, leading the Harvard philosopher to modify views he had put forth earlier in his foundational textbook, *Principles of Psychology*, published in 1890.[71] For Myers, what James called 'the consciousness of the ordinary field' accounted for only a fraction of the total consciousness available. Myers's extra-marginal consciousness was both non-pathological and multiple without being hierarchical. There existed a limen or 'threshold' where our everyday or 'supraliminal' consciousness met the 'subliminal'.[72] Myers considered his findings to be comparable with the contemporaneous discoveries of portions of the electromagnetic spectrum – radio waves in 1886 and X-rays in 1895 – and the realisation that the human eye was only able to see a fraction of the light available.[73] Unlike the eye, however, Myers saw consciousness as being shaped by two very different needs: 'a naturalistic and social way via our supraliminal self' and 'a spiritual or "transcendental" way via our subliminal Self'.[74] As the human race evolved, it might develop in either direction with the former limiting the functioning of the mind to an even smaller portion of the consciousness spectrum and the latter expanding it.[75]

Various levels of personality were thus a constitutive rather than an exceptional part of human life. These differences were not always pathological. Myers summarised his assumptions thus:

> There exists a more comprehensive consciousness, a profounder faculty, which for the most part remains potential only [. . .] no Self of which we can here have cognisance is in reality more than a fragment of a larger Self, – revealed in a fashion at once shifting and limited through an organism not so framed as to afford its full manifestation.[76]

Psychical research into phenomena such as telepathy revealed the subliminal gaining ascendency over the supraliminal consciousness. Other modes of encountering the world became possible.

Eliot read *The Varieties of Religious Experience* while he was a student at Harvard. James had recently retired from the university and Jain has explained that the apprentice poet had far more in common with the broader intellectual interests of older figures on the Harvard faculty, including James and Eliot's own doctoral supervisor Josiah Royce, than the younger and typically more specialised recruits.[77] In his notes on religion and mysticism, Eliot fastened on to aspects of *The Varieties of Religious Experience* that revealed James's debt to Myers. In a passage that Eliot noted down, James wrote:

> our normal waking consciousness, rational consciousness as we call it, is but one special type of consciousness, whilst all about it, parted from it by the filmiest of screens, there lie potential forms of consciousness entirely different.[78]

James's 'potential forms of consciousness entirely different' recalls Myers's multiplicity of consciousness, while the 'filmiest of screens' dramatises the arbitrariness of Myers's 'limen'. The mind reveals itself as akin to a sprawling country house with hidden rooms that the subject himself might never have unlocked, but which were nevertheless open to God. Limen and screen anticipate, though delineated with far greater technical precision, what Eliot would later refer to as the 'frontiers of consciousness' beyond which he envisioned the poet working.[79]

Evelyn Underhill's *Mysticism*, another study Eliot read in 1912 at Harvard, shares Myers's and James's understanding of the mind. Underhill argued that the transformation of the mystic was achieved by God acting through a 'spiritual spark' or 'transcendental faculty' that 'remains below the threshold in ordinary men'.[80] The idea of a 'transcendental faculty' situated 'below the threshold' drew on Myers's subliminal mind and James's 'potential forms of consciousness entirely different'. In a passage that Eliot recorded, Underhill observed that 'visions and voices' are 'ways in which the subconscious activity of the spiritual self reaches the surface-mind'.[81] Some of the phantasmagorical phenomena associated with mysticism are best construed as not independently verifiable visual phenomena to which a third party could attest, but rather upsurges from 'below the threshold' of the mystic's own mind.

There are analogies between Underhill's understanding of vision and the composition of *Ash-Wednesday*. Absorbed in Anglo-Catholic culture, Eliot witnessed the bubbling up of the yew tree, nun and garden god from his subliminal mind. James and Underhill alike argue that even if 'visions and voices' have a psychological origin they were not thereby devoid of the value religious traditions have attributed to them.[82] Eliot likewise affirmed that the dreams that inspired the sequence were of natural origin. They came from the workings of his own subconscious. The psychological origin of the imagery does not mean that Eliot's probing of these dreams cannot be used by readers to reflect on their own religious perspectives. At another time or with another subject, God might choose to speak through the subliminal mind to produce a vision. For Janet, by contrast, all such religious talk was damned by association, given his connection of the subconscious and pathology.

The intersections of Myers's and Eliot's thought are even starker in the lectures collected and revised in his 1933 volume *The Use of Poetry and the Use of Criticism*. The connection arises in Eliot's account of John Dryden's poetic 'invention'. Responding to the dictionary definition of 'invention' – which included the word 'devising' – Eliot wrote:

> the word 'devising' suggests the deliberate putting together out of materials at hand; whereas I believe that Dryden's 'invention' includes the sudden irruption of the germ of a new poem, possibly merely as a state of feeling.[83]

While 'invention' does not exclude the 'deliberate putting together out of materials at hand', it focuses on something akin to a 'Eureka!' moment: 'the sudden irruption of the germ of a new poem' or an unexpected and revealing arrival. *Irruption* was a word favoured by Myers to describe the invasion of the normal waking consciousness, often triggered in moments of stress, by deeper movements from beyond the threshold: the 'irruption of subliminal into supraliminal life'.[84] The *Oxford English Dictionary*, however, neglects the psychological usage, offering only the 'action of bursting or breaking in' (*OED* 1). Myers's usage was picked up by James, who most likely passed it on to Eliot.[85] Later in *The Use of Poetry and the Use of Criticism*, the poet spelt out these psychological associations:

> That there is an analogy between mystical experience and some of the ways in which poetry is written I do not deny [. . .] I know, for instance, that some forms of ill-health, debility or anaemia, may (if other circumstances

> are favourable) produce an efflux of poetry in a way approaching the condition of automatic writing – though, in contrast to the claims sometimes made for the latter, the material has obviously been incubating within the poet, and cannot be suspected of being a present from a friendly or impertinent demon. [. . .] To me it seems that at these moments, which are characterised by the sudden lifting of the burden of anxiety and fear which presses upon our daily life so steadily that we are unaware of it, what happens is something *negative*: that is to say, not 'inspiration' as we commonly think of it, but the breaking down of strong habitual barriers – which tend to reform very quickly. Some obstruction is momentarily whisked away. The accompanying feeling is less like what we know as positive pleasure, than a sudden relief from an intolerable burden.[86]

To James's 'margins' and Myers's 'limen', Eliot adds his own 'habitual barriers'. His understanding of creativity as a process by which consciousness is invaded by other parts of the mind also runs through the opposition between 'incubating within the poet' and the 'friendly or impertinent demon'. Rather than owing anything to the presence of a substantial 'demon', the influx arises in the manner of Underhill's 'visions and voices' from another part of the self. The irruption enjoys some solidity and stature insofar as it involves the 'breaking down of strong habitual barriers'. For all its association with 'ill-health, debility or anaemia', the influx cannot be dismissed. Never merely a symptom, the break-in rather injects new and otherwise inaccessible knowledge. Without such irruptions, Eliot would not have written *Ash-Wednesday*.

Eliot's return to the subliminal mind constituted a reconsideration of the creative process. In a later preface, he underlined the relationship between *The Use of Poetry and the Use of Criticism* and earlier critical essays such as 'Tradition and the Individual Talent' and 'The Metaphysical Poets'.[87] The emphasis in his first critical pieces had fallen on technique and the 'the intensity of the artistic process'.[88] The later Eliot, however, felt that he had overemphasised the degree to which poetry came from a 'deliberate putting together out of materials at hand'.[89]

Eliot's reassessment of creativity was accompanied by a recognition as to the limits of an artist's power. Eliot would not remain the reserved diagnostician of the quatrain poems. His art needed the unlooked for, the unexpected and the painful. The dream symbolism of *Ash-Wednesday*, the vision in the garden of 'Burnt Norton', and the reflections on failed relationships in 'Little Gidding' are the fruits of his later approach. These moments also channel scenes from earlier in Eliot's career. Given the poet's own strained marital circumstances, the couple's conversation in 'A Game of Chess' always sat awkwardly with the tenets of the 'Impersonal theory of poetry'.[90] The aesthetic decision to emphasise personal irruptions amounted to a rejection of modernist epiphany or the idea that literature might replace revelation in a secularising world by offering access to a 'secular sacred'.[91] Poets are not mystics. They might experience irruptions from the subliminal mind as mystics do, but the common origins of mystical and creative insight should not obscure their differences. The younger Eliot had hoped, too, that poetry would serve as a form of therapy. Its distance from the poet's own emotional struggles and critical attitude to society at large might offer some resolution to the dissociations he diagnosed. The later Eliot was far more sanguine about the prospects of poetry as a kind of leaven for change in social attitudes.

The treatment of the veiled lady or the 'nun' of the recurrent dream in *Ash-Wednesday* nevertheless offers a sense of what for poetry remains possible. The female figure draws from Marian devotions and shares a familial resemblance with Dante's Beatrice. For all that, she remains stubbornly unassimilable. Eliot himself claimed to have become 'fully aware' of her 'significance' only after reading a book by the literary critic, Colin Still.[92] Still was concerned with the veiled figures in Shakespeare's late plays. He argued that:

> The drawing aside of the Veil is the ascent of the consciousness from reason to intuition; and we may equate the Veil itself with the RING OF FIRE which divides the AIR from the AETHER [. . .] I have already argued somewhat fully that AETHER is the Celestial Paradise; so that the ascent thither is a passing behind the Veil into the very Presence of God (or the gods).[93]

Religious symbols are multivalent. The Virgin Mary is the tireless protector of the family, the healer of Lourdes, and the sensuous beauty of innumerable artworks. One distinguishing feature of her role in Roman or Anglo-Catholicism has been her approachability. She is not the austere Theotokos, the imposing symbol of divine and imperial power familiar from Byzantine art.[94] By contrast, Eliot's dream figure represents a border or boundary. She is curiously distant, ambiguous and even infuriating. The sequence asks later, prayerfully:

> Will the veiled sister between the slender
> Yew trees pray for those who offend her
> And are terrified and cannot surrender
> (p. 95).

These words are at once a plea to a powerful figure ('Please pray for those in need') and a sigh of exasperation at the figure's inaction ('Are you going to intercede for us or not? What exactly is your role here?'). The triplet recalls the polysyllabic rhymes of 'The Love Song of J. Alfred Prufrock' ('come and go' | 'Michelangelo') or even 'The Love Song of St. Sebastian' ('mangled you' |

'strangled you') and registers discord, colouring the speaker's request with overbearing anxieties (p. 5, p. 6, p. 266). At the stage in the speaker's journey recounted here, the nature of the 'veiled lady' has only partially emerged; the speaker's frustration is audible in the rhymes.

Eliot's insistence on a natural rather than a supernatural origin for the veiled lady leaves the scene open to a range of interpretations. The austere figure might owe something to the pressures of childhood developmental trauma from which the mind worked to protect the writer. Deep, imaginative reflection on Christian symbolism on the writer's part might well have shaped the nun's reserved behaviour. Eliot's appreciation of a more secular source, the dramatic ambiguities and theatrical pyrotechnics of Shakespeare's late plays, might likewise contribute to the scene's staging. The significance of the Marian figure does not come to Eliot fully formed from orthodoxy alone. Religious symbolism is not merely transposed from a faith context. Given the potentially all-too-human context for the vision, the speaker's frustration with the veiled figure is at once completely understandable and, as the jangling rhymes suggest, thoroughly impertinent considering her possible divine pedigree. Counterintuitively, perhaps, Eliot's insistence on the distance between poetry and mysticism allows for an intermingling of the sacred and the secular. Disavowing special insight into matters divine, Eliot's poem shifts religion into the byways and throughways of the everyday in a fashion that not only devalues apparently religious symbols, but also raises up mundane matters.

Shaping (Un)Conscious Christianity: Social Forms of Religion

New Christian Types

In his essay, 'Religion and Literature', first published in 1935, Eliot wished for 'a literature which should be *un*consciously, rather than deliberately and defiantly, Christian'.[95] He added that many 'deliberately and defiantly' Christian texts, such as G. K. Chesterton's fictions, were so framed because they were published 'in a world which is definitely not Christian'.[96] Eliot had reservations about such works. The religious and cultural context of the 1930s encouraged polemical literature with all the attendant simplification. Such literature marginalised itself. In limiting themselves to religious matters, writers of religious literature appeared ignorant of the passions that drove others, both inside and outside their tradition. One could not, however, simply decide to write '*un*consciously Christian' literature. It was dependent upon social conditions and thus outside one's own control. It required the construction of a new society where leaders attended to cultural formation and inculcated practices, symbols and values. Drawing on Christian sociology, Eliot's *The Idea of a Christian Society*, published four years later in 1939, endeavoured to outline just such an arrangement. The hybrid discipline of Christian sociology wedded aspects of the emergent social sciences to theological principles in pursuit of social reforms.[97] Social critique stands at some distance from the struggles over interior life, the questioning as to whether a vision came from God or from a fevered brain, in which the psychology of religion featured.

The new '*un*consciously' Christian writing has a counterpart in twentieth-century theology. The distinction between conscious and unconscious acts was central to the theological reckoning with Christianity's relationship with other world religions, on the one hand, and atheism, on the other. In the mid-1960s, the Jesuit theologian Karl Rahner, for instance, outlined the idea of the 'anonymous Christian'. This was a figure who:

> on the one hand has *de facto* accepted of his freedom this gracious self-offering on God's part through faith, hope, and love, while on the other he is absolutely not yet a Christian at the social level (through baptism and membership of the Church) or in the sense of having consciously objectified his Christianity to himself in his own mind (by explicit Christian faith resulting from having hearkened to the explicit Christian message).[98]

The concept of the anonymous Christian enabled Rahner both to affirm that 'salvation cannot be gained without reference to God and Christ' and to recognise the salvific value in other religious traditions.[99] To be an anonymous Christian is to express one's openness to the 'gracious self-offering on God's part through faith, hope, and love' or what Rahner elsewhere termed the 'supernatural existential', the sense that 'any moment of insight is not an end in itself, but just the beginning of an ongoing process of discovery and understanding'.[100] Having responded to the invitation, the anonymous Christian need not have 'consciously objectified his Christianity' through the profession of a creed or membership of a church. Members of other faiths can be construed as anonymous Christians in opposition to, or even in disregard of, the expectations and values to which they may consciously adhere.

The anonymous Christian serves a different purpose to the '*un*consciously Christian' in Eliot's thought, even if the terminology is partly shared. In addressing religious pluralism, however problematically, Rahner sidesteps Eliot's emphasis on inculturation. Even more strikingly, the German Protestant theologian and anti-Nazi dissident Dietrich Bonhoeffer formulated, in his *Letters and Papers from Prison* written during the internment that preceded his execution in 1945, the idea of an 'unconscious Christianity'. For Bonhoeffer, the phrase asserted that:

> People outside the church community who model true humanity unbeknownst to themselves both draw on and model Christian virtues [. . .] like integrity, courage to state the truth, respect for others, an intuitive sense for the proper action required by any given situation, and acting righteously rather than talking piously.[101]

While anonymous as much as confessing Christians access Christian salvation, Rahner's language of anonymity emphasised a difference in status between the two. Anonymous Christians lack something confessing Christians have. Rahner values Christianity over other religious traditions and thus construes confessional Christianity as inherently superior to the anonymous version. Bonhoeffer's unconscious Christians, by contrast, are not only adherents of other religions, but also atheists and agnostics. They grasp more firmly than even confessing Christians the essential truths of the Christian religion. Their intuitive grasp of certain moral principles reveals the hollowness of much conscious religiosity. The unconscious Christian is not so much a second-class figure as a model for a community whose very cultural forms and practices threaten to drown out the true call of their tradition. The '*un*consciously Christian' in Eliot, by contrast, followed from the absorption of Christian culture, the very forms and practices about which Bonhoeffer worried, to such a degree that it was no longer necessary to think about one's religion overtly.

Despite the differences between them, the verbal similarities between the poet's and theologians' usages are worth noting because they reveal an idiosyncratic feature of Eliot's '*un*consciously Christian'. *Unconscious*, for the theologians, concerns religious observance that is 'unintentional; not deliberate or planned' (*OED* 4). In Rahner's account, life circumstances have intervened such that it is impossible or unpractical for an anonymous Christian to live as a confessing Christian. In Bonhoeffer, conscious attention to institutional forms of Christianity can even distract from the moral truths one might otherwise intuit. Eliot's '*un*consciously Christian' incorporates, albeit in a different context, the absence of deliberation. Social institutions outlined in *The Idea of a Christian Society* are adapted to make Christian life habitual. Ordinary people live out a Christian vocation with little fuss. The concern with societal groups, broadly speaking the masses, politicians and elites, reveals Eliot's essay in Christian sociology to be a corporatist work. Its theme is the relationship between religion and the community. For Eliot, a change in social arrangements in turn instigates a change in outlook. *Unconscious* in the sense of 'mental or psychological processes of which a person is not aware but which influence emotions and behaviour' (*OED* 6) comes into view. Eliot's fascination with the formative role that religion plays in the psyche reasserts itself in *The Idea of a Christian Society*, particularly when he discusses the religious elites or the Community of Christians; outlines the importance of religious orders; and draws on principles from *The Idea of a Christian Society* in a paper on the Christian imagination produced for the Christian think tank named the Moot. Even in a work that is ostensibly focused on the role of orthodoxy in developing and maintaining social order, Eliot was not blind to the attractions of 'spilt mysticism'.

A Communion of Saints in The Idea of a Christian Society

One central tenet of Eliot's planned society in *The Idea of a Christian Society* was its hierarchical or 'graded' nature.[102] Eliot outlined three groups: first, the Community of Christians, a group of religious elites who framed the long-term goals of the society and had special responsibility for education; secondly, the Christian State, where politicians, civil servants and the leaders of civil life framed social goals using categories from Christian thought; and thirdly, the Christian Community, or the masses, whose habitual Christian faith exerted certain expectations on the politicians leading the society (p. 695). The Community of Christians promotes orthodoxy and develops, in negotiation with an established church, forms of social life that enable ordinary people to live out their religion. In a society so framed, expectations and values are inculcated in the Christian Community and these in turn exert a restraining influence on the political class.

The social arrangements set out in *The Idea of a Christian Society* deliberately clash with principles cherished by liberal, democratic states. The essay begins with a concern for the community, rather than with the individual actors of liberal society and the democratic forms to which such individualism appeared wedded. More strikingly still, it challenges, insofar as it outlines a structural role for a group of religious elites, the esteem in which equality is held. For David Bradshaw, the role conferred upon an unelected group empowered to shape society brings Eliot 'perilously close to promoting a totalitarian theocratic state'.[103] *The Idea of a Christian Society* struggles to value non-Christian cultures or to construe minorities as anything other than a problem to be managed. In praising the 'unity of religious background' in *After Strange Gods*, published five years earlier in 1935, Eliot lamented that 'reasons of race and religion combine to make any large number of free-thinking Jews undesirable'.[104] Eliot's Christian society appears not merely totalitarian in the abstract, but rather shockingly close to the anti-Semitic National Socialist totalitarianism that *The Idea of a Christian Society* had ostensibly set out to challenge.

While responding to contemporary Nazi and Soviet totalitarianisms, Eliot never conceived of *The Idea of a Christian Society* as a programme to be implemented. He was 'not', he insisted, 'concerned with the means for bringing a Christian Society into existence' or 'with making it appear desirable' (p. 685). *The Idea of a Christian Society* is no party manifesto. He intended to hold up a mirror to a contemporary society that contained remnants of historical Christendom to show how far short it fell from being a Christian society. The example of Maurras looms large in Eliot's plans, particularly in the role assigned to an established church in maintaining social order.

There are nevertheless striking differences between *The Idea of a Christian Society* and Maurras's thought, the most significant development being that

Eliot's societal grades are to be understood 'in connexion with the problem of *belief*'. Maurras, by contrast, was an atheist in the positivist tradition of Auguste Comte with little interest in religious ideas outside the social order they instigated. Eliot explained the connection between his grades and belief:

> Among the men of state, you would have as a minimum, conscious conformity of behaviour. In the Christian Community that they ruled, the Christian faith would be ingrained, but it requires, as a minimum, only a largely unconscious behaviour; and it is only from the much smaller number of conscious human beings, the Community of Christians, that one would expect a conscious Christian life on its highest social level (p. 697).

The transformed outlook follows from a system of education that trains people 'to think in Christian categories' (p. 697). Importantly, Eliot's society would 'not compel belief and would not impose the necessity for insincere profession of belief' (p. 697). 'Christian categories' shaped individual worldviews, social institutions and ultimately give rise to a form of belief. The Community of Christians and the church with the support of the state and the masses would frame social life to reflect a basic Christian pattern or what Eliot called elsewhere 'the belief' in 'holy living and holy dying, in sanctity, chastity, humility, austerity'.[105] The pattern was to be sustained and supported by wider intervention in and regulation of economic and social life (pp. 735–37).[106]

Different modes of belief would thereafter emerge. Christian life is habitual for the masses that constitute the Christian Community. *Belief* here is akin to the 'habit of trusting to or having confidence' in the society in which one lives and its relationship with God (*OED* 2). Nobody thinks about religious matters very much. Christian principles can be practised almost accidentally; the Christian Community is more or less '*un*consciously Christian'. The 'men of state', by contrast, articulate the ideas and values that undergird the Christian outlook to explain their actions. They must be careful not to justify decisions in terms that undermine the religious principles of the majority. Such *belief* is closer to a 'set of propositions held to be true' (*OED* 4a). The designs of the Community of Christians make everything possible. The group exemplifies 'conscious Christian life on its highest social level'. Participation in the Community of Christians depends on the intensity and creativity of an individual's relationship with their religion. Its members exhibit a deep creative engagement with Christianity, which is indicative of *belief* in the sense of the 'trust that the believer places in God; the Christian virtue of faith' (*OED* 1a). They make intuitive links within the tradition and map out a path for development true to the founding charism. The present study has repeatedly contrasted religious observance as, on the one hand, a form of assent to traditional authority structures and, on the other, what the sociologist Robert N. Bellah has termed the 'internalization of authority'.[107] In *The Idea of a Christian Society* both forms are present, but at different levels: the former among the Christian Community and the latter among the Community of Christians.

The Idea of a Christian Society treats differences in belief as part of natural variation. The society proposed by the essay 'would be', Eliot explained, one 'in which the natural end of man – virtue and well-being in community – is acknowledged for all, and the supernatural end – beatitude – for those who have the eyes to see it' (p. 700). Everyone sees the world in Christian categories, but belief at its highest level only takes hold among a small group. The presence of religious contemplative orders is thus important to the design of the society. Eliot explained:

> I should not like it to be thought, however, that I considered the presence of the higher forms of devotional life to be a matter of minor importance for such a society. [. . .] I cannot conceive a Christian society without religious orders, even purely contemplative orders, even enclosed orders. And, incidentally, I should not like the 'Community of Christians' of which I have spoken, to be thought of as merely the nicest, most intelligent and public-spirited of the upper middle class – it is not to be conceived on that analogy (p. 715).

For Stefan Collini, 'the incongruously archaic image of the cloistered, celibate monk' symbolises the difference between Eliot's Community of Christians on the one hand and 'the nicest, most intelligent and public-spirited of the upper middle class' – those figures associated with the liberal intellectual tradition that *The Idea of a Christian Society* set out to overturn – on the other.[108] Eliot allowed that those exhibiting the requisite intensity of belief should rise from the Christian Community to the Community of Christians. His elite were not to correspond, he explained, to either the secular social elite or even the ranks of Oxbridge-educated Anglican clerics. His advocacy of spiritual mobility drew on the breadth of his own religious network. Eliot made regular retreats at Kelham Theological College, which was run by the Anglo-Catholic religious order, the Society of the Sacred Mission (SSM). Kelham served as the site of the SSM's monastic house and as an educational institute that prepared working and lower middle-class men for missionary work.[109] The SSM was convinced, as David A. Dowland has noted, 'that "lower" social groups had a unique value to the Church'.[110] In order to live out its mission, the order felt that the Church of England needed to 'employ lower-class men' and the SSM dedicated itself to training such figures.[111] Institutions such as the SSM, defiantly orthodox in persuasion and committed to diversifying the ranks of the clergy, would doubtless have their representatives among the Community of Christians.

The key characteristic of group members was nevertheless neither class nor educational background, but rather the intensity of belief. Strong belief mattered to more than the individual from whom it emanated. Eliot thought the 'ordinary man' needed 'the opportunity to know that the religious life existed, that it was given its due place, would need to recognise the profession of those who have abandoned the world, as he recognises the professions practised in it' (p. 175). Religious orders made concrete the higher levels of belief that were otherwise absent from the Christian Community. Far from being a mere quirk, the 'incongruously archaic' monk is integral to Eliot's hierarchic society. The monk reveals what the basic exposure to Christianity, enjoyed by everyone through their schooling and via the framing of social life, could ultimately become. Religious orders are held up as an example to emulate and to induce humility among the Christian Community about the religious commitments of its members. They are spiritual role models reworking the significance once accorded to the speaker of 'The Love Song of St. Sebastian' and to Saint Narcissus, who Eliot had previously held up as representative types. The difference between the figures from these two periods is not only that the monks are orthodox while the pseudo-martyrs are heretical, but also that the former in keeping with the corporatist designs of *The Idea of a Christian Society* is depicted as a model for a whole community, while the appeal of the latter is far more partial and idiosyncratic.

The foundation upon which the higher levels of religious belief and practice built was as important to art as to religion. Eliot outlined these ideas in a paper written in 1941 and entitled 'Revival of Christian Imagination'. The paper, presented at a gathering of the Moot, responded to an essay written by another member, the sociologist Karl Mannheim.[112] Mannheim's piece took a pluralist approach to the understanding of religion in society. He argued that for some people religion centred on intense experiences; for others, it was bound up with human relationships; and for a third group, it was part of a way life.[113] Eliot made use of these categories, but dispensed with Mannheim's pluralism, organising them into 'a sort of hieratic order' which, he acknowledged, was to 'depart from Mannheim's intentions towards them'.[114] Different approaches to religion became variations in quality or intensity. For most, Christianity is merely a way of life; for the more advanced, it is at work in their relationships and daily habits; and for the most intense, it bursts out into 'personal ecstatic mystical communion with God' with each subsequent step marking progress in the 'stages of contemplative life'.[115] In the third stage, the development of a foundation of Christian observance provides the necessary conditions for more advanced forms of religious commitment.

The response to Mannheim aids an understanding of '*un*consciously Christian' literature. Such writing becomes possible when a given writer is no longer inescapably confronted with the exclusion of Christianity from public life. In the proposed society, Christianity would be everywhere and no case for its inclusion would be required. More importantly, the pervasiveness of Christianity within the social environment thereafter worked at a subconscious level on a given writer such that its influence becomes visible in strange creative irruptions shaped by exposure to the tradition. According to Hadjiyiannis, Eliot's attention to subterranean concerns taps into a broader history of political thinking on the right, influenced by Henri Bergson's philosophy and mediated through figures such as T. E. Hulme and Georges Sorel, that recognised that intellectualism alone was not sufficient for the formation of political ideologies.[116] A Christian society helped produce both non-polemical Christian literature and an emergent literature of the Christian subconscious. For these higher levels of engagement to become possible, the background hum of the Christian Community was necessary.

The subliminal mind was central to how Eliot conceptualised *The Idea of a Christian Society*. While he described it as 'political philosophy', *The Idea of a Christian Society* concerned not the 'the conscious formulation of the ideal aims of a people', but rather 'the substratum of collective temperament, ways of behaviour and unconscious values which provide the material for the formulation' (p. 691). The opposition of *conscious* and *unconscious* reappears. Rather than specific aims or doctrines, Eliot concerns himself with the societal structures that shape habitual, non-deliberative actions. He had recourse to the language of James and Myers. The phrase 'substratum of collective temperament' is suggestive of a non-pathological alternative mode of consciousness running alongside conscious, everyday deliberation. Eliot outlined societal grades that imposed a hierarchy on the otherwise flat structures of a liberal society that preached equality. These grades shaped institutions important to society members. Eliot also attended to the impact of these structures and institutions on the deeper layers of the mind. Subliminal formation enables him to find places for a religion of authority and the '*internalization of authority*'. In *The Idea of a Christian Society* the latter does not follow from the breakdown of the former; rather, the former provides the condition necessary for the latter. Orthodoxy gives birth to mysticism. The broadening of the individual subliminal consciousness into the 'substratum of collective temperament' is the counterpart to Eliot's evocation of 'the mind of England' in 'The Metaphysical Poets'. The social structures of a Christian society would do what Eliot's quatrain poems could not: heal 'the mind of England'.[117] The rupture represented by the 'dissociation of sensibility' appears to be simultaneously religious, a break in the pattern of Christian life, and psychological insofar as these social shifts impact upon the mental worlds of those living in the changed society. The art a society produces merely reflects these broader conditions.

In the community envisioned by *The Idea of a Christian Society*, art and religion enjoy a mutually supportive relationship. Responding to Mannheim, Eliot claimed that 'the Imagination is essentially religious'.[118] He explained:

> I think that the disintegration of the Imagination is manifest by the separation between those people who cultivate the arts [. . .] and those who cultivate the religious sensibility. The tendency is then for the religious sensibility to be stunted, and for the arts to perish slowly – as the religious imagination atrophies, the imagination *tout court* disappears also. The arts, in their decline, pass through the stage of sensationalism; theology and philosophy which cease to be nourished by the imagination descend into verbalism.[119]

The 'religious sensibility' risks becoming mere conformity to a preconceived orthodoxy and losing the inspiration represented by genuinely creative thought. It needs the creative impetus of the imagination. Likewise, 'sensationalism' is evident when art becomes idiosyncratic, parochial and detached from what really matters. A Christian collective temperament helps art and religion alike avoid these pitfalls. The rise of a religious and artistic elite prevents habitual religious devotion from becoming stale. Informed by an embedded Christianity, creative work avoids the idiosyncrasy that might otherwise attend it. Public concerns shape such art and art in turn speaks to that same public.[120] Artists have principles to work with and a public to write for and the quality of the art thereby advances just as a baseline Christianity makes possible a greater frequency and intensity of 'mystical communion' among the population.

In *The Idea of a Christian Society,* Eliot focused on the religious community rather than the religious commitments of individuals. He endeavoured to 'picture, not a society of saints, but of ordinary men, of men whose Christianity is communal before being individual' and stressed that representatives of the Christian State are to be chosen for their qualifications rather than the quality of their faith because a 'regiment of Saints is apt to be too uncomfortable to last' (p. 714, p. 696). Saints embody a religious extreme. They exhibit an idiosyncratic approach in matters of religion at odds with Eliot's focus on the religious life of the community. *The Idea of a Christian Society* nevertheless attends to not only shared values, but also the capacity to produce, through the lives of religious pattern setters, unexpected and creative exemplifications of those values. Saints are not feted for their own sake. Their example, as with that of vowed religious, inspires the Christian Community. The religious insights of their life and thought, as interpreted by the Community of Christians and the established church, refine corporate religious life. The public and the private, the mystical and the orthodox, come together in such figures. While he had long distanced himself from the poetics of 'The Love Song of

St. Sebastian' and 'The Death of Saint Narcissus', Eliot continued to react to the forces that influenced their composition, searching out ways in which society might produce true saints.

SECULAR CONSOLATIONS: PATTERNS OF MYSTICISM IN *FOUR QUARTETS*

Missing Mystics in the Age of Modernism

From an orthodox perspective, saints and mystics were always exceptional. The assumption that such figures were few and far between jarred with the profusion of unchurched mysticism in the twentieth century. D'Arcy, for instance, advised that mystics were always 'rare' figures, who had 'undergone a long religious discipline, a dark night of the soul, before they have emerged on the shining plateaux where they have experimental union with God'.[121] The apparent multiplication of mysticisms in the age of modernism followed from the mislabelling of a range of deeply felt religious emotions. Eliot agreed. Only a 'few', he wrote in a review of an edition of St John of the Cross's works published in 1934, 'ever reach a stage so advanced' that they can 'adopt' the mystic as 'their guide'.[122] He advised modern readers to turn to the Carmelite not as a how-to, but rather for what he had gleaned about God from a profound 'experimental union'.[123] Likewise, the graded conception of Christian belief Eliot outlined in *The Idea of a Christian Society* recognised the importance of differences in belief within the Christian community. A society only produces a few saints and mystics, but their rarity makes them a source of inspiration.

Differences nevertheless emerged between D'Arcy and Eliot. D'Arcy believed that the volume of mysticism in modern society was overestimated. Eliot's concern was that mysticism was becoming increasingly rare, even on the verge of disappearing altogether. In his 1941 paper on the 'Revival of Christian Imagination', he explained:

> We have the evidence, first, of the marked differences of type between the mysticism of different peoples and different periods: no one could confuse the mysticism of Spain with that of Germany, or the mysticism of the twelfth and thirteenth centuries [. . .] with that of the seventeenth; second, that a period which produces one or two great mystics is apt to produce a host of lesser mystics or enthusiasts as well. Furthermore, I believe that an historical study of the genesis of religious movements would confirm the importance of the social background in its religious aspect; as well as the more obvious relevance of economic and other social conditions and motives [. . .] It is not perhaps an accident that instead of great devotional writers, we have rather distinguished writers about devotional literature, though it would be unfair to suggest that von Hügel was no more than that.[124]

These 'social conditions' bear comparison to the hierarchical steps Eliot identified in Mannheim's article. Mystics such as St John of the Cross grew up with the background noise of religion always in their ears; it inspired their own music as adults. Among modern writers, mysticism was not, however, an outlet for a deeply religious adolescence. Their interest typically emerged later in life. To these moderns, the intensity of mysticism offered what organised religion, at least of the kind recalled from childhood Sunday schools, did not.[125] By then, it was too late. There was no seed buried within to be nurtured. The twentieth century produced only 'distinguished writers about devotional literature' and not 'great devotional writers' because the background music had fallen silent. The commentator could not become the mystic.[126]

A consequence of the social change to which Eliot attended was an outpouring of what he took to be *ersatz* mysticisms. In an essay reflecting on revelation published in 1937, Eliot described the rise of *'psychological mysticism'* which he considered 'a phenomenon of decadence rather than of growth'.[127] Reference to the *'psychological'* here recalls Eliot's fascination with Charcot in the martyr poems. Psychological mystics attend to their own internal irruptions, rather than lifting their eyes to the heavens. While D'Arcy saw the proliferation of mysticism as a problem of religious illiteracy, Eliot understood the emergence of what the present study has termed 'spilt mysticism' as an indictment of social change. New mysticism reveals a society not merely neutral in matters of religion, but rather actively hostile. Christian mysticism had been replaced by something else altogether. In a range of critical writings from the mid-1930s onwards, Eliot traversed the distance between Christian mysticism and contemporary society. Even as he read the mystics ever more closely, attended religious retreats and participated in Anglican worship, Eliot underscored the alien nature of the mystical outlook, which contemporaries struggled even to understand let alone practice.

Episodes and Processes in 'East Coker'

Disregarding Eliot's own critical positioning in the mid- to late-1930s, a popular and scholarly consensus has designated *Four Quartets*, Eliot's major poetic work of his later period, as itself a mystical work. Childs, for instance, detects within the poem 'a pattern in which meditation upon intellectual concerns culminates in an experience of mystical knowledge that answers the concerns in question'.[128] More broadly, as Geoffrey Hill has complained, the work has been canonised as a work of 'Anglican literary "spirituality"' in ways that jar with the careful distinction Eliot himself drew between irruptions from the subliminal mind and mystical union with God.[129] James thought it possible that God might work through the subliminal mind, but he did not equate the activity of the subliminal mind with the movement of God. *The Varieties of Religious Experience* distinguished the psychological mechanisms underlying religious phenomena from the value ascribed to them. Eliot rightly worried that readers would run the two together again.

Reading *Four Quartets* as a mystical text gains credence from its allusions to mystical writers. The gnomic wisdom of 'East Coker', for instance, paraphrases a passage from St John of the Cross's *Ascent of Mount Carmel*:[130]

> You say I am repeating
> Something I have said before. I shall say it again.
> Shall I say it again? In order to arrive there,
> To arrive where you are, to get from where you are not,
>   You must go by a way wherein there is no ecstasy.
> In order to arrive at what you do not know
>   You must go by a way which is the way of ignorance.
> In order to possess what you do not possess
>   You must go by the way of dispossession.
> In order to arrive at what you are not
>   You must go through the way in which you are not.
> And what you do not know is the only thing you know
> And what you own is what you do not own
> And where you are is where you are not
> (p. 189).

Paul Murray finds in these lines a 'profound' and 'intense *theological* vision' that assumes '"two contraries . . . cannot co-exist in one person"'.[131] In service of the 'intense *theological* vision', all things worldly must be excised to allow for a single-minded focus on God. Murray worries whether the mystic 'was not a dangerous guide for someone with Eliot's unhappy and introverted temperament'.[132] Like those of the mystic they paraphrase, Eliot's lines ask the reader to undergo a process of intellectual purification. Murray sets aside Eliot's claim that 'few persons' are 'advanced' enough to take St John of the Cross as a guide and the fact that the society that had shaped Eliot's audience was very different from that which the saint inhabited.

In eliding St John's and Eliot's concerns, Murray flattens the passage. Two voices are audible: the mystic's gnomic wisdom and the fussing of the narrator. The latter is characterised by a parenthetical, self-correcting syntax: 'You say I am repeating | Something I have said before. I shall say it again. | Shall I say it again?' The lines are coloured by both heavy caesurae and a hesitant, self-questioning tone. The narrator's voice contrasts with the mystic's riddles, which are marked by coincidence of line and sense unit; across two-line units, the adverbial clauses ('In order to possess what you do not possess') complete the first line and the main clause the second ('You must go by the way of dispossession'). The mystic's voice betrays a studied calm that serves as a counterpoint to the narrator's befuddlement. Far from acting as a guide, the mystic gestures in a direction otherwise closed off to the poem. The Carmelite neither reveals the core message of the poem nor provides it with a linguistic strategy. His voice, notably distinct from the harried utterances of the speaker, is merely tried out for a moment.

The significance of St John of the Cross comes instead from the dialogue his presence initiates. Elsewhere, Eliot speaks about moments of spiritual intensity:

> As we grow older
> The world becomes stranger, the pattern more complicated
> Of dead and living. Not the intense moment
> Isolated, with no before and after,
> But a lifetime burning in every moment
> And not the lifetime of one man only
> But of old stones that cannot be deciphered
> (p. 191).

The passage glances at brief, powerful moments of mystical insight. The disruption at the line break in the midst of the adjectival phrase 'intense moment | Isolated' affords us a grand, if nevertheless brief, reveal. 'Isolated', signalling the hermit's fervour, presents the 'moment' as singular and transformative, while also hinting at ostracism and loneliness. The overrun snaps back attention on the 'intense moment' at the very instant that the experience appears to have been left behind. The speaker has enjoyed moments of illumination, but they have left him cut off from others. These moments of illumination recall the irruptions of *The Use of Poetry and the Use of Criticism* and *Ash-Wednesday*. They are a feature of Eliot's life and writing to which critics from Lyndall Gordon and Ronald Schuchard to James Longenbach have attended.[133] The verse resists the idea that they are 'not' to be continued.

The sequence nevertheless opposes the 'intense moment' to the notion of a broader 'pattern'. In the sense of a 'decorative or artistic design' or an 'elaboration of form', the *pattern* of *Four Quartets* reaches back ('piety towards the dead') and stretches forward ('solicitude for the unborn') in time (*OED* 9a). A studied calm, quite different to the disruptive line break of 'intense moment | Isolated', is retained when discoursing on 'pattern'. While 'a lifetime burning in every moment' is a phrase wrought to an emotive pitch, momentary flashes of intensity are brought under control as the verse slips into the qualifications of 'And not the lifetime of one man only' – a phrase that expands on 'lifetime' and sidesteps the ferocity of 'burning' – and the imagery of 'old stones' that gestures back to the enigmatic monuments on Salisbury Plain. Counter-intuitively, Eliot links a term charged with Christian resonance to Stonehenge, that druidic monument of ancient Britain. The unbroken heritage invoked by such symbolism, however misleadingly, dampens the flames the passage lit.

Pattern also denotes an 'example or model to be imitated' or 'a person' who 'is worthy of copying; an exemplar; an archetype' (*OED* 2a). In the latter sense, St John of the Cross is incorporated into the sequence's broader design. In his analysis of recent studies of spirituality, William B. Parsons distinguishes between the 'mystical *experience*' and the 'mystical *process*'.[134] The latter 'expands the episodic' to find the meaning of mystical experience 'in the context of the course of a religious life and in the cultivation of various dispositions, capacities, virtues, and levels of consciousness'.[135] There are losses in the shift from one to the other. In *Four Quartets*, the sense of radical change that turns on an instant, reminiscent of the moments of martyrdom or murder in Eliot's early poems, is replaced by interpretation, reinterpretation and ascetic practice. St John of the Cross was one of the central systemisers of the mystical process and his achievements attach to the patient, wise voice audible in the sequence.

Within *Four Quartets*, the seductive 'intense moment' stands alongside the visions to which the poem attends from the dry pools of 'Burnt Norton' to the 'daunsinge' figures of 'East Coker' and the metaphysical transformations effected by the pastiches of seventeenth-century lyrics. For all their idiosyncrasy and distinctiveness, the sequence attempts to incorporate these intensities into the broader 'pattern' afforded Eliot by virtue of his Christianity in ways that recall the shift from the isolated, idiosyncratic intensities of the martyr poems to the broader social thought of *The Idea of a Christian Society*. As a sequence, *Four Quartets* practices stylistic asceticism. Eliot incorporated the intense and often very personal lyric 'Burnt Norton', which grew out of the crisis occasioned by the separation from his wife and his reunion with Emily Hale, into the sequence of *Four Quartets*. The later quartets, by contrast, are publicly minded pieces, more rhetorical than lyrical, addressing the wartime situation in Britain. The earlier sensual, confessional intimacy gives way to a larger pattern. Thematically, structurally and stylistically, the poem stages a tussle between 'spilt mysticism' and 'wavering orthodoxy'. Like Hügel and the later Underhill, *Four Quartets* attempts an accommodation between the contemporary celebration of immanence and the mediation of institutional religion.

Mystics at War in 'Little Gidding'

Critics have often found the ascetic method Eliot employs to negotiate the tension between immanence and mediation problematic. For F. R. Leavis, the asceticism of *Four Quartets* was indicative of Eliot's 'fear of life and contempt (which includes self-contempt) for humanity'.[136] These feelings arose, Leavis thought, from an 'untenable conception of the spiritual', which ultimately compromised Eliot's commitment as a poet to both language and the community language enabled.[137] Shira Wolosky concurs; 'the ideal of Silent Union', Wolosky writes, 'demotes language and displaces meaning from this world into another one'.[138] The corporatist dimension of Eliot's Christianity suggests that his alleged equation of spirituality and anti-communitarianism is more problematic than might otherwise appear.

Marina MacKay has, more recently, taken a different tack in her attempt to separate the poem's religious commitments from its engagement with the wartime context. She challenges Ronald Schuchard's reading of the lines: 'Why should we celebrate | These dead men more than the dying?' (p. 206), for instance, arguing that Schuchard is 'forgetful of the immediate context' insofar as he construes these lines as part of the relationship between 'the dying (that is, the living) and the dead'.[139] Given the transitoriness of human life, she accepts that glossing 'dying' as 'living' is 'theologically plausible'.[140] We all die a little bit each day and human concerns pale when set alongside eternal matters. She argues that such a position, were Eliot to have held it, would nevertheless have represented 'unthinkable callousness at the beginning of 1942'.[141] Millions were dying, not in the ordinary run of a finite human life, but rather prematurely during a world war. *Four Quartets* might well be a classic of Anglican spirituality, but it is also, as MacKay insists, a war poem. Her approach to the issue Leavis identified is to disentangle the two, freeing the poem from the weight of religious interpretations.

One consequence of Eliot's disavowal of poetry as a form of mysticism was his willingness to allow for interplay between the sacred and the secular. Dissociation of the religious and the wartime becomes unnecessary. After all, such a separation is contrary to the impetus behind *The Idea of a Christian Society*, which saw the secular structures of society framed by liberal democracies as an impediment to an appreciation of the sacred and thus in need of reform. If social reform was required to save the sacred, the sacred, too, could speak to the secular. Despite the distance in context, outlook and time between Julian of Norwich and the author of *The Cloud of Unknowing* on the one hand and a contemporary Londoner living through the Blitz on the other, the allusions to medieval mysticism in 'Little Gidding' enabled Eliot to reach out to a wartime public, whom in 1942 had good reason to expect defeat.

The language of mysticism forms an appeal to shared memory. Eliot described his allusions to the English vernacular mystics as a means of avoiding 'a certain romantic Bonnie Dundee period effect' and claimed he wanted 'to check this and at the same time give greater historical depth to the poem by allusions to the other great period, i.e. the 14th century'.[142] The fourteenth-century English mystics were a counterpart to seventeenth-century metaphysical poets; their inclusion gave 'Little Gidding' a variety of reference that helped distance the poem from pastiche. The fourteenth century represented, for Eliot, a 'great period' in English cultural history and thus afforded the poem 'greater historical depth'. It was also a period of distinguished devotional writing. The religious background music of that time had been turned up loud and had, in line with the theories Eliot rehearsed in *The Idea of a Christian Society*, inspired these figures to produce their own compositions.

Eliot thus gestured towards what he took to be common Christian heritage as a bulwark against present exigency. The sociologist of religion Danièle Hervieu-Léger has argued that the 'future of religion', following the shift in modes of belief akin to those outlined in the present monograph, is bound up with the problem of 'collective memory' in the face of a modernity that valorises change and works against processes of recollection.[143] She goes on to speak of how the '*normative* character' of any collective memory (its editing, sifting and reimagining) is reinforced by a given religious group's understanding of itself as a '*lineage* of belief'.[144] The recollection of the past is an 'essentially religious act', which 'gives meaning to the present and contains the future'.[145] Hervieu-Léger distances herself from religions of hierarchical authority. She is critical of understandings of religious practice defined by formal membership of a given religious institution within which members grant assent, whether implicit or explicit, to positions articulated by religious authorities. Instead, she pictures a group coalescing around a common memory that is edited on an ongoing basis in the retelling of a shared story. The emphasis she places upon memory rather than institutional membership enables Hervieu-Léger to retain a respect for history and tradition, while recognising the breakdown of institutional authority through the twentieth century in matters of religion.[146]

The allusions of *Four Quartets* ask readers to share in religious memory. Ronald Bush has warned against understanding Eliot's allusiveness as a mere demonstration of erudition in which genuine emotion is subjugated to a scholarly appreciation of the poet's command of the canon.[147] Drawing on the lectures Eliot delivered in America during the academic year running from 1932 to 1933, Bush writes:

> Eliot suggests [. . .] that allusions are an organic part of the modernist writer's synchronizing procedures, in which 'memories, both from reading and life', are 'charged with emotional significance'. The emphatic link between reading, life, and memory is crucial here, for it speaks to the way allusions carry a 'personal saturation value' that differs [. . .] from poet to poet and from poem to poem [. . .] In the Harvard notes on Joyce, he more specifically acknowledges the price that the emotional essence of such 'synchronisation' exacts in poetic 'clarity'. But for Eliot, whose work actively invites the collaboration of the reader into the act of interpretation, it is a cost he knows he has to pay.[148]

Four Quartets transposes the idea of the 'personal saturation value' associated with literary criticism into something akin to the collective memory to which Hervieu-Léger attends. The allusions to the mystics invoke what *The Idea of a Christian Society* was written to recover, the lost religiously informed 'substratum of collective temperament'. The allusions to the mystics and thought world they represent offer some consolation in the face of wartime defeat, even to readers who were not confessing Christians. Strains of a background music that had become all but inaudible are heard once more. The poem attempts consolation not via the ministrations of the religious elite but through triggering a memory response among its readers. The response might well hit one with the force of an irruption from the subliminal mind, as if it were an uprush of meaning from the collective memory. Not everyone, as Bush recognises, can be expected to react identically. For some, specific allusions will bear little significance, if they are noticed at all. Still more may share Leavis's valuation of Eliot's 'spiritual commitments' and respond to the allusions as stifling and stuffy, recalling uncomfortable Sunday school classes. Eliot accepts the risk. Addressing what he understood as a country that evinced largely different values and found itself in the midst of a national crisis, Eliot produced a public poem that invoked a Christian past.

It is misleading to treat the fragmented voices of the medieval mystics scattered through *Four Quartets* as representatives of authoritative doctrine demanding assent.[149] Literary allusions work differently and Eliot conceived of the relationship between literature and religion in quite other terms. The close of 'Little Gidding' instead confronts the wartime situation with soaring rhetoric that interweaves voices from earlier quartets and allusions to medieval mysticism:

> Not known, because not looked for
> But heard, half-heard, in the stillness
> Between two waves of the sea.
> Quick now, here, now, always—
> A condition of complete simplicity
> (Costing not less than everything)
> And all shall be well and
> All manner of thing shall be well
> When the tongues of flames are in-folded
> Into the crowned knot of fire
> And the fire and the rose are one.
> (p. 209)

In its original context, Julian of Norwich's 'All shall be well' takes its place within the 'grandest possible' narrative that the mystic develops about sin and suffering, namely that everything that has happened and ever will happen – whatever the outcome – will fit with everything's being 'well' in the broader frame of God's providence.[150] To an unsympathetic observer, the phrase may appear flippant, insufficient or even in bad taste. 'How can that be true in the face of all this destruction?', a reader might be led to ask.[151] The allusion nevertheless gestures towards a body of religious thinking – alludes to a longer view or a greater plan – that provides a measure of comfort when little else could. The phrase is at once hopeless and full of hope. Eliot is unwilling to venture the latter without the protection of the former. The theodicy can always be shrugged off.

The balancing act between the two turns on an interpretation of 'when' in 'All manner of thing shall be well | *When* the tongues of flame are in-folded. . .' (my italics). Eliot's 'when' can be heard as a simple relative: All 'shall be well' when these conditions (the tongues, the knot, the fire and the rose) are met. 'When' firmly excludes 'if'. Using a rhetorical, public style of writing, the speaker, styled as an assured prophet, explains that the burning city will inevitably in the long run or at a deeper level be transformed, signified here by the Christian symbols of the inverted crown and the rose.[152] The close of *Four Quartets* is *dogmatic*, which often veers between the imposition of 'dogmas or opinions in an authoritative, imperious, or arrogant manner' and 'characterized by or consisting of dogma; doctrinal' (*OED* 4b & 2). Sometimes named the 'Pope of Russell Square', Eliot had to do with both senses of the word. The assurance with which transformation is expected borders on arrogance.

An interest in doctrine need not, however, become imperious. Anthony Domestico, for instance, notes that *The Criterion* treated Karl Barth's work as an exemplar of a 'living theology'; that is, 'not just theology that affects, and is affected by, lived experience', but also – and perhaps counter-intuitively given Barth's unwavering insistence on the primacy of revelation – 'theology that acknowledges its own provisional nature'.[153] The softer, more self-aware perspective helps us hear 'when' differently. It functions as a 'reference to a future time' (*OED* 4b) and thus a form of strained hope. Instead of dictating to a despairing country that all 'shall be well' so long as one accepts some basic doctrinal principles – a notion at a far remove from what Julian understood herself to be doing – the voice becomes gentle, conciliatory, striving for common ground. The speaker positions himself alongside the reader and together in solidarity the speaker and reader look out at the burning city. Eliot inspires his readers with the mystics. As with the religious orders held up in *The Idea of a Christian Society*, their advanced state is not a boon for themselves alone or even for their own segment of society; their presence inspires a broader community, incorporating people like and unlike themselves. Recalling the faith exhibited by past inhabitants of the land, speaker and reader alike wait and watch for a transformation that they are all too aware might never come. The extremity of wartime London works against any form of triumphalism. Doctrinal certainties are called into question by the vulnerability of the city.

The 'pattern | Of timeless moments' that Eliot stiches together in *Four Quartets* unites the perspectives on religion described over the course of the present chapter. The poem consoles, while recognising the futility of imposing dogmatic demands upon an irreligious populace. Confronted by chilling extremity the brief invocation of collective saturation value represented by the mystics grants readers momentary access to shared memory. *Four Quartets* is a public poem. It channels collective memory to help its readers come to terms with an anticipated national loss on an unimaginable scale. The poem becomes a form of church, ministering to those both with and without existing religious affiliation. It does not, however, attempt to replace revelation with aesthetic experience in the manner of the modernist epiphany. Eliot's explorations in the psychology of religion, politics and sociology taught him that modern religious life was not defined by the emergence of new religions and the inevitable decline of traditional ones alone. The role of the churches was itself changing and Eliot imagined a mutually supportive relationship between poetry and its institutional counterpart.

An End to Religious Quest

Ash-Wednesday, *The Idea of a Christian Society* and *Four Quartets* all post-date Eliot's baptism and confirmation, which took place on consecutive days at a parish church in Oxford in summer 1927.[154] Having received the sacraments, Eliot quickly worried about how his actions might be perceived. His former Harvard teacher, Irving Babbitt, in England on a visit, persuaded him that a declaration in print was necessary.[155] In response, Eliot presented himself, in the preface to *For Lancelot Andrewes*, published the following year, as a 'classicist in literature, royalist in politics, and anglo-catholic in religion'.[156] For a later critic of Eliot's work such as Jewel Spears Brooker, the baptism and creedal statement initiated Eliot's embrace of a 'straightforward, no-nonsense' Anglo-Catholicism and the end of his youthful pursuit of 'substitutes' for religion.[157] Not all commentators, however, have been so sympathetic. Virginia Woolf famously opined on meeting Eliot in early 1928 that a 'corpse would seem to me more credible than he is', adding 'there's something obscene in a living person sitting by the fire and believing in God'.[158] More broadly, Eliot's actions appeared to jar with, or even to betray, his role as 'the poet for a new age of doubt, skepticism, and irony', even if, as Jeffrey M. Perl has argued, Eliot can be understood as a 'Christian skeptic'.[159] The poet withdraws from a 'new age' into what C. K. Stead has called a 'life-denying form of Christian asceticism' or plots, in the words of Roger Luckhurst, a 'conservative trajectory' away from modernity 'towards a disciplinarian religious belief that curtails the radicalism of modernisms'.[160] Eliot's tricolon nevertheless alludes to a summary of Maurras's programme that he had encountered in the *Nouvelle Revue Française* many years earlier: 'classique, catholique, monarchique'.[161] His declaration of an apparently newfound faith was framed after the pattern of a notorious atheist. There are, it would appear, as many continuities as discontinuities between the pre- and post-1927 Eliot.

The present chapter has emphasised the former. The psychology of religion fed Eliot's doctoral work and early martyr poems; it remained, too, a prominent influence on his later literary criticism, social criticism and poetry. Moreover, to construe the religious dimension of Eliot's life in terms of a lifelong spiritual quest is as misleading as casting his baptism as a radical break with what went before. Such an interpretation betrays the influence of a secular outlook that construes religion as a private matter. The present chapter has instead examined the intersection of Eliot's life and processes of religious change. Eliot witnessed the rise of the academic study of non-Christian religions at European and American universities; the challenge to the authority of institutional religions both from outside in the form of the hostility of secular governments and from within through invocations of immanence; and the decline in church attendance and the rise of new or alternative religions. This is not to mention the wider processes that, while not overtly concerned with religion, nevertheless influenced it from urbanisation to changes in economic life and the consequences of the First World War.

Eliot, like many of the figures in the present book, was attracted by some of these new developments, while also believing that the traditional facets of religion provided a solution to several challenges generated by the new order. The boundaries between mysticism and orthodoxy, secular and sacred, public and private were shifting at the turn of the twentieth century. Poetry such as *Ash-Wednesday*, which alludes to the Catholic liturgy while nevertheless eschewing the label 'religious', witnesses to this shift in outlook. The respective pulls of mysticism and orthodoxy explain why Eliot can at times sound like a spiritual seeker and other moments like a High Churchman. There was often something of the seeker in the Anglo-Catholic and a hankering for aspects of traditional religion even among the unchurched mystic. The commonality between mysticism and orthodoxy is approached from a different angle in the following chapter. Given her attractions to psychic research, spiritualism and the occult, H.D. exemplifies a seeker mentality and yet, she, too, during a period of artistic, personal and social turmoil, returned to the Moravian Christianity of her childhood as a resource for both artistic inspiration, improved self-understanding and social critique.

Notes

1. Spurr, p. 214.
2. T. S. Eliot to Rev M. C. D'Arcy SJ, 24 May 1930, in *The Letters of T. S. Eliot*, 9 vols (London: Faber & Faber, 1989–), 5: *1930–31*, ed. by Valerie Eliot and John Haffenden, p. 201 (p. 201); T. S. Eliot to Maurice Leahy, 17 May 1930, in *Letters*, 5, pp. 188–89 (p. 188).
3. Eliot to D'Arcy, 24 May 1930, p. 201.
4. Eda Lou Walton, 'T. S. Eliot Turns to Religious Verse', *New York Times Book Review*, July 1930, in *T. S. Eliot: The Critical Heritage*, ed. by Michael Grant, 2 vols (London: Routledge & Kegan Paul, 1982), 1, pp. 253–55.

5. Spurr, p. 214.
6. See T. S. Eliot, 'Religion and Literature', in *Tradition and Orthodoxy*, pp. 218–29 (pp. 219–20).
7. Eliot, 'Religion and Literature', pp. 219–20.
8. T. S. Eliot to George Bell, 20 July 1930, in *Letters*, 5, pp. 257–58 (pp. 257–58).
9. Eliot to Bell, 20 July 1930, pp. 257–58.
10. See Martha Noel Evans, *Fits and Starts: A Genealogy of Hysteria in Modern France* (Ithaca, NY: Cornell University Press, 1991), p. 24.
11. See Cristina Mazzoni, *Saint Hysteria: Neurosis, Mysticism, and Gender in European Culture* (Ithaca, NY: Cornell University Press, 1996), p. 26.
12. See Taves, *Fits, Trances, and Visions*, p. 277.
13. Eliot to Bell, 20 July 1930, p. 257.
14. Hulme, p. 62; Kenneth Asher, *T. S. Eliot and Ideology* (Cambridge: Cambridge University Press, 1995), pp. 36–37.
15. Asher, p. 34.
16. Shortall, pp. 54–55.
17. Shortall, p. 55.
18. Shortall, p. 55.
19. T. S. Eliot, 'Dante', in *Complete Prose, 3: Literature, Politics, Belief, 1927–1929*, ed. by Frances Dickey, Jennifer Formichelli and Ronald Schuchard, pp. 700–46 (p. 718); Eliot, '*After Strange Gods*', p. 40.
20. See Shortall, pp. 60–84.
21. The present section expands arguments rehearsed in Callison, 'Dissociating Psychology', 1029–59.
22. Eliot, 'Clark Lectures', p. 653, p. 707.
23. See Donald J. Childs, *T. S. Eliot: Mystic, Son and Lover* (London: Athlone, 1997), pp. 152–85. For the classicism-versus-romanticism debate, see David Goldie, *A Critical Difference: T. S. Eliot and John Middleton Murry in English Literary Criticism, 1919–1928* (Oxford: Clarendon Press, 1998), pp. 96–105.
24. Sinclair, p. 270.
25. See Elaine Showalter, *The Female Malady: Women, Madness, and English Culture, 1830–1980* (London: Virago, 1985), pp. 150–55.
26. Paul Richer, 'L'hystérie dans l'art', in *Études cliniques sur la grande hystérie ou hystéro-épilepsie* (Paris: Delahaye et Lecrosnier, 1885), pp. 914–56 (p. 956); Evans, p. 35.
27. As a young woman, St Margaret of Cortona lived as the mistress of a nobleman. Accounts of her life occasion exhortations to sexual purity. See Antonio Francesco Giovagnoli, *The Life of Saint Margaret of Cortona* (Philadelphia: Cunningham, 1888), pp. 7–16; Alban Goodier, SJ, 'St. Margaret Of Cortona: The Second Magdalene – 1247–1297', in *Saints for Sinners* (Garden City, NJ: Image Books, 1959), pp. 20–32.
28. See Evans, pp. 13–14.
29. See Mazzoni, pp. 17–53.
30. See Taves, *Fits, Trances, and Visions*, p. 278; James, pp. 1–25.
31. James, p. 21.
32. Ronald Schuchard, *Eliot's Dark Angel: Intersections of Life and Art* (Oxford: Oxford University Press, 1999), p. 219n.

33. T. S. Eliot to Conrad Aiken, 25 July 1914, in *Letters*, 1: *1898–1922*, ed. by Valerie Eliot and Hugh Haughton, rev. edn, pp. 48–51 (p. 49).
34. T. S. Eliot, 'The Love Song of St. Sebastian', in *The Poems of T. S. Eliot: The Annotated Text*, ed. by Christopher Ricks and Jim McCue, 2 vols (London: Faber & Faber, 2015), 1, pp. 265–66 (p. 265). Further references to Eliot's poems are to this edition and volume; references are given after quotations in the text.
35. See Evans, p. 42.
36. T. S. Eliot, 'Baudelaire in our Time', in *Literature, Politics, Belief*, pp. 71–82 (p. 73).
37. See, for example, T. S. Eliot, 'A Review of *Egoists, A Book of Supermen*, by James Huneker', in *Apprentice Years*, pp. 24–25 (p. 24); T. S. Eliot, '*Syllabus of a Course of Six Lectures on Modern French Literature, Frederick Hall, 1916*', in *Apprentice Years*, pp. 471–76 (p. 473); T. S. Eliot, 'Baudelaire', in *Complete Prose, 4: English Lion, 1930–1933*, ed. by Jason Harding and Ronald Schuchard, pp. 155–67 (p. 161).
38. Ellis Hanson, *Decadence and Catholicism* (Cambridge, MA: Harvard University Press, 1997), p. 127.
39. Manju Jain, *T. S. Eliot and American Philosophy: The Harvard Years* (Cambridge: Cambridge University Press, 1992), pp. 160–61.
40. See T. S. Eliot, notes on religion and mysticism, in *T. S. Eliot Papers, 1878–1958*, MS Am 1691.129, Houghton Library, Harvard University. 'Je n'avais pas vingt ans encore et je foulais, ce me semble, sous les pieds le monde vaincu', Henri Delacroix, *Études d'histoire et de psychologie du mysticisme. Les grands mystiques chrétiens* (Paris: Félix Alcan, 1908), p. 4. Delacroix quotes from St Teresa of Ávila's *Le livre de la vie*. The translation is mine.
41. Delacroix, p. 13.
42. T. S. Eliot to Conrad Aiken, 31 December 1915, in *Letters*, 1, pp. 80–82 (p. 82).
43. Eliot, 'The Metaphysical Poets', p. 380.
44. Nancy K. Gish, 'Discarnate Desire: T. S. Eliot and the Poetics of Dissociation', in *Gender, Desire, and Sexuality in T. S. Eliot*, ed. by Cassandra Laity and Nancy K. Gish (Cambridge: Cambridge University Press, 2004), pp. 107–29 (p. 113).
45. See Murray McArthur, 'Symptom and Sign: Janet, Freud, Eliot, and the Literary Mandate of Laughter', *Twentieth Century Literature*, 56 (2010), 1–24.
46. T. S. Eliot, 'A Neglected Aspect of Chapman', in *Perfect Critic*, pp. 548–58 (p. 553).
47. T. S. Eliot, 'Style and Thought: An Unsigned Review of *Mysticism and Logic and Other Essays*, by Bertrand Russell,' in *Apprentice Years*, pp. 690–94 (p. 690).
48. T. S. Eliot, 'A Commentary (June 1928),' in *Literature, Politics, Belief*, pp. 416–20 (p. 417).
49. Ezra Pound, 'Remy de Gourmont', in *Literary Essays of Ezra Pound*, ed. by T. S. Eliot (London: Faber & Faber, 1954), pp. 339–358 (p. 351).
50. See Louis Menand, *Discovering Modernism: T. S. Eliot and His Context*, 2nd edn (Oxford: Oxford University Press, 2007), p. 170.
51. Remy de Gourmont, 'La sensibilité de Jules Laforgue', in *Promenades littéraires* (Paris: Mercure de France, 1904), pp. 105–10 (pp. 105–6). The translation here and below is mine.
52. Gourmont, 'La sensibilité de Jules Laforgue', pp. 105–6.
53. Gourmont, 'La sensibilité de Jules Laforgue', pp. 105–6.
54. Eliot, 'The Metaphysical Poets', p. 380.

55. See Elton Mayo, *The Psychology of Pierre Janet* (London: Routledge and Kegan Paul, 1951), pp. 30–31.
56. James, p. 233.
57. See Taves, *Fits, Trances, and Visions*, p. 257.
58. See Mayo, p. 30; Eugene Taylor, *William James on Consciousness Beyond the Margin* (Princeton: Princeton University Press, 2011), pp. 40–43.
59. Pierre Janet and Raymond Fulgence, *Névroses et idées fixes*, 2 vols (Paris: Félix Alcan, 1898), 2, pp. 176–78. The translation is mine. For Eliot's notes, see Eliot, notes on religion and mysticism, in *T. S. Eliot Papers, 1878–1958*.
60. T. S. Eliot, 'Tradition and the Individual Talent', in *Perfect Critic*, pp. 105–14 (p. 109).
61. Eliot, 'The Metaphysical Poets', p. 380.
62. Eliot, 'A Neglected Aspect of Chapman', p. 553.
63. See Jean-Jacques Rousseau, *The Collected Writings of Rousseau*, ed. by Roger D. Masters and Christopher Kelly, 13 vols (Hanover, NH: University Press of New England, 1990–2010), 6: *Julie, or the New Heloise: Letters of Two Lovers Who Live in a Small Town at the Foot of the Alps*, trans. and ann. by Philip Stewart and Jean Vaché; Rousseau, *Collected Writings*, 13: *Emile: or On Education*, trans. and ed. by Christopher Kelly and Allan Bloom.
64. Christos Hadjiyiannis, *Conservative Modernists: Literature and Tory Politics in Britain, 1900–1920* (Cambridge: Cambridge University Press, 2018), pp. 46–47.
65. See Asher, pp. 36–38; Hadjiyiannis, pp. 45–51; Goldie, pp. 96–104; Schuchard, pp. 52–69.
66. Eliot, 'The Metaphysical Poets', p. 381.
67. Evans, p. 12.
68. Ann L. Ardis, *Modernism and Cultural Conflict, 1880–1922* (Cambridge: Cambridge University Press, 2002), p. 17.
69. James, p. 233.
70. T. S. Eliot, 'The Use of Poetry and the Use of Criticism: Studies in the Relation of Criticism to Poetry in England', in *English Lion*, pp. 574–694 (p. 669).
71. See Taylor, *James on Consciousness*, pp. 40–96.
72. Edward F. Kelly and others, *Irreducible Mind: Toward a Psychology for the 21st Century* (Lanham, MD: Rowman & Littlefield, 2007), p. 77.
73. See Kripal, p. 60.
74. See Kripal, pp. 67–8.
75. See Kripal, pp. 66–70.
76. Frederic W. H. Myers, *Human Personality and Its Survival of Bodily Death*, 2 vols (London: Longmans Green, 1903), 1, p. 12, p. 15. Quoted in Kelly, p. 73.
77. Jain, p. 166.
78. James, p. 388; see Eliot, notes on religion and mysticism.
79. T. S. Eliot, 'The Music of Poetry', in *Complete Prose*, 6: *The War Years, 1940–1946*, ed. by David E. Chinitz and Ronald Schuchard, pp. 310–25 (p. 314).
80. Underhill, 1911, p. 93.
81. Underhill, 1911, p. 271; Eliot, notes on religion and mysticism.
82. Childs trivialises Underhill's argument by summarising it thus: 'visions are not necessarily reliable'. Childs, *Mystic, Son and Lover*, p. 43. Underhill outlines a psychological model that resists efforts to equate origins with value.

83. Eliot, 'The Use of Poetry and the Use of Criticism', p. 616.
84. Myers, 2, p. 132.
85. James, p. 173, p. 176, p. 180, p. 235.
86. Eliot, 'The Use of Poetry and the Use of Criticism', pp. 685–86.
87. See Eliot, 'The Use of Poetry and the Use of Criticism', p. 575.
88. Eliot, 'Tradition and the Individual Talent', p. 109.
89. Eliot, 'The Use of Poetry and the Use of Criticism', p. 616.
90. Eliot, 'Tradition and the Individual Talent', p. 108.
91. See, for example, Lewis, p. 19; Mutter, p. 77. For modernism and the epiphany, see Beja; Nichols; Kim.
92. T. S. Eliot to Colin Still, 13 May 1930, in *Letters*, 5, pp. 170–72 (p. 171).
93. Colin Still, *Shakespeare's Mystery Play: A Study of* The Tempest (London: Cecil Palmer, 1921), p. 101, pp. 110–11.
94. Miri Rubin, *Mother of God: A History of the Virgin Mary* (New Haven, CT: Yale University Press, 2010), pp. 43–49.
95. Eliot, 'Literature and Religion', p. 221.
96. Eliot, 'Literature and Religion', p. 221.
97. See, for example, Joseph A. Scimecca, *Christianity and Sociological Theory: Reclaiming the Promise* (London: Routledge, 2018), pp. 119–35; Susan E. Henking, 'Sociological Christianity and Christian Sociology: The Paradox of Early American Sociology', *Religion and American Culture: A Journal of Interpretation*, 3 (1993), 49–67. See also T. S. Eliot, 'The Idea of a Christian Society', in *Tradition and Orthodoxy*, pp. 683–747 (p. 686). Further references to this essay are from this edition and are given after quotations in the text.
98. Karl Rahner, 'Observations on the Problem of the "Anonymous Christian"', in *Theological Investigations*, 23 vols (New York: Crossroads, 1961–92), 14: *Ecclesiology, Questions in the Church, the Church in the World*, trans. by David Bourke, pp. 280–94 (p. 283).
99. Karl Rahner, 'The One Christ and the Universality of Salvation', in *Theological Investigations*, 16: *Experience of the Spirit: Source of Theology*, trans. by David Morland, pp. 119–224 (p. 218).
100. David Pitman, *Twentieth Century Christian Responses to Religious Pluralism: Difference is Everything* (Farnham: Ashgate, 2014), p. 94.
101. Jens Zimmerman, *Dietrich Bonhoeffer's Christian Humanism* (Oxford: Oxford University Press, 2019), p. 59.
102. T. S. Eliot, 'Notes Towards the Definition of Culture', in *Complete Prose*, 7: *A European Society, 1947–1953*, ed. by Iman Javadi and Ronald Schuchard, pp. 194–287 (p. 221).
103. David Bradshaw, 'Politics', in *T. S. Eliot in Context*, ed. by Jason Harding (Cambridge: Cambridge University Press, 2011), pp. 265–74 (p. 272). See also Hadjiyiannis, p. 96.
104. Eliot, '*After Strange Gods*', p. 20.
105. T. S. Eliot, 'Christianity and Communism', in *English Lion*, pp. 422–31 (p. 428).
106. See Collini, 'Where Did it All Go Wrong?', pp. 247–74.
107. Bellah, 'Religion and Belief', p. 224.
108. Stefan Collini, *Absent Minds: Intellectuals in Britain* (Oxford: Oxford University Press, 2006), p. 316.

109. See Peter Ackroyd, *T. S. Eliot: A Life* (New York: Simon and Schuster, 1984), p. 207.
110. David A. Dowland, *Nineteenth-Century Anglican Theological Training: The Redbrick Challenge* (Oxford: Clarendon Press, 1997), p. 107.
111. Dowland, p. 107.
112. For the Moot, see Jonas Kurlberg, *Christian Modernism in an Age of Totalitarianism: T. S. Eliot, Karl Mannheim and the Moot* (London: Bloomsbury Academic, 2019).
113. See T. S. Eliot, 'Revival of Christian Imagination', in *War Years*, pp. 239–44 (p. 240). The essay to which Eliot responded is collected in Karl Mannheim, *Diagnosis of Our Time: Wartime Essays of a Sociologist* (London: Routledge, 1943), pp. 122–42.
114. Eliot, 'Revival of Christian Imagination', p. 242.
115. T. S. Eliot, 'A Review of *The Mystical Doctrine of St. John of the Cross*', in *Tradition and Orthodoxy*, p. 108 (p. 108).
116. Hadjiyiannis, pp. 15–16.
117. Eliot, 'The Metaphysical Poets', p. 380.
118. Eliot, 'Revival of Christian Imagination', p. 242.
119. Eliot, 'Revival of Christian Imagination', p. 242.
120. This summarises a version of the argument offered by Gill, pp. 219–49.
121. D'Arcy, *Nature of Belief*, p. 232.
122. Eliot, 'Review of *The Mystical Doctrine*', p. 108.
123. Eliot, 'Review of *The Mystical Doctrine*', p. 108.
124. Eliot, 'Revival of Christian Imagination', p. 240, p. 242.
125. For the importance of the influence of Sunday school on the religious imagination, see T. S. Eliot, 'Why Mr. Russell Is a Christian: A Review of *Why I Am Not a Christian*, by the Hon. Bertrand Russell', in *Literature, Politics, Belief*, pp. 160–63.
126. A. E. Waite accused Evelyn Underhill of being too academic in her approach. 'If only she owed less to the past, less to her patient reading up and more to her proper self, we should have had the book that we are wanting more than all'; one 'misses', Waite continues, 'the sense of something that has come to its author individually, whether through the intellect or otherwise'. A. E. Waite, 'A Garden of Spiritual Flowers', *New Age* 9, no. 6 (8 June 1911), 137–39 (p. 138).
127. Eliot, 'Introduction to *Revelation*', pp. 472–96 (p. 483).
128. Childs, *Mystic, Son and Lover*, p. 198.
129. Geoffrey Hill, 'Dividing Legacies', in *Collected Critical Writings*, ed. by Kenneth Haynes (Oxford: Oxford University Press, 2008), pp. 366–79 (p. 379).
130. Compare John of the Cross, *Ascent of Mount Carmel*, trans. by E. Allison Peers, 3rd edn (Garden City, NY: Image Books, 1958), p. 72.
131. Murray, p. 97, p. 98. Murray quotes from John of the Cross, p. 27.
132. Murray, p. 99.
133. See Lyndall Gordon, *Eliot's Early Years* (Oxford: Oxford University Press, 1977), p. 52, p. 61; James Longenbach, *Modernist Poetics of History: Pound, Eliot, and the Sense of the Past* (Princeton: Princeton University Press, 1987), p. 220, pp. 212–13; Schuchard, pp. 3–24.
134. Parsons, *Freud and Augustine*, p. 15.

135. Parsons, *Freud and Augustine*, p. 16.
136. Leavis, p. 205.
137. Leavis, p. 205.
138. Shira Wolosky, *Language Mysticism: The Negative Way of Language in Eliot, Beckett and Celan* (Stanford, CA: Stanford University Press, 1995), p. 49.
139. Marina MacKay, *Modernism and World War II* (Cambridge: Cambridge University Press, 2007), p. 88; Schuchard, p. 194.
140. MacKay, p. 88.
141. MacKay, p. 88.
142. T. S. Eliot to John Hayward, 2 September 1942, quoted in Helen Gardner, *The Composition of* Four Quartets (London: Faber & Faber, 1978), p. 70.
143. Danièle Hervieu-Léger, *Religion as a Chain of Memory*, trans. by Simon Lee (Cambridge: Polity Press, 2000), p. 123.
144. Hervieu-Léger, p. 124, p. 125.
145. Hervieu-Léger, p. 125.
146. See Bellah, 'Religion and Belief', pp. 216–29.
147. Ronald Bush, '"Intensity by association": T. S. Eliot's Passionate Allusions', *Modernism/ modernity*, 20 (2013), 709–727 (p. 719).
148. Bush, p. 719.
149. See DuPlessis, *Genders, Races, and Religious Cultures*, p. 156; Luckhurst, p. 444. The remainder of the present section expands upon Callison, 'Sacred Ground', pp. 375–88.
150. Denys Turner, *Julian of Norwich, Theologian* (New Haven, CT: Yale University Press, 2011), p. 46.
151. Turner, *Julian of Norwich*, p. 11.
152. The public voice constitutes the second of Eliot's voices of poetry. See T. S. Eliot, 'The Three Voices of Poetry', in *European Society*, pp. 817–833 (p. 817).
153. Domestico, pp. 29–30.
154. Spurr, p. 111.
155. Asher, p. 56; Spurr, pp. vii–viii.
156. T. S. Eliot, 'Preface to *For Lancelot Andrewes: Essays on Style and Order*', in *Literature, Politics, Belief*, pp. 513–14 (p. 513).
157. Jewel Spears Brooker, *Mastery and Escape: T. S. Eliot and the Dialectic of Modernism* (Amherst: University of Massachusetts Press, 1994), pp. 126–27.
158. Virginia Woolf to Vanessa Bell, 11 February 1928, in *The Letters of Virginia Woolf*, ed. by Nigel Nicolson with Joanne Trautmann, 6 vols (London: Hogarth, 1975–80), 3: *A Change of Perspective, 1923–1928*, pp. 456–58 (pp. 457–58).
159. John Xiros Cooper, *The Cambridge Introduction to T. S. Eliot* (Cambridge: Cambridge University Press, 2006), p. 111; Jeffrey M. Perl, *Skepticism and Modern Enmity: Before and After Eliot* (Baltimore: Johns Hopkins University Press, 1989), p. 110.
160. C. K. Stead, *Pound, Yeats, Eliot, and the Modernist Movement* (New Brunswick, NJ: Rutgers University Press, 1986), p. 229; Luckhurst, p. 444.
161. Asher, p. 36.

3

REVERSION THERAPY: THE PERSONALISM OF H.D.'S RETURN TO RELIGION

In the eyes of her fellow Imagists, H.D.'s early poetry was otherworldly. Reviewing her first volume *Sea-garden* in 1917, John Gould Fletcher wrote:

> The great mystics, whether they call themselves Christians or pagans, have all this trait in common – that they describe in terms of ordinary experience some super-normal experience. The unpractised reader, picking up H.D.'s *Sea-garden* and reading it casually, might suppose it was all about flowers and rocks and waves and Greek myths, when it is really about the soul, or the primal intelligence, or the *Nous*, or whatever we choose to call that link that binds us to the unseen and uncreated.[1]

Fletcher's characterisation of H.D.'s verse echoed a talking point from F. S. Flint's 'The History of Imagism', published in 1915. Flint's piece, written at the behest of Ezra Pound, portrayed the Imagists as a hermetic sect clustered around an unwritten 'doctrine of the Image', producing verse marked by a meditative temperament and a cloistered reserve.[2] Lashed by Pound's editorial pen, Imagism became a form of stylistic asceticism that prepared writers and readers for a new reality.[3] H.D. took her place among the 'great mystics'.

Sea-garden's religious insights were shared by D. H. Lawrence, a close associate of H.D.'s. T. S. Eliot remarked that 'the recognition that even the most primitive feelings should be part of our heritage' is 'the explanation and justification' for Lawrence.[4] Elsewhere, he explained that Lawrence 'wished to go as low as possible in the scale of human consciousness, in order to find something that he could assure himself was *real*.[5] In these spiritual quests, accretions and accumulations, intervening layers of civilisation, are stripped away in order to reveal the vital forces lurking beneath the surface. Mysticism is often the name conferred on what is discovered. Charles Taylor considers the procedure a characteristically secular strategy, even if H.D. and Lawrence opposed the materialism with which the secular is often associated.[6] Peeling off layers of tradition in the name of immediacy removes what is distinctive about religious traditions, making the ground more favourable to secular arguments. One might identify at the heart of all religions a humanistic core centred on justice; then claim that enlightened rationality is better able to deliver on such promises because it is free from the embedded prejudices of traditional religions. Likewise, so long as the mysticism uncovered beneath the accretions of tradition is equated with emotive or noetic experience, it remains open to debate as to whether religion or, say, art functions as the best conduit to such experiences.[7] Why fast, give alms or reflect on scripture, when you can access religion through *Sea-garden*?

The fascination with religious experience among writers on modernism has contributed to secularisation. Thinking about the Moravian history outlined in H.D.'s *The Gift*, for instance, Adalaide Morris argues that 'Moravian doctrine' is 'less a dogma than a design for living', which is focused on 'the binding power of love'; 'eros', she continues, 'determined not only Moravian rituals of connection like the love feast and the kiss of peace but also the daily arrangements of their economy'.[8] The Moravians were a Protestant sect that claimed an older lineage. In the mid-eighteenth century, they founded H.D.'s hometown, Bethlehem, Pennsylvania; the history of the sect fascinated the poet through the 1940s. Morris outlines a variety of experiences of religion: from participation in religious worship to the valences of everyday life under a theocracy. She nevertheless opposes properly modernist religious phenomena to restrictive 'doctrine' or 'dogma', sidestepping the presumed corruption of organised religions. Institutional religion encourages adherents to respect principles, conduct themselves in certain ways and participate in communal worship. These elements, notwithstanding the radical welcome a given religious community might choose to extend, establish boundaries around the sacred in a way that a volume of poetry does not. *Sea-garden* ushers in a new equality of access to the spiritual.

The religious immediacy of H.D.'s verse opens out on to a form of perennialism. Religions the world over have a common core. Fletcher insists on the interchangeability of the Christian 'soul', the Kabbalist 'primal intelligence' and the Plotinian '*Nous*', all of which are labels for 'that link that binds us to the unseen and uncreated'. These concepts play distinct roles within their respective thought systems and as a result are very different from each other. The connection between them is an emotional and existential experience: a recognition of humankind's limitations, a sense of awe at the possibilities of the natural world and a desire to pass beyond the changeable to connect with something more permanent. The longing for unity that Fletcher describes is constant across time and space, shaping a range of religious doctrines even if those doctrines have themselves given rise to different intellectual justifications, hermeneutic traditions and forms of cultural practice.[9] H.D. takes her place among the 'great mystics' because the aesthetic effect of her poetry corresponds to the emotional reality informing these doctrines. Religion becomes a label for an intense human experience.

The emotional-religious concerns of Fletcher's review contribute to the 'crystalline' aesthetic of H.D.'s early verse and speak to a modernist response to broader shifts in religious culture.[10] William B. Parsons notes that the increased academic attention conferred upon Asian religions at European and American universities from the late nineteenth century onwards facilitated work in comparative religions.[11] The idea shared by twentieth-century theorists such as William James, Rudolf Otto and Mircea Eliade that all religions had a mystical core was one of the fruits of initial work in comparative religions. Modernism, too, participated in the process, not only following Fletcher in attending to authentic or 'primitive' religious experiences rather than what Pericles Lewis calls the 'false refinements' of institutional religion, but also positioning itself through terms such as epiphany as a conduit to such experiences.[12] A focus on religious experience and the rise of an autonomous artistic sphere blurred the boundaries between the aesthetic and religious in ways that were central to modernist style and its critical legacy.

The present chapter argues that H.D.'s well-documented stylistic shift away from the 'crystalline' aesthetic was sustained by a changed attitude towards religion and the spiritual directness of her early work. The perennialism identified by Fletcher was later complicated by H.D.'s midlife reimagining of her Moravian heritage. The chapter opens with the conditions for that rediscovery, namely H.D.'s unexpected encounter with the Moravians in Denis de Rougemont's 1939 study, *L'Amour et l'Occident*. An English edition appeared the following year as *Passion and Society*.[13] Rougemont presented the Moravians as part of an ancient heretical church of love. Struck as she was by the mismatch between the daring of Rougemont's narrative and the primness of her own upbringing, H.D.'s work offers a rich and complex portrait of her return to religion, opening a window on to what the sociologist of religion Danièle Hervieu-Léger has called 'a transformation in the mode of believing'.[14] A reclaimed and reworked Moravianism equipped H.D. to challenge aspects of Freudian psychoanalytic theory and to mount, in *Helen in Egypt*, a public, religiously informed critique of interwar militarism. Contrary to Lawrence Rainey's contention that H.D.'s religious interests were a consequence of withdrawal from the public realm, the present chapter argues that H.D.'s Moravian background enabled H.D. to engage the public in a new way.[15] In her Moravian phase, H.D. is not interested in stripping away, but rather adding, building and combining. H.D.'s accretive approach produced a more intricate picture of twentieth-century religion and a nuanced version of modernity.

Rediscovering the Moravians: Between Credibility and Credulity

Encountering Denis de Rougemont's Passion and Society

Christianity is a religion of the book and conversions to it have often prominently featured texts. Augustine's *Confessions* is a case in point. Drawing heavily on that spiritual classic in her biography of the saint, the novelist Rebecca West notes how on one occasion Augustine heard a child chanting the phrase *'Take . . . up . . . and . . . read!'* repeatedly, which led him to open the Bible at the verse: 'Not in rioting and drunkenness, not in chambering and wantonness, not in strife and envying. But put ye on the Lord Jesus Christ, and make not provision for the flesh, to fulfil the lusts thereof' (Romans 13: 13–14).[16] Following the incident, light 'flooded' Augustine's heart and ensured that his will 'moved like a living thing' once more.[17] The encounter with the book was 'the sign' for which Augustine 'had waited'.[18] God spoke to Augustine through the incident, entreating the future bishop to leave off debauchery and to commit to a Christian life.

West, however, was unwilling merely to describe the transformative moment. She felt called upon to analyse it too. She followed her description of the scene with an observation:

> It is well to note that Ambrose had been called to baptism and the episcopate when [. . .] a child's voice had chanted again and again, 'Bishop Ambrose! Bishop Ambrose!' It is well to note, too, that the Epistles of St. Paul were the foundations of Ambrose's preachings. One might think that the omen might have been more fortunate, for indeed it would be difficult to open the Epistles of St. Paul and not find some encouragement to adhere to the Church, and it would have been better for the world if Augustine's eyes had fallen on a text that added graciousness to purely negative moral admonition and gaunt invitation to enrol under the right banner.[19]

The intensity and power of Augustine's reorientation is dissipated by his biographer's recognition that the abrupt change was artfully patterned. West notes the allusions to Augustine's mentor Ambrose. The scene depicts an unexpected event: an extraordinary meeting of the human and the divine, mediated by an open book. Augustine's writerly concern was not, however, confined to his relationship with God; he also stressed his worldly connection with Ambrose. The biographer is moved, too, to moralise. West's sense that it was unfortunate that Augustine's attention was drawn to a verse of 'negative moral admonition' is deflationary. She records the transformative power of conversion, but also identifies the story's limitations. The text pulls in different directions, credibility and credulity, scepticism and sincerity, simultaneously.

An encounter with Rougemont's *Passion and Society* in 1939 produced a similarly complex response in H.D.'s life and thought. H.D read the text in 1939 when it was published in French, and then re-read it in English, when the translation appeared the following year.[20] The effect on her, as for many readers, was powerful.[21] In November 1940, she explained to her friend, George Plank:

> Also, I am asking Br to order for you a vol. called Passion and Society by Denis de Rougemont. [. . .] I read it in Vaud wondering WHAT manner of Frenchman could have written it – but of course there it was, de Rougemont is French-swiss. The translation, I have is wonderful – the French is '*L'amour et l'occident*', Love and the West does not translate. I hope Logan lives to read it. But maybe its religious background would not appeal so much – it will to you. De R. brings in old Shakers too and Milton and has a go at the subconscious he-man school which Logan will like, too.[22]

'I read it in Vaud wondering WHAT manner of Frenchman could have written it' records the shock and surprise the book occasioned. H.D. would elaborate on the connection with English poetry alluded to in 'De R. brings in old Shakers too and Milton' in *By Avon River*, published in 1949, where she presented Shakespeare's writing and Elizabethan lyric as companions to troubadour writing. They mediate the teachings of what she refers to in *The Gift* as the 'Invisible Church' (p. 265n). She draws on Rougemont, as Lara Vetter observes, 'to broaden her meditation on Elizabethan poetry'.[23] *Passion and Society* would shape her creative interests for years to come just as Augustine, too, set out in a new direction after his bookish encounter.

Rougemont's book stimulated a new concern for a religious tradition. H.D. assumed Rougemont's religious themes were congenial to Plank. Subsequent correspondence shows H.D. turning to Plank for help with the research recorded in the notes she wrote for her creative memoir *The Gift* from 1943 to 1944.[24] The body of the text was completed from 1941 to 1943.[25] H.D. requested Plank's help late in the project precisely because they had discussed the 'religious background' to Rougemont's work from 1940 onwards. All H.D.'s Moravian works were shaped by *Passion and Society* because it shed new light upon H.D.'s upbringing. She would thereafter see the Moravians as representatives of Rougemont's invisible church. Like Augustine's encounter with the Bible, H.D.'s reading of *Passion and Society* had lasting effects. A re-envisaged Moravian past enabled her to overcome writer's block, laying the groundwork for the prose works, *The Gift* and *The Mystery*, and the poetry of *Trilogy* and *Helen in Egypt*.

H.D.'s encounter with Rougemont and West's critical look at Augustine's conversion also betray notable differences. West distinguished Augustine's assumptions from her perspective as a modern commentator. The poetic compression with which she renders Augustine's insight clashes with the matter-of-fact language used to set out her own reservations. While credulity and sincerity are features of Augustine's worldview, West, as a modern author, evokes credibility and scepticism for her readers. The critical intertexture anticipates the concerns of her readers; the benefit of using West's biography rather than turning directly to *Confessions* lies in its narrowing of the distance between Augustine and the modern reader. In H.D., however, these interpretive difficulties are present in the conversion itself. H.D. remembered the Moravians from her childhood, but as an adult she had drifted from them. Upon her recollection and loss, a new version of the Moravians-as-invisible-church was superimposed. The power of the vision resided in its distance from what H.D. remembered; her sense that these new possibilities could not previously have been conceived of by her, her parents or her siblings. To recall Richard Kearney's account of anatheism, there is a connection between absence and presence with the latter counter-intuitively facilitated by the former. H.D.'s story mixes Augustine's conversion and West's commentary such that modern scepticism, far from being a subsequent addition, becomes integral to the conversion experience itself. In creative terms, H.D. would render these complications in *The Gift*, *The Mystery* and significant moments of *Trilogy*.

Passionate Cathar-sis: Rougemont's Historical Narrative

H.D.'s return to the Moravians was facilitated by the historical element of *Passion and Society*. Rougemont sought to isolate the theological and ritual underpinnings of an understanding of love developed by the Cathars, a twelfth-century dualist sect based in southern France. The Roman Catholic Church pronounced them heretics and they became closely associated with the lives and work of the troubadour poets.[26] Catharist love, Rougemont argued, exerted influence on attitudes to romance, even in the present, distorting views of marriage. The sect was an unnamed third party in numerous recent divorces. The historical-theological influence of the Cathars produced a society-wide overvaluation of romantic passion: 'Men and women to-day, in being creatures of passion, expect an overwhelming love to produce some revelation either regarding themselves or about life at large' (p. 293). Rougemont's account of passion recalls what the present study has termed 'spilt mysticism'. Catharist love challenged official teaching; it also emphasised directness and immediacy over mediation. Like the subtraction stories rehearsed earlier, passionate love makes accessible the revelation previously mediated by institutional religion.

The Cathar's celebration of passion was the centrepiece of an alternative religion. Modern romance represented the 'last vestige of the primitive mysticism' associated with the Cathars (p. 293). The mysticism of modern romance derived from the classical idea of eros, which was 'complete Desire, luminous Aspiration, the primitive religious soaring carried to its loftiest pitch, to the extreme exigency of purity which is also the extreme exigency of Unity' (p. 74). The emphasis on the otherworldly and non-mediated differentiates Rougemont's eros from its more common equation with sexual love, which in Diotima's famous speech from Plato's *Symposium*, for example, acts as a stage in the ascent from the physical to the metaphysical. For the Cathars, sex was only ever a distraction. Eros is driven by a desire to leave the created world, which seems tarnished, evil and limited, to achieve a mystical reunion with the world of spirit. The steps of eros do not so much bring a pilgrim closer to what is divine as allow him to peek out over the top and visualise his own annihilation.

The Cathars instituted a set of social practices that shaped the literature of romance. *Passion and Society* opens with an analysis of the myth of the 'parting lovers', Tristan and Iseult, whose adulterous love threatens to break apart a kingdom. Rougemont attends not only to the social upheaval the pair countenance, but also the limited time they spend with each other in various versions of the story. He concludes: 'Tristan and Iseult do not love one another'; instead '*What they love is love and being in love*' (p. 51). These lovers are party to a love that, far from acknowledging an embodied other, uses that other as a conduit for the aforementioned 'primitive religious soaring' (p. 74). These mythical figures are at the mercy of 'a desire that never relapses, that nothing can satisfy' (p. 74). The lovers have no real interest in each other. They think only of a reunion with spirit. These assumptions inform the doctrine of the '*fruitfulness of suffering*', which was central to the Catharist worldview (p. 247).

While harkening back to the heretical revival of eros, the contemporary celebration of passion was inevitably dissociated from the religious group that had shaped it. Modern romance was what the Victorian anthropologist Edward Burnett Tylor called a 'survival': a ritual practice separated from its original context in ways that made its initial meaning unrecoverable.[27] Relationships can never deliver on their salvific, revelatory promises precisely because these claims are shaped by an inaccessible theological, ritual and cultural context. For the modern lover cut off from the Catharist ritual, passion can only ever be disorientating. Hollywood's celebration of romance as a source of revelation is a secularised form of the passion to which the Cathars attended. The prominence of mysticism in contemporary discourse is not so much a challenge to nineteenth-century materialism as itself a product of secularisation.

The difficulty Rougemont faced was connecting an obscure historical movement with contemporary social attitudes. To do so, he drew on histories of the occult that had also been important to Pound. Outlining a process of historical transmission that captured the breadth of influence the Cathars had exerted, Rougemont established, as Leon Surette explains, 'a chain of succession reaching back to high antiquity and forward into the present'.[28] H.D. was endeared to Rougemont because his historical narrative incorporated the Moravians. On the flyleaf of her copy of *Passion and Society*, she noted where the Moravians were discussed. They were, Rougemont argued, one of several sects that 'denied the dogma of the Trinity – at least in its orthodox form'; they 'evinced a high-flown spirituality'; 'professed a doctrine of "radiant joy"'; and 'were anticlerical, cultivated poverty and vegetarianism, and displayed an egalitarian spirit, extending in some instances to complete communism' (p. 169). The Moravians were agents of historical transmission, keeping alive the practices associated with the Cathar's version of love.

H.D. nods to the Moravians' role as historical agents in *The Gift*. In a note to the text, she veers away from the linear historical narrative developed by Rougemont towards something universalist in her claim that 'the Invisible Church' can 'never really be destroyed, any more than you can destroy a river that runs underground' (p. 265n). For Rougemont, the historical narrative was a means to an end, but H.D. was fascinated by the connections he made. She endeavoured to find new links for herself, writing, for instance, a long note to *The Gift* expanding on the significance of the use by both the Moravians and the Knights Templar of the 'Lamb of God' in their seal [Figures 3.1 and 3.2].

Figure 3.1 *Seal of the Moravian Church*, ca. 1870, GriderColl.f.55.9, DP Collection of Drawings and Prints, Visual Materials, Moravian Archives, Bethlehem, PA. Digital image courtesy of the Moravian Archives, Bethlehem, PA..

Figure 3.2 *Seal Cast of The Temple, Bristol*, ca. 1200–1299, impression taken from original seal matrix in Bristol Museum, ca. 1850–1915, Museum of the Order of St John. Digital image courtesy of Museum of the Order of St John and the University of Birmingham.

She corresponded on the issue with Plank prior to completing *The Gift*, urging him to share any other examples of the lamb in Roman Catholic imagery. The connection suggested the plot for her novel *The Mystery* and fleshed out what she calls in *Trilogy* the 'search for historical parallels'.[29] Her difference from Rougemont owes something to her unexpected discovery of the Moravians. If her childhood religion was part of the occult network she had once discussed with Pound, then surely there were other connections to be found if she only looked hard enough.

Reimagining Childhood Religion

Rougemont's esoteric historical narrative was stridently criticised by reviewers, even if readers welcomed the social critique represented by his discussion of marriage.[30] The present chapter concerns itself with an element of his study that might otherwise be passed over because it reveals the extent to which H.D.'s Moravian period represented a return to, and a revisioning of, the tradition she knew from her own recollections and from family lore. A photograph taken in 1887 of a dressed altar in the Moravian Central Church, Bethlehem, a year after H.D. was born [Figure 3.3], provides some insight into the pre-return version of the Moravians. The altar was decorated to celebrate the one-hundredth anniversary of the Society for Propagating the

Gospel. The community's missionary activity went back to 1737 when Count Nikolaus Ludwig von Zinzendorf, a German landowner and religious visionary, began the work that resulted in the founding of Bethlehem (as a mission to the Indigenous Americans) and missions in the Caribbean, Central America, South Africa, German East Africa, the Himalayan Mountains, Australia, Jerusalem and Newfoundland.[31] H.D.'s *The Gift* celebrates the Moravian community's visionary, imaginative and creative faculties, particularly as manifested in the work of women. In the photograph, the creative dimension of community life is evident in the fantastic arrangement of plants interspersed with the oil paintings of long-dead Moravian worthies; the living, green arrangement underscores the vibrancy of the missionary work. The mixture of oils and shoots honours the past and underscores how live the Moravian missionary tradition remains. The visual language of the altar invokes the Moravian putz tradition, which saw members of the community celebrate Christmas by assembling a nativity scene constructed from hand-carved wooden figures and moss gathered from the surrounding woods [Figure 3.4]. These festive decorations dominate a photograph of the Moravian Sunday schools [Figure 3.5]. The walls of Moravian Central Church were usually bare, recalling the Quaker chapel of H.D.'s vision in *Trilogy*: 'a spacious, bare meetinghouse' marked by 'eighteenth-century | simplicity and grace'.[32] During the festive season, the Moravians demonstrate a sensitivity to the aesthetic at odds with either the Quakers or the reformed tradition. The image at the centre of the photograph turns the scene into an act of devotion; far from simply gawping at the camera, the community gathers around a nativity scene staged in the church.

The visible space of the *sesquicentennial Christmas celebration* photograph is structured by the creativity celebrated in *The Gift*. H.D.'s memoir offers, as Jane Augustine argues, a narrative of 'female empowerment' that 'embodies' a 'belief in an eternal creative feminine spirit'.[33] It provides the basis for what Friedman terms H.D.'s 'Moravian gyno-poetics'.[34] Undoubtedly, some of the critic's 'eternal creative feminine spirit' went into the staging of the missionary display. Yet the paintings behind the altar jar with the supposed nature of H.D.'s vision. Apart from one image of Johann Nitschmann and his wife Susanna, all the figures celebrated here are men. Zinzendorf, for example, is in the centre and Christian Seidel, a major presence in *The Gift*, is level with the founder on the far right of the picture. The initial eighteenth-century Bethlehem settlement was organised not by nuclear families but rather communal groups or 'choirs', where children lived separately from their parents. Married couples likewise lived separately with transformative social effects: 'Parents, including women busy with ministering, set out to do mission work without their children'; women 'could live separately, to some degree independent of male control, and there were numerous positions as choir leaders that women could and did fill'.[35]

MODERNISM AND RELIGION

Figure 3.3 H. B. Eggert, *Central Moravian Church, Bethlehem, decorated for the one-hundredth anniversary of the Society for Propagating the Gospel*, ca. 1887, PhotC PA 706, Visual Materials, Moravian Archives, Bethlehem, PA. Digital image courtesy of the Moravian Archives, Bethlehem, PA.

Figure 3.4 H. B. Eggert, *Sesquicentennial Christmas Decorations, Moravian Church*, ca. 1891, PhotColl PA 703, Visual Materials, Moravian Archives, Bethlehem, PA. Digital image courtesy of the Moravian Archives, Bethlehem, PA.

Figure 3.5 H. B. Eggert, *Sesquicentennial Christmas Celebration, Moravian Sunday Schools*, Bethlehem, PA, ca. 1891, PhotColl PA 704, Visual Materials, Moravian Archives, Bethlehem, PA. Digital image courtesy of the Moravian Archives, Bethlehem, PA.

As a result female 'piety flourished in the Single Sisters Choir'.[36] As the community developed, women continued to play roles in a wide range of church-related activities, particularly the religious education that was a prominent element of missionary work. Comparable labour is evident in the Sunday school photograph where the sea of children's faces part and numerous older women, the class teachers, emerge, standing next to groups of either girls or boys of a similar age. The 1887 display celebrating the Moravian missionary society, however, neglects the contributions of women. Of course, religious symbolism, as Caroline Walker Bynum notes, does not rely on straightforward identification alone; the veneration of the founders no doubt provoked complex and multivalent responses among men and women alike.[37] Nevertheless, while the Moravians informed H.D.'s 'gyno-poetics', the connection was not made because of H.D.'s childhood memories. By the late nineteenth century, Moravian culture in Bethlehem reflected the social patterns evident across American society, including the veneration of men's work, the undermining of women's labour and the division of male and female spheres of activity. In the Sunday school photograph, for instance, the male teachers are charged with the older boys, while their female counterparts attend to the girls and the younger children.

De-radicalisation is also evident in the changing patterns of Moravian worship. H.D.'s grandfather Francis Wolle died when the would-be poet was six. The young H.D., her family and numerous Moravian dignitaries were invited to the funeral service, which was held at the Central Moravian Church depicted in the Sunday school photograph. The service included hymns such as 'Jesus Lord of life and Glory', 'How Bright these glorious spirits shine', 'Forever with the Lord', 'Asleep in Jesus' and 'When I shall gain permission', which were taken from *The Liturgy and Hymns of the American Province of the Unitas Fratrum*, published in 1872.[38] Hymn singing enjoyed a prominent role in Moravian worship, but it also had a darker history.[39] Augustine discusses the significance of the late 1740s or the 'Sifting Time'.[40] This period of Moravian history was characterised by an intensity of religious devotion to which H.D.'s poem 'Hymn' also gestures, centring on a sensuous attention to Christ's body in the Moravian's 'blood and wound' theology.[41] Paul Peucker has argued that the Sifting Time was also marked by sexual licence that was inspired by Moravian theology.[42] Record of the scandal can be found in a number of hymns that were subsequently removed from Moravian hymnbooks. Given the community's self-censorship, these hymns were absent in the book from which H.D. sang at services and inaccessible to anyone who did not seek them out. The 'actual extravagances' of the Sifting Time are alluded to and refashioned in *The Gift* (p. 178). Looking back on what she remembered from her upbringing, H.D. recollected a more traditional theology; she told Freud that, at that time, the 'Hell from the Bible stories seemed a real place'.[43] The Moravians she discovered in *Passion and Society* were the negative image of her childhood: what seemed conventional, was scandalous; what was solid, was fluid; and what was traditional, was hidden.

Rewriting Conversion in The Gift and The Mystery

The force of H.D.'s rediscovery of the Moravians is registered in a chapter of *The Gift* entitled 'The Secret'. The chapter attends to the interactions between the narrator, Hilda, then a young girl, and her grandmother, Mamalie, who is in a state of delirium. The older woman mistakes the young girl for her own sister; speaking to the child as a confidant, she reveals the existence of an 'inner church' within the Moravian community dedicated to the worship of the '*Sanctus Spiritus*' (p. 170). With limited comprehension, the young Hilda attempts to convey what she hears. The central event of the 'inner church' was a meeting between the Moravian settlers and a delegation from the Indigenous American Lenape people on whose land Bethlehem was founded. The meeting between the Lenape and the Moravians exposes a shared religious outlook:

> The S on the Cup was the *Sanctus Spiritus* that the inner church has worshipped and Christian Seidel (the first one) had been an inner member or an initiate of that church.
>
> The inner members of the lodges and cults of the friendly tribes – and for that matter, maybe of the unfriendly – spoke the same language. The serpent shaped like an S, carved on the pole outside their lodges or painted in their picture writing, was the same serpent [. . .] The inner band of initiates, worshiped the same Spirit, the *Sanctus Spiritus* (p. 170).

The S on the cup used in the Moravian communion service and the carved snakes outside the Lenape lodgings point to a connection across cultures, as the Lamb of God symbol used by the Templars and Moravians did. While the shared Lamb of God symbol is occasioned by historical transmission, the connection between the Lenape and the Moravians exemplifies religious perennialism; the Moravian's *Sanctus Spiritus* and the Lenape's 'Great Spirit' are, according to *The Gift*, the 'same'.

The commonality is revealed by the word 'Spirit'. *The Gift* outlines 'a war of the Spirit or for the Spirit, the Spirit was the Indian's Great Spirit and the Spirit was (for the inner band of United Brethren) a Spirit like the Holy Ghost, which nobody seemed really to understand but which they understood' (p. 163). 'Spirit' is an intentionally vague word, referring to anything from the souls of the dead to the third person of the Trinity. In Augustine's account of H.D.'s response to the Moravians, the feminine gender of the Holy Spirit and its elevation to equality with the Father is central.[44] By contrast, in Indigenous American religious tradition, the 'Great Spirit', as Alfred A. Cave notes, is often 'portrayed as the omnipotent, omnipresent creator and ruler of the universe'.[45] Among the Lenape, the Great Spirit emerged during the eighteenth century and, as Cave adds, 'cannot be found in the traditional Indigenous American tribal folklore that has been compiled over the centuries'.[46] It drew instead on 'ideas' of Christian religion 'conveyed' by missionaries.[47] Indigenous American prophets adapted the jealous God of the Hebrew scriptures as well as later Christian concepts of the afterlife. Their invocations of the Great Spirit endeavoured to compel Indigenous American auditors to re-engage with a range of indigenous rites and practices, suitably reworked to meet the demands of the time.

The judgemental aspects of the 'Great Spirit' are omitted from *The Gift*. Picking up on the earlier excursions on symbolism, the importance of Spirit lies in the aesthetic. Mamalie notes that a ritual exchange of women and names followed the coming together of the Lenape and the Moravians. Anna von Pahlen, a Moravian, was symbolically given to the Lenape, taking on the name 'Morning Star'; the 'Morning Star' of the Lenape was likewise given to the Moravians, taking the name 'Angelica', which 'was another name of Anna von Pahlen' (p. 171). The two communities unite to celebrate their common spirit, an act made possible by the work of women otherwise obscured in the decoration of the altar in Figure 3.1.

The shared ritual stands opposed to the violence that inhered in the meeting of these communities and to which *The Gift* alludes. The exchange of women provides the basis for a promise: the Lenape's forgiveness of the European settlers' crimes and the agreement of both parties to honour each other in the future. The treaty would have 'changed the course of history' (p. 168). The ultimate failure of the promise, Hilda notes, owed something to traditionalists within the Moravians – recalling the censorship of the Moravian prayer book – for whom the porous boundaries, the shared appreciation of spirit, between the Lenape and the Moravians represented a 'scandal' or 'witchcraft' (p. 171), and to the actions of other Indigenous Americans in perpetrating a massacre of settlers at '*Gnadenhuetten*' (p. 181).

By ignoring the asymmetry between the Moravians and the Lenape to blame both sides equally for the failed promise, H.D. obscures the revisionary intent of her own religious perennialism. Leigh Eric Schmidt has traced the emergence of a 'universal and timeless' mysticism through its designation as a 'solitary subjectivity' shorn of 'distinct practices'.[48] The concept proved useful to an American society divided in the wake of the Civil War. Emphasis on both personal experience and freedom from specific theologies, practices and worldviews reduced the potential for friction between different groups.[49] In *The Gift*, H.D. projects Schmidt's 'universal and timeless' mysticism further back in time so that, far from being a problematic undertaking marked by unevenly distributed power, the work of Moravian missionaries to convert Indigenous Americans became a process of mutual discovery. Each group led the other to uncover otherwise hidden elements of their own tradition. The meeting of the two cultures is the companion to H.D.'s encounter with Rougemont; it facilitates a return to their respective traditions from a new vantage point.

These are not the concerns of H.D.'s childhood, but rather those of the Imagist H.D. extended and developed through her encounter with Rougemont. They reveal the degree to which she re-made the Moravians in her own image. A similar dynamic is visible in the notes she collated on the Moravians after 1940. The text that attracted her attention was *A Candid Narrative of the Rise and Progress of the Herrnhuters, call'd Moravians, or Unitas Fratrum*, published in 1753 by the anti-Moravian polemicist Henry Rimius. Throughout his polemic, Rimius presented the Moravians as a conspiratorial sect. They 'have not the Truth in View, but the Execution of a favourite Plan', he warned in a passage marked in H.D.'s notes.[50] In the controversialist's analysis, Zinzendorf's 'Plan' had political objectives. Zinzendorf's teachings were merely a tool to facilitate the establishment of an *'Empire within an Empire'* as Rimius picked up on Zinzendorf's status as a titled landowner and his problematic history with Roman Catholicism.[51] In founding Bethlehem, Zinzendorf was setting up a theocracy over which he would rule as the chief interpreter of God's will.

The 'Plan', as H.D. encountered it, was nevertheless polyvocal. The body of Rimius's polemic outlines Zinzendorf's designs for political disruption, but in his footnotes Rimius also reproduces Zinzendorf's own words, ostensibly as evidence. In support of his own arguments, Rimius cited the following text – one that H.D. noted down – from Zinzendorf's sermons:

> Marriages are a capital Article of the Society, they are a *primum principium, ut ita dicam* of the whole Society, the Root of the Society's Tree; and we must always consider them as the most precious Depositum from the Hand of our Lord, as the greatest Mystery of all human Things deposited with us, and whereof the Key is given us: why? not on Account of the exterior Circumstances, but for the Sake of the principal Plan, which the Lord, who knew every Thing, had in his own Breast.[52]

In the body of the text, the polemicist observes that couples in the Moravian community were often matched through the casting of lots. Clerical interference in marriage amounted to a perversion of the proper order of society. The practice undermined free choice. Parents were also denied a say in whom their children married, which restricted the formation of alliances that might otherwise challenge the position of Zinzendorf and his family. To Rimius's mind, Zinzendorf's mention of Christ's 'principal Plan' was merely a convenient cover for establishing autocratic control over every unit of the new society.

A more sympathetic reading of the Count's designs was offered by Joseph Taylor Hamilton, a historian of Bethlehem whom H.D. herself read. He equated the repetition of Christ's plan in Zinzendorf's works with 'the conception of the grace of the Son of God, whereby personal fellowship with Him and unfeigned following of Him are made possible and acceptance with God is realized'.[53] More recently, Peucker has noted that during the Sifting Time the 'conception of grace' identified by Hamilton contributed to the building 'eschatological expectation' within the community.[54] Through the intimacy of cohabitation and the symbolic interpretation of a couple's sex life, marriage (as the 'capital Article of the Society') facilitated fellowship with Christ, enabling the intuition of God's plan in everyday life. Rimius asked that Zinzendorf's words be seen through the hermeneutic lens established by his polemic. Yet the separation on the page between body text and footnote creates space for a different approach. Zinzendorf's intuitive grasp of Christ's plan rubs up against the calculating motives Rimius ascribed to him.

H.D. was drawn to the conspiratorial dimension of Rimius's work, not least because of the 'chain of succession' material she discovered in Rougemont. In her notes, she highlighted passages containing the words 'plan', 'secrecy' and 'initiates', but she did not share her eighteenth-century source's political suspicions.[55] She focused, instead, on evidence from Zinzendorf that the polemicist reproduces. Freed from Rimius's polemic, 'plan', 'secrecy' and 'initiates' came to represent the intentions of the Moravians to execute a secret programme to which they – whether through occult transmission or inspiration from a divine source – had been granted access. Concerned with 'world peace', H.D.'s fascination with the 'plan' finds her, following the example of David Jones and T. S. Eliot, turning to religion to invoke neither narrowly denominational matters nor the valences of a private spirituality, but rather the world around her.

Both H.D.'s book-length Moravian works, *The Gift* and particularly the later novel *The Mystery*, written from 1949 to 1951 but not published until 2009, are fascinated by an idea of conversion or reorientation marked by the recognition of an unfurling plan.[56] *The Mystery* depicts the shock and surprise that follow from such a moment. Set in Prague after the suppression of the Jesuits and in the run up to the French Revolution, *The Mystery* opens with St Germain, a French Jesuit, living in exile. Germain, disguised as a member of another religious order (a Dominican lay brother), is at work in the cathedral school, awaiting the completion of a plan executed with his co-conspirator, Cardinal Rohan. In disguise, Germain had joined the Freemasons to obtain information about both the Freemasons' heretical practices and the coming revolution in France and shared it with Rohan. Rohan, in turn, intends to pass the information to the Pope, exploiting the goodwill that follows to lobby for an end to the suppression of the Jesuits. During the novel, Germain experiences psychic events that complicate the initial plan, resembling those that H.D. herself recounted in *Tribute to Freud* and *Majic Ring*. These are triggered by his meeting with a Moravian, Elizabeth de Watteville (also in disguise), who is visiting Prague secretly to undertake archival research on her familial sect.

Over the course of the book, Germain identifies a metaphysical plan involving Elizabeth, centring on parallels between Elizabeth and her grandfather. Zinzendorf had been prosecuted in Protestant Bohemia for practising Roman Catholic devotions and Elizabeth likewise blurs denominational boundaries. Elizabeth's decision to light candles in the Roman Catholic cathedral shocks her cousin. The exchange reads:

> 'You light candles? My dear Elizabeth —'
> 'Shouldn't I?'
> 'I don't think so.'
> 'Well, I do it when there's no one about.'[57]

The scene is modelled on an exchange between H.D. and Bryher, where the latter 'did not approve of a "protestant" making a gesture toward Our Lady'. H.D. however understood the Virgin Mary as '"Our Lady universally", a Spirit – from the days of Numa and what-not'.[58] H.D.'s response is shaped by *Passion and Society*, particularly the fact that for the troubadours the Virgin Mary became the 'Lady of Thoughts' (p. 104, p. 106). As she is transformed into a symbol for the Catharist religion, the mother of the incarnate Lord becomes a figurehead set apart from all creation. While Rougemont understands the transformation as the product of specific historical circumstances, H.D.'s 'Lady' is bound up with the universalist language of 'the Invisible Church' that 'can never really be destroyed' (p. 265n). As an initiate in the invisible church through her Moravian heritage, H.D. grasps the continuity in which Mary is implicated. Elizabeth shares Bryher's incomprehension insofar as she offers, when called out for her actions, not H.D.'s justification for her devotional catholicity but merely a nod to propriety: 'I do it when there's no one about'. Given that she is disguised as a Roman Catholic noblewoman, her claim to light candles in secret rather misses the point. The significance of her actions must be drawn out by Germain.

Elizabeth's incomprehension follows from her role as the conduit for revisions to Germain's plan. Germain calls her 'Our Lady', a designation that maintains a Catholic pedigree, while also alluding to the 'Lady of Thoughts' of the troubadours. The terminology points toward Germain's understanding of Elizabeth as a figure central to the Church of Love about which he learned while undercover with the Freemasons. He experiences a vision of medieval Florence that helps him understand Elizabeth's role:

> You were Monna Vanna when I saw you first, wrapt in meditation, in the Chapel of Saint Wenceslas. She was a screen, a veil; Johanna, Primavera was a screen, a veil for Beatrice. She could appear where she was not. I saw her, on a bridge in Venice.[59]

Monna Vanna, Johanna and Primavera are all 'screens' for Dante's Beatrice – as, indeed, is Elizabeth. The screen or the 'veiled love' was a cynical device employed in *Vita Nuova* to obscure the true object of attention from the public view. Dante initially selected a 'screen' lady to mask his connection with Beatrice, asserting that he 'thought of making this lovely lady a screen to hide the truth'.[60] Moravians, troubadours, Dante and the Freemasons are all, *The Mystery* assumes, secret tributaries of the Church of Love or screens for an otherwise secret organisation. Here the idea of a secret church has been combined with both Rougemont's historical narrative and H.D.'s interest in astral projection or doubling to make a form of religious bricolage. Astral doubling, according to Matte Robinson, is the idea that 'the astral body' is 'an exact double of the physical, a separate "vehicle" of the consciousness', which offers '*whole-body* projected experiences of the other realms'.[61] Elizabeth is at once a historical bubbling up of the same religious stream that ran through Florence, an instantiation or screen of an otherwise hidden church and an astral double. Germain and Beatrice appear in multiple places simultaneously and the novel suggests, somewhat unconvincingly, that tensions between Guelph and Ghibelline in medieval Florence could have been eased by a recognition of the identity, as screens or veils of the same figure, of the ladies of each party.

The climax of the narrative finds Germain in bed, first in the Florentine trance, then talking to Elizabeth about the Moravian mission to the Indigenous Americans and finally reflecting alone. What Germain's supine meditations uncover is 'a mysterious plan of world unity without war' by which he found himself 'compelled', a counterpart to the broken promise between the Moravians and the Lenape in *The Gift*.[62] The revised plan subsumes and repurposes his agreement with Rohan and it does so insofar as Elizabeth-as-screen situates his concerns in the context of a longer subterranean religious history.

Germain's trance is the counterpart to the incomprehension of *The Gift*'s child narrator. The supposed forgiveness of the Moravians for the crimes of the settlers, for instance, is recounted in *The Gift* in prose of stylised uncertainty. Hilda says:

> Only this was something different, though I couldn't tell just how, only that it made Mamalie shiver and then say that, about Shooting-star forgiving them or something. I think maybe, it was a sort of dream, maybe it did not happen. Maybe even, I made it up alone there on the bed while Mamalie was sitting at the window, maybe Mamalie didn't even say anything at all, maybe it is like that time when I saw the Old Man on Church Street and he sent his sleigh and Mama said it never happened (p. 175).

The repetition of 'maybe' helps render the bemusement of the child as she looks on at her grandmother telling her a fantastic story during her delirium.

The naivety of the narrator absolves the narrative of some responsibility. The full context for the dispensation issued by 'an Indian priest who is called Shooting-star' is omitted as is an account of his role; in his propensity to grant collective pardons, the figure resembles a medieval pope or cardinal issuing indulgences (p. 174). The repetition points to a persistent hedging in H.D.'s work between what Suzanne Hobson has called the 'credible' and the 'incredible'.[63] H.D. proposes something fantastic and simultaneously opines that it might be mere fantasy. Germain's time-travel, for instance, takes place during a period of sickness. In Éliphas Lévi's occult work *The History of Magic*, H.D. read about the historical Germain and his double; her novel undoubtedly draws on these historical associations. The fictionalised version of Germain in *The Mystery* is also, given H.D.'s evocation of medicine or pathology, the product of scepticism.[64] Germain's visions are not all in his head; the novel turns on the importance of his doubles and screens. Yet it is not altogether out of his head either. As Robinson demonstrates, H.D. does not dismiss astral doubling (it became increasingly important to her later in life), but she does not wholeheartedly endorse the idea either. Even as she revels in the fantastical, H.D. anticipates explaining herself to a modern commentator akin to West on Augustine.[65]

H.D.'s mature work is thus defined by the confusion that radiates from contact with the supernatural in a world that seemed to have largely dispensed with it. Gauri Viswanathan has outlined 'an idea of conversion that signifies its use not just for strategic (or instrumentalist) purposes, nor even as a turn toward one's own roots, but rather as the embrace of multiple positions'.[66] H.D.'s conversion enables her to be at once close to and removed from the phenomena she describes. Her discovery of the Moravians in Rougemont provided an alternative lens through which to view her childhood, but it did not erase the fact that her life had been different to what *Passion and Society* described. Far from equating conversion with the single-mindedness of the zealot, Viswanathan emphasises a multiplicity of association. *The Gift* and *The Mystery* are likewise conversion novels concerned not so much with the worldview, thought system or community to which the conversion announces entry as with the intellectual and emotional act of holding on to the new life and the old life at the same time.

Vagaries of Vision in Trilogy

The concerns that shaped H.D.'s approach to conversion also inform her writing about vision in *Trilogy*. In 'The Flowering of the Rod', Mary (a composite of the biblical Marys but most reminiscent of Mary Magdalene) causes Kaspar (one of the biblical magi but here more merchant than king) to have a vision. He catches sight of light glancing off Mary's loose hair. The visionary insight it affords is then recounted:

> he saw the many pillars and the Hearth-stone
> and the very fire on the Great-hearth,
>
> and through it, there was a sound as of many waters,
> rivers flowing and fountains and sea-waves washing the sea rocks,
>
> and though it was all on a very grand scale,
> yet it was small and intimate,
>
> Paradise
> before Eve. . .[67]

H.D. spent a career writing about the coastline. Fletcher judged the 'everlasting grind of the sea on the rocks' to be one of the major notes of *Sea-garden*.[68] At various points in her early lyrics, the sea offers a form of self-annihilation, threatening to 'hurl' itself over the speaker in 'Oread', or else cuts a frightening figure that 'gnashed its teeth' in 'Hermes of the Ways'.[69] *Trilogy* transforms the earlier 'crystalline' mode by replacing the violence of the sea swell with the sweetness of 'a sound as of many waters' and the purification of 'washing' as H.D. attempts to render the halcyon fantasy of prelapsarian times to which Kaspar's Mary-inspired vision affords access. The transformation is disorientating. The vision of a 'Paradise | before Eve' points to a time that is mythologically rich and conceptually significant. Language and the world it names are intrinsically related. The vision is a conduit to something 'very grand': Edenic, prelapsarian. Yet at the same time it remains 'small and intimate': familiar, comforting, provoking a slight sense of déjà vu. The oxymoron registers Kaspar's uncertainty. The terms in which he wishes to frame his situation do not quite fit.

The poem is fascinated by the inability to place experience. Shifting from the vision to its impart, *Trilogy* evokes the incomprehension of the Moravian novels. The poem seeks to understand the vision:

> no one would ever know
> if it could be proved mathematically
>
> by demonstrated lines,
> as an angle of light
>
> reflected from a strand of a woman's hair,
> reflected again or refracted
>
> a certain other angle –
> or perhaps it was a matter of vibration

> that matched or caught an allied
> or exactly opposite vibration
>
> and created a sort of vacuum,
> or rather a *point* in time –
>
> he called it a fleck or flaw in a gem
> of the crown that he saw
>
> (or thought he saw) as in a mirror;
> no one would know exactly
>
> how it happened,
> least of all Kaspar.[70]

The multiple maybes of *The Gift* find a counterpart in the repetition of 'no one would know' and 'or'. If the 'sounds as of many waters' and the oxymorons 'very grand' and 'small and intimate' mark the poem's attempt to render what Hobson calls the 'incredible', then these hesitations mark the arrival of the 'credible'.[71] The undercutting of the visionary evident here is close to the prosy, jaded voice of *Four Quartets*, resigned to the fact that 'The poetry does not matter' (p. 187). And yet the tone here is distinct from Eliot's; as the verse slowly unwinds, the speaker relishes alternative interpretations of the vision. The poem notes:

> no one would ever know
> if it could be proved mathematically
>
> by demonstrated lines,
> as an angle of light
>
> reflected from a strand of a woman's hair,
> reflected again or refracted
>
> a certain other angle[72]

A long sentence is broken up across multiple lines, saying in effect: 'we can't prove that some manipulation of light caused the vision'. The pauses introduced by line breaks make the verse cautious, hesitant, meditative even, as the reader halts at the white spaces to link the sinuous lines into a coherent statement. Combined with the repetition of 'angle' and 'reflection', the line breaks are almost stage directions; we might imagine the speaker trying to work out the trajectory of the light that produced the visual phenomenon, breaking after 'reflected again or refracted', perhaps, to make the requisite shapes with her hands. The diction, too, lays claim to a scientific pedigree ('reflected', 'refracted', 'vibration', 'vacuum') that distances the passage from the unknowing maybes of *The Gift*. Yet these words are often paired with opposites or alternatives: reflection 'or' refraction, 'allied' or 'opposite', vibration 'or' vacuum. While this vocabulary ostensibly contributes to the analytic air of the passage, the speaker's credibility is undermined by the sheer range of phenomena under consideration. It could be one thing or something very different. We cannot say for sure. Kaspar, too, plays a double part. He is the seer contemplating 'Paradise I before Eve' and something of a comic dupe in 'no one would know I how it happened I least of all Kaspar'. The last phrase reads like a punchline, looking on with a wry smile at a character who, for all his visionary credentials and mythological stature, fails to comprehend what is going on. The joke is on him.

The mixture of the intense and the verbose in *Trilogy* ushers in a new form of religious poetry. The hybrid form is not what Louis L. Martz, the editor of H.D.'s *Collected Poems*, described in *The Poetry of Meditation: A Study in English Religious Literature of the Seventeenth Century*, where the focus on a religious theme, the teasing out of detail, is indicative of imaginative discipline.[73] In *Seven Types of Ambiguity*, William Empson observed that religious poetry such as George Herbert's 'The Sacrifice' often reflects simultaneously the assumptions of a given religious framework and a questioning of that same system.[74] *Trilogy*, by contrast, conveys visionary richness, while probing, querying or teasing that same vision. The sequence moves from the incredible to the credible and back again. What is repressed and returns in Empson is a deliberate method here. H.D.'s poetry treats religion not like a religious organisation shaping 'boundaries' and 'exerting their authority to distinguish what they approve as proper individual religious practice from all else', but as a far more malleable phenomenon bound up with the struggles of individual believers pulled in various directions.[75] The result is poetry of neither the believer (whether in Moravian Christianity, spiritualism or the occult) nor the materialist (for whom religion has long since served its purpose). It is, somehow, both of those poetries at once.

AGAINST DIAGNOSIS: H.D. AND FREUD ON RELIGION

Between Prohibition and Nurture: Religion in Tribute to Freud

While it was Rougemont's book that paved the way for her return to the Moravians, H.D.'s reflection on her childhood religion also formed part of her analysis with Freud, which ran from 1933 to 1934. During their time together, H.D. and Freud bonded over shared geographical connections. The founder of psychoanalysis was born in the land from which the Moravians were exiled. At times during their conversations, Freud approached H.D.'s heritage in ways that were conversant with his major statements on religion in works such as

The Future of an Illusion, published in 1927. H.D. documented her analysis in two works: 'Writing on the Wall', written in 1944 and published in Bryher's journal *Life and Letters* from 1945 to 1946, and 'Advent', assembled in December 1948 from the notebooks H.D. had kept while in analysis with Freud; it was not published until it was collected with 'Writing on the Wall' in an expanded posthumous edition of *Tribute to Freud* in 1974.[76] In her reflections on her analysis, H.D. detailed how Freud had conceived of her 'religion in terms of myth'.[77] Myths were, for him, transformations of the pleasure-seeking urges that society demanded individuals repress; he framed his most famous discovery, the Oedipus Complex, in mythic terms. In a comparable vein, Freud's teacher, Jean-Martin Charcot, wrested control of the Christian mystics from the Roman Catholic Church and depicted these revered figures as driven by not their closeness to God but rather undiagnosed hysteria. For Freud, too, Moravian belief was best understood not kneeling at the altar but rather lying on an analyst's couch.

At other times, the conversations between poet and analyst moved out of a diagnostic mode. H.D. recalled Freud saying: 'If every child had a lighted candle given, as you say they were given at your grandfather's Christmas Eve service, by the grace of God, we would have no more problems . . . That is the true heart of all religion'.[78] The comment jars with Freud's public persona as an arch-materialist for whom religion was to be considered a delusion. While it had once served an important purpose by helping to repress antisocial urges, religion was, Freud claimed, increasingly ineffective as a form of social glue in the modern world.[79] Psychoanalysis was on standby waiting to fill the gap.[80] Freud and H.D.'s exchange represents an alternative approach where religion is seen as more than a series of prohibitions. While he frequently interprets culture in terms of childhood psychosexual development and parental relationships, Freud also recognised, as James DiCenso notes, that 'parental influence' includes 'not only the personalities of the actual parents but also the family, racial and national traditions handed on through them, as well as the demands of the immediate social *milieu* which they represent'.[81] While the 'personal presence of some parental-type figure is essential' to a child's development, Freud saw that 'parental figures are not merely individuals, but bearers of culture'.[82] The emphasis on the interaction between the individual and culture through 'parental-type figures', rather than a single-minded emphasis on the child's psychosexual relationship with them, has shaped the work of subsequent generations of psychoanalysts.

H.D.'s exchange with Freud on religion anticipates these later developments. H.D.'s grandfather was a distinguished minister of the Moravian Church. The gentle aestheticism of the Christmas Eve service, the handing on of a 'lighted candle', suggests that culture can be conveyed in ways other than the harsh prohibitions that marked what Freud considered the religion of the 'common man' and which ultimately flowed from the Oedipus Complex.[83] Freud's sense that Moravian practice reveals the 'true heart of all religion' provides psychological warrant for an alternative. In *Civilization and Its Discontents*, Freud made reference to what he called the 'oceanic feeling', which, as Parsons has argued, can be understood 'as the preservation of the limitless ego-feeling of primary narcissism'.[84] It thus reveals, as Freud observes, 'a much more intimate bond between the ego and the world about it'.[85] The Christmas Eve service invokes, then, not the later stage of human development represented by the Oedipus Complex, but rather an earlier period in a child's life, the formation of the ego.[86] The developmental stage in question was the subject of the ego psychology pursued by subsequent generations of psychoanalytic theorists including figures such as Erik Erikson.[87] Distancing himself from the link Freud established between the role of the parent in a child's psychosexual development and the prohibitive dimension of religion, Erikson, through his life-cycle theory, traced the ways in which religious practices such as the Moravian church service relate to the individual's emergent sense of self.[88]

These two psychoanalytic approaches to religion, the prohibitive and the nurturing, provide different ways of understanding a dream H.D. recounted in *Tribute to Freud*. With imagery drawn from her family's illustrated Bible [Figure 3.6], H.D.'s dream involved a princess discovering a baby in a basket

Figure 3.6 Gustave Doré, 'Moses in the Bulrushes', Exodus 2. 1–10. Digital image courtesy of The Pitts Theology Library, Candler School of Theology, Emory University.

floating in a river. Freud's interpretation is striking. He eschewed the straightforward gender identification of H.D. with the princess or between the infant Moses who went on to lead his people out of Egypt and the Jewish founder of psychoanalysis. Instead, he argued that the poet identified with the baby boy in the basket. Based on an analysis of her dream, H.D. wished, Freud contended, to be 'the founder of a new religion'.[89] H.D. was connecting, Freud thought, Moses's maleness, his having a penis, to his potency as a religious leader; she yearned for what Moses had and what he did.

Responding to such interpretations, scholarship has emphasised both the prominence of penis envy in H.D.'s analysis and her resistance to the assumptions about femininity the concept entailed. As far back as 1969, Norman N. Holland drew attention to an episode from *Tribute to Freud* where Freud showed H.D. a damaged statue of the Greek goddess Athena and called her 'perfect' except for the fact that *'she has lost her spear'*.[90] By talking to her about his statue of Athena, Holland argued that Freud encouraged the poet to confront the unconscious operation of penis envy in her psyche.[91] Two of H.D.'s most prominent interpreters, Susan Stanford Friedman and Rachel Blau DuPlessis, concur with Holland about the subtext of the conversation. They nevertheless highlight H.D.'s challenge to Freud's assumptions:

> This troubling interchange between analyst and analysand is as close as H.D. gets in *Tribute to Freud* to revealing that they ever discussed Freud's related theories of penis envy, the girl's castration complex, and rejection of the female body. In the context of these theories, Freud's message to H.D. in handing her the statue operates on two levels, both of which express his belief in female inferiority. First, Pallas Athené (woman) is 'perfect', except for her lack of a spear (penis); with a penis, she would reach the 'perfection' of uncastrated man (whole or complete statue). Second, woman is 'perfect' only in the imperfection of the castration to which she is biologically destined. It is an ironic perfection which Freud insists on for women, one created precisely by the absence of the phallic mark of power.[92]

The authors go on to argue that H.D.'s poem 'The Master' responds to Freud's description of his Athena statue, approaching the female body and sexuality in terms other than the 'inferiority' Freud ascribes it. The claim that H.D. wished to be 'the founder of a new religion' can also be interpreted as a critique of Freudian assumptions. Spoken by Freud, the assessment has the pejorative associations that follow from his diagnostic approach to religion. H.D.'s religious yearnings are a symptom. The observation nevertheless appears in *Tribute to Freud* not in direct or reported speech, but in a fragmentary question spoken in H.D.'s own voice: 'Do I wish myself, in the deepest or subconscious layers of my being, to be the founder of a new religion?'[93] Taken out of Freud's mouth and put into H.D.'s own, the dismissive reading is not authoritative. The wish to be a 'founder of a new religion' might well be taken as evidence of creative potential rather than neurosis such that the question is followed, a reader may imagine, by an enthusiastic affirmation. H.D.'s wish is not a symptom but a sign of strength.

H.D.'s return to the Moravians, first in analysis with Freud and then later under the sign of Rougemont, continues the challenge to Freudian thought. H.D. separates her perceived wish to be a 'founder of a new religion' from Moses's maleness and the corresponding lack his naked body exposed. The vibrant, female-orientated creativity of the Moravians represented in *The Gift* by Mamalie's story, alongside the rituals of exchange in the meeting of the Moravians and the Lenape, appears to fulfil that wish. Yet H.D.'s religion is neither 'new' nor her creation alone. H.D.'s preferred terminology is that of initiation, which is not only what Hilda's grandmother recounts in her story of the secret church but also what the speech represents for the young Hilda. She becomes an initiate of a secret church. She is welcomed into an existing order of sign and symbol like Germain in *The Mystery* or indeed the children of all culture-bearing parental figures. The emphasis here falls on not H.D.'s omnipotence, her ability to create from nothing, but rather more subtle mediations between subject and tradition. *The Gift* is interested in what the return to the Moravians enables the narrator to become.

H.D.'s midlife filiation with the Moravians was a response to her analysis. She talked with Freud about the strange psychic phenomena she experienced: a vision where she saw writing projected on to a wall, moments where she was inhabited or possessed by spirits and meetings with mysterious figures who later vanished. These are the subjects of H.D.'s later writing. They occurred in the wake of a period of intense suffering and following her departure from England for Greece in the aftermath of the First World War. During H.D.'s analysis, Friedman notes that Freud was more interested 'in exploring the significance of psychic phenomenon' than 'his better-known position as the defender of the ego against the onslaught of symptomatic hallucination' might suggest, even as she argues that H.D. was not much concerned with whether these experiences were 'internally or externally projected'.[94] Yet, the tradition of psychological responses to religion in which Freud wrote invoked origins in order to devalue or rather revalue experiences. While they represent a response to Freud, *The Gift* and the other Moravian writings are best considered as not direct engagements with penis envy and related concepts, but rather part of a far broader reframing of religion that resists psychological reductionism. Unlike traditional religions with their structures of authority, a psychoanalytic approach is attuned to the attempt, as Robert N. Bellah put it, 'to find a religious form that genuinely expressed' one's 'own individuality'.[95] Freud is H.D.'s conduit to a version of what Friedrich von Hügel termed the mystical element of religion, the very element with which Jones was concerned. At the same time, however,

H.D. resisted Freud's presentation of religion as the product of Oedipus. Freud himself recognised such limitations in his own theory as evinced by the self-described limits of *The Future of an Illusion*, which concerns itself merely with the common man's religion, and in the glance at the pre-Oedipal stages of development in *Civilization and Its Discontents*. H.D.'s Moravian works reframe religious issues to recognise the centrality of vision. Like James in *The Varieties of Religious Experience*, H.D. resisted the invocation of origins as a means of dismissing the value she assigned to certain experiences.

Re-(w)rites in H.D.'s 'Hymn'

H.D.'s positioning of both Freud and her own religion made for a rich engagement with the Moravian hymnal tradition. First published in 1950 in *Life and Letters*, H.D.'s poem 'Hymn' was later included in H.D.'s *Selected Poems* published by Grove Press. It post-dates the work included in *Collected Poems* and is omitted from later editions of *Selected Poems*. It is quoted in full below:

Hymn
(For Count Zinzendorf, 1700–1760)

Of unguent in a jar,
We may ensample myrrh;

So were His fragrance stored,
Sealed up, compact, secure,

In flawless alabaster,
But for the spear;

This is the wound of grace,
This is the nesting-place

Of the white dove,
This is the wound of love;

The spear opened for us
The rose of purple fire,

The rose of iciest breath,
White rose of death;

The spear opened for us
The narrow way

Into the dust,
To the eternal day.[96]

The poem is in dialogue with the Moravian blood-and-wound devotional tradition, which combined Christian bridal mysticism that drew on the Song of Songs and pietist dedication to Christ's suffering.[97] From the eighteenth-century religious fusion, a hymnal tradition emerged that centred on a sensuous celebration of Christ's 'Spear slit' or the hole made in his side during the crucifixion. These hymns were often accompanied by liturgical actions such as the physical probing by members of the congregation of sculpted versions of the wounds. In her notebooks, H.D. recorded a translation of a hymn that exemplifies the blood-and-wound tradition, reading: 'Husband; mayest thou feel or meet with great Tenderness at the Side, which is open for the Lamb's spouse, since the Spear has pushed into it, and which is the object of married people'.[98] The text brings out the explicit connection between Christ's wounds and another bodily opening, the vagina. On the cross, Christ is penetrated by Longinus's spear and the act is subsequently repeated in the Moravian liturgy. It is analogous, too, to the penetrative sex of the heterosexual marriage bed: the 'Tenderness at the Side' where 'the Spear has pushed into it, and which is the object of married people'. Christ is nevertheless androgynous. He is at once the penetrating 'Husband' and the wife penetrated.[99] These explicit hymns formed the soundtrack to the sexual licentiousness of the Sifting Time. The willingness of the Moravians to use sex as an analogy for the Easter mysteries and to push the boundaries of the kind of sex invoked outraged Rimius and elicited his anti-Zinzendorf polemics.

H.D.'s poem responds to blood-and-wound hymnal tradition. 'Hymn' originally carried the subtitle 'From the Bohemian' as if it were a translation of an unspecified source text.[100] Later, the claim was softened to merely a dedication to Zinzendorf. The poem reworks the Moravian concern with blood and wounds. In the Moravian imagination, the wound is a 'slit', an 'opening' and a 'swat': an absence, a hole or a lack that must be filled. Similar assumptions inform Freud's concept of penis envy with his otherwise 'perfect' spear-less statue of Athena. In the Christian story, the side hole was created by an act of violence that Moravian devotions repeat. 'Hymn' subverts the penetrative logic in a move that, perhaps, claims precedence in Zinzendorf's presentation of Christ as simultaneously husband and wife. The poem concerns not the pushing in of foreign objects, but the release of what is held inside, the 'fragrance stored'. The fragrance emanates mysteriously from its container. The moment recalls *Trilogy*, which ends with the scent of the 'most beautiful fragrance, | as of all flowering things together' arising from an uncertain source.[101] The poem builds up layered images: a 'rose' of 'purple fire' and 'iciest breath' and 'the nesting-place | of the white dove'. The imagery emphasises not the penetrated vaginal openings of the Moravian Sifting Time, but the coiling, bunching and unfurling of the labia, which is pictured here as flowers and nests.

The sexual connotations of the imagery attach themselves to the repeated phrase 'The spear opened'. *Opened* might well be understood as the making of 'a hole or incision' (*OED* 5a). The spear pierces the flesh, wounds the body and mars the beauty. Yet *to open* is also 'to spread out or apart' (*OED* 4a), which recalls the 'rose' that is 'parted wide' in H.D.'s poem 'The Master'.[102] Moravian devotions are re-imagined in terms of mutuality; the wound responds to the spear. The entry of the 'wound' in the fourth stanza rescores the poem's sound. The discordant consonance of the opening six lines ('jar' | 'myrrh', 'stored' | 'secure', 'alabaster' | 'spear') cedes control to the perfect rhymes of 'grace' | 'place' and 'dove' | 'love' as the fragrance wafts free. Far from being a mere negation, the wound institutes a restorative harmony.

'Hymn' evokes both Freud's views of the female body and Zinzendorf's wound theology. In keeping with Friedman and DuPlessis on 'The Master', 'Hymn' functions as a feminist reworking of the phallocentric traditions of both psychoanalysis and the Moravians. While classical psychoanalysis can be framed in terms of fixed precepts such as those governing Oedipus, Freud also recognised the culture-bearing power of a child's parents in ways that complicate the mechanistic aspects of his thought. Religion, too, is more than a collection of dogmas and principles.[103] The heteronormativity of Moravian blood-and-wound theology may well have been disconcerting for the bisexual H.D., but she nevertheless finds creative opportunities in these texts. The Moravian tradition is the forum in which she negotiated her mature relationship with psychoanalysis.

Throughout the present chapter, religion has featured as among other things: a particular set of feelings; a community organised around both natural and supernatural goals; a form of cultural memory; and a kind of therapy. For some, these various essays at definition are interlocking and overlapping; for others, they are either mutually exclusive or else antithetical to religion altogether. Jones, Eliot and H.D. all transform their respective traditions, but differences emerge between them. While he made daring connections in his meditations on Catholic tradition, Jones's worldview, major life decisions and devotional practice are comprehensible to other Catholics. H.D.'s Moravian Christianity was different. Orthodoxy, in her case, is more waning than wavering. H.D. nevertheless shows how even an idiosyncratic religious interest has public significance. She challenges the secular assumption that religion, perhaps in the form of mysticism or spirituality, must be confined to the private sphere. *The Gift* serves as a rejoinder to what H.D. considered dangerous psychological reductionism. The final section of the present chapter shows how H.D.'s religious filiations enabled her to challenge the militarism of the twentieth century and to imagine in *Helen in Egypt* a new form of society.

Community and Action: Personalism and the End of War
Alternatives to Individualism

While the present chapter has focused on the historical narrative inscribed in *Passion and Society*, H.D. scholars have cited the link Rougemont established between love and war as the site of his most significant influence on the poet, particularly in relation to *Helen in Egypt*. Friedman makes overt reference to Rougemont as she outlines H.D.'s realisation that 'the opposing forces of Love ("L'Amour") and Death ("La Mort") structure human existence and explain the origins of the Trojan War', arguing that over the course of *Helen in Egypt* the two are united.[104] The forces at work are themselves multifaceted. They are culturally conditioned insofar as love is, as H.D. sees it, the prerogative of the feminine as exemplified by Helen. Achilles, by contrast, represents death, formed in the patriarchal structures of 'the Command'.[105] These forces are also versions of the drives Freud identified in *Civilization and Its Discontents*: 'the instinct to preserve living substances and to join in ever larger units' and the 'instinct seeking to dissolve those units and to bring them back to their primeval, inorganic state'.[106] *Helen in Egypt* positions the male militarism that drove ancient epic, the twentieth century's wars and much else in-between as an expression of the death instinct. In its revisioning of the epic form, *Helen in Egypt* enmeshes the actions dependent upon the death drive in the broader web of associations characteristic of a feminised eros. Georgina Taylor has argued that the 'examination of internal drivers, privileged over external event' and 'a profound awareness' of 'the need to combat external violence at its source' are characteristic of women's war writing.[107] By charting the changes experienced by its eponymous hero, *Helen in Egypt* identifies the transformations of the self that are best suited to cutting off militarism at its source.

A comparable outlook is central to a particular form of feminism. Focusing on Dora Marsden's journal *The Egoist* for which H.D. at one time acted as literary editor, Lucy Delap describes what she terms the 'feminist avant-garde', which was characterised by 'a desire to seek liberation not through "externals", such as rights granted by men, but through internal transformation of one's psyche and sexual being'.[108] Delap's 'internal transformation' expands Taylor's suggestion that an awareness of 'internal drivers' could challenge the twentieth century's violent tendencies. *Passion and Society* has been positioned as a framework for understanding the transformation the character of Helen experiences over the course of *Helen in Egypt*.

In the context of modernism and religion, the privileging of internal development coalesces with understandings of the secular. Religion, such an approach assumes, is a private matter reflective of the richness of an individual's interiority. Rougemont, however, was a major proponent of personalism, a philosophical, political and theological movement that endeavoured to chart a path between the individualism of liberal society and the communitarian mentality of communism.[109] *Passion and Society* holds up relationships between persons as a counterpoint to the celebration of the individual on the one hand and the group on the other and, indeed, as a challenge to the militarism with which H.D. was concerned. The context is important for understanding the close of *Helen in*

Egypt where, after she has cast off her lover Paris, Helen and Achilles unite in marriage. Readings focusing on Helen's internal development have struggled to reckon with the ascetic tone of H.D.'s description of the union, which, the present chapter argues, reflects aspects of *Passion and Society*.[110] My argument presents Rougemont's personalist outlook as an alternative to the withdrawn interiority outlined above.[111]

As noted earlier, *Passion and Society* opposes two forms of love: eros and agape. The former is characterised by a yearning to free oneself from earthly constraints, while the latter is marked by a mutuality and reciprocity between persons. Eros formed the basis of a heretical religion, Rougemont contended, practised by the Cathars and passed on through various sects, including the Moravians. Warfare, too, as seen in everything from the chivalric code to the cult of heroism, revealed a dissatisfaction with life on earth. 'There is no need', Rougemont observes, 'to invoke Freudian theories in order to see that the war instinct and eroticism are fundamentally allied: it is so perfectly *obvious* from the common figurative use of language' (p. 247). Passion and war are two sides of the same coin, both antithetical to embodied, worldly life and built upon faith in the fruitfulness of suffering.

The alternative to passion and war, Rougemont contends, is agape. Such love centres on, and recognises the dignity of, other persons. It represents a commitment to the earthly life that eros would dismiss. For Rougemont, agape had been promoted by the Christian churches through marriage. It was also one element of the broader project of personalism, an 'ism' that once rivalled existentialism in notoriety. Jean-Paul Sartre is alleged to have said to Rougemont, on meeting him in New York during the Second World War, 'you Personalists are the victors; in France now everyone is a Personalist'.[112] Agape not only gave rise to a particular kind of interpersonal or even social organisation, but also a new kind of politics. Samuel Moyn has shown how early understandings of human rights were informed by notions of the 'dignity of the person' that flowed from Emmanuel Mounier, a central figure in personalism, via Jacques Maritain.[113]

The central idea of personalism is that of the person. Mounier defined the person as:

> *a spiritual being, constituted as such by its manner of existence and independence of being; it maintains this existence by its adhesion to a hierarchy of values that it has freely adopted, assimilated, and lived by its own responsible activity and by a constant interior development; thus it unifies all its activity in freedom and by means of creative acts develops the individuality of its vocation.*[114]

As many commentators have remarked, the definition confuses as much as it clarifies.[115] 'Spiritual', 'interior development' and 'creative acts' reflect the pervasiveness of mysticism. Setting himself in opposition to the social planning and state invention required in communism, Mounier also insisted that the person acts 'freely' and enjoys 'freedom'. Still more terms point in a different direction altogether. Reference to 'responsible activity' underlines the ethical requirements placed on persons who recognise a 'hierarchy of values'. While liberal individualism assumes an equality of access, personalism, like Eliot's *The Idea of a Christian Society*, emphasises the graded nature of existence.[116] Some activities, institutions and traditions have more value than others and recognition of hierarchy makes community possible. The definition of a person draws on tensions like those outlined in Hügel; Mounier runs together Hügel's institutional and mystical elements or what more broadly might be understood as the social cohesion represented by the religions of authority with the inward depth characteristic of religions of the spirit.

Religion was not, however, a discrete activity. For Mounier, a combination of the institutional and mystical was vital for forming persons who were not bound to spheres of activity narrowly defined as religious. The juxtaposition of the communal and institutional on the one hand and the individual and mystical on the other constituted the 'creative tensions' with which the properly formed person wrested. 'These conflicts were potentially creative', as Emmanuelle Hériard Dubreuil has observed in a doctoral thesis on Rougemont's spiritual politics, 'and solving conflicts shaped the character of a person'.[117] The formative influence of 'action' and 'activity' ensures their significance to personalism, even if contemplation and reflection are more typically associated with terms such as 'spiritual' and 'interior development'.

Passion and Society's discussion of marriage is indicative of such formation. The person was formed vertically and horizontally. In addition to charting how individuals in their depths are united with the hierarchies of value that tower over them, the personalists also attended to communion between persons standing side-by-side. For Mounier, community is a place where

> each person would at all times be able to achieve his fruitful vocation in the totality and in which the communion of all in the totality would be the living outcome of the efforts of each one. [. . .] Love would be the primary tie and not any constraint or any economic or 'vital' interest or any extrinsic apparatus. Each person would there find, in the common values transcending each one's own limitations of place and time, the tie that binds all the members in the whole.[118]

In Mounier's thought, the 'hierarchy of value' to which individuals bind themselves is represented by not a religion of authority, but rather something closer to Josiah Royce's understanding in *The Sources of Religious Insight* of a church as a shared project that unites individuals and universalises their goals (pp. 277–78). Mounier's community excludes an interventionist state apparatus; here each person pursues their own vocation without obstruction. The resulting tension is addressed in two ways: first through the practice of 'Love' or the recognition of the dignity of personhood in the other; secondly, through adhesion to 'common values transcending each one's own limitations' that include among them those principles that shape formed persons. Mounier recognises not merely the right to pursue one's own vocation, but rather the centrality of that pursuit to the dignity of personhood.

Marriage was central to Rougemont because it set these tensions in relief. Agape or married love consists of 'some action, a putting in order, a purification' (p. 240). Rougemont goes on to define marriage, deploying terminology taken from Søren Kierkegaard's reflections on faith, as a 'wager', emphasising the risk it involves (p. 311).[119] The wager of marriage is absurd. The parties become vulnerable as those who refuse such decisive action are not. Despite everyone's best intentions, a marriage might fail. One cannot know how either partner will develop, where one's vocation and that of the other might lead or the challenges life together will entail. Marriage is akin to a school for would-be persons or a transformative process from which sufficiently formed persons emerge. Through it, a person became legible as a person via the public exercise of a freely chosen act of self-limitation. Those who pursue passion by contrast are not coherent, Rougemont thought; they are merely carried away on a wave of Hollywood romance without ever exercising personal choice.

Heretical Origins of War

Human passion, for Rougemont, revealed a longing for death. Such a longing is also prominent in matters of war. Turning to one form of military engagement, Rougemont explains how chivalry 'stood for an attempt to endow instinct with a kind of correct deportment' (p. 261). The practice of war and the idea of restraint are aligned. He thinks of tournaments and the custom where a knight carried 'the veil or a fragment of the dress of his lady, and sometimes after the lists handed this to her stained with his blood' (p. 255). The chivalric code, like the language of courtly love, imposes limits on the war instinct that yearns for death; a tournament circumscribes how violence may be visited on another. The chivalric code does not dampen instinct but rather inflames it. With one eye on his lady's token, a knight undertakes ever more daring and dangerous acts, freely risking life and limb. Passion and heroism, love and war, have both been shaped by and give expression to the human desire to abandon earthly existence. The intensity of feeling in such matters has been carefully manipulated by specific traditions over history, but these traditions – and here lies the problem – have in turn been uprooted by modern thought and practice. We are left with survivals that cannot be fully explained.

While it expends much effort on expounding a thirteenth- and fourteenth-century heresy, *Passion and Society*'s focus is the present. Looking at the rise of the Nazis in Germany, Rougemont sought to diagnose his times, using his understanding of the war instinct as a survival of a religious heresy. The problems of the 1930s could be traced back to the conduct of the First World War. Total war had provided a newly depersonalised context for ancient practices. A tournament's constraints on conduct disappear in modern warfare. The mechanisation of war places soldiers in a new relationship with the war instinct itself. Far from enabling troops to live out their own death wishes by inflicting suffering on another while making themselves vulnerable to the same treatment, modern warfare hid or obscured its victims and thus tended to '*neutralize the actual passion for war* in the hearts of fighting men', dehumanising both sides in a given conflict (p. 274). Rougemont's discussion recalls Mounier's 'world of the impersonal', which centred on 'individuals without character', 'general ideas and vague opinions' and 'neutral positions and "objective knowledge"'.[120] The neutralising process in Rougemont ultimately stored up problems for post-war society, instigating 'a period of wandering *libidos* in quest of new spheres of activity' (p. 276).

Totalitarian politics emerged as one of these 'new spheres'. The nation or party takes on the libidinal role in the face of the irradiated passions of the populace. Now, the nation or party as desiring subject wants ever more living space or ever greater access to natural resources and inevitably comes into conflict with other nations. There are analogies here with Tristan and Iseult; just as the lovers refuse to admit that their passion is for love itself rather than the partner, so the totalitarian desire for war and ultimately death remains in most cases unconscious, dictating policy while the zombified population looks on in thrall (pp. 277–78). The libidinal state longs for destruction, that of others and its own. Unsatisfied yearning is the fruit of a romantic passion translated from the troubadours to the modern world. In Rougemont's other field of enquiry, the ultimate outcome is a state of permanent war.

The allusion to the Great War and the consequent rise of the Nazis raises the stakes in the case Rougemont makes for marriage. Undertaking the wager of marriage enables the living out of agape. Given what marriage demands and the persons it reveals, a society that celebrates marriage is shaped differently to one driven by passion. A new way of living, one that recognises the other in their dignity, is the way to end twentieth-century wars. The political structure that recognised the dignity of the person was not the centralised nation state, but rather a federalism of several regions organised into a political unity.[121] Such a system permits regions to govern themselves with autonomy and a significant degree of independence. Like Jones earlier, Rougemont uses insights derived from religion to address far more than denominational concerns. The idea of marriage as a wager was an application to a new scenario of Kierkegaard on the absurdity of faith, which provided a model for social and political organisation. Religion here is not a carefully defined space set apart from the secular public sphere. Without demanding allegiance to Christian dogma per se, it infuses, forms and shapes everything.[122]

New Asceticism: Helen in Egypt *and the Sacrifice of Marriage*

Rougemont's broad political, philosophical and theological understanding of marriage is central to *Helen in Egypt*.[123] One of the poem's interpretative challenges has been what to make of the union of Helen and Achilles at the close. The Helen of the final book turns her back on what Friedman calls a 'joyous act of springtime love' with her lover, Paris.[124] The poem stages the respective pulls of Paris and Achilles on Helen's attentions with the former calling out for his lover in a way that remains unmatched by Achilles. Paris says:

> why, why would you deny
> the peace, the sanctity
> of this small room,
>
> the lantern there by the door?
> why must you recall
> the white fire of unnumbered stars,
>
> rather than that single taper
> burning in an onyx jar,
> where you swore
>
> never, never to return,
> (*"return the wanton to Greece"*),
> where we swore together
>
> defiance of Achilles
> and the thousand spears,
> we alone would compel the Fates,
>
> we chosen of Cytheraea;
> can you forget the pact?
> why would you recall another?
> (p. 142)

Paris opposes the candlelit intimacy of his love affair with Helen in the 'sanctity | of this small room' with the cosmic intensity of his former partner's yearning for Achilles. He works hard to formalise the most famous of adulterous unions through repeated reference to the vows they 'swore', their unique and special status ('we alone would compel the Fates, | we chosen of Cytheraea'), and the shift over the course of the passage from the second person – why have 'you' betrayed me? – to the first-person plural – 'we' made a commitment to live in opposition to the martial death cult of Greece represented by 'Achilles | and the thousand spears'. The references to their warmly lit haunts (the 'lantern,' 'the onyx jar') underscore the earthy nature of the relationship in contrast with what Paris takes to be the insubstantial nature of Helen's connection with Achilles, lit by 'the white fire of unnumbered stars'. Paris pleads and suffers for Helen's love, while Achilles remains withdrawn, removed and distant. Paris's description of Helen's bedazzlement remembers Helen and Achilles's first meeting. When Helen first catches sight of him on the beach, Achilles is described as the '*Star in the night*' to whom (p. 17) 'God willed' Helen be joined (p. 102); Achilles's mother, the nymph Thetis, also advises Helen to 'Seek not another Star' (p. 105). Achilles is in the firmament, far removed from the intimacy of Helen and Paris's romance. Paris casts Achilles as inhuman, set apart and unreachable. Helen, Paris contends, loves only her feelings for Achilles, while Paris offers that which Rougemont thought impossible: happy mutual love.

Helen ultimately chooses Achilles. Her tone nevertheless represents a striking contrast to Paris's impassioned appeals. Speaking of her marriage to Achilles, Helen says:

> the sun and the seasons changed,
> and as the flower-leaves that drift
> from a tree were the numberless
>
> tender kisses, the soft caresses,
> given and received; none of these
> came into the story
> (p. 289).

The unwinding of a simile that compares the volume and delicacy of falling leaves to a lover's caress contemplates the sensuality of a romantic partnership in terms Paris would have recognised. Such tenderness represents, for Helen, only the briefest of moments. The poem quickly jerks free from the reverie in the syntactic recapitulation of 'none of these | came into the story'. All that one might dare to hope to gain from a marriage can be put out of mind. The conventions of romance ('tender kisses, the soft caresses') are briefly entertained before their dismissal in favour of an ascetic commitment to what Helen calls the 'epic, heroic' (p. 289).

Helen's decision to eschew mutuality and intimacy has been understood as the persistence of 'female thraldom', which 'occurs with startling, even dismal frequency throughout H.D.'s published and unpublished works'.[125] For Terry Eagleton, 'the consoling illusion that fulfilment can be achieved without fundamental rupture and rebirth' is a major challenge a reader must overcome in engaging with a text such as *Helen in Egypt*.[126] Ideas of self-sacrifice, particularly in marriage, are highly gendered as Woolf's observation that 'Killing the Angel in the House was part of the occupation of a woman writer' recognised.[127] Helen meets these objections by linking her ascetic actions to a broader social project, namely Rougemont's reformulated idea of marriage. Helen and Achilles's wager serves as the basis for a new kind of social organisation.

Their marriage stands opposed to the threat of endless war, which bubbles up repeatedly throughout the poem. In a choral section, the complexity of the relationship between love and war is played out in the sound patterns of the verse, so that 'the rhythms must speak for themselves' (p. 178):

> War, Ares, Achilles, Amor;
> [...]
> could Achilles be the father of Amor,
> Begotten of Love and of War?
> (p. 179).

'War, Ares, Achilles, Amor': in the thread of nouns (proper and otherwise), love and war are linked through both the assonance that facilitates the entry of a new god of love ('Amor') into a list constructed from terms associated with battle ('War, Ares, Achilles'), and the multilingual rhyme of the English 'War' and the Latin 'Amor'. The auditory similarity hints at unity as if the two were linked forever. Yet rhymes work through both similarity and difference; identical words do not rhyme, and the difference between 'War' and 'Amor' is further underlined by the fact that the rhyme moves across linguistic boundaries.[128] H.D.'s usage remembers the distinct twist *Passion and Society* gave the terms. A yearning for an end to earthly life is at the heart of unsatisfying relationships and ceaseless war. The auditory connection suggests that a change in one area affects the other. 'Was Troy lost for a kiss, | or a run of notes on a lyre?', Helen asks elsewhere (p. 230). The question can be read as merely rhetorical. Love, war and art are part of a cycle that cannot be broken; *Helen in Egypt* is merely the latest iteration. H.D.'s work is nevertheless as much dramatic poem as it is lyric and narrative. While relaying the poet's reflections on love and war and re-telling the story of the fall of Troy, the poem also expresses the outlooks of the characters it develops. Read in Helen's voice, these lines are not merely resigned in the face of the inevitable. She asserts her agency as a character. 'Was Troy lost for a kiss and a song? I won't let that happen again', Helen seems to say. Helen and Achilles's union is not a perpetuation of the doomed cycle, but rather a challenge to it.

The mixing of forms, the coming together of the dramatic, lyric and narrative elements, deepens the connection between the two central figures. In the narrative, the connection between Helen and Achilles is thin; their only form of interaction is Achilles's attack on Helen at the outset. The dramatic and lyrical elements of the poem nevertheless allow Helen and Achilles to understand each other in far richer terms. The staggered meetings of the figures are presented as moments of shock around which their lives are subsequently reordered. Achilles recalls how the sight of Helen set him apart from his surroundings. From the battlefield, Achilles watched Helen walk about the ramparts and one day caught her eye. Achilles explains:

> I stooped to fasten a greave
> that was loose at the ankle,
>
> when she turned; I stood
> indifferent to the rasp of metal,
> and her eyes met mine;
>
> you say, I could not see her eyes
> across the field of battle,
> I could not see their light
>
> shimmering as light on the changeable sea?
> all things would change but never
> the glance she exchanged with me.
> (p. 54)

Indifference, as *Four Quartets* reminds us, is distinct from the spiritual virtue of detachment which it resembles 'as death resembles life' (pp. 205–6). Achilles has not consciously distanced himself from the militarism of the Greeks, obtained a newfound peace or progressed along a spiritual path. All that he once cared about, the demands of 'the Command', has suddenly fallen away (p. 61). It no longer touches him. H.D. repeatedly uses 'rasp' to characterise battle, but the drive towards synonymy has another effect; 'the rasp of metal' falls short of naming war as if the great hero Achilles is now a stranger in the ranks, able to speak only in euphemisms. Achilles's moment with Helen is timeless, eternal. Its significance is captured by the change of vocabulary. Achilles turns a putative question from an unconvinced observer dripping with cynicism – something like: 'How did you see her from that far away?' – into a lyrical meditation. In place of his usual martial language, Achilles betrays a feeling for the aesthetic with his notion of Helen's eyes 'shimmering as light on the changeable sea'.

The aesthetic sense was precisely what Helen felt Achilles, the committed soldier, lacked when they first met. He had 'never spoken of Beauty', she complains (p. 39). Their meeting changes Helen's life as the earlier encounter changed his, but the soldier's militaristic past impinges on her withdrawn reflection. She adds:

> Much has happened
> in timeless-time,
> here in the Amen-temple,
>
> but he had not questioned me,
> he had never spoken of Beauty;
> the rasp of a severed wheel
>
> seemed to ring in the dark,
> the spark of a sword on a shield,
> the whirr of an arrow,
>
> the crack of a broken lance,
> then laughter mingled with fury,
> as host encountered host
> (p. 39)

In the opening lines, Helen unhurriedly considers her budding relationship with Achilles in a syntax that relies on apposition to expand upon itself: each line bringing a further piece of information about the setting and the interactions of the two lovers, subtly adjusting the picture with each addition. Her seclusion in the Amen-temple and her dedication to 'Beauty' is nevertheless soon interrupted. The martial world of Achilles intrudes on her meditations via the arrival of new diction (the swords, arrows and lances) and the repetition of noun phrases that follow one after the other in disciplined succession in the final lines of the quotation. Intimate fluidity is replaced by marshalled order. In H.D.'s own recording of these lines, she switches between two dramatic voices: a soft, conversational voice for the first five lines and a deeper, almost mechanical rhetorical voice for the remainder.[129] The dramatisation of Helen's speech incorporates Achilles's tones too, serving as an auditory record of the blending of perspectives thematised across the work. Achilles's shellshock, his inability to close his ears to the ring of the sword and whir of the arrow, is as much a part of Helen's experience as his own.

The poem dramatises the relationality of persons that Rougemont thought central to marriage. Helen goes out of herself to try on Achilles's militaristic outlook, his experience of war and his trauma, before returning changed.

Achilles, under Helen's guidance, begins to speak and think in ways that life in 'the Command' would otherwise have made impossible (p. 61). They pursue their own vocations but are changed by their confrontations with the other. The characters are not mere representations of opposing forces: a feminine world of love and beauty and a masculine universe of military values. They try on and try out their otherness. Their actions instantiate Mounier's observation that the 'world of the impersonals is a world of *laissez-faire* indifference, but the world of "others like myself" is one of willing and often heroic sacrifice for a common cause'.[130] At the close of the poem, Achilles and Helen, the exemplification of Greek militarism and the face that launched a thousand ships, come together not out of passion or mutual love, but rather from a recognition of the cost of war and a desire to produce a form of social organisation that will end the cycle. The decisiveness of Helen at the close of the poem distinguishes *Helen in Egypt* from *The Gift* or *The Mystery*. The poem does not dwell on what could have been or the valences of possible plans; it dramatises a moment of decisive action undertaken for the social good.

Helen and Achilles's union thus offers an alternative myth to that of Tristan and Iseult. Tristan and Iseult's pursuit of an adulterous passion that soars above earthly concerns threatens a fragile kingdom. In contrast, the wager of Helen and Achilles's agape-informed marriage, their hope that their uneasy union will bring about a more peaceful society, is justified by communitarian concerns. Achilles gives over his search for the mother image, the type that Rougemont considers a central feature of passionate love (p. 89). Helen, too, gives over her attachment to Paris (p. 23). Rougemont understood myth as the expression of collective social practice; to interpret a myth is to understand what drives the group that expressed itself, however obliquely, through the myth. The connection between cultural experiences and expression might be true of any work of art. Myth is marked by the *'power which it gains over us'*; it is best understood, Rougemont adds, as a form of *'compulsion'* (p. 92). *Helen in Egypt* is itself a myth that instantiates Rougemont's celebration of a different form of love and a new kind of society. The peculiar mix of philosophy, politics and theology that shaped Mounier and Rougemont's personalism fed H.D.'s major poem and serves as a counterweight to what the present study has termed 'spilt mysticism'.

A (Re)Imagist H.D.

Helen in Egypt brought H.D.'s Moravian period to a close. While her earlier Moravian works were marked by her excitement at revisiting her childhood religion from a new vantage point, H.D.'s late epic is defined by a newfound seriousness. Helen rejects the celebration of passionate love that the Cathars had made the basis for a whole religion. The poem offers a myth built from new forms of association, which calls out the assumptions that underwrote two world wars.

The late H.D. stands at a far remove from her incarnation as an Imagist. H.D.'s early poetry is marked by its reserve. Through the withdrawal of her crystalline, otherworldly verse, H.D. uncovered timeless truths akin to those at the heart of the world's great mystical traditions. *Helen in Egypt* understands religion differently. In mythologising Rougemont's marriage wager, H.D. disputed not only the idea that religious traditions were timeless – that 'Christian marriage', say, was always and had always been one thing – but also and more importantly that religion was best construed in terms of a subtraction narrative that unearthed a perennial core. Personalism was important to H.D. because it drew on a range of sources, theology among them, to speak to the present moment. The personalists' concepts of action, community and the person spoke to a society that had been failed, so they thought, by liberal individualism and which was presently threatened by statist communism. Facing multiple crises, Rougemont and his associates described not a return to a pre-modern Christendom, but rather a reformed modernity leavened with religious ideas. The very traditions that the subtraction approach to religion would sheer off offered, in the personalist's description of the situation, otherwise inaccessible resources for dealing with modern problems.

Reformulating the relationship between the public and the private confers a new role upon religious poetry. H.D.'s Imagist verse can be read in terms of the modernist epiphany. In sketching out a prehistory of the concept, M. H. Abrams, for instance, cited William Wordsworth's early work, which, he argued, included 'encounters when a natural or human object unexpectedly shows forth a meaning beyond propositional statement'.[131] John Gould Fletcher, in his review of *Sea-garden*, suggested that H.D.'s reflections on coastlines, woods and flowers are similarly revelatory. They provide an accessible route into truths that were otherwise the preserve of the world religions. Fletcher reframes religion as primarily a mode of extraordinary experience. Works of art likewise generate powerful aesthetic experiences, particularly those that, in the terminology Virginia Woolf employed in her essay on 'Modern Fiction', pursue the 'spiritual' and eschew materialism.[132] In Fletcher's argumentative frame, aesthetic experiences might well provide access to the same objects as religious experiences. Ultimately, the respective objects of religion and art are one and the same.

The unwieldiness of *Helen in Egypt* challenges such assumptions. Given her rediscovery of the Moravians, H.D. could not countenance the identity of religion and aesthetic experience. It left out too much of what was important to her about religion. Moreover, she imagined her poetry not as a form of withdrawn spiritual practice, but rather as a way of re-envisioning society. Her mythic writing detailed new forms of social organisation. Its complications, digressions and prose-like qualities, very different to the highly wrought work of the earlier period, speak to her attempt to engage with such questions.[133] While her late poetry was built on astral doubling, conversions and visions, H.D. was not content to isolate extraordinary experience, whether aesthetic, religious or a combination of the two, as the key tenet of religion or, for that matter, of poetry. The following chapter charts a comparable attempt within the twentieth century's nascent retreat movement, an undertaking contemporaneous with H.D.'s return to the Moravians, to unite the cultivation of experiences deemed special and an experimental social project.

Notes

1. John Gould Fletcher, 'H.D.'s Vision', *Poetry* 9, no. 5 (February 1917), 266–69 (p. 267).
2. F. S. Flint, 'The History of Imagism', *The Egoist* 2, no. 5 (May 1915), 70–71 (p. 71); see also James Longenbach, *Stone Cottage: Pound, Yeats and Modernism* (Oxford: Oxford University Press, 1991), pp. 31–33.
3. See Robert Duncan, *The H.D. Book*, ed. by Michael Boughn and Victor Coleman (Berkeley: University of California Press, 2012), pp. 319–20.
4. Eliot, *'The Idea of a Christian Society'*, p. 716.
5. Eliot, 'Introduction to *Revelation*', p. 487.
6. Taylor, *Secular Age*, p. 26.
7. Taylor, *Secular Age*, p. 355.
8. Adalaide Morris, *How to Live/what to Do: H.D.'s Cultural Poetics* (Champaign: University of Illinois Press, 2008), p. 131.
9. See Taves, *Religious Experience Reconsidered*, pp. 17–22; for a critique, see Nicholas Lash, *Easter in Ordinary: Reflections on Human Experience and the Knowledge of God* (Charlottesville: University of Virginia Press, 1988), p. 47.
10. H.D., 'H.D. by Delia Alton', *The Iowa Review*, 16 (1986), 180–221 (p. 184). For the 'crystalline' in H.D., see Susan Stanford Friedman, *Penelope's Web: Gender, Modernity, H.D.'s Fiction* (Cambridge: Cambridge University Press, 1990), pp. 54–58.
11. Parsons, *Freud and Augustine*, pp. 143–44.
12. Lewis, p. 25.
13. *L'Amour et l'Occident* was published in Paris by Plon in 1939. The text was translated and published by Faber & Faber the following year. The first English edition appeared as Denis de Rougemont, *Passion and Society*, trans. by Montgomery Belgion (London: Faber & Faber, 1940). The American edition appeared as Denis de Rougemont, *Love and the Western World*, trans. by Montgomery Belgion (New York: Harcourt, 1940). Subsequent English editions have used the American title. H.D. used the Faber edition. Further references to Rougemont's text are from the Faber edition and are given after quotations in the text. H.D.'s copy is held at the Beinecke Library, Yale University <http://hdl.handle.net/10079/bibid/602571> [accessed 1 March 2022]. H.D.'s marginal notes are referenced according to the page number of *Passion and Society* upon which they appear.
14. Hervieu-Léger, p. 74.
15. See Lawrence Rainey, *Institutions of Modernism: Literary Elites and Public Culture* (New Haven, CT: Yale University Press, 1998), p. 163.
16. Rebecca West, *St Augustine* (London: Davies, 1933), p. 83.
17. West, *Augustine*, p. 83.

18. West, *Augustine*, p. 84.
19. West, *Augustine*, pp. 83–84.
20. Susan Stanford Friedman, *Psyche Reborn: The Emergence of H.D.* (Bloomington: Indiana University Press, 1981), p. 309n.
21. For the reception of *Passion and Society*, see Luisa Passerini, *Women and Men in Love: European Identities in the Twentieth Century*, trans. by Juliet Haydock with Allan Cameron (New York: Berghahn Books, 2012), pp. 174–228.
22. H.D. to George Plank, 25 November 1940, YCAL MSS 28, Series 1, Box 3, folder 49, George Plank Papers, Yale Collection of American Literature, Beinecke Rare Book and Manuscript Library, Yale University. The following year H.D. wrote to Bryher: 'Will you PLEASE post me on, *Passion and Society*? It should be in my bedroom, in the glass-door book-shelf. I was looking up words, I copied down from the vol., on various heresies'. H.D. to Bryher, 25 May 1941, GEN MSS 97, Box 15, Bryher Papers, Yale Collection of American Literature, Beinecke Rare Book and Manuscript Library, Yale University.
23. Lara Vetter, introduction to H.D., *By Avon River*, ed. by Lara Vetter (Gainesville: University Press of Florida, 2017), pp. 1–42 (p. 4).
24. 'I am having fun with an appendix to my book, *The Gift*'. H.D. to George Plank, 5 February 1944, YCAL MSS 28, Series 1, Box 3, folder 50, George Plank Papers; 'Can you tell me how that Lamb with the Banner originated? [. . .] Can you trace it in your popery?' H.D. to George Plank, 5 February 1944, Series 1, Box 3, folder 50, George Plank Papers.
25. Jane Augustine, 'A Note on the Text and Its Arrangement', in *The Gift*, pp. ix–xi.
26. For a comparable narrative, see Pound, 'Psychology and Troubadours', pp. 87–100.
27. Edward Burnett Tylor, *Primitive Culture: Researches into the Development of Mythology, Philosophy, Religion, Language, Art, and Custom*, 2 vols (London: Murray, 1871), 1, pp. 70–139; see also Larsen, pp. 22–27.
28. Rougemont relied on Eugène Aroux's *Dante hérétique* (1854) and Joséphin Péladan's *De Parsifal à don Quichotte: le secret des troubadours* (1906). Pound used these in *The Spirit of Romance* (1913). See Surette, p. 104.
29. H.D., *Trilogy: The Walls Do Not Fall; Tribute to the Angels; The Flowering of the Rod*, with an introduction and readers' notes by Aliki Barnstone (New York: New Directions, 1998), p. 51.
30. For criticism of Rougemont's historiography, see C. S. Lewis, 'review of *Passion and Society*, by D. de Rougemont, trans. M. Belgion, Faber & Faber and review of *The Bride of Christ*, by Claude Chavasse, Faber & Faber', *Theology*, 40 (1940), 459–61.
31. For late nineteenth-century Moravian missions, see Joseph Taylor Hamilton, *A History of the Missions of the Moravian Church, During the Eighteenth and Nineteenth Centuries* (Bethlehem, PA: Times Publishing, 1901), pp. 200–8.
32. H.D., *Trilogy*, p. 25.
33. Jane Augustine, introduction to *The Gift*, pp. 1–28 (p. 1)
34. Friedman, *Penelope's Web*, p. 352.
35. Aaron Spencer Fogleman, *Jesus is Female: Moravians and Radical Religion in Early America* (Philadelphia: University of Pennsylvania Press, 2008), p. 90. The effects of these arrangements on women's lives in the Moravian settlement at Winston-Salem,

North Carolina are outlined in Johanna Miller Lewis, 'Equality Deferred, Opportunity Pursued: The Sisters of Wachovia', in *Women of the American South: A Multicultural Reader*, ed. by Christie Anne Farnham (New York: New York University Press, 1997), pp. 74–89.
36. Fogleman, p. 90.
37. See Caroline Walker Bynum, *Jesus as Mother: Studies in the Spirituality of the High Middle Ages* (Berkeley: University of California Press, 1982).
38. Bethlehem Church Register, vol. 6, ChReg 207, Church Registers, Collections, Moravian Archives, Bethlehem, PA.
39. Anderson, pp. 68–71.
40. Augustine, introduction to *The Gift*, p. 13.
41. H.D., 'Hymn', in *Selected Poems of H.D.*, ed. by Norman Holmes Pearson (New York: Grove Press, 1957), pp. 69–70.
42. Paul Peucker, *A Time of Sifting: Mystical Marriage and the Crisis of Moravian Piety in the Eighteenth Century* (University Park: Penn State University Press, 2015), pp. 3–4.
43. H.D., *Tribute to Freud*, intro. by Kenneth Fields with a forward by Norman Holmes Pearson (Boston: Godine, 1974), p. 124.
44. Augustine, introduction to *The Gift*, pp. 9–10.
45. Alfred A. Cave, *Prophets of the Great Spirit: Native American Revitalization Movements in Eastern North America* (Lincoln: University of Nebraska Press, 2014), p. 2.
46. Cave, pp. 2–3.
47. Cave, p. 5.
48. Schmidt, p. 287.
49. Schmidt, p. 287.
50. Henry Rimius, *A Candid Narrative of the Rise and Progress of the Herrnhuters, call'd Moravians, or Unitas Fratrum* (London: Linde, 1753), p. 11.
51. Rimius, p. 15.
52. Quoted in Rimius, p. 52. Reproduced in H.D. 'Zinzendorf Notes', YCAL MSS 24, Box 24, H.D. Papers, YCAL MSS 24, Box 24, Yale Collection of American Literature, Beinecke Rare Book and Manuscript Library, Yale University.
53. Joseph Taylor Hamilton, *A History of the Church Known as the Moravian Church, or, The Unitas Fratrum, or, The Unity of the Brethren, During the Eighteenth and Nineteenth Centuries* (Bethlehem, PA: Times Publishing, 1900), p. 190.
54. Peucker, p. 113.
55. H.D. 'Zinzendorf Notes'.
56. Jane Augustine, 'A Note on the Edition', in H.D., *The Mystery*, ed. by Jane Augustine (Gainesville: University Press of Florida, 2009), pp. ix–xi (p. x).
57. H.D., *The Mystery*, p. 32.
58. H.D. to Norman Holmes Pearson, 11 September 1944, in *Between History and Poetry: The Letters of H.D. and Norman Holmes Pearson*, ed. by Donna Krolik Hollenberg (Iowa City: University of Iowa Press, 1997), pp. 43–44 (p. 43).
59. H.D., *The Mystery*, p. 69.
60. Dante, *Vita Nuova*, trans. by Mark Musa, new edn (Bloomington: Indiana University Press, 1973), p. 8.

61. Matte Robinson, *The Astral H.D.: Occult and Religious Sources and Contexts for H.D.'s Poetry and Prose* (London: Bloomsbury Academic, 2016), p. 15.
62. H.D., *The Mystery*, p. 74.
63. Suzanne Hobson, 'Credulous Readers: H.D. and Psychic-Research Work', in *Incredible Modernism: Literature, Trust and Deception*, ed. by John Attridge and Rod Rosenquist (Farnham: Ashgate, 2013), pp. 51–67 (p. 53).
64. H.D., *The Mystery*, p. 149n.
65. See Robinson, p. 4.
66. Gauri Viswanathan, *Outside the Fold: Conversion, Modernity, and Belief* (Princeton: Princeton University Press, 1998), p. 37.
67. H.D., *Trilogy*, p. 155.
68. Fletcher, p. 267.
69. H.D., *Collected Poems*, p. 55, p. 39.
70. H.D., *Trilogy*, pp. 165–66.
71. Hobson, 'Credulous Readers', p. 53.
72. H.D., *Trilogy*, pp. 165–66.
73. See Martz, p. 321.
74. See William Empson, *Seven Types of Ambiguity*, 3rd edn (London: Chatto & Windus, 1953), p. 232.
75. McGuire, p. 6.
76. See H.D., 'A Note on the Text', in *Tribute to Freud*, p. xlvi.
77. H.D., *Tribute to Freud*, p. 123.
78. H.D., *Tribute to Freud*, p. 13.
79. See Sigmund Freud, 'The Future of an Illusion', in *The Standard Edition of the Complete Psychological Works of Sigmund Freud*, 24 vols (London: Hogarth, 1953–74), 21: *The Future of an Illusion, Civilization and Its Discontents and Other Works (1927–1931)*, pp. 3–58 (p. 37).
80. William B. Parsons, *Freud and Religion: Advancing the Dialogue* (Cambridge: Cambridge University Press, 2021), p. 105. Friedman construes the discussion of the Christmas Eve service as an oblique reference to the psychoanalytic concept of penis envy. Susan Stanford Friedman, 'The First Week – March 1–5, 1933', in *Analyzing Freud: Letters of H.D., Bryher, and their Circle* (New York: New Directions, 2002), pp. 31–33 (p. 32). What follows is an alternative interpretation.
81. Sigmund Freud, 'An Outline of Psycho-analysis', in *The Standard Edition*, 23: *Moses and Monotheism, An Outline of Psycho-Analysis and Other Works (1937–1939)*, pp. 141–208 (p. 146). Quoted in James DiCenso, *The Other Freud: Religion, Culture and Psychoanalysis* (London: Routledge, 1999), p. 24.
82. DiCenso, p. 24.
83. Sigmund Freud, 'Civilization and Its Discontents', in *The Standard Edition*, 21: *The Future of an Illusion, Civilization and Its Discontents and Other Works (1927–1931)*, pp. 59–148 (p. 74).
84. Freud, 'Civilization and Its Discontents', pp. 64–65; Parsons, *Freud and Augustine*, p. 58.
85. Freud, 'Civilization and Its Discontents', p. 68.
86. See Susan Stanford Friedman, 'The Fourth Week – March 20–27, 1933', in *Analyzing Freud*, pp. 119–23 (pp. 120–21).

87. Parsons, *Freud and Religion*, pp. 189–90.
88. Parsons, *Freud and Religion*, pp. 191–96.
89. H.D., *Tribute to Freud*, p. 37.
90. H.D., *Tribute to Freud*, p. 69.
91. Norman N. Holland, 'H.D. and the "Blameless Physician"', *Contemporary Literature*, 10 (1969), 474–506 (pp. 485–86).
92. Rachel Blau DuPlessis and Susan Stanford Friedman, '"Woman Is Perfect": H.D.'s Debate with Freud', *Feminist Studies*, 7 (1981), 417–430 (p. 421). Friedman has written about the Athena scene more recently. See Friedman, 'The First Week', p. 32.
93. H.D., *Tribute to Freud*, p. 37.
94. Friedman, 'The Fourth Week', p. 119.
95. Bellah, 'Religion and Belief', p. 219.
96. H.D., *Selected Poems*, p. 69.
97. See Craig D. Atwood, 'Understanding Zinzendorf's Blood and Wounds Theology', *Journal of Moravian History*, 1 (2006), 31–47; Paul Peucker, 'The Songs of the Sifting: Understanding the Role of Bridal Mysticism in Moravian Piety During the Late 1740s', *Journal of Moravian History*, 3 (2007), 51–87; Peter Vogt, '"Honor to the Side": The Adoration of the Side Wound of Jesus in Eighteenth-Century Moravian Piety', *Journal of Moravian History*, 7 (2009), 83–106.
98. H.D. 'Zinzendorf Notes'.
99. See Fogleman, pp. 73–104.
100. H.D., 'Hymn (From the Bohemian)', *Life and Letters*, 64, no. 151 (March 1950), 213 (p. 213).
101. H.D., *Trilogy*, p. 172.
102. H.D., *Collected Poems*, p. 456.
103. For the newfound prominence of dogma in the modern era, see Harrison, pp. 83–115.
104. Friedman, *Psyche Reborn*, p. 256.
105. H.D., *Helen in Egypt* (New York: New Directions, 1974), p. 61. Further references to this poem are to this edition and are given after quotations in the text.
106. Freud, 'Civilization and Its Discontents', pp. 118–19.
107. Georgina Taylor, *H.D. and the Public Sphere of Modernist Women Writers, 1913–1946: Talking Women* (Oxford: Oxford University Press, 2001), pp. 164–65.
108. Lucy Delap, *The Feminist Avant-Garde: Transatlantic Encounters of the Early Twentieth Century* (Cambridge: Cambridge University Press, 2007), p. 7.
109. John Hellman, *Emmanuel Mounier and the New Catholic Left 1930–1950* (Toronto: University of Toronto Press, 1981), p. 5.
110. See Rachel Blau DuPlessis, 'Romantic Thralldom in H.D.', *Contemporary Literature*, 20 (1979), 178–203.
111. My argument builds on Elizabeth Anderson's account of community in H.D.'s understanding of the Moravians. Anderson, pp. 61–94.
112. Quoted in Dudley Andrew and Steven Ungar, *Popular Front Paris and the Poetics of Culture* (Cambridge, MA: Harvard University Press, 2005), p. 140.
113. See Moyn, pp. 25–64. Mounier and Maritain nevertheless had very different positions, see Shortall, pp. 50–84 and Hellman, pp. 48–51.

114. Emmanuel Mounier, *A Personalist Manifesto*, trans. by Monks of St John's Abbey (London: Longmans Green, 1938), p. 68. Italics in the original.
115. Hellman, p. 79.
116. Taylor, *Secular Age*, p. 370.
117. Emmanuelle Hériard Dubreuil, *The Personalism of Denis de Rougemont: Spirituality and Politics in 1930s Europe* (unpublished doctoral thesis, University of Cambridge, 2005), p. 188.
118. Mounier, p. 95.
119. Passerini, p. 194.
120. Mounier, p. 90.
121. Dubreuil, p. 205.
122. See Shortall, pp. 74–76.
123. This section expands arguments rehearsed in Jamie Callison, 'Redefining Marriage in Interwar Britain: Internal Transformation and Personal Sacrifice in the Poetry of H.D.', in *Marriage Discourses: Historical and Literary Perspectives on Gender Inequality and Patriarchic Exploitation*, ed. by Jowan A. Mohammed and Frank Jacob (Berlin: De Gruyter, 2021), pp. 187–206.
124. Friedman, *Psyche Reborn*, p. 255.
125. DuPlessis, 'Romantic Thralldom', p. 179.
126. Terry Eagleton, *Radical Sacrifice* (New Haven, CT: Yale University Press, 2018), p. 8.
127. Virginia Woolf, 'Professions for Women', in *Selected Essays*, pp. 140–45 (p. 142).
128. See *The Princeton Handbook of Poetic Terms*, ed. by Roland Greene and Stephen Cushman, 3rd edn (Princeton: Princeton University Press, 2016), p. 294.
129. H.D., *Helen in Egypt*, read by the author, recorded in Zurich, 1955, PennSound, MP3, 37 min., 52 sec. <https://writing.upenn.edu/pennsound/x/HD.php> [accessed 1 March 2022], Pallinode 3.3.
130. Mounier, p. 92.
131. Abrams, p. 390.
132. Woolf, 'Modern Fiction', p. 10.
133. H.D., 'H.D. by Delia Alton', p. 184; Friedman, *Penelope's Web*, pp. 54–58.

4

SILENT PROTEST:
THE RETREAT MOVEMENT, 1920–45

In a 1928 letter to William Force Stead, the Church of England priest who had baptised and confirmed him the year before, T. S. Eliot wrote 'I feel that I need the most severe' and 'the most Latin, kind of discipline, Ignatian or other'; 'nothing', he added, 'could be too ascetic, too violent, for my own needs'.[1] 'Latin' here might function as a synonym for Roman Catholic (the Latin church); the European regions where Romance languages are spoken (in short a non-English kind of discipline); or the medieval monasticism that gave rise to the 'Latinate mysticism' about which Eliot spoke in his 1927 Clark lectures. The connection with medieval monasticism coats Eliot's contemporary spiritual decisions with a historical gloss; like his turn to metaphysical lyrics as an inspiration for modernist verse, the poet invoked classic mystical writing to reimagine his spiritual life. As a new Anglican, Eliot sought out techniques to help him realise his faith in everyday life.

His yoking of discipline, asceticism and violence might nevertheless appear troubling. As a spiritual director, Evelyn Underhill reminded her charges that asceticism should be preceded by a recognition, however brief and transient, of spiritual joy. The connection between asceticism and joy guarded against the former spilling over into self-destruction.[2] Asceticism requires voluntary self-limitation in service of a broader goal and thus undermines, as Terry Eagleton has recognised, the belief that 'fulfilment can be achieved without a fundamental rupture and rebirth' upon which much contemporary theorising of the self is based.[3] The practice has thus been treated somewhat critically. One influential understanding of early Christian asceticism, for instance, describes how ascetics strive to situate themselves within the drama of Christ's passion as 'a way of subjugating the subject to the law' of the gospels.[4] The links critics have made between Eliot's own religious belief and his reputedly disciplinarian outlook – the move in *After Strange Gods*, for example, to fashion orthodoxy and heresy as terms of critical appraisal – might owe as much to the adoption of these ascetic techniques as to long-standing political positions about order and progress.[5]

Those who had heard Eliot's Clark lectures in 1927 would nevertheless have been surprised to find in the poet's letter to Stead a thread running between St Ignatius, asceticism and discipline. In the lectures, Eliot had opposed monastic mysticism that facilitated 'the development and subsumption of emotion and feeling through intellect into the vision of God' to the vernacular Spanish mysticism of St Teresa of Ávila, which he found guilty of substituting 'divine love for human love'.[6] During the lecture, St Ignatius had been placed squarely in the second category.[7] According to Ronald Schuchard, Eliot's reclassification of St Ignatius responded to an exchange between Eliot and one of his auditors, an American Jesuit priest named Fr Francis Joseph Yealey.[8] Under Yealey's guidance, Eliot reassessed, Schuchard explains, the significance of St Ignatius and the purpose of his *Spiritual Exercises*.[9]

While Yealey's intervention was undoubtedly helpful, the Anglo-Catholic Eliot had access to other sources of Ignatian influence. The saint was the guiding light of the retreat movement and particularly the Anglo-Catholic organisation, the Association for Promoting Retreats (APR). A retreat, as Dorothy Day, a Roman Catholic proponent of the practice, explained, 'is an annual exercise' that is 'conducted by a leader'; there are 'conferences, spiritual exercises, hours of prayer in the chapel, and a life lived in common, and in silence'.[10] 'The most famous retreat', Day continued, 'is that of St Ignatius'.[11] Eliot would go on mostly silent visits to the theological college of the Society of the Sacred Mission (SSM) at Kelham, Nottinghamshire through the 1930s and attend organised retreats with the Society of St John the Evangelist, otherwise known as the 'Cowley Fathers', in Oxford and at Nashdom Abbey in Buckinghamshire.[12] As Day's words suggest, retreat, as a silent practice based on reflection and meditation rather than study and discussion, took place under the sign of St Ignatius. Eliot's reclassification of the saint from a romantic-adjacent mystic to a viable spiritual guide follows from the meeting of his own theorising about religion with new forms of religious practice.[13]

The APR was cognisant not only of the problematic associations of asceticism, but also the concerns potential retreatants might have about such practices. Retreat after the Ignatian pattern was therefore reimagined for a new audience. The present chapter outlines two different attempts to make Ignatian retreat new: the first practised by the APR in England and the second by Day's Catholic

Worker organisation in North America. In describing these retreats, the present chapter has recourse to both the APR's quarterly journal, *The Vision*, and Day's drafts for an unpublished account of the Catholic Worker retreat and her recently published retreat notebooks.[14] The transatlanticism at work in the present chapter not only underlines the breadth of the retreat movement, but also reveals how ideas that influenced David Jones, Eliot and H.D. travelled. Retreat can be understood as an institutional form that reflects many of the tensions at work in the literature discussed throughout the present study.

Retreat was shaped by the conflict between mysticism and orthodoxy. The buildings, specialised staff and the organisational networks of existing churches were leveraged in service of a mission based on personal contemplation. The twentieth century produced a torrent of unchurched mysticism that offered an alternative to institutional religion. The retreat movement can be understood as part of a strategy enacted by religious authorities to capture contemporary spiritual energy for its own cause. Numerous studies of 'Christian Mysticism' appeared at and around the turn of the twentieth century, which imposed borders and boundaries around the broader, nonconfessional mysticism that had concerned Underhill in her 1911 bestseller.[15] Despite its historical analogues, retreat is thus best understood as a new phenomenon that bore witness to a shift in modes of belief. The present chapter offers a brief overview of two forms of retreat before going on to outline the thematic commonalities among not only APR and Catholic Worker retreats, but also retreats and the modernist poems discussed earlier. It concludes by linking what appears to be an act of private devotion to a broad range of public projects in ways that demand a reassessment of the relationship between modernism and religion.

Tradition and Innovation: A Brief History of Retreat

On Location: The APR's Experiments with Retreat

The retreat movement was not always well received. One writer in *The Vision* claimed that to 'those in authority' the movement appeared to be 'a mere recrudescence of monastic notions unfortunately revived by the "high-church" party'.[16] The nostalgic quality of retreat served as a companion to the emphasis the '"high-church" party' placed upon ritual. For theological modernisers, by contrast, such practices were considered trivial or even primitive. Precedents for a deliberate withdrawal from society for religious reasons preceded medieval 'monastic notions', notably Jesus's forty days in the desert and the austerities of the desert fathers. In the narrative preferred by 'those in authority', however, those practices had been surpassed by more developed forms of Christianity. Returning to an earlier stage of Christian development would only be destructive considering the pressures exerted on organised religion by secularisation. More recently, the focus on the interconnections between religion and the everyday has also cast an unflattering light on forms of religious practice that insist that the truest, most revealing patterns of religious insight, are to be found in withdrawal from domestic duties and political engagement, given the assumptions about gender, socio-economic standing and relative power that are embedded in such an outlook. Christianity has not progressed beyond the need for retreat, rather problematic aspects of Christian practice have been exposed by secular critique. A return could only be prompted by naivety or wilful ignorance.

Those better versed in APR's work knew that the movement incorporated much that was genuinely new and not mere nostalgia, even if that brought its own problems. One letter writer noted the existence of a small Anglican retreat culture before 1914. These retreats were typically arranged by Anglican monastic communities, three days in duration and attended by people attracted to a monastic rule.[17] Retreats after 1914 were *'entirely different'*.[18] They last 'for practically one day' and were attended by 'all sorts and conditions of men, women and juveniles, chiefly people with only an elementary school education and no experience whatever of sustained devotion and meditation'.[19] Retreat had become a mass movement, but it had not adapted to its new context. Retreats had been shortened from a full three days to a weekend that typically began late Saturday afternoon and ended on either Sunday evening or Monday morning, but the shape of the retreat itself was modelled on the pre-1914 form.

The pre-1914 retreats had their roots in the Oxford Movement, the nineteenth-century revival of Catholic themes and religious practices in Anglican life. The Society of the Holy Cross, led by the ritualist Charles Lowder, offered yearly retreats for clerical members of the nominally secret society in the late 1850s.[20] Lowder had been inspired by the societies formed by the French priest Vincent de Paul and his use of St Ignatius's *Spiritual Exercises*. In the following years, retreat was often recommended or even required in dioceses sympathetic to ritualism.[21] Retreat practice in England was thus inspired by European Roman Catholicism, though in time gestures towards home-grown religious communities such as Little Gidding would soften the status of retreat as a continental import.[22] During their retreats, ritualist sympathisers, often isolated in rural parishes and far removed from likeminded colleagues, united for a few days of life in common and returned to their parishes conscious of a shared mission.[23] In light of the call of the *Spiritual Exercises* to enter emotionally and imaginatively into the Christian story, Ignatian retreats were part of the Oxford Movement's attempt to increase Christian observance and to promote inward identification with Christian doctrines.

Yet something happened to retreat over the course of the twentieth century. In 1902, retreat was a salve for priests, providing 'frequent opportunities' for the 'strengthening of the interior life' and serving as 'the best safeguard the Church can have against a Priesthood barren of the gifts and power of the spirit'.[24] By the mid-1930s, there were fifty-three Anglican retreat houses across England and the majority catered to lay participants.[25] The APR's slogan said nothing about ministers: 'Give us a Retreat House on the outskirts of every town in England. In two generations we will show you a Church revived in vision and power and a nation with a new outlook upon religion'.[26] The re-empowerment of the Anglican Church relied on not the development of a saintly clergy but rather greater lay participation. Retreat leaders looked to the mass market. 'The object of Retreat is to awake and strengthen', J. A. Bouquet claimed, 'a *sense* of Vocation in every class and sort of Christian'.[27] The APR not only met charges of nostalgia, but also resisted some of the challenges associated with a growing appreciation for everyday religion. The APR did not claim that the true locus of religion was to be found in withdrawal, but rather argued that the process of stepping away for reflection allowed for a remaking of religious subjects thereafter capable of engaging with the everyday in richer and more fruitful ways. Through the practice of retreat, the everyday is not so much devalued as revalued.

The APR was also concerned with place. The comparative quiet of the 'outskirts' of towns and cities where the ideal retreat house would be located sustained an environment conducive to meditation and reflection, even as these houses depended upon urban populations for the necessary volumes of support. The quiet of retreat confronted what was deemed damaging and unhealthy economic activity. *The Vision* noted that 'our so-called civilization gets more and more complicated, more and more noisy. It is like one of those mills where the noise of the looms makes it impossible for the workers to hear each other speak'.[28] The modern world thrums with the machinery of an industrial age, drowning out the voices of those closest to us, marring human bonds and ultimately harming humankind's relationship with God. In quiet, one is alone with God and thereby closest to oneself. The city, however, imposes limits upon human flourishing. By virtue of its location, the urban parish church was unable to minister to such needs. Eliot's lunchtime visits to Christopher Wren's London monuments – the 'Inexplicable splendour of Ionian white and gold' of *The Waste Land* (p. 64) – exacerbated the spiritual yearning he experienced in his years at Lloyds Bank. These churches proved unable to deliver on what they promised. The retreat movement came into being in response. The focus was never only leaving the home, setting aside the everyday and disregarding specific experiences of marginalisation; as a lay practice, retreat was envisaged as a-going-away-and-a-coming-back.

The Sound of Retreat: Silencing the Catholic Worker

The quiet of the APR retreat house was not a by-product of their respective locations. The APR understood their retreats as Ignatian in character. As with the earliest Anglican retreats, they looked to the *Spiritual Exercises* as a guide. A typical APR retreat was undertaken at a dedicated retreat house and included communal church services and several short addresses from the director designed to inspire reflection (Figure 4.1). Aside from the addresses, practical announcements and liturgies, retreats were conducted in silence.

MODERNISM AND RELIGION

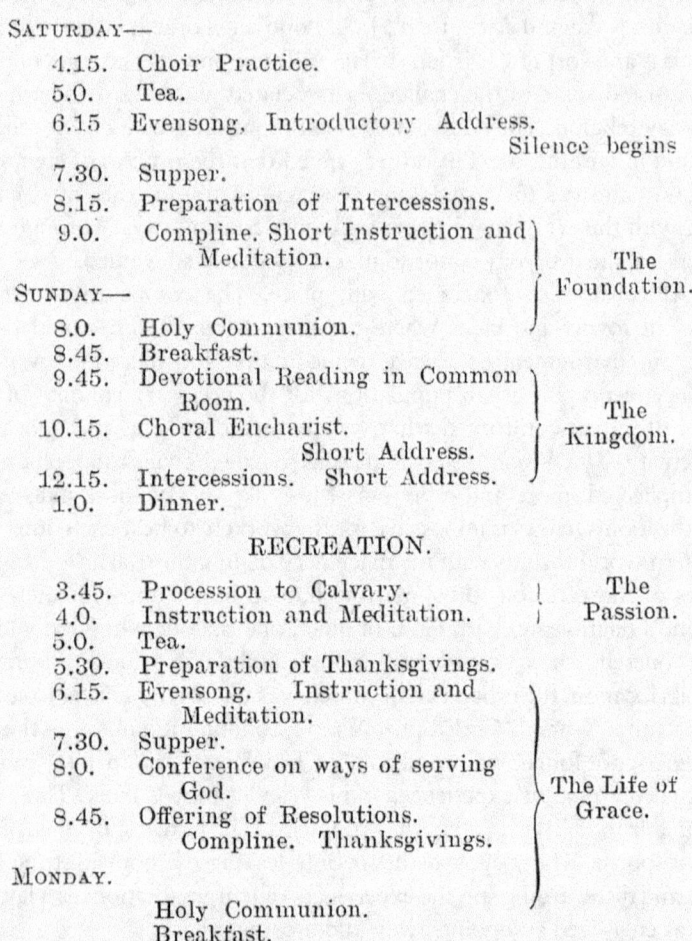

Figure 4.1 A Suggested Timetable for a Weekend Retreat for Beginners. Reproduced from Alan H. Simpson, *Short Retreats for Beginners: A Handbook for Conductors* (London: Association for Promoting Retreats, 1931), p. 51. Digital image courtesy of United Lutheran Seminary, Gettysburg and Philadelphia.

Silence was also a feature of Catholic Worker retreats from 1940 onwards. The Catholic Worker movement, founded in 1933 by Day and another layperson Peter Maurin, is known for its newspaper and charitable works, particularly the houses of hospitality that aided the poor during the Great Depression. The organisation practised – and continues to practise – 'a communitarian Christianity, which stresses the necessity to live in community as Jesus did and the importance of individual action (personalism) to achieve social justice; pacifism and nonviolence; and voluntary poverty, which stems from a de-emphasis on material possessions'.[29] Initially, Maurin delivered a 'program' of 'little lectures' on issues such as 'poverty and community' twice a day to Workers.[30] The arrangement led Day to describe the Catholic Worker's way of life rather 'smugly' as 'living a retreat'.[31] Day's understanding of retreat dramatically shifted when she heard through Maisie Ward, of the British Catholic publisher Sheed & Ward then establishing a New York office, about a silent retreat modelled on St Ignatius's *Spiritual Exercises*.[32] The priest who delivered Ward's retreat had been inspired by a Jesuit priest, Onesimus Lacouture.[33] The Catholic Worker went on to establish a close relationship with two of Lacouture's disciples, Fr Pacifique Roy and Fr John Hugo, and Day attended retreats in the Lacouture tradition in 1940 and 1941.[34]

Both the early retreats Day attended and those she incorporated into the Catholic Worker followed the pattern laid down by Lacouture. His retreats were ten days in length and represented a creative adaption of the *Spiritual Exercises* organised into three sections, though he rarely went beyond the first on detachment and purification.[35] Lacouture's conferences focused on overcoming natural in favour of supernatural motives. Retreatants were also exposed to spiritual exercises that they could practice in silence to effect self-transformation.[36] Later in the sequence, Lacouture expounded his 'doctrine of samples': the way in which the natural world provided limited glimpses of the supernatural. The fact that the later themes received less attention, however, brought Lacouture under theological suspicion. He was accused of denying the goodness of creation and ultimately forbidden by his superiors from offering further retreats.[37] The ascetic overtones of Lacouture contrast with the APR's understanding of silence. One article in *The Vision* assured readers that in silence a retreatant may 'actually hear the voice of God' as if silence itself were filled with divine presence.[38] Elsewhere in the APR literature, the emphasis fell on the restorative powers of silence as contrasted with the overwhelming noise of modern life. The Catholic Worker, by comparison, was austere and purgative; silence is at once the location for, and the medium of, the spiritual work with which a retreat is charged.

Given some of the differences in their design, the setting for Catholic Worker retreats was also somewhat different to the APR's suburban retreat houses. The following description of St Anthony's Village appears in Day's retreat notebook for 1942.[39] It served as the locale of one of the earliest Ignatian-style retreats she made. The venue was:

> an hour's ride by bus northeast of Pittsburgh. You get off the bus and walk a mile or so uphill – a long climb on a hot day. The Village is one of children, and nuns, and in the summer a few visiting priests and forty or so retreatants. It is here members of the C[atholic] W[orker] groups also had their retreat this summer. There are 10 acres of grounds, a salad and herb garden a little orchard – and many weeping willow trees. They are the kind of trees neither goats nor children can hurt. Down one side of the grounds there is even a hedge of these trees.[40]

Reaching the venue required an hour's bus ride into the farmland surrounding Pittsburgh and then a mile hike 'uphill'. St Anthony's Village was by no means as accessible as an APR retreat house. It was nevertheless idyllic thanks to the '10 acres of grounds, a salad and herb garden a little orchard – and many weeping willow trees'. Day's retreat lived in the quiet of the natural world; 'it is so beautiful, so peaceful here', she wrote of another retreat house, 'far from noise and traffic and the world'.[41] In her autobiography, Day outlined the first and largely unsatisfying retreat she ever made in an urban convent, which offered no outside space for reflection and was 'crushed in by the stone walls all about'.[42] Ultimately, she was left feeling hemmed in and claustrophobic, keen for it all to end. The shift from an urban to a rural location was thus foundational for Day's later successful retreat practice. The more challenging setting, the greater length and the nature of the content meant that Catholic Worker retreats exerted far greater demands upon retreatants than APR offerings. While they incorporated laypeople including Day herself, Catholic Worker retreats were aimed at Workers and thus assumed a level of commitment that the APR could not expect among weekend retreatants.

There were nevertheless continuities between the two retreats. For the APR, retreatants dedicated an extended period to religious observation. Ideally, the confrontation with silence triggered a reordering of priorities, instilled a new sense of conviction and enabled retreatants to return to everyday matters with a new outlook. One contributor to *The Vision* noted: 'few people' go on retreat 'without a mysterious sensation *of having been led to an occasion of choosing*; of having been tested; of having received a challenge to dedicate or withhold, to draw nearer or go back'.[43] Transformation was central to the Catholic Worker retreat too. The spiritual exercises practised at St Anthony's Village gave retreatants a way of approaching the secular world from a distinctly Catholic outlook. The dedication and singularity of purpose enshrined in the Catholic Worker retreat was so attractive that in 1948 Day endeavoured to withdraw from social justice work to live a life purely of retreat. Having completed what amounted to a one-year sabbatical, she recognised a need for both aspects of the Catholic Worker's mission. She thereafter sought to integrate the practical action of social justice work and the spiritual action of retreat.[44] Like its APR counterpart, the Catholic Worker retreat was defined by rhythms of withdrawal and return.

Religious Reflections: Themes of Retreat
Sacred Ground: The Place of Retreat

The APR understood its work as a departure from the typical methods employed by the Church of England.[45] In early numbers of *The Vision*, Canon Alan H. Simpson, the founding editor, opposed the APR to the established bureaucratic competence of the Anglican Church. He argued that it was 'in such things as stillness and withdrawal that our confidence must rest, precisely because they are the clear opposite of the ordinary world notions of efficiency'.[46] He added that the 'talk of Committees produces minutes and resolutions; the silence of retreats produces consecrated lives'.[47] The rhythms of withdrawal and return offered an alternative model for responding to the crisis of decreasing church attendance. Those who had fallen away, or who were at risk of falling away, were invited to rediscover their faith in withdrawal; setting aside paperwork and initiatives, the APR facilitated these personal journeys and offered a new way of living a Christian life. Simpson explained:

> God is realized most directly in seclusion and quiet [. . .] Looking back upon the old days it seems, indeed, strange to many of us now that we should have come to rely so exclusively as we did upon organisations, clubs, missions, – upon everything in short that is not quiet – for the deepening and extending of our Christian faith and life.[48]

The crisis was to be addressed not by imitating the administrative state's bureaucratic procedures, but rather through the expansion of Christian identity. New forms of Christian life required a greater time commitment; retreat served as an additional mode of worship over and above weekly or semi-regular church attendance. It also demanded greater attention. Christian identity might well be marked by the practices to which one adheres (christenings, marriages and funerals; Easter and Christmas), but such a designation was bestowed by virtue of geographical location or family background. In retreat, religion played a role in the self-conception of individuals. In Eliot's parlance, retreat raised Christianity above unconscious levels, making it a subject of reflection and a source of action.

The expansion of retreat required different forms of space. The rural parish church was a site of special significance for the Church of England. In his reflections on rural life, John Middleton Murry argued that the high regard in which rural populations held their local church had little to do with religion. The parish church had afforded a rural community the opportunity to engage with a man of a certain social status and breadth of education; it was the relative cultural sophistication afforded the minister by virtue of his background, Murry contended, that endeared the parish to its church. The new prominence of theological schools in the formation of clergy had diminished the Church of England's reputation among rural communities.[49] Retreat was an attempt to engage on a different level with would-be congregants, not quite in terms of Murry's country parson, but at a far remove from what he considered divisive theological intensity. Through their retreat houses, the APR made available new forms of space outside, or at least as a supplement to, the parish church.

The Catholic Worker, too, valued rural sites. In a diary entry for 1 August 1948, Day expressed a deep affection for the Catholic Worker's Maryfarm at Newburgh, New York State. Day exclaimed:

> Let us hope that Maryfarm at Newburgh will give a taste for the simplicity of life on the land and the courage to face it, and that other Maryfarms throughout the country will be performing the same function. A place to make retreats, to learn to meditate, to think in the heart, 'to be quiet and see that I am God', a place to learn to work, and a place to go from, as apostles, and make a life for the family.[50]

For the Catholic Worker, 'the simplicity of life on the land' contrasted with the competing interests, complex challenges and range of stimuli of urban life. Maryfarm was on the one hand, a 'place to make retreats, to learn to meditate' and on the other a 'place to learn to work'. Retreatants contributed farm labour. Catholic Worker farms planted and harvested their own vegetables, which they in turn brought to the communal table. Manual labour cleansed. It offered respite from both the intellectual labour a journalist such as Day undertook in the city and the intensity of the spiritual exercises practised on retreat. Day wrote:

> In the country the material and the spiritual have their proper relationship. There one can wholeheartedly say that the material is good; it is good to enjoy the material things of this world; that one can see the world and God Who made it, and not be a materialist and separate from Him.[51]

Farm labour, for Day, was a mechanism that prevented one from feeling 'separate from' God.

The APR, by contrast, presented retreat as a form of leisure. A striking feature of *The Vision* under the editorship of Miles Sergeant from the mid-1930s until the outbreak of the war was that the journal carried advertisements for

Figure 4.2 *The Chapel, The House of Mercy, Horbury, Yorkshire*. Reproduced from *The Vision*, 72 (October 1937), p. 8. Digital image courtesy of the author.

specific retreat houses, involving photographs and a short description of the house. Accompanying a photo depicting the chapel at the House of Mercy, Horbury, Yorkshire [Figure 4.2], for instance, the text explained that the house 'stands in a very large and beautiful garden' and noted that 'Horbury is only three miles from Wakefield, and buses run frequently, so it is easy of access'.[52] The weekend retreats were 'very popular' in the summer and, the copy advised, 'people write to book their rooms months beforehand'.[53] The House of Mercy was, in the world of the APR at least, a must-visit location. Another contributor asked, 'are we so poor that we can afford a holiday but *not* a Retreat?', and the advertisements urged prospective visitors to combine the two.[54] Twenty years into the movement, *The Vision* had established a marketplace for retreat providers.

The retreat house system parallels work in heritage preservation. *The Vision*, for instance, published a report of a retreat at Leiston Abbey, Suffolk (a site now stewarded by English Heritage) [Figure 4.3]. The report recounted in detail the effect of the setting on the retreat:

> The ruins of S. Mary's Abbey made a perfect setting for the Retreat held there the first week in September. The ideal those master-builders of old sought to express in perfect form and the vision which inspired their work both remain and are still for us, although the fabric is broken, the delicate traceries gone and windows and arches stand open to the

MODERNISM AND RELIGION

Figure 4.3 *Leiston Abbey Ruins*, Suffolk, England, 2009, photograph, 43.2 × 28.8 cm. Digital image courtesy of geogphotos/ Alamy Stock Photo.

sky [. . .] The spirits of those who had worshipped in that old building with its thatched roof in days long gone seemed very near and made an atmosphere beyond description. As we knelt in expectant silence awaiting the Message we had brought thither to hear we felt that truly we were upon holy ground. The loveliness of our surroundings, the perfect weather, the brilliant sunshine and moon-lit evening, the deep sense of peace and the silence broken only by robins and martins all helped us to realize more fully the joy of life which was the subject of the conductor's first address.[55]

Far from the purgative silence of a Catholic Worker retreat, the partially broken quiet is filled with delight in nature and a connection with historical religious worship. The description of the service is responsive to aspects of romantic literature; it celebrates the fullness of the natural world. The potential rival source of insight is carefully incorporated into the Mass. The 'Message we had brought thither to hear', the celebration of the Mass, is enlivened by the presence of nature – 'the loveliness of our surroundings, the perfect weather, the brilliant sunshine and moon-lit evening, the deep sense of peace and the silence broken only by robins and martins' – which calls to mind, perhaps, God's creative power. The service becomes a thanksgiving for the 'joy of life'. The ruins also invoke past worshippers. The 'spirits of those who had worshipped in that old building' seemed 'very near'. While present-day churches may be emptying, the modern faithful reassure themselves by repopulating, via acts of memory and imagination, these modern scenes with historical figures. For Anglo-Catholics, it was particularly exciting to worship in an abbey ruined during the Reformation. The service re-enacted a recusant drama, putting participants in touch with the religious history from which denominational factionalism had cut them off.

As shown by practices such as pilgrimage, tourism and religion are interchangeable.[56] The retreat represented a departure from promulgating religious content and towards the sanctioning of space for human-divine contact, or what William Inge, Dean of St Paul's, called the development of 'God-consciousness' that many now considered 'a normal part of the healthy inner life'.[57] Challenging Lewis's claim that, for modernists, churches were museums recording forms of experience rapidly facing extinction, the retreat movement deployed the museum or the heritage sector to invigorate religious life.[58] The fruits of such thinking are evident in Eliot's meditation on Little Gidding: 'You are here to kneel | Where prayer has been valid' (p. 202). The historical precedent – the sense of the site having been validated by past worshippers – authorises prayer for a broader range of people than usual during a time of national emergency. Looking beyond the specific objects of Christian worship, prayer brings national history into focus. Eliot was an observant Anglo-Catholic, but 'Little Gidding' does not ask readers to view an impending wartime disaster through a doctrinal lens. Instead, Anglo-Catholic concerns provide a language that enables the scale of the loss to be broached.

Healing Silence: Restorative Retreats

Retreat was often greeted with a mixture of excitement and suspicion. Durtal, the protagonist of J. K. Huysmans's novel *En Route*, receives advice from a Roman Catholic priest while preparing to make a retreat at a monastery. The priest advises:

> Thank Him in getting rid of your nature as soon as possible, and leaving the house of your conscience empty for Him. The more you die to yourself the better will He live in you. Prayer is the most powerful ascetic means by which you can renounce yourself, empty yourself and render yourself humble in this matter; pray therefore without ceasing at La Trappe.[59]

Durtal is fascinated by the possibilities of spiritual discipline; yet, for him, even anticipating the physical austerities waiting at the monastery is trying. The morning after his conversation with the priest, Durtal 'awoke ill' such that 'furious neuralgia bored his temples like a gimlet'.[60] The novel neither commends his commitment nor condemns his weakness; it does, however, attend to the convergence of illness and asceticism in Durtal's journey towards conversion. At one point during his retreat, Durtal trips over several monks spread out on the floor. He describes the scene:

> On the ground human forms were lying, in the attitudes of combatants, mowed down by grape shot, some flat on their faces, others on their knees, some leaning their hands on the ground as if stricken from behind, others extended with their fingers clenched on their breast, others again holding their heads or stretching out their arms.[61]

Are these contorted figures – struck down with their faith, dead to the world – demonstrating the extent of their devotion? Or are they experiencing a neuralgic or catatonic fit? For Huysmans, nervous illness and extreme devotion were products of 'a materialistic age that offers no vent to the spiritual aspirations of the people'.[62] Attracted by both piety and scepticism, Huysmans incorporated suspicion of ascetic practice into his conversion narrative.

Asceticism was also a central feature of the Catholic Worker retreat. Farm labour required a physical austerity that brought the retreatant closer to God. Day's retreat made use, too, of ascetic spiritual exercises that were understood as not so much 'penance' as 'a means of perfecting the soul'.[63] These exercises assumed a rigid distinction between natural and supernatural motives or between acts undertaken from one's own desire and from love of God. In her retreat notebooks, Day looked askance at the 'pagan mentality' of those driven by 'natural motives'.[64] 'To enjoy things of this world and try to avoid mortal sin', she explained, is 'as impossible as to jump' from the Empire State Building and 'expect to stop before we get hurt'.[65] Human concerns, needs and wants at best obscure God's will and at worst conspire against it. They are not a point of departure for the religious life, but rather obstacles to its fulfilment. To overcome these limitations, Day recommended what her teacher Hugo called 'pruning'.[66] The work ensured that the 'part of the soul that delights in the world' was 'stifled' or 'eradicated'.[67] The intellect and the affect were thereby reorientated towards the supernatural.

For Day, asceticism was about more than merely personal holiness. 'Of course I will not save my soul alone', she wrote, 'wherever we are we are with people. We drag them down, or pull them up. Or we get dragged down or pulled up'.[68] Living in a community and working in challenging circumstances, Workers needed to attend to their own religious commitments. Losing one's way affected the mission of the whole community. 'We can do nothing today without saints, big ones and little ones', Day observed, and the ascetic work of retreat made and sustained such saints.[69] The importance Day conferred upon action, community and the dignity of persons came to her through her co-founder Maurin's mediation of Emmanuel Mounier's personalism.[70] Transformed by asceticism, the Catholic Worker community worked for the social good in ways that recall H.D.'s *Helen in Egypt*. Under the influence of personalism, H.D.'s eponymous hero hoped that an ascetic act might terminate the cycle of war. Day herself was a pacifist and her newspaper famously carried, in the run up to the first anniversary of the events of December 1941, a headline that read 'Forget Pearl Harbor'.[71] The emergence of Day's pacifism and her commitment to retreat coalesced in the early 1940s; asceticism confirmed her in her principled stance, even as her position proved divisive within the Catholic community.[72]

The Vision published a few accounts of asceticism. In an article from 1928, the author described the 'spiritual training' necessary to 'advance', linking retreat 'with prayer and mortification and with the response of the soul to the ordinary operations of grace'.[73] An earlier paper from 1925 addressed the idea of fasting. The author claimed fasting:

> introduces into the spiritual combat a plain and simple point at which the will can begin to be effective, and from which its energy can be extended to more subtle and difficult spheres [. . .] The man who can observe a bodily discipline in small matters of abstention gains a power of mastery that can be used in far more important conflicts.[74]

Durtal had found what the article calls 'bodily discipline' disconcerting. Alongside terms such as 'combat', 'mastery' and 'conflicts', the phrase has a militaristic ring. Asceticism reveals a form of spiritual heroism where practitioners purify themselves for God, using mortifications to recreate Christ's passion. Asceticism becomes, what Michel Foucault calls, 'a way of subjugating the subject to the law'.[75] One of the question marks that hangs over such an approach is, how do manufactured austerities relate to suffering brought on individuals or communities involuntarily? For her part, Day reflected at length on 'the gulf between her more or less voluntary, ascetic acceptance of suffering as a choice and that of the truly destitute'.[76]

What is striking about the APR's relationship with asceticism, however, is just how little *The Vision* had to say on the topic. The first number of the journal appeared in 1920 and it took five years for the magazine to publish an article on the asceticism so central to Day's retreat. For the APR, the preferred register was that of joy rather than austerity. 'Is not the silence of a Retreat very trying?', posed the journal in its frequently asked questions section; 'No', it answered, 'that is only true of the first hour or so. After that most people find it wonderfully helpful and refreshing'.[77] Another correspondent explained that 'the joy of the silence' was visible on the faces of those returning from retreat.[78] In a retreat for children at St Winnifred's Home for Girls, Wolverhampton, a published report observed 'a complete absence of strain in any direction, naturalness and simplicity of spiritual response, and a gladness overflowing through all'.[79] Likewise, in a retreat for men and young adults, 'there was no need of a *rule* of silence', the report contended; we 'craved for silence, and in our common experience we understood each other with that deeper understanding which has no need of words'.[80] Elsewhere, *The Vision* noted that retreat was 'for renewal as well as for rest'; and rest and renewal were linked to 'stillness' in which 'the Vision of God is awakened or restored, and the rest is found in a new power of service'.[81] The decision to marginalise asceticism was no doubt propagandistic. The new movement required participants and steered clear of divisive material, perhaps with the understanding that asceticism might be broached later. Yet, the distance between the APR and the Catholic Worker is so great as to suggest deeper motivations. Huysmans's sympathetic attitude towards spiritual seeking led him to treat both extreme religious devotion and hysteria as symptoms of the spiritual condition of the age, whereas elsewhere asceticism (the practice of or desire for) was cited by unsympathetic critics influenced by Charcot as evidence of the underlying pathology of religious devotion. Day shrugged off the characteristically modern critique of the dangers of asceticism, while the APR's pitch acknowledged it as decisive. The language of *The Vision* brushed over the associations of asceticism, mysticism and spiritual experience with disease and sought instead to connect retreat with health and wellness.

The APR's interest in spiritual health set the tone for Underhill's retreat preaching. In addition to authoring numerous well-respected studies of mysticism and establishing herself as a spiritual director, Underhill was also an in-demand retreat leader. One of her retreat addresses, delivered at Pleshey, Essex, in 1932, opened with the observation that some 'are rather troubled about the amount of space the healing of the sick takes in the Gospels'.[82] The biblical texts then became a model for understanding the modern self. Underhill described the troubled soul:

> That is our model for dealing with the results of weakness and sin. The patient is really a moral invalid, the type of all nerve-ridden impotent souls defeated by circumstances and worn by inner conflicts, restored to his full stature by the healing power of God and his own act of faith in that healing power.[83]

In Underhill, the 'patient' or 'moral invalid' stands in stark contrast to the heroic ascetic of Day's retreat. Retreat, for Underhill, offered respite to 'nerve-ridden impotent souls defeated by circumstances and worn by inner conflicts'. In the quiet of retreat, one identified such conflicts, backed away from them and turned to God for help. While Day in her autobiography emphasised the 'choice' a retreatant made to act from supernatural motives, Underhill focused on an 'act of faith' in God's healing power.[84]

Unproductive Value: Gratuitousness of Retreat

The skilful use of silence helped make retreat a mass movement. While Anglo-Catholicism played a prominent role in the Church of England in the first half of the twentieth century, its influence was divisive.[85] Two attempts to revise the *Book of Common Prayer* to incorporate Anglo-Catholic themes were defeated in parliament in the late 1920s, following a national campaign taken up by church groups and MPs that made the case for the Protestant character of the Church of England and its worship.[86] Silence, by contrast, ministered to Anglican modernists such as Inge, who had interests in spirituality and mysticism, and the Anglo-Catholics of the SSM alike. A preached retreat would have struggled to retain such a broad appeal. 'It is true that the Retreat movement of recent years was revived by the Catholic section of the Church', *The Vision* itself acknowledged, 'but it would be entirely wrong to say that it is in any way restricted in these days; for every part of the Church is offering Retreat to its members in an almost startling and indeed most encouraging manner'.[87]

Silence was not, however, accepted unanimously. *The Vision* carried several pieces questioning whether the emphasis was appropriate for a movement that included religious beginners from all classes and backgrounds: 'we make a very grave mistake if we identify too closely the ordinary retreat with the Ignatian form', Underhill counselled.[88] 'It is time we freed ourselves from this slavery to what is considered the "correct thing" in the matter of silence', added another.[89] The alternative was to turn the retreat into a conference to create a forum for adult religious instruction. The challenge posed to national health by the decline of organised religion was a product of poor religious education. Adult catechesis could be offered during retreats to impart some religious content to the masses, filling up otherwise empty vessels.

Catholic Worker retreats moved in the opposite direction. Having started with a conference model under the influence of Maurin, Day turned to Ignatian practice following her discovery of Lacouture. The embrace of silent retreat led some, both inside and outside the organisation, to complain that the Catholic Worker was 'retreating from the world, living in ivory towers'.[90] As with the letter writers above, these critical voices considered silence inappropriate or even self-indulgent; it might be fine for monks and nuns, but not for spiritual beginners or social activists.

While there are numerous historical examples of groups and individuals observing silence for religious reasons, the practice had been limited to extraordinary figures, vowed religious or those in clerical orders. The APR and the Catholic Worker, by contrast, promoted silence among the laity. To some, silent retreat seemed at best a wasted opportunity to evangelise and at worst actively harmful. The time would have been far more usefully and productively spent, so the argument went, on basic instruction or much-needed social action. A conference is educational and thus quantifiable. Social action can make a quantitative and qualitative difference. A retreat, by contrast, is gratuitous. Nothing is accomplished. Reflecting on contemporary attitudes, Day supposed that the 'world will leave us alone, saying – after all they are not doing anything. Just a bunch of smug fools praying'.[91] For Jones, as a modernist artist and poet, the pejorative characterisation of gratuitous activity as 'not doing anything' revealed the blinkered nature of the contemporary outlook. Jones defined art, creativity and sign-making with reference to their gratuitous, non-purposeful character that, for him, served as an analogy for God's creative work. Art was not an optional add-on to human experience or the preserve of a few gifted elites; it defined human beings made in the image of their creator. While, for Jones, the Eucharistic rite played a special role in celebrating human nature, the APR made a similar claim for retreat. In their unnecessary, even wasteful, guises, art and retreat alike are an affront to the rationalised, utilitarian efficiency of modernity.

The Vision repeatedly countered critics of the Ignatian character of retreat. J. Wareham maintained:

> To make a little conference part of a retreat is to make that retreat something different from what a retreat really is. It is not that it would be something entirely useless, but that it would not be a retreat. A retreat is a time alone with God, and it is for such times that our souls are athirst.[92]

Silence served a purpose, albeit a purposeless one. The APR and its members hoped that retreat would have a range of effects on society. Yet, transformation was only possible if the space for an encounter between human and divine was maintained; it must not be replaced with forms of activity more easily measured and described. Against both religious and social objections, retreats made the development of an unquantifiable relationship with God the centrepiece of the activity, democratising what had typically been available to those eligible for inclusion in Eliot's Community of Christians. Reflecting the tensions outlined in the present study between 'spilt mysticism' and 'wavering orthodoxy', the mass retreat movement cultivated the interior life while retaining contact with institutional religion.

Retreat In and Out of the World

An editorial in an early number of *The Vision*, published in 1921, observed 'Our greatest present need is quiet; not because we want a religion of sheer mysticism, but because we want a real motive of practical action'.[93] The opposition between 'sheer mysticism' and 'practical action' assumes a disconnect between the mystic and the world that was pervasive at the turn of the twentieth century and remains influential today. In *The Star of Redemption*, for instance, Franz Rosenzweig caricatured the mystic as one whose 'soul opens for God, but because it opens only for God, it is invisible to all the world and shut off from it'.⁹⁴ Mysticism becomes 'a cloak of invisibility' to rival criticisms of Day's retreats as so many 'ivory towers'. The present study, by contrast, has argued that 'sheer mysticism' was also connected to 'practical action'. While retreat may appear to be 'a bunch of smug fools praying', its formative influence facilitated types of political engagement not otherwise captured by the paradigms of either the left or the right.

Divine Worship and National Unity in the APR

While the present chapter has emphasised the experimental features of retreat, the practice remained connected to established patterns of worship. 'The Retreat opens the way back into the life of grace for thousands who have drifted from it', one contributor to *The Vision* explained, 'but it is not merely to find a self-contained religion of Retreat and little or nothing else'; instead, it 'restores or awakens an appreciation of all the normal ways of the Church's ministry to souls'.⁹⁵ The APR recognised that church attendance had declined, but the aim was never to develop an Anglican-lite version of Christian worship. Instead, the energy and enthusiasm of retreatants helped make 'the normal ways of the Church's ministry to souls' seem viable to other members or would-be members of a given parish.

The 'normal ways' were incorporated into the experimental form. During a weekend retreat, retreatants heard addresses from the retreat director, engaged in silent reflection and participated in communal acts of worship. Silence thus acted as preparation for evensong and Holy Communion. These services, for which the retreatant extensively prepared, took on greater significance. A contemporary report on an Easter retreat emphasised the connection between innovative and traditional modes of worship:

> First, the great uplifting act of Eucharistic worship, with all the adornment possible by way of music and ceremonial. In the conditions of Retreat it seemed very specially to lift up all present into the joy of those who ever worship before the throne of God. And then the pilgrimage made to the Calvary, singing the Litany of the Sacred Passion. This came as a prelude to meditating in the stillness of the Chapel on the meaning of the Cross, and was a real help to an understanding of its message, deeper than could have been brought by any mere words of explanation.⁹⁶

'Eucharistic worship, with all the adornment' was 'very special' in the context of retreat, while silence and stillness became a 'real help to an understanding' of the wider Maundy Thursday liturgy. In Anglo-Catholic liturgical and theological thought, as Barry Spurr explains, 'the Incarnate Lord Himself is truly contained in, with and under the elements of bread and wine by virtue of the priest's consecration of those elements at the Mass, which are then received by the communicant'.[97] The rite enables the retreatant to see, touch and consume God. During the early years of the retreat movement, Anglo-Catholicism itself expanded, bringing in new members who might have had little previous exposure to the real presence.[98] For some, the silence of retreat simply allowed for a better understanding of what Jones described as 'the amazing nature of what our theology proposes'.[99]

The confrontation with Anglo-Catholic worship alongside the encounter with God in silence transformed retreatants. The change was palpable. One contemporary commentator observed that a group of retreatants return 'as a body into its parish bringing with it the light of a new experience, and that explosive force of witness which can only come from people who have together shared a vision'.[100] Their 'enthusiasm' acted like leaven among regular congregations, inspiring others to make a retreat themselves and enriching the whole community's religious life. Parochial retreats, which were made by a few members of a given parish at the same time, were popular among the clerical subscribers to *The Vision*. Returning retreatants functioned like the religious orders in Eliot's *The Idea of a Christian Society*, demonstrating what faith could be at its higher levels and inspiring others to make ever greater commitments.

For some commentators, faith commitments overflowed into a life of service. One commentator observed that 'worship is not, as is so commonly supposed, a mere pinnacle of devotion', but rather 'a principle of action'.[101] Underhill, in an address to the annual conference of the APR, insisted that 'spiritual life in its fullness must move to and fro between adoration and action: direct and loving intercourse with God must inspire its service of men'.[102] Transformed retreatants, it was to be hoped, would go out into the community in service. While Anglo-Catholicism has often been portrayed as fussily concerned with ritualistic niceties, the social commitments of its practitioners, particularly in working class areas of England, have increasingly been documented.[103] The APR, however, did not systematically develop the connection between retreat and action. These observations printed in *The Vision* must be taken as gestures in the direction that certain APR members would have liked to take retreat.

A far more prominent concern in the APR was the sense that the Church of England was in trouble and that the retreat movement could help. While it could not address 'reasoned unbelief', retreat reached out to those whose lives were characterised by 'Godlessness' or 'life without God'.[104] Engaging the godless was not simply a case of assisting individuals or shoring up numbers in the pews. In an article from 1926, a commentator observed that the 'decay' of religion would result in the loss 'from national life' of 'the main stream of unifying influence' and went on to argue that the APR was doing God's work 'by bringing the nation to regain and strengthen definite Christian religion as the only possible unifying bond of its life'.[105] The unifying character of a national religion is a theme familiar from Eliot's writings. In addressing godlessness, retreat was not only helping to 'strengthen definite Christian religion', but also restoring the unity of a national culture. Retreat might appear to be a private undertaking. It is a long way, for instance, from the Church of England mobilising a political campaign against a pressing social issue such as the liberalisation of divorce laws as it did in 1919 and was ultimately unable to do in 1937.[106] Yet, the shift is best understood not as a move from public to private, but as a re-conception of the way in which religion related to public discourse.

The Catholic Worker's Spiritual Action

While the APR's retreat was treated with suspicion by church authorities at its outset, the practice had, by the later 1930s, become part of the Anglican establishment. In 1935, contributors to *The Vision* complained that 'there is not the same enthusiasm for bringing others into retreat that there used to be in those who had just made a retreat' because retreat had become merely 'part of the normal Christian life'.[107] In 1937, the movement put itself at the service of an initiative framed by Cosmo Lang, the Archbishop of Canterbury, entitled the 'Recall to Religion', which was 'a nationwide evangelistic campaign' that was 'inaugurated to coincide with the coronation' of George VI.[108] For Day, however, the retreat movement and, in her case, American national goals were resolutely opposed. Poverty and pacifism served to distinguish the Catholic Worker from other 'Church-sanctioned avenues of progressive engagement' familiar from 1930s American Catholicism insofar as they challenged key facets of American life, namely consumer consumption and military commitment, at a time when Catholicism was attempting an accommodation with mainstream American life.[109]

The challenge posed by retreat arose from the transformation it effected among its practitioners. Day described retreat as 'a place of *action*' that is 'spiritual action'. Day's 'spiritual action' is comparable to the 'taking of cities', 'revolution' and the 'Corporal Works of Mercy'.[110] 'Spiritual action' was the third term in a tripartite division of work handed down by Lacouture and his students: manual, intellectual and spiritual.[111] The distance between manual and intellectual work is captured in the difference between farm labour and writing for the *Catholic Worker* newspaper; the location of retreat and its role in the life of Day and Maurin's organisation ensured that those involved in the latter did not lose touch with the former. Spiritual work, by contrast, registers the change wrought by ascetic spiritual exercises, which endeavoured to stifle natural motives and to cultivate supernatural ones. Day explained the change in her retreat notes: 'If I wash dishes for love of God – supernaturalized. If I pray for nat[ural] motive[s] no good. How can I know? When love is active principle. A supernatural motive. Every activity can be made supernatural'.[112] The Catholic Worker diverges from the APR retreat here. For the APR, God was accessible, at hand, nearby. One only had to look carefully. Day dismissed such an idea. Natural motives always obscured God. Retreatants failing to commit to spiritual work inevitably attempted to pass off their own earthly desires as the promptings of God's will. One cannot find God, Day contended, without discernment and the systematic application of self-control. Retreat was where one developed these supernatural motives.

'Spiritual action' transformed the motives with which an agent undertook a given task. Washing the dishes and washing the dishes for God may appear indistinguishable from the outside, but below the surface the two are separated by a qualitative difference. Actions driven by supernatural motives are not performed because they fulfil the agent's own desires, respond to the requests of others or fulfil a practical purpose. They are undertaken with reference to God's will and through God's love. The poor are always in need of help. One might be moved to meet their needs from empathetic, ethical or even political imperatives. In the Catholic Worker's houses of hospitality, however, the poor were helped for the love of God. Spiritual action set Day's charity apart from the state-sponsored welfare activities of Franklin D. Roosevelt's New Deal, which the Catholic Worker characterised as too abstract in its approach and justification. It dehumanised, Day contended, those it set out to help. Denis de Rougemont's personalist insight that human relationships were the medium through which one both developed and acknowledged the dignity of personhood, both of oneself and of others, bears on Day's conception of retreat. The spiritual action made possible by retreat becomes the basis for a new form of community situated between the individualism of liberal society and the collectivism of state communism.

Looking beyond America alone, the Catholic Worker imagined a new way of being Catholic in a secular society. One important theological resource for mapping new forms of engagement was the neo-scholastic assertion that 'the natural order exhibits a rational structure that is intelligible to human reason without the aid of revelation'.[113] As Sarah Shortall observes, non-believers and Catholics alike could 'discern the same set of truths about the social order that were prescribed by natural law, even if they disagreed on the origin of that law'.[114] The philosopher Jacques Maritain worked with representatives of secular society on the Universal Declaration of Human Rights, which was accepted by the General Assembly of the United Nations in 1948. While Maritain himself approached rights from a wish to protect what he took to be the God-given dignity of humankind, other contributors worked on the same proposal within the very Enlightenment-based rights paradigm that Catholic theology opposed. Day, for her part, resisted the separation of the natural and supernatural through which Maritain justified his collaboration. For her, it was incumbent upon Catholics to act always and everywhere from supernatural promptings. Day offered a way of being fully and completely Catholic from inside out. The Catholic Worker was an organisation constructed from the tensions apparent in its name. Its most visible activities were associated with the 'Worker': its houses of hospitality, communal farms and voluntary poverty. Retreat nevertheless ensured that these activities, rather than becoming the work of just another civil society organisation, flowed from the Catholic in the Worker's nomenclature.

The Poetry of Retreat

The APR retreat addressed two distinct audiences. For committed Anglicans, retreat provided a means of deepening their existing faith, while for those living in a godless state it served as an invitation to make a change. The opportunities afforded by retreat reflected both contemporary interests in mysticism or spirituality and the traditional teachings of the Church of England. Retreat was not, however, an apologetic; 'reasoned unbelief' went unchallenged.[115] While theological suppositions underwrote the practice, neither speculative reason nor divine revelation were the most prominent forces behind retreat either. The thinking that informed the movement resembled Eliot's Christian sociology, which attended to the social, cultural and even emotional realities that the author deemed necessary to drive artistic, intellectual and political endeavours.

As a collection of social practices that reorientated its members, the retreat movement disappointed several liberal democratic expectations. It suggested alternative ways of living, resisting what Charles Taylor has called 'the buffered self' and 'the immanent frame'.[116] Secular societies sought to replace the supernatural dimension of human experience and, in so doing, taught individuals to see themselves outside of, or separate from, the world they inhabit. Retreatants at an APR or Catholic Worker retreat discovered that God could find a way into one's life once more, not only during the retreat itself but also in the return to everyday life that followed. Even if the APR proved unable to link the practice of retreat and the social commitments of Anglo-Catholicism in the manner of Day, both the APR and the Catholic Worker resisted aspects of the society in which they participated: the flattening out of signification and value, a single-minded focus on reason and utility, excessive individualism and the celebration of *Homo economicus*.

As the previous chapters have demonstrated, the modernist poetry of Jones, Eliot and H.D. not only resists a similar slate of terms, but also reaches for a religious register that is part mystic, part orthodox in nature. The forms of the long poems discussed in the present study are mechanical; their stylistic unevenness reveals creaking joints, which connect constituent parts of sequences written in different contexts, times and frames of mind. The resulting unevenness bears comparison to the hybrid form of retreat itself. The *Spiritual Exercises*, a sixteenth-century aid to reflection that helped a community of vowed religious elect particular vocations, shaped a practice that empowered lay people to meet the challenges posed by a newly secular society.[117] Retreat is more modern bricolage than time-honoured tradition. The repurposing of retreat accounts for the strain running through the contributions to *The Vision* that struggle to find value in yoking a rule of silence to a mass religious movement and informs Day's attempt to unite the apparently contradictory elements of the Catholic Worker's mission.

The poetry of retreat, if that label is to be applied to the work of Jones, Eliot and H.D., must be understood in counterintuitive terms. Far from dedicating itself to epiphany, the work of the poets to which the present study attends is driven by an awareness of the ruptures occasioned by the secular, whether that be described as Eliot's 'dissociation of sensibility', Jones's 'The Break' or Taylor's 'immanent frame', and the contradictions generated by the overlapping structures of the new and the old orders.[118]

Notes

1. T. S. Eliot to William Force Stead, 10 April 1928, in *Letters, 4: 1928–29*, ed. by Valerie Eliot and John Haffenden, pp. 127–28 (p. 128).
2. See Callison, 'Directing Modernist Spirituality', pp. 39–54.
3. Eagleton, p. 7.
4. Michel Foucault, *The Hermeneutics of the Subject: Lectures at the Collège de France 1981–1982*, ed. by Frédéric Gros, trans. by Graham Burchell (Basingstoke: Palgrave Macmillan, 2016), p. 317.
5. See Eliot, *After Strange Gods*, pp. 15–55.
6. Eliot, 'Clark Lectures', p. 653, p. 707.
7. Eliot, 'Clark Lectures', p. 632, p. 637.
8. Schuchard, pp. 165–66.
9. Schuchard, pp. 169–70.
10. Dorothy Day, 'All is Grace' [also titled: 'Spiritual Adventure'], The Dorothy Day Papers, The Dorothy Day – Catholic Worker Collection, Papers: Manuscripts, c. 1914–1975, D-3, Box 4, Folder 3, Special Collections and University Archives, Raynor Memorial Library, Marquette University.
11. Day, 'All is Grace'.
12. Spurr, pp. 152–53.
13. See Childs, *Mystic, Son and Lover*, pp. 152–85.
14. *The Vision: A Quarterly Magazine Issued by the Association for Promoting Retreats*; Day, 'All is Grace'; Dorothy Day, 'Retreat Notebooks', in Benjamin T. Peters, *Called to be Saints: John Hugo, The Catholic Worker, and a Theology of Radical Christianity* (Milwaukee, WI: Marquette University Press, 2016), pp. 259–582.
15. See William Inge, *Christian Mysticism: Considered in Eight Lectures Delivered before the University of Oxford* (London: Methuen, 1899); Eleanor C. Gregory, *An Introduction to Christian Mysticism* (London: Allenson, 1901); Rev. W. Major Scott, *Aspects of Christian Mysticism* (New York: Dutton, 1907); William Henry Dyson, *Studies in Christian Mysticism* (London: Clarke, 1913).
16. 'A Plea for Really Modern Thought', *The Vision*, 35 (August 1928), 1–5 (p. 5).
17. See Experientia Docet, 'To the Editor: The Rule of Silence', *The Vision*, 30 (May 1927), 15–17 (p. 17).
18. Experientia Docet, 'To the Editor', p. 17.

19. Experientia Docet, 'To the Editor', p. 17.
20. John Tyers, 'Ignatian and Silent: A Brief Survey of the Development of the Practice of Retreat in the Church of England, 1858–2008', *Theology*, 113 (2010), 267–75 (pp. 267–68).
21. Tyers, p. 268.
22. See J. Wareham, 'Retreats and the Centenary', *The Vision*, 53 (November 1933), 3–5 (pp. 3–4).
23. See Nigel Yates, *Anglican Ritualism in Victorian Britain, 1830–1910* (Oxford: Oxford University Press, 1999), pp. 70–150.
24. *The Official Year-Book of the Church of England, 1902* (London: Society for Promoting Christian Knowledge, 1902), p. 13. Quoted in Tyers, p. 269.
25. Tyers, p. 270.
26. 'Notes', *The Vision*, 3 (August 1920), 1–3 (p. 3).
27. J. A. Bouquet, 'Retreat and Vocation', *The Vision*, 31 (August 1927), 6–10 (p. 7).
28. Evelyn Underhill, 'The Need of Retreat', *The Vision*, 49 (January 1932), 3–7 (p. 4).
29. Nancy L. Roberts, *Dorothy Day and the* Catholic Worker (Albany: State University of New York Press, 1985), p. 7.
30. Dorothy Day, *The Long Loneliness: The Autobiography of Dorothy Day* (New York: Harper & Row, 1981), p. 245.
31. Day, *Long Loneliness*, p. 245.
32. Day, *Long Loneliness*, p. 245.
33. Day, *Long Loneliness*, p. 245.
34. Day, *Long Loneliness*, pp. 246–58. Sandra Yocum Mize, '"We Are Still Pacifists": Dorothy Day's Pacifism during World War II', in *Dorothy Day and the Catholic Worker Movement: Centenary Essays*, ed. by William J. Thorn and others (Wisconsin, WI: Marquette University Press, 2001), pp. 465–73 (p. 469). For the Lacouture tradition, see Peters, *Called to be Saints*; Jack Lee Downey, *The Bread of the Strong: Lacouturisme and the Folly of the Cross, 1910–1985* (New York: Fordham University Press, 2015).
35. Downey, p. 85.
36. Downey, p. 90.
37. Downey, p. 93.
38. 'Martha in Retreat', *The Vision*, 14 (May 1923), 1–4 (p. 2).
39. Day, 'Retreat Notebooks', 261.
40. Quoted in Peters, *Called to be Saints*, p. 53.
41. Dorothy Day, *On Pilgrimage* (Grand Rapids, MI: Eerdmans, 1999), p. 141.
42. Day, *Long Loneliness*, p. 243.
43. 'Retreat and the Claims of God', *The Vision*, 5 (February 1921), 4–7 (p. 5).
44. See Brigid O'Shea Merriman, *Searching for Christ: The Spirituality of Dorothy Day* (Notre Dame, IN: University of Notre Dame Press, 1994), p. 148.
45. An earlier version of the present section appears in Callison, 'Sacred Ground', pp. 375–88.
46. 'Stillness, Vision, Service', *The Vision*, 5 (April 1920), 14–17 (p. 15).
47. 'Retreat and Progress', *The Vision*, 7 (August 1921), 1–3 (p. 3).
48. 'Retreats for Children and Young People', *The Vision*, 10 (May 1922), 9–13 (p. 9).
49. John Middleton Murry, *Community Farm* (London: Nevill, 1952), pp. 238–39.

50. Day, *Pilgrimage*, p. 112.
51. Dorothy Day, *House of Hospitality* (London: Sheed & Ward, 1939), p. 159.
52. 'The House of Mercy, Horbury, Yorks.', *The Vision*, 72 (October 1937), 8–9 (p. 9).
53. 'The House of Mercy, Horbury, Yorks.', p. 9.
54. 'Holidays and Change of Air', *The Vision*, 27 (August 1926), 4–7 (p. 7).
55. 'A Retreat at S. Mary's Abbey, Leiston, Suffolk', *The Vision*, 8 (November 1921), 7–8 (pp. 7–8).
56. See Brooke Schedneck, 'Religious and Spiritual Retreats', in *The Routledge Handbook of Religious and Spiritual Tourism*, ed. by Daniel H. Olsen and Dallen J. Timothy (London: Routledge, 2022), pp. 247–61.
57. Inge, introduction to *Light, Life and Love*, p. lviii.
58. See Lewis, pp. 1–22.
59. J. K. Huysmans, *En Route*, trans. by C. Kegan Paul (London: Kegan Paul, Trench, Trübner, 1896), pp. 142–43.
60. Huysmans, p. 143.
61. Huysmans, p. 171.
62. Hanson, p. 115.
63. Downey, p. 91.
64. Day, 'Retreat Notebooks', p. 313.
65. Day, 'Retreat Notebooks', p. 313.
66. Day, 'Retreat Notebooks', p. 507; Downey, p. 90.
67. Day, 'Retreat Notebooks', p. 507; Downey, p. 90.
68. Day, 'All is Grace'.
69. Day, 'All is Grace'.
70. Roberts, pp. 7–8.
71. See Louis Lee Lock, 'Forget Pearl Harbor, or a South Pacific Charter', *Catholic Worker*, December 1942, 3 (p. 3).
72. See Yocum Mize, pp. 465–73.
73. 'The Need of the Study of Ascetic Theology', *The Vision*, 36 (November 1928), 9–12 (p. 9, p. 11).
74. 'Retreat and the Rules of Life', *The Vision*, 23 (November 1925), 1–4 (p. 3).
75. Foucault, p. 317.
76. Downey, p. 175.
77. 'Some Questions and their Answers', *The Vision*, 1 (January 1920), 6 (p. 6).
78. Gilbert Shaw, 'To the Editor: The Rule of Silence', *The Vision*, 31 (August 1927), 10–13 (p. 12).
79. 'Coleshill Park, Birmingham', *The Vision*, 9 (February 1922), 6–7 (pp. 6–7).
80. 'A Retreat for Men and Lads: S. George's, Cullercoats', *The Vision*, 9 (February 1922), 4–5 (p. 5).
81. 'Waiting upon God', *The Vision*, 15 (August 1923), 1–3 (p. 2); 'Stillness, Vision, Service', p. 14.
82. Evelyn Underhill, '*Light of Christ: Addresses Given at the House of Retreat, Pleshey, in May, 1932*', in '*Fruits of the Spirit*', '*Light of Christ, with a Memoir by Lucy Menzies*', '*Abba, Meditations based on the Lord's Prayer*' (London: Longmans Green, 1956), pp. 9–107 (p. 58).
83. Underhill, *Light of Christ*, pp. 60–61.

84. Day, *Long Loneliness*, p. 256.
85. See Spurr, pp. 93–97.
86. See Maiden, pp. 133–62.
87. 'Retreat without Tears', *The Vision*, 70 (April 1937), 15–17 (p. 15).
88. Underhill, 'The Need of Retreat', p. 5.
89. Experientia Docet, 'To the Editor', p. 17.
90. Day, *Long Loneliness*, p. 245.
91. Day, 'All is Grace'.
92. J. Wareham, 'What a Retreat Really Is', *The Vision*, 47 (July 1931), 3–6 (p. 6).
93. 'Retreat and Progress', p. 3.
94. Rosenzweig, p. 207.
95. 'Stillness, Vision, Service', p. 5.
96. 'S. Winifred's, Wolverhampton: A Rescue and Preventive Home for Girls up to Sixteen Years of Age', *The Vision*, 9 (February 1922), 5–6 (p. 6).
97. Spurr, p. 100.
98. See Spurr, pp. 64–110.
99. Jones to Hague, 28 May 1974.
100. 'Parochial Retreats', *The Vision*, 14 (May 1923), 11–13 (p. 12).
101. 'The Worship of Retreat', *The Vision*, 13 (February 1923), 8–12 (p. 9).
102. Evelyn Underhill, 'The Need of Retreat', *The Vision*, 17 (February 1924), 1–4 (p. 2).
103. See Spurr, pp. 174–81.
104. 'Retreat and the Claims of God', *The Vision*, 4 (November 1920), 3–7 (p. 3).
105. 'What is a Nation?', *The Vision*, 27 (August 1926), 1–4 (p. 4).
106. See Lawrence Stone, *Road to Divorce: England, 1530–1987* (Oxford: Oxford University Press, 1990), pp. 390–401.
107. Miles Sergeant, 'From the Editor's Study', *The Vision*, 63 (July 1935), 1–2 (p. 1, p. 2).
108. Robert Beaken, *Cosmo Lang: Archbishop in War and Crisis*, with a forward by Rowan Williams (London: I. B. Tauris, 2012), p. 123.
109. Downey, p. 131. See also Leslie Woodcock Tentler, *American Catholics: A History* (New Haven, CT: Yale University Press, 2020), pp. 241–88.
110. Dorothy Day, 'Here and Now', in *By Little and By Little: The Selected Writings of Dorothy Day*, ed. by Robert Ellsberg (New York: Knopf, 1983), pp. 100–4 (p. 104).
111. Day, 'All is Grace'.
112. Day, 'Retreat Notebooks', p. 293.
113. Shortall, p. 55.
114. Shortall, p. 55.
115. 'Retreat and the Claims of God', *The Vision*, 4 (November 1920), 3–7 (p. 3).
116. Taylor, *Secular Age*, pp. 37–42, pp. 542–57.
117. For the *Spiritual Exercises*, see John W. O'Malley, *The First Jesuits* (Cambridge, MA: Harvard University Press, 1993), pp. 37–50.
118. Eliot, 'The Metaphysical Poets', p. 380; Jones, preface to *The Anathemata*, p. 15; Taylor, *Secular Age*, pp. 542–57.

CONCLUSION: THE DISTRACTION OF RELIGIOUS POETRY

In *Seven Types of Ambiguity*, published in 1930, William Empson offered a justly famous reading of George Herbert's 'The Sacrifice'. One verse reads:

> *O all ye who pass by, behold and see;*
> Man stole the fruit, but I must climb the tree;
> The tree of life to all, but only me:
> > Was ever grief like mine?[1]

Empson explained that Christ 'climbs the tree to repay what was stolen, as if he was putting the apple back; but the phrase implies rather that he is doing the stealing, that so far from sinless he is Prometheus and the criminal'.[2] The critic recognised a conventional theological idea at work in Herbert's text. A sin has been committed and requires atonement. In mounting the cross, Christ performs atonement; the act of reparation ('but I must climb the tree') rhetorically parallels the original sin ('Man stole the fruit'). Empson nevertheless heard dissenting murmurs in these lines. *Tree* becomes not only the cross (the site of the atonement) but also the tree of life in the Garden of Eden (which bore the forbidden fruit). In the alternative understanding, Christ does not place himself on the cross; he climbs the tree to steal an apple in solidarity with the human cause. Christ is not so much sinless as Promethean.

The interpretation was divisive. For Louis L. Martz, author of *The Poetry of Meditation: A Study in English Religious Literature of the Seventeenth Century* and H.D.'s future editor, Empson's reading revealed a Herbert who went beyond transposing into verse a traditional set of religious concerns. Martz noted, for instance, the way Herbert balanced 'the immensity of God's omnipotence and the immensity of God's love, the companion-powers of punishment and mercy'.[3] For other critics, such as the Renaissance specialist Rosemond Tuve, Empson's focus on the artistic predicament led him astray, encouraging him to see originality where there was only convention.[4] The necessary critical discernment, so the argument ran, could only be developed via immersion in the religious literature of the period; Empson, as a generalist, failed to respond to the textual cues an informed commentator would recognise.

The reading also smuggled in anachronistic secular humanist assumptions. In *Milton's God*, published in 1961, Empson portrayed the poet of *Paradise Lost* as a writer forever 'struggling to make his God appear less wicked'.[5] Likewise, in response to Tuve's criticism, Empson insisted that 'a Supreme God who takes pleasure in giving torture' was 'ineradicable' from Christianity.[6] No honest and intelligent person could think otherwise; Herbert was compelled to criticise the Christian doctrine to which he had dedicated his life. *Seven Types of Ambiguity* exemplifies, to use T. S. Eliot's words, how 'modern literature is corrupted' by 'Secularism'; 'it is simply unaware of, simply cannot understand the meaning of', Eliot explained, 'the primacy of the supernatural over the natural life'.[7]

Empson's solution to the conflict between Herbert as at-once dedicated Anglican and secret religious radical was to invoke modern psychology. Central to *Seven Types of Ambiguity*'s understanding of the creative process was 'the Freudian idea that language is capable of signifying patterns of meaning beyond the author's conscious awareness and deliberate control'.[8] The double-mindedness of 'The Sacrifice' is characteristic of poetic utterance, but by virtue of neither policy nor deliberation. The human mind is a divided place, driven by forces of which it is unaware; chaos spills onto the page, particularly when the mind is working at great intensity. Herbert was not a theologian rewriting Christology. Reflecting on these two scenes from religious history, Eden and Golgotha, he was unable to accept in the deepest recesses of his mind the official Christian teaching. 'The Sacrifice' is thus a divided work in which the poet unconsciously undermines the theological principles he set out to versify. The result recalls the tension between personal cries of despair and the dignity of ritual ordonnance in Eliot's *Ash-Wednesday*.

As Herbert unintentionally gave himself away in 'The Sacrifice', so Empson's reading says more than he realised about the relationship between modernism and religion. The hermeneutics of *Seven Types of Ambiguity* and *Milton's God* assume the resistance of poetry to doctrine, even among the most dedicated religious writers. Expressions of faith on the one hand and distrust of the assumptions, principles and stories of the same faith tradition on the other sit side-by-side on the page. 'The Sacrifice' is not a period piece that makes use of certain traditions of expression, so much as a proto-modern religious poem. What makes it so surprisingly contemporary is not its humanism per se, but rather the way in which the presence of a nascent humanism leaves the poem sounding unconvinced, even as it utters them, by the sentiments and theology it propounds. The present monograph has portrayed the pairing of religious commitment and consciousness of the limitations of faith traditions as a feature of religious change. The shifting religious outlook, affecting the emergence of new religions as much as engagement with institutional religions, helped make religion in the age of modernism new.

Wholesale religious change sat uncomfortably with traditional understandings of religious poetry. Eliot explained that:

> For the great majority of people who love poetry, '*religious* poetry' is a variety of *minor* poetry: the religious poet is not a poet who is treating the whole subject matter of poetry in a religious spirit, but a poet who is dealing with a confined part of this subject matter; who is leaving out what men consider their major passions, and thereby confessing his ignorance of them.[9]

Religious poetry is a self-limiting category. Rather than dealing with the 'major passions' or the 'whole subject', a religious poet is 'confined' to topics acceptable to a given religious community. Even if Christ-as-Prometheus was at the back of his mind, Herbert would not, in Tuve's view, have ventured to express the idea on the page because it ran counter to his readers' expectations. Eliot's initial hospitality to both Herbert and Gerard Manley Hopkins arose from his understanding of them as religious poets.[10]

Empson's reading of Herbert draws attention to the entwining of expressions of faith and the voicing of doubts. In writing about John Donne's 'Holy Sonnets', Paul Cefalu extends Empson's practice by noting a difference between 'being in doubt about your own salvation' and 'being in doubt about the very means or method of salvation', placing Donne in the second category.[11] To be in 'doubt about your own salvation' is Calvinistic: I do not know whether I am among those predestined for salvation because I have often acted like a reprobate. To betray 'doubt about the very means or method of salvation', however, is to challenge Calvinist assumptions, musing that maybe salvation does not work in quite the way one had supposed; the broader Reformation debates about the saving powers of faith on the one hand and of good works on the other exemplify such a divide. Victorian poetry was also famously shaped by doubt. For Kirstie Blair, Victorian poetry approaches faith and doubt in very different ways; it addresses the former 'in steady and regular rhythms' and the latter in 'irregular, unsteady, unbalanced rhythms'.[12] Faith here is trust in Christian revelation and traditional values, while doubt is occasioned by the way in which modern scientific discoveries, new social theories and particular ethical positions eroded such trust. Doubt is no longer centred on uncertainties about versions of Christian life, but rather the divide between religion or no-religion. Blair's 'regular rhythms' bespeak nostalgia as much as assurance or rather nostalgia for old assurance. Such poetry enabled Victorian readers to experience the comforting certainties of a religious upbringing that now seemed outdated.[13]

When addressing the religious challenges Donne faced, however, Eliot spoke of not doubt but distraction. Eliot fell back on a term that had medical or psychological associations: 'we feel that there is something else, some preoccupation, in Donne's mind, besides what he is talking about; his attention is not only often dispersed and volatile; perhaps it is so because it is really distracted'.[14] The shift in religious expectations from, say, Donne to Alfred, Lord Tennyson is matched by that from Tennyson to Eliot; given its ties with the Victorian age, doubt does not quite capture the phenomena in question. Instead, a psychological register serves the purpose. Eliot's Donne is pathologically unable to focus.[15] He is torn by competing demands upon his attention in a world in which all hierarchies of value seem to have broken down. Eliot's sensitivity to Donne's preoccupation was conditioned, it might be surmised, by his own experiences of negotiating the tensions between 'spilt mysticism' and 'wavering orthodoxy'.

Eliot's reading of Donne bears witness to what Charles Taylor considers a shift in the social imaginary whereby past expressions of religious faith are restructured.[16] Richard Kearney's *Anatheism: Returning to God After God*, with its presentation of a life lived without God but in which the sacred remains open to those willing to venture it, is evidently a product of the later shift. Eliot's *Four Quartets* similarly registers the change in the conditions of belief by, for example, juxtaposing a pastiche of a metaphysical lyric that might have been analysed in Martz's *Poetry of Meditation* with grudging and prosy blank verse that maintains 'The poetry does not matter' (p. 187), which serves to undermine the metaphysical aspirations of the lyrics that preceded it. The ability of a poem to transform – to offer glimpses of the divine – is at once invoked and denied. In form as much as content, *Four Quartets*, what Kevin J. H. Dettmar has called 'the most important Christian poem of the twentieth century', advertises its difference from past religious experiences and worldviews.[17]

The reorientation of religious life challenges the idea, famously formulated by Matthew Arnold, of poetry as a replacement for religion.[18] For Arnold, 'the great concern of life' was '*conduct*'.[19] Religious teaching, dogma and its exposition were merely later additions to an otherwise ethics-driven project: a means of inspiring religious subjects to live up to the demands placed upon them. Classic works of literature, particularly given the challenges to certain religious assumptions posed by modern science, were better placed than the Bible, doctrine or preaching to encourage and exhort. The relationship between religion and literature in Arnold's thought is very different to that evident in the 'secular sacred' approach to the study of modernism and religion.[20] The 'secular sacred' equates religion with the experience, feelings or ideas inspired by religious revelation, rather than Arnold's ethical prerogative. Modernist texts incorporate epiphanies and through their stylistic experimentation open new vistas of insight.

Rather than offering a replacement religion, David Jones's *The Anathemata* attempts to think through the nature of religion in a world changed from that which Donne or Tennyson knew. For Jones, the relationship between the Roman Catholic Church and the arts acted as a counterweight to the utilitarian impetus of modern society. *The Anathemata* celebrates gratuitous activity of all kinds, connecting human and divine creativity, reflecting on the Mass and ferreting out historical connections otherwise lost in acts of ratiocination. His poetry, as *The Grail Mass* suggests, was informed by the Catholic worldview that helped produce an influential understanding of human rights, an understanding that Jones himself attempted to bring to bear on the legacies of empire in a period of historical experiments in decolonisation. Religion was driven by its own internal dynamics, but it also provided a well-positioned vantage point from which one could view developments in contemporary culture and scope out potential interventions.

In the case of *The Anathemata*, terse stylistic juxtapositions facilitate the poem's engagement with culture. Within the poem, texts from different worlds rub against each other. Jones's religious verse is marked by ambitious coverage rather than self-imposed restriction. Eliot himself would have refused to call such poetry *religious*, seeing it instead as an attempt to outline 'a particular phase of the progress of one person'.[21] The present monograph, however, has surveyed the broader landscape of religious change through which such a pilgrim trekked. During the journey detailed over the proceeding pages, religious poetry was itself transformed. Through its associative method, *The Anathemata* unites the secular and the sacred in ways that eschew the careful divisions upon which neo-scholastic theology relied. Religion refused to be merely what Eliot called a 'confined part' and sought instead new ways to engage 'the whole subject matter of poetry' and the 'major passions' of readers.[22]

The case of Jones shows why the idea of *religious* poetry or indeed modernism and *religion* is important as a field of study. The perspectives, debates and aesthetic strategies outlined under those headings over the course of the present study are inaccessible from other points of entry. While politically Eliot was an anti-progressive Tory, the presentation of his interests as 'reactionary Anglo-Catholicism' flattens the contours of religious debate surveyed over the proceeding pages.[23] It obscures, for instance, the degree to which *The Idea of a Christian Society* responded idiosyncratically to developments in the psychology of religion or how Eliot deployed allusions to mystical writings in

'Little Gidding' in strikingly original ways so as to offer some consolation to a wartime audience facing an Allied defeat. In common with many European Catholics, Jones was attracted to aspects of fascism, even as he deplored the hate it fostered.[24] At the same time, however, he was an anti-imperialist who sought to protect and celebrate creativity wherever he found it. H.D., for her part, was an avant-garde feminist with a commitment to the 'internal transformation' of her 'psyche and sexual being' who nevertheless extolled, at the close of one of her major works, the social value of public self-sacrifice.[25] These complex positions are difficult if not impossible to parse using the conventional political language of progressive and reactionary or left and right. They can be best understood as a response to a series of cultural debates that sought to reposition bodies of religious thought and practice to meet the challenges of modernity. The notion of a distinctly religious response to modernity is exemplified by Dorothy Day's presentation of retreat as a spiritual school for retreatants. Remade by religious discipline, Catholic Workers sought to engage with society from a deeply considered religious perspective that confounded contemporary expectations.

The use of the *Spiritual Exercises* of St Ignatius of Loyola in the retreat movement stands apart from Martz's focus in *Poetry of Meditation* on the meditative practices of Ignatian devotional literature and their subsequent influence on metaphysical poetry. Martz argued that the sixteenth-century poet Robert Southwell, a Jesuit and recusant priest, introduced these meditative practices into English poetry.[26] The critic went on to describe the influence that the seventeenth-century poets who later took up Southwell's technique exerted on figures such as Jones, Eliot and H.D. The poetry of the twentieth century, quite as much as that of the seventeenth, made use of 'intense, imaginative meditation that brings together the senses, the emotions, and the intellectual faculties of man; brings them together in a moment of dramatic creative experience'.[27] In Martz's reading, meditation enabled the modern poet to overcome Eliot's 'dissociation of sensibility': to block out the distractions of the modern world and to unite sense, emotion and intellect in a single vision.[28] A form of religious practice underwent a process of secularisation. In Martz's hands, the supernatural dimension of the *Spiritual Exercises*, as important to St Ignatius himself as to the twentieth-century retreat movement that utilised his techniques, is razed; meditative practices that once served as a means of growing closer to God are repurposed as a creative writing technique.

The present monograph has resisted the merging of aesthetic and religious experience. It has argued for an alternative trajectory of Ignatian influence, namely the invocation of quiet, the rhythms of retreat-and-return and the redeployment of the *Spiritual Exercises* in a strikingly new setting – all factors that shaped the retreat movement. The repurposing of an old religious aid within a mass religious movement provides one way of understanding the divided, bricolage-like elements of the poetry discussed here. The inclusion in H.D.'s *Trilogy* of both an overpowering visionary encounter and a sceptical probing of that same vision (alongside the willingness to pass between the two without comment) underscores the mixed nature of a new form of religious poetry, which often tries to assert simultaneously mutually exclusive positions. None of the authors studied here attempted to draw boundaries between the religious and the non-religious, the sacred and the secular; these modernists thus resisted the partiality Eliot considered intrinsic to religious poetry. Together they challenged the secular elevation of rational discourse as the medium for public debate and the corresponding restriction of religion to the private sphere. In the work of the modernists discussed here, religious insight refuses to stay in its assigned place.

Notes

1. George Herbert, 'The Sacrifice', in *The Complete English Poems*, ed. by John Tobin (Harmondsworth: Penguin, 1991), pp. 23–31 (p. 29).
2. Empson, *Seven Types of Ambiguity*, p. 232.
3. Martz, p. 95.
4. See Rosemond Tuve, 'On Herbert's "Sacrifice"', *Kenyon Review*, 12 (1950), 51–75. Subsequently, Empson admitted it was 'absurd' to describe 'such a traditional poem' as 'unique', but otherwise stood by the reading. Empson, note for the third edition, in *Seven Types*, p. xvii.
5. William Empson, *Milton's God* (London: Chatto & Windus, 1961), p. 11.
6. William Empson, draft response to Rosemond Tuve, quoted in John Haffenden, *William Empson*, 2 vols (Oxford: Oxford University Press, 2005–2006), 2: *Against the Christians*, p. 435.
7. Eliot, 'Religion and Literature', pp. 219–20.
8. Donald J. Childs, *The Birth of New Criticism: Conflict and Conciliation in the Early Work of William Empson, I. A. Richards, Robert Graves, and Laura Riding* (Montreal: McGill-Queen's University Press, 2014), p. 29.
9. Eliot, 'Religion and Literature', pp. 219–20.
10. Eliot, 'Religion and Literature', p. 220. For Eliot's revised view of Herbert, see Schuchard, pp. 175–97.
11. Paul Cefalu, *Moral Identity in Early Modern English Literature* (Cambridge: Cambridge University Press, 2004), p. 116.
12. Kirstie Blair, *Form and Faith in Victorian Poetry and Religion* (Oxford: Oxford University Press, 2012), p. 1.
13. See Simon Goldhill, *A Very Queer Family Indeed: Sex, Religion, and the Bensons in Victorian Britain* (Chicago: University of Chicago Press, 2016), pp. 271–84.
14. Eliot, 'Clark Lectures', p. 693.
15. See Callison, 'Dissociating Psychology', 1048–50.
16. See Taylor, *Secular Age*, pp. 1–22.
17. Kevin J. H. Dettmar, '"An Occupation for the Saint": Eliot as a Religious Thinker', in *A Companion to T. S. Eliot*, ed. by David E. Chinitz (Oxford: Wiley-Blackwell, 2009), pp. 363–75 (p. 374).

18. Arnold, 'The Study of Poetry', p. 3.
19. Arnold, *Literature and Dogma*, p. 39.
20. See Lewis, p. 21.
21. Eliot to D'Arcy, 24 May 1930, p. 201. See also T. S. Eliot, 'A Note on *In Parenthesis* and *The Anathemata*, by David Jones', in *Complete Prose, 8: Still and Still Moving, 1954–1965*, ed. by Jewel Spears Brooker and Ronald Schuchard, pp. 44–46.
22. Eliot, 'Religion and Literature', pp. 219–20.
23. Harding, p. 198, p. 158; see also Hadjiyiannis, pp. 31–64.
24. For European Catholicism and fascism, see Chappel, pp. 22–58. For Jones and fascism, see Villis, pp. 9–26; Thomas Dilworth, 'David Jones and Fascism', *Journal of Modern Literature*, 13 (1986), 149–62.
25. Delap, pp. 6–7.
26. Martz, pp. 25–43.
27. Martz, pp. 179–210.
28. Eliot, 'The Metaphysical Poets', p. 380.

BIBLIOGRAPHY

ARCHIVAL SOURCES

Bryher, Papers, Yale Collection of American Literature, Beinecke Rare Book and Manuscript Library, Yale University, CT.

Church Registers (ChReg), Collections, Moravian Archives, Bethlehem, PA.

Day, Dorothy, Papers, Manuscripts, c. 1914–1975, The Dorothy Day–Catholic Worker Collection, Special Collections and University Archives, Raynor Memorial Library, Marquette University, WI.

DP Collection of Drawings and Prints, Visual Materials, Moravian Archives, Bethlehem, PA.

Eliot, T. S., Notes on Religion and Mysticism, Papers, 1878–1958, MS Am 1691.129, Houghton Library, Harvard University, MA.

Grisewood, Harman, Papers 1, Booth Family Center for Special Collections, Lauinger Library, Georgetown University, Washington, D. C.

———, Papers 2, Booth Family Center for Special Collections, Lauinger Library, Georgetown University, Washington, D. C.

H.D., Library, Yale Collection of American Literature, Beinecke Rare Book and Manuscript Library, Yale University, CT.

H.D., Papers, Yale Collection of American Literature, Beinecke Rare Book and Manuscript Library, Yale University, CT.

Jones, David, Letters to Harman Grisewood, General Collection, Beinecke Rare Book and Manuscript Library, Yale University, CT.

———, Letters to Jim Ede, Kettle's Yard Archive, University of Cambridge.

———, The Library of David Jones, National Library of Wales, Aberystwyth.
———, Papers, National Library of Wales, Aberystwyth.
Photocollections (PhotC), Visual Materials, Moravian Archives, Bethlehem, PA.
Plank, George, Papers, Yale Collection of American Literature, Beinecke Rare Book and Manuscript Library, Yale University, CT.

Published Works

Abrams, M. H., *Natural Supernaturalism: Tradition and Revolution in Romantic Literature* (New York: Norton, 1971).
Ackroyd, Peter, *T. S. Eliot: A Life* (New York: Simon and Schuster, 1984).
Adams, James Luther, 'Letter from Friedrich von Hügel to William James', *Downside Review*, 98 (1980), 214–36.
Allitt, Patrick, *Catholic Converts: British and American Intellectuals Turn to Rome* (Ithaca, NY: Cornell University Press, 1997).
Anderson, Elizabeth, *H.D. and Modernist Religious Imagination: Mysticism and Writing* (London: Bloomsbury Academic, 2013).
Andrew, Dudley and Steven Ungar, *Popular Front Paris and the Poetics of Culture* (Cambridge, MA: Harvard University Press, 2005).
Anonymous, 'Coleshill Park, Birmingham', *The Vision*, 9 (February 1922), 6–7.
———, 'Holidays and Change of Air', *The Vision*, 27 (August 1926), 4–7.
———, 'The House of Mercy, Horbury, Yorks.', *The Vision*, 72 (October 1937), 8–9.
———, 'Martha in Retreat', *The Vision*, 14 (May 1923), 1–4.
———, 'The Need of the Study of Ascetic Theology', *The Vision*, 36 (November 1928), 9–12.
———, 'Notes', *The Vision*, 3 (August 1920), 1–3.
———, 'Parochial Retreats', *The Vision*, 14 (May 1923), 11–13.
———, 'A Plea for Really Modern Thought', *The Vision*, 35 (August 1928), 1–5.
———, 'Retreat and the Claims of God', *The Vision*, 4 (November 1920), 3–7.
———, 'Retreat and the Claims of God', *The Vision*, 5 (February 1921), 4–7.
———, 'Retreat and Progress', *The Vision*, 7 (August 1921), 1–3.
———, 'Retreat and the Rules of Life', *The Vision*, 23 (November 1925), 1–4.
———, 'A Retreat at S. Mary's Abbey, Leiston, Suffolk', *The Vision*, 8 (November 1921), 7–8.
———, 'A Retreat for Men and Lads: S. George's, Cullercoats', *The Vision*, 9 (February 1922), 4–5.
———, 'Retreats for Children and Young People', *The Vision*, 10 (May 1922), 9–13.
———, 'Retreat without Tears', *The Vision*, 70 (April 1937), 15–17.

——, 'S. Winifred's, Wolverhampton: A Rescue and Preventive Home for Girls up to Sixteen Years of Age', *The Vision*, 9 (February 1922), 5–6.
——, 'Some Questions and their Answers', *The Vision*, 1 (January 1920), 6.
——, 'Stillness, Vision, Service', *The Vision*, 5 (April 1920), 14–17.
——, 'Waiting upon God', *The Vision*, 15 (August 1923), 1–3.
——, 'What is a Nation?', *The Vision*, 27 (August 1926), 1–4.
——, 'The Worship of Retreat', *The Vision*, 13 (February 1923), 8–12.
Ardis, Ann L., *Modernism and Cultural Conflict, 1880–1922* (Cambridge: Cambridge University Press, 2002).
Armstrong, Tim, *Modernism: A Cultural History* (Cambridge: Polity Press, 2005).
Arnold, Matthew, *Literature and Dogma: An Essay Towards a Better Apprehension of the Bible* (London: Smith Elder, 1873).
——, 'The Study of Poetry', in *Essays in Criticism: Second Series* (London: Macmillan, 1888), pp. 1–56.
Asher, Kenneth, *T. S. Eliot and Ideology* (Cambridge: Cambridge University Press, 1995).
Astley, H. J. D., 'Primitive Sacramentalism', *The Modern Churchman*, 16 (1926), 282–95.
Attwater, Donald, *'In the Beginning was the Word': A Plea for English Words in the Worship of the Roman Church* (London: R. D. Dickinson, 1944).
Atwood, Craig D., 'Understanding Zinzendorf's Blood and Wounds Theology', *Journal of Moravian History*, 1 (2006), 31–47.
Augustine, Jane, introduction to *The Gift by H.D.: The Complete Text*, edited by Jane Augustine (Gainesville: University Press of Florida, 1998), pp. 1–28.
——, 'A Note on the Text and Its Arrangement', in *The Gift*, pp. ix–xi.
——, 'A Note on the Edition', in *The Mystery*, edited by Jane Augustine (Gainesville: University Press of Florida, 2009), pp. ix–xi.
Babbitt, Irving, 'Buddha and the Occident' (1936), in *On Literature, Culture, and Religion: Irving Babbitt*, edited by George A. Panichas (Oxford: Routledge, 2017), pp. 224–70.
Baring, Edward, *Converts to the Real: Catholicism and the Making of Continental Philosophy* (Cambridge, MA: Harvard University Press, 2019).
Barmann, Lawrence F., *Baron Friedrich von Hügel and the Modernist Crisis in England* (Cambridge: Cambridge University Press, 1972).
Beaken, Robert, *Cosmo Lang: Archbishop in War and Crisis*, with a forward by Rowan Williams (London: I. B. Tauris, 2012).
Beja, Morris, *Epiphany in the Modern Novel* (Seattle: University of Washington Press, 1971).
Bellah, Robert N., 'Religion and Belief', in *Beyond Belief: Essays on Religion in a Post-Traditionalist World* (Berkeley: University of California Press, 1991), pp. 216–29.

———, *Religion in Human Evolution: From the Paleolithic to the Axial Age* (Cambridge, MA: Harvard University Press, 2011).
Berger, Peter L., *The Sacred Canopy: Elements of a Sociological Theory of Religion* (Garden City, NY: Doubleday, 1967).
Bidney, Martin, *Patterns of Epiphany: From Wordsworth to Tolstoy, Pater, and Barrett Browning* (Carbondale: Southern Illinois University Press, 1997).
Blair, Kirstie, *Form and Faith in Victorian Poetry and Religion* (Oxford: Oxford University Press, 2012).
The Book of Common Prayer: The Texts of 1549, 1559, and 1662, edited by Brian Cummings (Oxford: Oxford University Press, 2011).
Bouquet, J. A., 'Retreat and Vocation', *The Vision*, 31 (August 1927), 6–10.
Bradshaw, David, 'Politics', in *T. S. Eliot in Context*, edited by Jason Harding (Cambridge: Cambridge University Press, 2011), pp. 265–74.
Bramble, John, *Modernism and the Occult* (Basingstoke: Palgrave Macmillan, 2015).
Branch, Lori, 'Postsecular Studies', in *The Routledge Companion to Literature and Religion*, edited by Mark Knight (Oxford: Routledge, 2016), pp. 91–101.
Brooker, Jewel Spears, *Mastery and Escape: T. S. Eliot and the Dialectic of Modernism* (Amherst: University of Massachusetts Press, 1994).
Browning, Robert, *Browning: Selected Poems*, edited by John Woolford, Daniel Karlin and Joseph Phelan (Harlow: Pearson Longman, 2010).
Bruce, Steve, *Secularization: In Defence of an Unfashionable Theory* (Oxford: Oxford University Press, 2011).
Bush, Ronald, '"Intensity by association:" T. S. Eliot's Passionate Allusions', *Modernism/modernity*, 20 (2013), 709–727.
Butler, Cuthbert, *Religions of Authority and the Religion of the Spirit, with Other Essays* (London: Sheed & Ward, 1930).
Butts, Mary, 'The Heresy Game', *The Spectator*, 12 March 1937, 466–67.
Callison, Jamie, 'David Jones's "Barbaric-fetish": Frazer and the "Aesthetic Value" of the Liturgy', *Modernist Cultures*, 12 (2017), 439–62.
———, 'Directing Modernist Spirituality: Evelyn Underhill, the Subliminal Consciousness and Spiritual Direction', in *Modernist Women Writers and Spirituality: A Piercing Darkness*, edited by Elizabeth Anderson, Andrew Radford and Heather Walton (Basingstoke: Palgrave Macmillan, 2016), pp. 39–54.
———, 'Dissociating Psychology: Religion, Inspiration and T. S. Eliot's Subliminal Mind', *ELH*, 84 (2017), 1029–59.
———, 'Redefining Marriage in Interwar Britain: Internal Transformation and Personal Sacrifice in the Poetry of H.D.', in *Marriage Discourses: Historical and Literary Perspectives on Gender Inequality and Patriarchic Exploitation*, edited by Jowan A. Mohammed and Frank Jacob (Berlin: De Gruyter, 2021), pp. 187–206.

———, 'Sacred Ground: Orthodoxy, Poetry and Religious Change', in *Edinburgh Companion to Modernism, Myth and Religion*, edited by Suzanne Hobson and Andrew Radford (Edinburgh: Edinburgh University Press, 2023), pp. 375–88.

Caputo, John D., *Hermeneutics: Facts and Interpretation in the Age of Information* (London: Pelican Books, 2018).

Catechism of the Catholic Church, 2nd edition (Vatican City: Vatican Press, 1997).

Cave, Alfred A., *Prophets of the Great Spirit: Native American Revitalization Movements in Eastern North America* (Lincoln, NE: University of Nebraska Press, 2014).

Cefalu, Paul, *Moral Identity in Early Modern English Literature* (Cambridge: Cambridge University Press, 2004).

Certeau, Michel de, *The Mystic Fable: The Sixteenth and Seventeenth Centuries*, edited by Luce Giard, translated by Michael B. Smith, 2 vols (Chicago: University of Chicago Press, 1995–2015).

Chamedes, Giuliana, *A Twentieth-Century Crusade: The Vatican's Battle to Remake Christian Europe* (Cambridge, MA: Harvard University Press, 2019).

Chappel, James, *Catholic Modern: The Challenge of Totalitarianism and the Remaking of the Church* (Cambridge, MA: Harvard University Press, 2018).

Chesterton, G. K., *Orthodoxy* (London: Bodley Head, 1908).

Childs, Donald J., *The Birth of New Criticism: Conflict and Conciliation in the Early Work of William Empson, I. A. Richards, Robert Graves, and Laura Riding* (Montreal: McGill-Queen's University Press, 2014).

———, *T. S. Eliot: Mystic, Son and Lover* (London: Athlone Press, 1997).

Collini, Stefan, *Absent Minds: Intellectuals in Britain* (Oxford: Oxford University Press, 2006).

———, 'Where Did it All Go Wrong? Cultural Critics and "Modernity" in Inter-War Britain', in *The Strange Survival of Liberal England: Political Leaders, Moral Values and the Reception of Economic Debate*, edited by E. H. H. Green and D. M. Tanner (Cambridge: Cambridge University Press, 2011), pp. 247–74.

Cooper, John Xiros, *The Cambridge Introduction to T. S. Eliot* (Cambridge: Cambridge University Press, 2006).

Crawford, Robert, *Young Eliot: From St. Louis to* The Waste Land (London: Vintage, 2015).

Daly, Gabriel, *Transcendence and Immanence: A Study in Catholic Modernism and Integralism* (Oxford: Oxford University Press, 1980).

Dante, *Vita Nuova*, translated by Mark Musa, new edition (Bloomington: Indiana University Press, 1973).

D'Arcy, Martin C., *The Mass and the Redemption* (London: Burns, Oates & Washbourne, 1926).

———, *The Nature of Belief* (New York: Longmans Green, 1931).

Day, Dorothy, *By Little and By Little: The Selected Writings of Dorothy Day*, edited by Robert Ellsberg (New York: Knopf, 1983).
——, *House of Hospitality* (London: Sheed & Ward, 1939).
——, *The Long Loneliness: The Autobiography of Dorothy Day* (New York: Harper & Row, 1981).
——, *On Pilgrimage* (Grand Rapids, MI: Eerdmans, 1999).
——, 'Retreat Notebooks', in Benjamin T. Peters, *Called to be Saints: John Hugo, The Catholic Worker, and a Theology of Radical Christianity* (Milwaukee, WI: Marquette University Press, 2016), pp. 259–582.
De Gay, Jane, *Virginia Woolf and Christian Culture* (Edinburgh: Edinburgh University Press, 2018).
De la Taille, Maurice, *The Mystery of Faith: Regarding the Most August Sacrament and Sacrifice of the Body and Blood of Christ*, translated by Joseph Carroll, 2 vols (London: Sheed & Ward, 1940–1950).
——, 'An Outline of *The Mystery of Faith*', in *The Mystery of Faith and Human Opinion Contrasted and Defined*, translated by J. B. Schimpf (London: Sheed & Ward, 1934), pp. 3–37.
Delacroix, Henri, *Études d'histoire et de psychologie du mysticisme: Les grands mystiques chrétiens* (Paris: Félix Alcan, 1908).
Delap, Lucy, *The Feminist Avant-Garde: Transatlantic Encounters of the Early Twentieth Century* (Cambridge: Cambridge University Press, 2007).
Dettmar, Kevin J. H., '"An Occupation for the Saint": Eliot as a Religious Thinker', in *A Companion to T. S. Eliot*, edited by David E. Chinitz (Oxford: Wiley-Blackwell, 2009), pp. 363–75.
DiCenso, James, *The Other Freud: Religion, Culture and Psychoanalysis* (London: Routledge, 1999).
Dilworth, Thomas, *David Jones: Engraver, Soldier, Painter, Poet* (London: Jonathan Cape, 2017).
——, 'David Jones and the Chelsea Group', in *David Jones: A Christian Modernist?*, edited by Jamie Callison, Erik Tonning, Anna Johnson and Paul Fiddes (Leiden: Brill, 2018), pp. 107–22.
——, 'David Jones and Fascism', *Journal of Modern Literature*, 13 (1986), 149–62.
——, *Reading David Jones* (Cardiff: University of Wales Press, 2008).
——, *The Shape of Meaning in the Poetry of David Jones* (Toronto: University of Toronto Press, 1988).
Dix, Dom Gregory, *The Shape of the Liturgy*, 2nd edition (London: Dacre Press, 1947).
Domestico, Anthony, *Poetry and Theology in the Modernist Period* (Baltimore: Johns Hopkins University Press, 2017).
Dowland, David A., *Nineteenth-Century Anglican Theological Training: The Redbrick Challenge* (Oxford: Clarendon Press, 1997).

Downey, Jack Lee, *The Bread of the Strong: Lacouturisme and the Folly of the Cross, 1910–1985* (New York: Fordham University Press, 2015).

Dubreuil, Emmanuelle Hériard, *The Personalism of Denis de Rougemont: Spirituality and Politics in 1930s Europe* (unpublished PhD thesis, University of Cambridge, 2005).

Duncan, Robert, *The H.D. Book*, edited by Michael Boughn and Victor Coleman (Berkeley: University of California Press, 2012).

DuPlessis, Rachel Blau, *Genders, Races, and Religious Cultures in Modern American Poetry, 1908–1934* (Cambridge: Cambridge University Press, 2001).

———, 'Romantic Thralldom in H.D.', *Contemporary Literature*, 20 (1979), 178–203.

———, and Susan Stanford Friedman, '"Woman Is Perfect": H.D.'s Debate with Freud', *Feminist Studies*, 7 (1981), 417–30.

Dyson, William Henry, *Studies in Christian Mysticism* (London: James Clarke, 1913).

Eagleton, Terry, *Radical Sacrifice* (New Haven, CT: Yale University Press, 2018).

Eliot, T. S., '*After Strange Gods: A Primer of Modern Heresy*', in *The Complete Prose of T. S. Eliot: The Critical Edition*, edited by Ronald Schuchard, 8 vols, Project MUSE, <https://about.muse.jhu.edu/muse/eliot-prose/>, 5: *Tradition and Orthodoxy, 1934–1939*, edited by Iman Javadi, Ronald Schuchard and Jayme Stayer, pp. 15–55.

———, 'Baudelaire', in *Complete Prose*, 4: *English Lion, 1930–1933*, edited by Jason Harding and Ronald Schuchard, pp. 155–67.

———, 'Baudelaire in our Time', in *Complete Prose*, 3: *Literature, Politics, Belief, 1927–1929*, edited by Frances Dickey, Jennifer Formichelli and Ronald Schuchard, pp. 71–82.

———, 'Christianity and Communism', in *English Lion*, pp. 422–31.

———, 'The Clark Lectures. Lectures on the Metaphysical Poetry of the Seventeenth Century with Special Reference to Donne, Crashaw and Cowley', in *Complete Prose*, 2: *The Perfect Critic, 1919–1926*, edited by Anthony Cuda and Ronald Schuchard, pp. 609–761.

———, 'A Commentary (June 1928)', in *Literature, Politics, Belief*, pp. 416–20.

———, 'Dante', in *Literature, Politics, Belief*, pp. 700–45.

———, 'The Idea of a Christian Society', in *Tradition and Orthodoxy*, pp. 683–747.

———, '[Inconsistencies in Bergson's Idealism]', in *Complete Prose*, 1: *Apprentice Years, 1905–1918*, edited by Jewel Spears Brooker and Ronald Schuchard, pp. 67–89.

———, 'Introduction to *Revelation*, eds John Baillie and Hugh Martin', in *Tradition and Orthodoxy*, pp. 472–96.

———, *The Letters of T. S. Eliot*, edited by Valerie Eliot, Hugh Haughton and John Haffenden, 9 vols (London: Faber & Faber, 1989–).

———, 'The Metaphysical Poets', in *Perfect Critic*, pp. 375–85.

———, 'The Music of Poetry', in *Complete Prose, 6: The War Years, 1940–1946*, edited by David E. Chinitz and Ronald Schuchard, pp. 310–25.

———, 'A Neglected Aspect of Chapman', in *Perfect Critic*, pp. 548–58.

———, 'A Note on *In Parenthesis* and *The Anathemata*, by David Jones', in *Complete Prose, 8: Still and Still Moving, 1954–1965*, edited by Jewel Spears Brooker and Ronald Schuchard, pp. 44–6.

———, 'Notes Towards a Definition of Culture', in *War Years*, pp. 343–56.

———, '*Notes Towards the Definition of Culture*', in *Complete Prose, 7: A European Society, 1947–1953*, edited by Iman Javadi and Ronald Schuchard, pp. 194–287.

———, *The Poems of T. S. Eliot: The Annotated Text*, edited by Christopher Ricks and Jim McCue, 2 vols (London: Faber & Faber, 2015).

———, 'Preface to *For Lancelot Andrewes: Essays on Style and Order*', in *Literature, Politics, Belief*, pp. 513–14.

———, 'Religion and Literature', in *Tradition and Orthodoxy*, pp. 218–29.

———, 'Religion without Humanism', in *English Lion*, pp. 36–43.

———, 'A Review of *Conscience and Christ: Six Lectures on Christian Ethics*, by Hastings Rashdall', in *Apprentice Years*, pp. 428–30.

———, 'A Review of *Egoists, A Book of Supermen*, by James Huneker', in *Apprentice Years*, pp. 24–28.

———, 'A Review of *The Mystical Doctrine of St. John of the Cross*', in *Tradition and Orthodoxy*, p. 108.

———, 'Revival of Christian Imagination', in *War Years*, pp. 239–44.

———, 'Style and Thought: An Unsigned Review of *Mysticism and Logic and Other Essays*, by Bertrand Russell', in *Apprentice Years*, pp. 690–94.

———, 'Syllabus of a Course of Six Lectures on Modern French Literature, Frederick Hall, 1916', in *Apprentice Years*, pp. 471–77.

———, 'The Three Voices of Poetry', in *European Society*, pp. 817–34.

———, 'Tradition and the Individual Talent', in *Perfect Critic*, pp. 105–14.

———, '*The Use of Poetry and the Use of Criticism: Studies in the Relation of Criticism to Poetry in England*', in *English Lion*, pp. 574–694.

———, 'Why Mr. Russell Is a Christian: A Review of *Why I Am Not a Christian*, by the Hon. Bertrand Russell', in *Literature, Politics, Belief*, pp. 160–63.

Empson, William, *Milton's God* (London: Chatto & Windus, 1961).

———, *Seven Types of Ambiguity*, 3rd edition (London: Chatto & Windus, 1953).

Evans, Martha Noel, *Fits and Starts: A Genealogy of Hysteria in Modern France* (Ithaca, NY: Cornell University Press, 1991).

Experientia Docet, 'To the Editor: The Rule of Silence', *The Vision*, 30 (May 1927), 15–17.

Fletcher, John Gould, 'H.D.'s Vision', *Poetry* 9, no. 5 (February 1917), 266–69.

Flint, F. S., 'The History of Imagism', *The Egoist* 2, no. 5 (May 1915), 70–71.

Fogleman, Aaron Spencer, *Jesus is Female: Moravians and the Challenge of Radical Religion in Early America* (Philadelphia: University of Pennsylvania Press, 2008).

Fordham, Finn, 'Between Theological and Cultural Modernism: The Vatican's *Oath against Modernism*, September 1910', *Literature and History*, 22 (2013), 8–24.

Foster, Elizabeth A., *African Catholic: Decolonization and the Transformation of the Church* (Cambridge, MA: Harvard University Press, 2019).

Foucault, Michel, *The Hermeneutics of the Subject: Lectures at the Collège de France 1981–1982*, edited by Frédéric Gros, translated by Graham Burchell (Basingstoke: Palgrave Macmillan, 2016).

Frazer, J. G., *The Golden Bough: A Study in Magic and Religion*, 3rd edition, 12 vols (London: Macmillan, 1906–1915).

Freer, Scott, *Modernist Mythopoeia: The Twilight of the Gods* (Basingstoke: Palgrave Macmillan, 2015).

Freud, Sigmund, '*Civilization and Its Discontents*', in *The Standard Edition of the Complete Works of Sigmund Freud*, translated and edited by James Strachey in collaboration with Anna Freud, Alix Strachey and Alan Tyson, 24 vols (London: Hogarth Press, 1953–74), 21: *The Future of an Illusion, Civilization and Its Discontents and Other Works (1927–1931)*, pp. 59–148.

——, 'The Future of an Illusion', in *The Standard Edition*, 21, pp. 3–58.

——, 'An Outline of Psycho-analysis', in *The Standard Edition*, 23: *Moses and Monotheism, An Outline of Psycho-Analysis and Other Works (1937–1939)*, pp. 141–208.

Friedman, Susan Stanford, *Penelope's Web: Gender, Modernity, H.D.'s Fiction* (Cambridge: Cambridge University Press, 1990).

——, *Psyche Reborn: The Emergence of H.D.* (Bloomington: Indiana University Press, 1981).

Fry, Roger, '"A New Theory of Art", *Nation*, 7 March 1914', in *A Roger Fry Reader*, edited with an introduction by Christopher Reid (Chicago: University of Chicago Press, 1996), pp. 158–62.

Gardner, Helen, *The Composition of Four Quartets* (London: Faber & Faber, 1978).

Gasiorek, Andrzej, *A History of Modernist Literature* (Oxford: Wiley-Blackwell, 2015).

Getachew, Adom, *Worldmaking After Empire: The Rise and Fall of Self-Determination* (Princeton: Princeton University Press, 2019).

Gill, Eric, 'Christianity and Art (1927)', in *Art-Nonsense and Other Essays* (London: Cassell, 1929), pp. 216–249.

Giovagnoli, Antonio Francesco, *The Life of Saint Margaret of Cortona* (Philadelphia: Cunningham, 1888).

Gish, Nancy K., 'Discarnate Desire: T. S. Eliot and the Poetics of Dissociation', in *Gender, Desire, and Sexuality in T. S. Eliot*, edited by Cassandra Laity and Nancy K. Gish (Cambridge: Cambridge University Press, 2004), pp. 107–29.

Goldhill, Simon, *A Very Queer Family Indeed: Sex, Religion, and the Bensons in Victorian Britain* (Chicago: University of Chicago Press, 2016).

Goldie, David, *A Critical Difference: T. S. Eliot and John Middleton Murry in English Literary Criticism, 1919–1928* (Oxford: Clarendon Press, 1998).

Goldpaugh, Thomas, '"A Heap of All That I Could Find": David Jones' Fragmented Sacrament', in *David Jones: A Christian Modernist?*, edited by Jamie Callison, Erik Tonning, Anna Johnson and Paul Fiddes (Leiden: Brill, 2018), pp. 17–36.

———, and Jamie Callison, 'The Chronology of *The Grail Mass* Manuscripts', in *The Grail Mass and Other Works*, edited by Thomas Goldpaugh and Jamie Callison (London: Bloomsbury Academic, 2018), pp. 273–76.

———, and Jamie Callison, introduction to *The Grail Mass and Other Works*, pp. 1–24.

Goodier, SJ, Alban, 'St. Margaret Of Cortona: The Second Magdalene—1247–1297', in *Saints for Sinners* (Garden City, NJ: Image Books, 1959), pp. 20–32.

Gordon, Lyndall, *Eliot's Early Years* (Oxford: Oxford University Press, 1977).

Gourmont, Remy de, 'La sensibilité de Jules Laforgue', in *Promenades littéraires* (Paris: Mercure de France, 1904), pp. 105–10.

Greenberg, Clement, 'Avant-Garde and Kitsch', in *Art and Culture: Critical Essays* (Boston, MA: Beacon Press, 1961), pp. 3–21.

Greene, Roland, and Stephen Cushman, eds., *The Princeton Handbook of Poetic Terms*, 3rd edition (Princeton: Princeton University Press, 2016).

Gregory, Eleanor C., *An Introduction to Christian Mysticism* (London: Allenson, 1901).

Griffiths, Eric, *The Printed Voice of Victorian Poetry* (Oxford: Oxford University Press, 1988).

Guardini, Romano, '*The Spirit of the Liturgy*', in '*The Church and the Catholic*' *and* '*The Spirit of the Liturgy*', translated by Ada Lane (London: Sheed & Ward, 1935), pp. 119–211.

Hadjiyiannis, Christos, *Conservative Modernists: Literature and Tory Politics in Britain, 1900–1920* (Cambridge: Cambridge University Press, 2018).

Haffenden, John, *William Empson*, 2 vols (Oxford: Oxford University Press, 2005–2006).

Hague, René, *A Commentary on* The Anathemata *of David Jones* (Toronto: University of Toronto Press, 1977).

Hamilton, Joseph Taylor, *A History of the Church Known as the Moravian Church, or, The Unitas Fratrum, or, The Unity of the Brethren, During the Eighteenth and Nineteenth Centuries* (Bethlehem, PA: Times Publishing, 1900).

———, *A History of the Missions of the Moravian Church, During the Eighteenth and Nineteenth Centuries* (Bethlehem, PA: Times Publishing, 1901).

Hanson, Ellis, *Decadence and Catholicism* (Cambridge, MA: Harvard University Press, 1997).

Harding, Jason, *The Criterion: Cultural Politics and Periodical Networks in Inter-War Britain* (Oxford: Oxford University Press, 2002).

Harrison, Peter, *The Territories of Science and Religion* (Chicago: University of Chicago Press, 2015).

H.D. [Hilda Doolittle], *Analyzing Freud: Letters of H.D., Bryher and Their Circle*, edited by Susan Stanford Friedman (New York: New Directions, 2002).

———, *Between History and Poetry: The Letters of H.D. and Norman Holmes Pearson*, edited by Donna Krolik Hollenberg (Iowa City: University of Iowa Press, 1997).

———, *By Avon River*, edited by Lara Vetter (Gainesville: University Press of Florida, 2017).

———, *Collected Poems, 1912–1944*, edited by Louis L. Martz (New York: New Directions, 1983).

———, *End to Torment: A Memoir of Ezra Pound*, edited by Norman Holmes Pearson and Michael King (New York: New Directions, 1979).

———, *The Gift by H.D.: The Complete Text*, edited by Jane Augustine (Gainesville: University Press of Florida, 1998).

——— [as Delia Alton], 'H.D. by Delia Alton', *The Iowa Review*, 16 (1986), 180–221.

———, *Helen in Egypt* (New York: New Directions, 1974).

———, *Helen in Egypt*, read by the author, recorded in Zurich, 1955, PennSound, MP3, 37 minutes, 52 seconds, <http://writing.upenn.edu/pennsound/x/HD.php> [accessed 1 March 2022].

———, 'Hymn (From the Bohemian)', *Life and Letters*, 64, no. 151 (March 1950), 213.

———, *The Mystery*, edited by Jane Augustine (Gainesville: University Press of Florida, 2009).

———, *Selected Poems of H.D.* (New York: Grove Press, 1957).

———, *Tribute to Freud*, introduced by Kenneth Fields with a forward by Norman Holmes Pearson (Boston: Godine, 1974).

——, *Trilogy: The Walls Do Not Fall; Tribute to the Angels; The Flowering of the Rod*, with an introduction and readers' notes by Aliki Barnstone (New York: New Directions, 1998).
Hellman, John, *Emmanuel Mounier and the New Catholic Left 1930–1950* (Toronto: University of Toronto Press, 1981).
Henking, Susan E., 'Sociological Christianity and Christian Sociology: The Paradox of Early American Sociology', *Religion and American Culture: A Journal of Interpretation*, 3 (1993), 49–67.
Herbert, George, *The Complete English Poems*, edited by John Tobin (Harmondsworth: Penguin, 1991).
Hervieu-Léger, Danièle, *Religion as a Chain of Memory*, translated by Simon Lee (Cambridge: Polity Press, 2000).
Hill, Geoffrey, 'Dividing Legacies', in *Collected Critical Writings*, edited by Kenneth Haynes (Oxford: Oxford University Press, 2008), pp. 366–82.
Hobson, Suzanne, *Angels of Modernism: Religion, Culture, Aesthetics 1910–1960* (Basingstoke: Palgrave Macmillan, 2011).
——, 'Credulous Readers: H.D. and Psychic-Research Work', in *Incredible Modernism: Literature, Trust and Deception*, edited by John Attridge and Rod Rosenquist (Farnham: Ashgate, 2013), pp. 51–67.
——, and Andrew Radford, introduction to *Edinburgh Companion to Modernism, Myth and Religion*, edited by Suzanne Hobson and Andrew Radford (Edinburgh: Edinburgh University Press, 2023), pp. 1–18.
Holland, Norman N., 'H.D. and the "Blameless Physician"', *Contemporary Literature*, 10 (1969), 474–506.
Hollywood, Amy, *Sensible Ecstasy: Mysticism, Sexual Difference, and the Demands of History* (Chicago: University of Chicago Press, 2003).
Hugo, John J., *Applied Christianity* (New York: printed by the author, 1944).
Hügel, Friedrich von, Letter to William James, 10 May 1909, edited by James Luther Adams, *Downside Review*, 98 (1980), 214–36.
——, *Letters from Baron Friedrich von Hügel to a Niece*, edited by Gwendolen Greene (London: Dent, 1928).
——, *The Mystical Element of Religion as Studied in Saint Catherine of Genoa and Her Friends*, 2 vols (London: Dent, 1909).
Hulme, T. E., 'Romanticism and Classicism', in *The Collected Writings of T. E. Hulme*, edited by Karen Csengeri (Oxford: Clarendon Press, 1994), pp. 59–73.
Huysmans, J. K., *En Route*, translated by C. Kegan Paul (London: Kegan Paul, Trench, Trübner, 1896).
Inge, W. R., *Christian Mysticism: Considered in Eight Lectures Delivered before the University of Oxford* (London: Methuen, 1899).
——, introduction to *Light, Life and Love: Selections from the German Mystics of the Middle Ages* (London: Methuen, 1904), pp. ix–lxiv.

——, 'The Mysticism of Browning', in *Studies of English Mystics: St Margaret's Lectures, 1905* (London: John Murray, 1907), pp. 207–39.

——, 'The Mysticism of Wordsworth', in *Studies of English Mystics*, pp. 173–206.

Jain, Manju, *T. S. Eliot and American Philosophy: The Harvard Years* (Cambridge: Cambridge University Press, 1992).

James, William, *The Varieties of Religious Experience: A Study in Human Nature* (London: Longmans Green, 1902).

Jameson, Fredric, 'Modernism and Imperialism', in *Nationalism, Colonialism, and Literature*, introduced by Seamus Deane (Minneapolis: University of Minnesota Press, 1990), pp. 43–68.

Janet, Pierre, and Fulgence Raymond, *Névroses et idées fixes*, 2 vols (Paris: Félix Alcan, 1898).

Jantzen, Grace M., 'The Legacy of Evelyn Underhill', *Feminist Theology*, 2 (1993), 79–100.

——, *Power, Gender, and Christian Mysticism* (Cambridge: Cambridge University Press, 1995).

Jasper, David, *Heaven in Ordinary: Poetry and Religion in a Secular Age* (Cambridge: Lutterworth Press, 2018).

Jay, Martin, *Songs of Experience: Modern American and European Variations on a Universal Theme* (Berkeley: University of California Press, 2005).

Joas, Hans, *The Power of the Sacred: An Alternative to the Narrative of Disenchantment*, translated by Alex Skinner (Oxford: Oxford University Press, 2021).

John of the Cross, *Ascent of Mount Carmel*, translated by E. Allison Peers, 3rd edition (Garden City, NY: Image Books, 1958).

Jones, David, 'Absalom, Mass', in *The Grail Mass and Other Works*, edited by Thomas Goldpaugh and Jamie Callison (London: Bloomsbury Academic, 2018), pp. 209–12.

——, *The Anathemata: Fragments of an Attempted Writing*, 2nd edition (London: Faber & Faber, 1955).

——, 'Art and Democracy', in *Epoch and Artist: Selected Writings*, edited by Harman Grisewood (London: Faber & Faber, 1959), pp. 85–96.

——, 'Art in Relation to War', in *The Dying Gaul and Other Writings*, edited by Harman Grisewood (London: Faber & Faber, 1978), pp. 123–66.

——, 'Art and Sacrament', in *Epoch and Artist*, pp. 143–79.

——, *Dai Greatcoat: A Self-Portrait of David Jones in his Letters*, edited by René Hague (London: Faber & Faber, 1980).

——, 'The Grail Mass', in *The Grail Mass and Other Works*, pp. 25–152.

——, *Inner Necessities: The Letters of David Jones to Desmond Chute*, edited by Thomas Dilworth (Toronto: Anson-Cartwright, 1984).

——, *In Parenthesis* (London: Faber & Faber, 1937).

———, *The Kensington Mass* (London: Agenda Editions, 1975).
———, 'The Myth of Arthur', in *Epoch and Artist*, pp. 212–59.
———, 'Notes on the 1930s', in *Dying Gaul*, pp. 41–50.
———, preface to *The Anathemata*, pp. 9–43.
———, 'Religion and the Muses', in *Epoch and Artist*, pp. 97–106.
———, *The Roman Quarry and Other Sequences*, edited by Harman Grisewood and René Hague (London: Agenda Editions, 1981).
———, 'The Tribune's Visitation', in *The Sleeping Lord and Other Fragments* (London: Faber & Faber, 1974), pp. 42–58.
Jones, Huw Ceiriog, *The Library of David Jones: A Catalogue* (Aberystwyth: National Library of Wales, 1995).
Kane, Paula M., *Sister Thorn and Catholic Mysticism in Modern America* (Chapel Hill: University of North Carolina Press, 2013).
Kearney, Richard, *Anatheism: Returning to God After God* (New York: Columbia University Press, 2009).
———, 'Epiphanies of the Everyday: Toward a Micro-Eschatology', in *After God: Richard Kearney and the Religious Turn in Continental Philosophy*, edited by John Panteleimon Manoussakis (New York: Fordham University Press, 2006), pp. 3–20.
———, 'Epiphanies in Joyce', in *Global Ireland: Irish Literatures for the New Millennium*, edited by Ondřej Pilný and Clare Wallace (Prague: Litteraria Pragensia, 2005), pp. 147–82.
———, 'Imagination, Anatheism, and the Sacred, Dialogue with James Wood', in *Reimagining the Sacred: Richard Kearney Debates God with James Wood, Catherine Keller, Charles Taylor, Julia Kristeva, Gianni Vattimo, Simon Critchley, Jean-Luc Marion, John Caputo, David Tracy, Jens Zimmermann, and Merold Westphal*, edited by Richard Kearney and Jens Zimmermann (New York: Columbia University Press, 2015), pp. 19–45.
Kelly, Edward F., Emily Williams Kelly, Adam Crabtree, Alan Gauld, Michael Grosso and Bruce Greyson, *Irreducible Mind: Toward a Psychology for the 21st Century* (Lanham, MD: Rowman & Littlefield, 2007).
Kern, Stephen, *Modernism After the Death of God: Christianity, Fragmentation, and Unification* (Oxford: Routledge, 2017).
Kim, Sharon, *Literary Epiphany in the Novel, 1850–1950: Constellations of the Soul* (Basingstoke: Palgrave Macmillan, 2012).
Knight, G. Wilson, *Myth and Miracle: An Essay on the Mystic Symbolism of Shakespeare* (London: Burrow, 1929).
Knights, L. C., 'Shakespeare and Profit Inflations', *Scrutiny*, 5 (1936), 48–60.
Kripal, Jeffrey J., *Authors of the Impossible: The Paranormal and the Sacred* (Chicago: University of Chicago Press, 2010).
Kurlberg, Jonas, *Christian Modernism in an Age of Totalitarianism: T. S. Eliot, Karl Mannheim and the Moot* (London: Bloomsbury Academic, 2019).

Larsen, Timothy, *The Slain God: Anthropologists and the Christian Faith* (Oxford: Oxford University Press, 2014).
Lash, Nicholas, *Easter in Ordinary: Reflections on Human Experience and the Knowledge of God* (Charlottesville: University of Virginia Press, 1988).
Leavis, F. R., *The Living Principle: 'English' as a Discipline of Thought* (London: Chatto & Windus, 1975).
Lewis, C. S., 'Review of *Passion and Society*, by D. de Rougemont and trans. M. Belgion. Faber & Faber; Review of *The Bride of Christ*, by Claude Chavasse. Faber & Faber', *Theology*, 40 (1940), 459–61.
Lewis, Pericles, *Religious Experience and the Modernist Novel* (Cambridge: Cambridge University Press, 2010).
Lock, Louis Lee, 'Forget Pearl Harbor, or a South Pacific Charter', *Catholic Worker*, December 1942, 3.
Loisy, Alfred, *The Gospel and the Church*, translated by Christopher Home (London: Isbister, 1903).
Longenbach, James, *Modernist Poetics of History: Pound, Eliot, and the Sense of the Past* (Princeton: Princeton University Press, 1987).
——, *Stone Cottage: Pound, Yeats and Modernism* (Oxford: Oxford University Press, 1991).
Luckhurst, Roger, 'Religion, Psychical Research, Spiritualism, and the Occult', in *The Oxford Handbook of Modernisms*, edited by Peter Brooker, Andrzej Gąsiorek, Deborah Longworth and Andrew Thacker (Oxford: Oxford University Press, 2010), pp. 429–44.
McArthur, Murray, 'Symptom and Sign: Janet, Freud, Eliot, and the Literary Mandate of Laughter', *Twentieth Century Literature*, 56 (2010), 1–24.
MacCarthy, Fiona, *Eric Gill* (London: Faber & Faber, 1989).
McGuire, Meredith B., *Lived Religion: Faith and Practice in Everyday Life* (Oxford: Oxford University Press, 2008).
MacKay, Marina, *Modernism and World War II* (Cambridge: Cambridge University Press, 2007).
McNabb, O. P., Vincent, 'A New Theory of the Eucharistic Sacrifice', *Blackfriars*, 4 (1923), 1086–1100.
Maeterlinck, Maurice, 'The Awakening of the Soul', in *The Treasure of the Humble*, translated by Alfred Sutro (London: George Allen, 1898), pp. 23–42.
Mahmood, Saba, *Religious Difference in a Secular Age: A Minority Report* (Princeton: Princeton University Press, 2015).
Maiden, John G., *National Religion and the Prayer Book Controversy, 1927–1928* (Woodbridge: Boydell & Brewer, 2009).
Major, H. D. A., 'Sign of the Times', *The Modern Churchman*, 11 (1921), 148–64.
Mannheim, Karl, *Diagnosis of Our Time: Wartime Essays of a Sociologist* (London: Routledge, 1943).

Maritain, Jacques, 'Art and Scholasticism', in 'Art and Scholasticism' and 'The Frontiers of Poetry', translated by Joseph W. Evans (Notre Dame, IN: University of Notre Dame Press, 1974), pp. 3–115.
Marsden, Richard, ed., *The Cambridge Old English Reader* (Cambridge: Cambridge University Press, 2005).
Martz, Louis L., *The Poetry of Meditation: A Study in English Religious Literature of the Seventeenth Century* (New Haven, CT: Yale University Press, 1954).
Matthiesen, Michon M., 'De la Taille's *Mysterium Fidei*: Eucharistic Sacrifice and Nouvelle Théologie', *New Blackfriars*, 94 (2013), 518–37.
Mayo, Elton, *The Psychology of Pierre Janet* (London: Routledge and Kegan Paul, 1951).
Mazzoni, Cristina, *Saint Hysteria: Neurosis, Mysticism, and Gender in European Culture* (Ithaca, NY: Cornell University Press, 1996).
Menand, Louis, *Discovering Modernism: T. S. Eliot and His Context*, 2nd edition (Oxford: Oxford University Press, 2007).
Miles, Jonathan, *Backgrounds to David Jones: A Study in Sources and Drafts* (Cardiff: University of Wales Press, 1990).
——, and Derek Shiel, *David Jones: The Maker Unmade* (Bridgend, Wales: Seren, 1995).
Miller Lewis, Johanna, 'Equality Deferred, Opportunity Pursued: The Sisters of Wachovia', in *Women of the American South: A Multicultural Reader*, edited by Christie Anne Farnham (New York: New York University Press, 1997), pp. 74–89.
The Missal in Latin and English, Being the Text of the Missale Romanum with English Rubrics and a New Translation (London: Burns, Oates & Washbourne, 1950).
Morris, Adalaide, *How to Live/What to Do: H.D.'s Cultural Poetics* (Champaign: University of Illinois Press, 2003).
Mounier, Emmanuel, *A Personalist Manifesto*, translated by Monks of St John's Abbey (London: Longmans Green, 1938).
Moyn, Samuel, *Christian Human Rights* (Philadelphia: University of Pennsylvania Press, 2015).
Muir, Edward, *Ritual in Early Modern Europe* (Cambridge: Cambridge University Press, 2005).
Murray, Paul, *T. S. Eliot and Mysticism: The Secret History of* Four Quartets (New York: St Martin's Press, 1991).
Murry, John Middleton, *Community Farm* (London: Nevill, 1952).
Mutter, Matthew, *Restless Secularism: Modernism and the Religious Inheritance* (New Haven, CT: Yale University Press, 2017).
Myers, Frederic W. H., *Human Personality and Its Survival of Bodily Death*, 2 vols (London: Longmans Green, 1903).

Nichols, Ashton, *The Poetics of Epiphany: Nineteenth-Century Origins of the Modern Literary Moment* (Tuscaloosa: University of Alabama Press, 1987).

Official Year-Book of the Church of England, 1902 (London: Society for Promoting Christian Knowledge, 1902).

O'Malley, John W., *The First Jesuits* (Cambridge, MA: Harvard University Press, 1993).

O'Shea Merriman, Brigid, *Searching for Christ: The Spirituality of Dorothy Day* (Notre Dame, IN: University of Notre Dame Press, 1994).

Owen, Alex, *The Place of Enchantment: British Occultism and the Culture of the Modern* (Chicago: University of Chicago Press, 2004).

Parsons, William B., *Freud and Augustine in Dialogue: Psychoanalysis, Mysticism, and the Culture of Modern Spirituality* (Charlottesville: University of Virginia Press, 2013).

——, *Freud and Religion: Advancing the Dialogue* (Cambridge: Cambridge University Press, 2021).

Passerini, Luisa, *Women and Men in Love: European Identities in the Twentieth Century*, translated by Juliet Haydock with Allan Cameron (New York: Berghahn Books, 2012).

Pecklers, Keith F., *The Unread Vision: The Liturgical Movement in the United States of America, 1926–1955* (Collegeville, MN: Liturgical Press, 1998).

Perl, Jeffrey M., *Skepticism and Modern Enmity: Before and After Eliot* (Baltimore: Johns Hopkins University Press, 1989).

Peters, Benjamin T., *Called to be Saints: John Hugo, The Catholic Worker, and a Theology of Radical Christianity* (Milwaukee, WI: Marquette University Press, 2016).

Peucker, Paul, 'The Songs of the Sifting: Understanding the Role of Bridal Mysticism in Moravian Piety during the Late 1740s', *Journal of Moravian History*, 3 (2007), 51–87.

——, *A Time of Sifting: Mystical Marriage and the Crisis of Moravian Piety in the Eighteenth Century* (University Park: Penn State University Press, 2015).

Pitman, David, *Twentieth Century Christian Responses to Religious Pluralism: Difference is Everything* (Farnham: Ashgate, 2014).

Pius X, *Pascendi Dominici Gregis*: Encyclical Letter on the Doctrines of the Modernists, 8 September 1907, Vatican website <http://w2.vatican.va/content/pius-x/en/encyclicals/documents/hf_p-x_enc_19070908_pascendi-dominici-gregis.html> [accessed 1 March 2022].

Pius XI, *Quadragesimo Anno: On Reconstruction of the Social Order*, 15 May 1931, Vatican website <https://www.vatican.va/content/pius-xi/en/encyclicals/documents/hf_p-xi_enc_19310515_quadragesimo-anno.html> [accessed 1 March 2022].

Pius XII, 'The Internal Order of States and People', Christmas Message for 1942, in *The Major Addresses of Pius XII*, edited by Vincent Yzermans, 2 vols (St Paul, MN: North Central Publishing, 1961), 2, pp. 53–64.

Pound, Ezra, 'Psychology and Troubadours', in *The Spirit of Romance,* revised edition (New York: New Directions, 1952), pp. 87–100.

——, 'Remy de Gourmont', in *Literary Essays of Ezra Pound*, edited by T. S. Eliot (London: Faber & Faber, 1954), pp. 339–58.

Rahner, Karl, 'Observations on the Problem of the "Anonymous Christian"', in *Theological Investigations*, 23 vols (New York: Crossroads, 1961–92), 14: *Ecclesiology, Questions in the Church, the Church in the World*, translated by David Bourke, pp. 280–94.

——, 'The One Christ and the Universality of Salvation', in *Theological Investigations*, 16: *Experience of the Spirit: Source of Theology*, translated by David Morland, pp. 119–224.

Rainey, Lawrence, *Institutions of Modernism: Literary Elites and Public Culture* (New Haven, CT: Yale University Press, 1998).

Rashdall, Hastings, *Conscience and Christ: Six Lectures on Christian Ethics* (London: Duckworth, 1916).

Richer, Paul, 'L'hystérie dans l'art', in *Études cliniques sur la grande hystérie ou hystéro-épilepsie* (Paris: Delahaye et Lecrosnier, 1885), pp. 914–56.

Rimius, Henry, *A Candid Narrative of the Rise and Progress of the Herrnhuters, call'd Moravians, or Unitas Fratrum* (London: Linde, 1753).

Roberts, Nancy L., *Dorothy Day and the* Catholic Worker (Albany: State University of New York Press, 1985).

Robichaud, Paul, 'Avant-garde and Orthodoxy at Ditchling', *Renascence*, 69 (2017), 186–97.

——, *Making the Past Present: David Jones, the Middle Ages and Modernism* (Washington, D. C.: Catholic University of America Press, 2007).

Robinson, Matte, *The Astral H.D.: Occult and Religious Sources and Contexts for H.D.'s Poetry and Prose* (London: Bloomsbury Academic, 2016).

Rosenzweig, Franz, *The Star of Redemption*, translated by William W. Hallo (New York: Holt, Rinehart and Winston, 1970).

Rougemont, Denis de, *Passion and Society*, translated by Montgomery Belgion (London: Faber & Faber, 1940).

Rousseau, Jean-Jacques, *The Collected Writings of Rousseau*, edited by Roger D. Masters and Christopher Kelly, 13 vols (Hanover, NH: University Press of New England, 1990–2010), 6: *Julie, or the New Heloise: Letters of Two Lovers Who Live in a Small Town at the Foot of the Alps*, translated and annotated by Philip Stewart and Jean Vaché, 13: *Emile: or On Education*, translated and edited by Christopher Kelly and Allan Bloom.

Royce, Josiah, *The Sources of Religious Insight* (Edinburgh: T & T Clark, 1912).

Rubin, Miri, *Mother of God: A History of the Virgin Mary* (New Haven, CT: Yale University Press, 2010).

Rzepa, Joanna, *Modernism and Theology: Rainer Maria Rilke, T. S. Eliot, Czesław Miłosz* (Basingstoke: Palgrave Macmillan, 2021).

Sackville-West, Vita, *The Eagle and The Dove – A Study in Contrasts: St Teresa of Avila, St Thérèse of Lisieux* (Garden City, NJ: Doubleday Doran, 1944).

Schedneck, Brooke, 'Religious and Spiritual Retreats', in *The Routledge Handbook of Religious and Spiritual Tourism*, edited by Daniel H. Olsen and Dallen J. Timothy (Oxford: Routledge, 2022), pp. 247–61.

Schloesser, Stephen, *Jazz Age Catholicism: Mystic Modernism in Postwar Paris, 1919–1933* (Toronto: University of Toronto Press, 2005).

Schmidt, Leigh Eric, 'The Making of Modern "Mysticism"', *Journal of the American Academy of Religion*, 71 (2003), 273–302.

Schuchard, Ronald, *Eliot's Dark Angel: Intersections of Life and Art* (Oxford: Oxford University Press, 1999).

Schwartz, Adam, 'These Global Days: Review of *The Grail Mass and Other Works* by David Jones, ed. by Thomas Goldpaugh and Jamie Callison. Bloomsbury Academic, 2019. Hardcover, xi + 279 pp., $176', Russell Kirk Center Website, 6 October 2019 <https://kirkcenter.org/reviews/these-global-days/> [accessed 1 March 2022].

——, *The Third Spring: G. K. Chesterton, Graham Greene, Christopher Dawson, and David Jones* (Washington, D. C.: Catholic University of America Press, 2012).

Scimecca, Joseph A., *Christianity and Sociological Theory: Reclaiming the Promise* (Oxford: Routledge, 2018).

Scott, Rev. W. Major, *Aspects of Christian Mysticism* (New York: Dutton, 1907).

Sergeant, Miles, 'From the Editor's Study', *The Vision*, 63 (July 1935), 1–2.

Shaw, Gilbert, 'To the Editor: The Rule of Silence', *The Vision*, 31 (August 1927), 10–13.

Shortall, Sarah, *Soldiers of God in a Secular World: Catholic Theology and Twentieth-Century French Politics* (Cambridge, MA: Harvard University Press, 2021).

Showalter, Elaine, *The Female Malady: Women, Madness, and English Culture, 1830–1980* (London: Virago, 1985).

Simpson, Alan H., *Short Retreats for Beginners: A Handbook for Conductors* (London: Association for Promoting Retreats, 1931).

Sinclair, May, *A Defence of Idealism: Some Questions and Conclusions* (London: Macmillan, 1917).

Soud, W. David, *Divine Cartographies: God, History, and Poiesis in W. B. Yeats, David Jones, and T. S. Eliot* (Oxford: Oxford University Press, 2016).

Spengler, Oswald, *Decline of the West*, translated by Charles Francis Atkinson, 2 vols (London: Allen & Unwin, 1918).

Spurr, Barry, *'Anglo-Catholic in Religion': T. S. Eliot and Christianity* (Cambridge: Lutterworth Press, 2010).
Staudt, Kathleen Henderson, 'Incarnation Reconsidered: The Poem as Sacramental Act in *The Anathemata* of David Jones', *Contemporary Literature*, 26 (1985), 1–25.
Stead, C. K., *Pound, Yeats, Eliot, and the Modernist Movement* (New Brunswick, NJ: Rutgers University Press, 1986).
Still, Colin, *Shakespeare's Mystery Play: A Study of* The Tempest (London: Cecil Palmer, 1921).
Stone, Lawrence, *Road to Divorce: England, 1530–1987* (Oxford: Oxford University Press, 1990).
Strachey, Lytton, *Eminent Victorians: Cardinal Manning, Florence Nightingale, Dr Arnold, General Gordon* (London: Chatto & Windus, 1918).
Surette, Leon, *The Birth of Modernism: Ezra Pound, T. S. Eliot, W. B. Yeats, and the Occult* (Montreal: McGill-Queen's University Press, 1993).
Sword, Helen, *Ghostwriting Modernism* (Ithaca, NY: Cornell University Press, 2002).
Taves, Ann, *Fits, Trances, and Visions: Experiencing Religion and Explaining Experience from Wesley to James* (Princeton: Princeton University Press, 1999).
———, *Religious Experience Reconsidered: A Building-Block Approach to the Study of Religion and Other Special Things* (Princeton: Princeton University Press, 2009).
Taylor, Charles, *A Secular Age* (Cambridge, MA: Harvard University Press, 2007).
Taylor, Eugene, *William James on Consciousness Beyond the Margin* (Princeton: Princeton University Press, 2011).
Taylor, Georgina, *H.D. and the Public Sphere of Modernist Women Writers 1913–1946: Talking Women* (Oxford: Oxford University Press, 2001).
Tentler, Leslie Woodcock, *American Catholics: A History* (New Haven, CT: Yale University Press, 2020).
Tonning, Erik, *Modernism and Christianity* (Basingstoke: Palgrave Macmillan, 2014).
———, 'Old Dogmas for a New Crisis: Hell and Incarnation in T. S. Eliot and W. H. Auden', in *Modernism, Christianity and Apocalypse*, edited by Erik Tonning, Matthew Feldman and David Addyman (Leiden: Brill, 2015), pp. 236–59.
Tracy, David, 'God: The Possible/Impossible', in *After God: Richard Kearney and the Religious Turn in Continental Philosophy*, edited by John Panteleimon Manoussakis (New York: Fordham University Press, 2006), pp. 340–54.
Turner, Denys, *The Darkness of God: Negativity in Christian Mysticism* (Cambridge: Cambridge University Press, 1995).

——, *Julian of Norwich, Theologian* (New Haven, CT: Yale University Press, 2011).
Tuve, Rosemond, 'On Herbert's "Sacrifice"', *Kenyon Review*, 12 (1950), 51–75.
Tyers, John, 'Ignatian and Silent: A Brief Survey of the Development of the Practice of Retreat in the Church of England, 1858–2008', *Theology*, 113 (2010), 267–75.
Tylor, Edward Burnett, *Primitive Culture: Researches into the Development of Mythology, Philosophy, Religion, Language, Art, and Custom*, 2 vols (London: John Murray, 1871).
Tyrrell, George, preface to *XVI Revelations of Divine Love Shewed to Mother Juliana of Norwich* (London: Kegan Paul, Trench, Trübner, 1902), pp. v–xvii.
Underhill, Evelyn, '*Light of Christ*: Addresses Given at the House of Retreat, Pleshey, in May, 1932', in '*Fruits of the Spirit*', '*Light of Christ*, with a Memoir by Lucy Menzies', '*Abba, Meditations based on the Lord's Prayer*' (London: Longmans Green, 1956), pp. 9–107.
——, *The Making of a Mystic: New and Selected Letters of Evelyn Underhill*, edited by Carol Poston (Champaign: University of Illinois Press, 2010).
——, *Mysticism: A Study in the Nature and Development of Man's Spiritual Consciousness* (London: Methuen, 1911).
——, 'The Need of Retreat', *The Vision*, 17 (February 1924), 1–4.
——, 'The Need of Retreat', *The Vision*, 49 (January 1932), 3–7.
——, preface to *Mysticism: A Study in the Nature and Development of Man's Spiritual Consciousness*, 12th edition (New York: Dutton, 1930), pp. vii–xi.
Van Mierlo, Chrissie, *James Joyce and Catholicism: The Apostate's Wake* (London: Bloomsbury Academic, 2017).
Vetter, Lara, introduction to H.D., *By Avon River*, edited by Lara Vetter (Gainesville: University Press of Florida, 2017), pp. 1–42.
——, *Modernist Writings and Religio-scientific Discourse: H.D., Loy, and Toomer* (Basingstoke: Palgrave Macmillan, 2010).
Villis, Tom, *British Catholics and Fascism: Religious Identity and Political Extremism* (Basingstoke: Palgrave Macmillan, 2013).
Viswanathan, Gauri, *Outside the Fold: Conversion, Modernity, and Belief* (Princeton: Princeton University Press, 1998).
Vogt, Peter, '"Honor to the Side": The Adoration of the Side Wound of Jesus in Eighteenth-Century Moravian Piety', *Journal of Moravian History*, 7 (2009), 83–106.
Waite, A. E., 'A Garden of Spiritual Flowers', *New Age* 9, no. 6 (8 June 1911), 137–39.
Walker Bynum, Caroline, *Jesus as Mother: Studies in the Spirituality of the High Middle Ages* (Berkeley: University of California Press, 1982).

Walton, Eda Lou, '"T. S. Eliot Turns to Religious Verse", *New York Times Book Review*, July 1930', in *T. S. Eliot: The Critical Heritage*, edited by Michael Grant, 2 vols (London: Routledge & Kegan Paul, 1982), 1, pp. 253–55.

Wareham, J., 'Retreats and the Centenary', *The Vision*, 53 (November 1933), 3–5.

———, 'What a Retreat Really Is', *The Vision*, 47 (July 1931), 3–6.

Weber, Max, *The Protestant Ethic and the Spirit of Capitalism*, translated by Talcott Parsons (London: Routledge, 1930).

West, Rebecca, *A Letter to a Grandfather* (London: Hogarth, 1933).

———, *St Augustine* (London: Davies, 1933).

Williams, Raymond, *Keywords: A Vocabulary of Culture and Society*, revised edition (Oxford: Oxford University Press, 1985).

Wolosky, Shira, *Language Mysticism: The Negative Way of Language in Eliot, Beckett, and Celan* (Stanford, CA: Stanford University Press, 1995).

Woolf, Virginia, *The Letters of Virginia Woolf*, edited by Nigel Nicolson and Joanne Trautmann, 6 vols (London: Hogarth Press, 1975–1980).

———, 'Modern Fiction', in *Selected Essays*, edited by David Bradshaw (Oxford: Oxford University Press, 2009), pp. 6–12.

———, 'Professions for Women', in *Selected Essays*, pp. 140–45.

Yates, Nigel, *Anglican Ritualism in Victorian Britain, 1830–1910* (Oxford: Oxford University Press, 1999).

Yocum Mize, Sandra, '"We Are Still Pacifists": Dorothy Day's Pacifism during World War II', in *Dorothy Day and the Catholic Worker Movement: Centenary Essays*, edited by William J. Thorn, Phillip M. Runkel and Susan Mountin (Wisconsin, WI: Marquette University Press, 2001), pp. 465–73.

Zimmerman, Jens, *Dietrich Bonhoeffer's Christian Humanism* (Oxford: Oxford University Press, 2019).

INDEX

Abrams, M. H., 11, 162
agape love, 152, 154, 155, 161
Allitt, Patrick, 36
anamnesis, 39–40, 44–5, 47
anatheism, 17–19, 23, 127, 199
Anderson, Elizabeth, 13, 20, 68
Anglesey, Wales, 66–7
Anglican Church (Church of England)
   Astley, 38–9
   Book of Common Prayer, 37–9, 185
   Churchman's Union, 38
   Eliot, 6, 13, 76–7, 78, 101, 106, 110, 169
   mission, 10, 101
   modernists, 6, 37–9, 185
   Rashdall, 6, 39
Anglo-Catholicism
   Association for Promoting Retreats (APR), 170–3, 175–80, *179*, 183–9, 191
   Church of England, 38, 185
   Eliot's *Ash-Wednesday*, 76–7, 93, 114, 115

Eliot's other writing, 6, 95, 181, 200–1
Eliot's retreats, 101, 106, 170, 181
anonymous Christian, concept of, 97–8
antimodernism, 12, 17, 36, 51, 62
Ardis, Ann L., 90
Arnold, Matthew, 6–7, 11, 39, 199–200
Arts and Crafts movement, 43
asceticism
   Eliot, 109, 114
   H.D., 152, 156, 158
   Imagism, 122
   retreat movement, 169–70, 175, 181–4, 189
Association for Promoting Retreats (APR), 170–3, 175–80, *179*, 183–9, 191
Astley, H. J. D., 38–9
astral doubling, 139, 140, 162
atheism, 18, 69, 78, 97, 98, 100, 114
Attwater, Donald, 57, 58
Augustine, *Confessions*, 125–6, 127
Augustine, Jane, 131, 133, 134
avant-garde, 11, 151, 201

226

INDEX

Babbitt, Irving, 49–50, 88, 114
baptism, 114, 115, 169
Barmann, Lawrence F., 53
Barth, Karl, 113
belief
   introduction to, 8–9, 20–1
   and doubt, 19, 114, 198–9
   Eliot, 97, 99–105, 111, 113, 114, 170, 199
   extra-belief ('*Aberglaube*'), 7, 23, 39
   Kierkegaard on faith, 154, 156
   lay belief, 50, 68
   Maurras, 78, 100
   reasoned unbelief, 188, 191
Bell, Clive, 35, 36, 43
Bellah, Robert N., 3, 24, 100–1, 147
Bergson, Henri, 41, 103
Biblical references
   Exodus 2: 1–10, *145*
   Genesis 1:1, 44
   Romans 13: 13–14, 125
   Song of Songs, 149
Blair, Kirstie, 198–9
blood-and-wound tradition, 133, 149–50
Bonhoeffer, Dietrich, 97–8
Book of Common Prayer, 37–8, 185
Bouquet, J. A., 173
Bradshaw, David, 99
Bramble, John, 68
bricolage, 46, 50, 68, 139, 191, 202
British Empire, 38, 62, 64, 67
Brooker, Jewel Spears, 114
Browning, Robert, 10, 56, 84
Bryher (Annie Winifred Ellerman), 138, 144
Buddhism, 49–50
'buffered self', 3, 10, 191
Bush, Ronald, 111–12
Butts, Mary, 12
Bynum, Caroline Walker, 133

Cathars, 127–9, 138, 152, 161
Catholic Worker retreats, 170–1, 175–7, 178, 182–3, 185–6, 189–92, 201
Cave, Alfred A., 134–5
Cefalu, Paul, 198
Certeau, Michel de, 20
Chappel, James, 12, 60, 62
Charcot, Jean-Martin
   Eliot influenced by, 85, 86, 89, 90, 106
   hysteria, 80–4, 144, 184
Chesterton, G. K., 12, 36, 96
Childs, Donald J., 79, 106
church
   attendance, 22, 115, 177, 181, 187, 188
   Royce's definition of, 14, 15, 153
   see also Anglican Church (Church of England); institutional religion; Moravian Church; Roman Catholic Church
Church of England *see* Anglican Church (Church of England)
Churchman's Union, 38
collective memory, 111–12, 114
collective temperament, 103–4, 111
Collini, Stefan, 101
communism, 129, 151, 153, 162, 190
communitarianism, 110, 151, 161, 175
consciousness
   astral doubling, 139, 140, 162
   dissociation of sensibility, 85–9, 90, 95, 103, 192, 201
   Eliot, 77, 92–5, 123
   God-consciousness, 9–10, 181
   multiple layers/forms, 87, 90–2, 109
   poetic consciousness, 11, 88
   streams of consciousness, 3
   subconsciousness, 3, 4, 92–3, 103, 146
   superhuman conscious reality, 14
   unconscious motivations, 96–8, 100, 102–3, 146, 155, 177, 197
conversions, 125–7, 137, 140, 162, 182
corporatism, 60–1, 62, 98, 102, 104, 109–10
craft skills, 43–4, 60–1, 67

227

creation story, 41, 43–4, 49, 186
The Criterion, 86, 113
crucifixion, 35, 45–7, 48, 62–3, 149–50, 196

Daly, Gabriel, 52
Dante, 12, 139
D'Arcy, Fr Martin C., 8, 9, 10, 45, 76, 105, 106
Dawson, Christopher, 50, 51
Day, Dorothy
    action, 177, 178, 182, 187, 189–90
    asceticism, 182–3, 184
    Ignation practice, 175–6, 185–6
    retreat concept, evolution of, 170, 175–7, 190, 192, 201
De Gay, Jane, 43
death instinct, 151, 154–5, 158, 159
Delacroix, Henri, 84–5
Delap, Lucy, 151
democracy, 12, 61, 62, 99, 110, 191
Dettmar, Kevin J. H., 199
DiCenso, James, 144
Dilworth, Thomas, 37, 57, 69
dissociation of sensibility, 85–9, 90, 95, 103, 192, 201
Ditchling, Sussex, 41, 43, 60, 61
Dix, Dom Gregory, 37–8, 39, 40, 44
Domestico, Anthony, 113
Donne, John, 198, 199
Doolittle, Hilda *see* H.D. (Hilda Doolittle)
Doré, Gustave, 'Moses in the Bulrushes', 145
Dowland, David A., 101
dramatic poetry, 56–7, 63, 65, 82, 158–61
'The Dream of the Rood' (anon.), 46
Dryden, John, 93
Dubreuil, Emmanuelle Hériard, 153
DuPlessis, Rachel Blau, 13, 146, 150

Eagleton, Terry, 158, 169
ecstasy, 80–1, *80, 81*, 102

The Egoist, 151
Eliot, T. S.
    After Strange Gods, 99, 170
    Anglicanism, 6, 13, 76–7, 78, 101, 106, 110, 169
    Ash-Wednesday, 76–8, 79, 93–5, 108, 114, 115, 197
    baptism, 114, 115, 169
    and Charcot, 85, 86, 89, 90, 106
    on D. H. Lawrence, 122–3
    'The Death of Saint Narcissus', 84, 85, 89, 105
    dissociation of sensibility, 85–9, 90, 95, 103, 192, 201
    'A Game of Chess', 94
    'Hysteria', 90
    The Idea of a Christian Society, 78, 96, 98–105, 109–11, 113, 188, 200
    and James, 92, 93, 103, 106
    'The Love Song of J. Alfred Prufrock', 85, 95
    'The Love Song of St. Sebastian', 82–4, 89, 95–6, 102, 104–5
    martyr poetry, 78, 82–5, 90, 106, 109, 115
    metaphysical poetry, 85–90, 109, 110, 199
    'The Metaphysical Poets', 85, 86, 88, 90, 94
    Moot, 98, 102
    orthodoxy, 12, 98–9, 102–5, 109, 115, 170, 199
    'Religion and Literature', 96
    'Revival of Christian Imagination', 102, 105
    'Sweeney Erect', 89, 90
    'Tradition and the Individual Talent', 50, 79, 94
    unconsciously Christian texts, 96–8, 100, 102–3
    The Use of Poetry and the Use of Criticism, 79, 93, 94, 108
    The Waste Land, 7, 85, 173
    see also *Four Quartets* (Eliot)

INDEX

emotion
  introduction to, 6–10, 13–16, 42
  dissociation of sensibility, 85–9, 90, 95, 103, 192, 201
  Eliot, 77, 79, 98, 105, 111, 170, 191
  Imagism, 123–4
Empson, William, 143, 196–7, 198
epiphanies
  definition, 11
  Eliot, 94, 114
  Imagism, 124, 162
  transference, 22–4, 42, 45, 200
Erikson, Erik, 145
eros, 123, 128, 151–2
ethics *see* morals and ethics
Eucharist *see* Mass/Eucharist
Evans, Martha Noel, 90
extra-belief ('*Aberglaube*'), 7, 23, 39

faith *see* belief
fascism, 61, 155, 201
females *see* women
femininity, 131, 134, 146, 151, 157–8, 161
feminism, 150, 151, 201
First World War, 46–7, 48, 115, 147, 155
Fletcher, John Gould, 122, 123–4, 141, 162
Flint, F. S., 122
Foucault, Michel, 183
Four Quartets (Eliot), 15–16, 17, 79, 106–14, 159, 199
  'Burnt Norton', 94, 109
  'East Coker', 107–8, 109
  'Little Gidding', 94, 110, 112, 181
France, 78, 90, 127, 152
Frazer, J. G., *The Golden Bough*, 38, 46–7, 48, 60

Freer, Scott, 68
Freud, Sigmund
  Civilization and Its Discontents, 145, 148, 151
  The Future of an Illusion, 144, 148
Freudian psychoanalysis, 124, 133, 143–8, 149–50, 151, 197
Friedman, Susan Stanford, 131, 146, 147, 150, 151, 156
Fry, Roger, 35, 36, 43, 69

Gasiorek, Andrzej, 12
gender
  femininity, 131, 134, 146, 151, 157–8, 161
  masculinity, 146–7, 151
  retreat movement, 172
  see also women
The Gift (H.D.)
  introduction to, 123, 126
  conversions, 127, 135, 137, 140
  lamb of God imagery, 129–30
  Mamalie, 134–5, 139, 147
  public or private religion, 150
  women's roles, 131, 133, 147
Gill, Eric, 41, 43, 60, 61
Gish, Nancy, 86
Goldpaugh, Thomas, 36, 65
Gourmont, Remy de, 86–8, 90
gratuitousness
  creation story, 41, 43–4, 186
  Jones, 57, 59, 60–1, 65, 200
  of retreat, 185–6
Greek language, 39, 40, 57
Greenberg, Clement, 11
Greene, Gwendolen, 54–6
Grisewood, Harman, 49–50
Guardini, Romano, 58

Hadjiyiannis, Christos, 88, 103
Hague, René, 49, 59
Hamilton, Joseph Taylor, 136–7
Hanson, Ellis, 84
Harding, Jason, 13

229

H.D. (Hilda Doolittle)
  introduction to, 1, 3, 12, 13, 15
  'Advent', 144
  avant-garde feminism, 151, 201
  By Avon River, 126
  'The Flowering of the Rod', 140
  Helen in Egypt, 17, 124, 126, 151–2, 156–62, 183
  'Hymn', 133, 148–50
  'The Master', 146, 150
  Moravians, depictions of, 130–1, 133–5, 137–43, 147–50, 161
  The Mystery, 126, 127, 130, 137–40, 147, 161
  Sea-garden, 122, 123, 141, 162
  Tribute to Freud, 137, 144, 145–7
  Trilogy, 68, 130, 131, 140–3, 149, 202
  see also The Gift (H.D.)
Herbert, George, 'The Sacrifice', 143, 196–7, 198
Hervieu-Léger, Danièle, 111, 124
Hill, Geoffrey, 106
historical elements
  Eliot, 88, 108, 110, 111–12, 114
  H.D., 129–30, 140, 151–2
  Hügel, 16–17, 52
  Jones, 48, 49, 51, 57, 63, 64, 67
  of Mass/Eucharist, 39–40
  retreat settings, 179–81
  Rougemont, 127, 128–9
Hobson, Suzanne, 21, 140, 142
Holland, Norman N., 146
Hollywood, Amy, 1
Holy Spirit, 14, 35, 40, 51, 134
House of Mercy, Horbury, Yorkshire, 179, *179*
Hügel, Friedrich von
  associates, 51
  Letters from Baron Friedrich von Hügel to a Niece, 53–4
  The Mystical Element of Religion, 2, 16–17, 52–5, 58, 82

Hugo, Fr John, 175, 182
Hulme, T. E., 9, 11, 78, 103
human dignity, 61–2, 68, 152, 154, 155, 190
human nature, as sign-making, 35, 45, 49, 59–61, 67, 69
human rights, 18, 62, 68, 152, 190, 200
humanism, 196, 198
Huysmans, J. K., 83–4, 85, 89, 181–2, 184
hymns, 133, 148–9
hysteria
  Charcot, 80–4, *80*, 144, 184
  Huysmans, 83–4, 85, 89, 182, 184
  'Hysteria' (Eliot), 90

Ignatian retreats, 169, 170, 172, 173, 175–6, 191, 201
Imagism, 122–4, 136, 162
immanence, 9, 109, 115, 175
  immanent frame, 10, 12, 191, 192
imperialism, 37, 38, 48, 62–5, 67–8, 200–1
Indigenous Americans, 131, 134–6, 139–40, 147
individuals, increasing focus on
  introduction to, 3–6, 9–10, 12–17, 20
  anonymous Christians, 97–8
  H.D., 143–4, 145, 147, 151, 153
  Hügel, 17, 52, 53, 54–5
  inner journeys, 9–10, 43, 54–5, 181, 184
  Jones, 36, 55, 57, 61
  personality, 12, 78, 79, 87, 92
  retreat movement, 175, 177, 181, 184, 185, 191
  see also liberal individualism; personal religion
Inge, William, 9–10, 181, 185
institutional religion
  introduction to, 2–6, 8–10, 14, 18–23

attendance, 22, 115, 177, 181, 187, 188
Eliot's *The Idea of a Christian Society*, 78, 98, 100, 101, 103
Hügel's institutional element, 2, 16–17, 52–5
and memory, 111, 114
Mounier, 153
see also Anglican Church (Church of England); Moravian Church; retreat movement; Roman Catholic Church
irruptions, 5, 93–5, 103, 106, 112

Jain, Manju, 84, 92
James, William
  and Eliot, 92, 93, 103, 106
  Principles of Psychology, 91
  scientific study of religion, 5–6, 13–14, 16, 82
  and Underhill, 2, 4–5, 7, 93
  The Varieties of Religious Experience, 2, 4–5, 7–8, 10, 13, 15–16, 82, 92, 106
Janet, Pierre, 86, 87, 90–1, 93
Jantzen, Grace, 3, 15
Jasper, David, 23
Jay, Martin, 6, 7
Jerusalem, 64
Jesus Christ
  crucifixion, 35, 45–7, 48, 62–3, 149–50, 196
  incorporation into, 58
  Last Supper, 35, 45, 47, 48, 49, 61
  Moravian Church, 136–7, 149–50
Jones, David
  'Absalom, Mass', 55–6, 59, 65
  The Anathemata, 39–40, 51, 57–61, 65–6, 68, 200
  'Art and Democracy', 61
  'Art and Sacrament', 35, 44, 60
  The Grail Mass, 34, 37, 62–5, 69, 200
  human nature as sign-making, 35, 45, 49, 59–61, 67, 69

imperialism, 37, 48, 62–5, 67–8, 200–1
Mass/Eucharist, 34–6, 39–41, 43–7, 49, 51, 55–60, 69
mysticism, 1–2, 8, 9, 55, 57–8, 69
In Parenthesis, 46–7, 48
'The Roman Dinner Conversation', 64–5
The Roman Quarry, 49–50
'The Tribune's Visitation', 62–4, 65
Joyce, James, 11, 43, 50, 66–7
Julian of Norwich, 53, 112, 113

Kant, Immanuel, 6
Kearney, Richard, *Anatheism*, 17–19, 23, 127, 199
Kern, Stephen, 20, 21
Kierkegaard, Søren, 154, 155
Knight, G. Wilson, 8
Knights, L. C., 12
Knights Templar, *130*, 134
Kripal, Jeffrey J., 4–5

Lacouture, Onesimus, 175, 185, 189
Laforgue, Jules, 86–7
lamb of God imagery, 129, *129*, *130*, 134
Lanfranco, Giovanni, *Ecstasy of St Margaret of Cortona*, 81, *81*, 82
Lang, Archbishop Cosmo, 189
languages
  of Mass/Eucharist, 40, 56, 57, 58
  mixing of, 39, 67, 158
  naming, 141
Last Supper, 35, 45, 47, 48, 49, 61
Latin language, 40, 56, 57, 67, 158
Lawrence, D. H., 122–3
lay persons, 36, 50, 57–8, 68, 172–3, 176, 191
Leavis, F. R., 15–16, 109, 110, 112
Leiston Abbey, Suffolk, 179–81, *180*
Lenape people, 134–6, 139, 147

Leo XIII, Pope, 61
Lévi, Éliphas, 140
Lewis, Pericles, 7, 22, 124, 181
  'secular sacred', 22, 23, 95, 200
liberal individualism
  and Catholic corporatism, 60
  Eliot's *The Idea of a Christian Society*, 99, 101, 103, 110, 153
  retreat movement, 190, 191
  Rougemont, 151, 162
  Rousseau, 88
  Taylor, 3
Life and Letters, 144, 148
literary modernism
  introduction to, 11, 15, 18, 50, 67–8, 90
  Butts, 12
  Fletcher, 122, 123–4, 141, 162
  Flint, 122
  Hulme, 9, 11, 78, 103
  Imagism, 122–4, 136, 162
  Joyce, 11, 43, 50, 66–7
  Lawrence, 122–3
  long poem form, 34, 37, 191
  Murry, 79, 177–8
  Pound, 1, 20, 86, 122, 128, 130
  Sinclair, 10, 79–80
  see also Eliot, T. S.; epiphanies; H.D. (Hilda Doolittle); Jones, David; Woolf, Virginia
liturgical movement, 57–8
liturgical poetry, 40
liturgy
  Eliot's allusions to, 77–8, 115
  offerings, 47
  see also baptism; marriage; Mass/Eucharist
The Liturgy and Hymns of the American Province of the Unitas Fratrum, 133, 135
lived religion, 36, 50, 68, 69
  bricolage, 46, 50, 68, 139, 191, 202
long poem form, 34, 37, 191

love
  agape, 152, 154, 155, 161
  Cathars, 127–9, 152, 161
  Eliot, 170
  eros, 123, 128, 151–2
  H.D.'s *Helen in Egypt*, 158, 161
Lowder, Charles, 172
Luckhurst, Roger, 21, 114

McArthur, Murray, 86
MacCarthy, Fiona, 43
McGuire, Meredith B., 36, 50, 68
MacKay, Marina, 110
Maeterlinck, Maurice, 24
Mahmood, Saba, 10
Maiden, John G., 37
Mannheim, Karl, 102, 104
Maritain, Jacques, 41, 60, 152, 190
marriage
  in H.D.'s writing, 149, 152, 156–8, 160–1, 162
  Moravian marriages, 127, 131, 136–7
  Rougemont, 127, 152–4, 155–6, 158, 160–1, 162
martyr poems, 78, 82–5, 90, 106, 109, 115
Martz, Louis L., *The Poetry of Meditation*, 143, 196–7, 199, 201
Mary, 95, 138, 140–1
Maryfarms, 178
masculinity, 146–7, 151
Mass/Eucharist
  Church of England, tensions, 37–9
  Jones, 34–6, 39–41, 43–7, 49, 51, 55–60, 69
  languages of, 40, 56, 57, 58
  priest's role, 35, 37, 40, 45, 57, 187–8
  retreats, 180, 186, 187–8
materialism
  Freud, 144
  H.D., 123, 143
  retreat movement, 175, 178, 182
  vs spirituality, 43, 162
  Wordsworth, 11

INDEX

Mattheison, Michon M., 45
Maurin, Peter, 175, 183, 185
Maurras, Charles, 78, 99–100, 114
mediation, 12, 13, 109, 125, 127–8, 147
medievalism
  guilds, 60
  monasticism, 12, 169, 170, 171
  mysticism, 2, 83, 110, 112
  philosophy, 35, 41
  settings, 138, 139
meditation
  Eliot's poetry, 106, 142, 181, 201
  H.D.'s writing, 126, 159, 160, 201
  Imagism, 122
  Jones's poetry, 57, 65–7, 150, 201
  retreat movement, 170, 172, 173, 178
  theological/religious, 53, 150
memory, collective, 111–12, 114
Menand, Louis, 86
metaphysical poetry, 85–90, 109, 110, 199
metaphysics, 128, 138
Michel, Virgil, 57–8
militarism, 124, 151, 159, 161; see also war
Milton, John, 126, 197
mission
  Church of England, 10, 101
  Moravian Church, 131, 133, 134–6, 139
modernism
  introduction to, 3, 12, 17, 21, 22, 200
  see also antimodernism; literary modernism; theological modernism
modernist poetry
  definition, 11, 12, 191
  proto-modern religious poems, 197–8
modernist religion, definition, 68, 198
modernity
  challenges of, 6, 12, 19–20, 201
  Eliot, 111, 114, 115
  Prayer Book debate, 38
  retreat movement, 186
  and Roman Catholicism, 52, 62, 69
Rougemont, 162
monasticism
  Eliot, 101–2, 113
  medieval, 12, 169, 170, 171
  retreat movement, 170, 171, 172, 181–2
Moot, 98, 102
morals and ethics
  anonymous Christians, 98
  Arnold, 6–7, 11, 39, 199–200
  Kearney, 18, 23
  personalism, 153, 154, 162, 175, 183
  see also practical action; social action; spiritual action
Moravian Church
  blood-and-wound tradition, 133, 149–50
  in H.D.'s writing, 130–1, 133–5, 137–43, 147–50, 161
  history of, 123, 130–1, *132*, 144
  lamb of God imagery, 129, *129*, 134
  The Liturgy and Hymns of the American Province of the Unitas Fratrum, 133, 135
  missions, 131, 133, 134–6, 139
  Rougemont, 124, 126–7, 129, 133–4, 140, 152
  Seidel, Christian, 131, 134
  Sifting Time, 133, 137, 149
  Society for Propagating the Gospel, 130, *132*
  women's roles, 131, 133, 147
  Zinzendorf, 131, 136–7, 138, 148, 149, 150
Morris, Adalaide, 123
Mounier, Emmanuel, 152–3, 155, 161, 183
Moyn, Samuel, 62, 152
Murray, Paul, 107
Murry, John Middleton, 79, 177–8
Mutter, Matthew, 22–3
Myers, Frederic W. H., 5, 91, 92, 93, 103

mysticism
  introduction to, 1–5
  Cathars, 127–8
  Eliot's *Four Quartets*, 106–9, 112–14
  Eliot's *The Idea of a Christian Society*, 78, 102–5, 109–11, 113, 200
  Eliot's other writing, 77–80, 92–6, 169–70, 199
  H.D., 122–4, 135, 149, 150, 162
  Hügel's mystical element, 2, 16–17, 52–5, 58
  Jones, 1–2, 8, 9, 55, 57–8, 69
  Mounier, 153
  psychological explanations, 4, 5, 77, 81–6, 93–4, 106–7
  retreat movement, 169–71, 184–7, 191
  world religions, 18–19, 79–80, 123–4
  see also spilt mysticism
mystics and saints, 1, 4, 8, 77, 81–2, 104–5

narrative lyric poetry, 84, 157–8
neo-scholasticism, 8, 17, 47, 52, 53–4, 190, 200

occultism, 20, 21, 50, 128, 130, 137, 140
O'Connor, Fr John, 41
Oedipus Complex, 144, 145, 148, 150
Old English poetry, 46
orthodoxy *see* religious orthodoxy; wavering orthodoxy
Owen, Alex, 1, 2
Oxford Movement, 172

Parsons, William B., 4, 109, 124, 145
passion, 127–8, 152, 154–5, 161
pathology
  asceticism, 181–2, 184
  Eliot, 77, 82, 84, 87–8, 199
  H.D., 140
  Janet and Myers, 90–3, 103
  see also hysteria

penis envy, 146, 149
perennialism, 123–4, 134, 135, 162
Perl, Jeffrey M., 114
person, definition of, 152–3
personal religion
  bricolage, 49–50
  Hügel, 2, 16–17, 51, 52–5, 58, 69
personalism, 78, 151–4, 161, 162, 175, 183, 190
personality, 12, 78, 79, 87, 92
Peucker, Paul, 133, 137
Pius XI, Pope, 61, 62
Pius XII, Pope, 62
Plank, George, 126, 130
pluralism, 97, 102, 123–4; *see also* world religions
poetic consciousness, 11, 88
Pollaiuolo, Antonio and Piero del, *The Martyrdom of Saint Sebastian*, 82, 83
post-Impressionism, 35, 36, 42, 43
post-secularism, 18, 19
Pound, Ezra, 1, 20, 86, 122, 128, 130
practical action, 15, 153, 187, 188; *see also* social action
prayer, 10, 19, 40, 54, 85, 181, 183
Prayer Book *see* Book of Common Prayer
priests
  in Jones's poetry, 36, 56, 60
  replaced by therapists, 77
  role in Mass/Eucharist, 35, 37, 40, 45, 57, 187–8
  vestments, 39, 40, 43, 45
primitive religious experience, 7, 38, 122, 124, 127–8, 171
private religion *see* public or private religion
Protestantism, 6, 7, 34, 37–9, 123, 138, 185

psychology
  dissociation of sensibility, 85–9, 90, 95, 103, 192, 201
  explanations for religious phenomena, 4, 5, 77, 81–6, 93–4, 106–7
  Freudian psychoanalysis, 124, 133, 143–8, 149–50, 151, 197
  of religion, 78, 87, 97, 115, 200
  and religion, wider debate, 79–80, 86
public or private religion
  conclusion, 202
  Eliot and art, 104, 112, 113, 114, 115
  H.D., 137, 150, 151, 154, 156, 162, 201
  introduction to, 11, 15–16, 19
  Jones, 68–9
  retreat movement, 171, 189
  see also individuals, increasing focus on; institutional religion; personal religion; social context

Quakers (Religious Society of Friends), 131
quatrain poems, 78, 89–90, 94

Rahner, Karl, 97–8
Rainey, Lawrence, 124
Rashdall, Hastings, 6, 39
real presence, doctrine of, 35–6, 38, 40, 43, 45, 49, 188
realism, definitions of, 35, 41–2
Reformation, 40, 181, 198
Regnard, Paul, *Attitudes Passionnelles Extase*, 80
religion
  developmental stages of, 7, 38–9, 51, 63, 64
  redescription of, 4–6, 8–10, 20–1
  see also institutional religion; world religions
religious experience
  modernist fascination, 123–4
  response to art, 24, 42, 162
  and science, 4–7, 8–10, 20–1, 52, 58, 198–9
  science of (James), 4–6, 8, 13–14, 16, 82
  see also epiphanies; mysticism; spilt mysticism; spirituality
religious orthodoxy
  Eliot, 12, 98–9, 102–5, 115, 170
  Jones, 34, 36–7, 69
  retreat movement, 171, 186
  see also wavering orthodoxy
religious poetry
  Eliot, 76–8, 79, 197–8, 200, 202
  H.D., 143, 162, 202
  Jones's Eucharist analogy, 35–6
religious tradition see institutional religion
retreat movement, 3, 12, *174*
  Association for Promoting Retreats (APR), 170–3, 175–80, *179*, 183–9, 191
  Catholic Worker retreats, 170–1, 175–7, 178, 182–3, 185–6, 189–92, 201
revelation
  and aesthetic experience, 42, 95, 114
  Barth, 113
  Cathars, 127, 128
  Eliot, 77–8, 84, 85, 95, 106
  epiphanies as, 11
  H.D., 162
  Hügel, 52
  modernism definition, 21, 200
rhyme, 83–4, 95–6, 150, 158
Rimius, Henry, 136, 137, 149
Robichaud, Paul, 67
Robinson, Matte, 139
Roman Catholic Church
  on Cathars, 127
  Catholic Action programme, 78
  Catholic social teaching, 61, 62
  Catholic Worker retreats, 170–1, 175–7, 178, 182–3, 185–6, 189–92, 201
  church-state separation, 12
  Hügel, 16–17, 51–3

Roman Catholic Church (*Cont.*)
  Huysmans's depiction of, 181–2
  Jones and Mass, 34–6, 39–41, 43–7, 49, 51, 55–60, 69
  Jones's faith (general), 1, 34, 50
  lamb of God imagery, 130
  mystics and saints, 1, 4, 8, 77, 81–2
  Roman Missal, 40, 44
  Virgin Mary, 95, 138, 140–1
Roman Empire, 63, 65, 67
Roman Missal, 40, 44
romance, 127–8, 154, 157
romanticism, 9, 11, 20, 79, 88, 180
Rosenzweig, Franz, 15, 69, 186
Rougemont, Denis de, *Passion and Society*
  Cathars, 127–9, 138, 152, 161
  love, war and marriage, 127, 150–6, 158, 160–1, 162
  Moravian Church, 124, 126–7, 129, 133–4, 140, 152
  personalism, 151–2, 161, 162, 190
Royce, Josiah, 4, 13–16, 92, 153

Sabatier, Auguste, 7
sacraments, 38–9; *see also* baptism; marriage; Mass/Eucharist
sacramentum soldier's oath, 63, 65
sacred/secular *see* 'secular sacred'; secular/sacred interplay
sacrifice
  of Christ, 37, 38–9, 40, 45–8
  'The Sacrifice' (Herbert), 143, 196–7, 198
  self-sacrifice, 158, 161, 201
St Anthony's Village, 175–6
St Catherine of Siena, 82
St Ignatius of Loyola, *Spiritual Exercises*, 170, 172, 173, 175, 191, 201
St John of the Cross, 105, 106, 107–8, 109
St Teresa of Ávila, 79, 84–5, 170
St Winnifred's Home for Girls, Wolverhampton, 183–4

saints *see* mystics and saints
Sartre, Jean-Paul, 152
Schleiermacher, Friedrich, 7, 11
Schloesser, Stephen, 12, 41
Schmidt, Leigh Eric, 135
scholasticism, 41; *see also* neo-scholasticism
Schuchard, Ronald, 108, 110, 170
Schwartz, Adam, 20, 21, 34
science
  H.D.'s use of language, 143
  and religion, 4–7, 8–10, 20–1, 52, 58, 198–9
  of religion (James), 4–6, 8, 13–14, 16, 82
  see also pathology; psychology
Second World War, 110, 113, 152
'secular sacred', 22, 23, 95, 200
secular/sacred interplay, Eliot, 77, 78, 79, 110, 115
secularisation, 18, 22, 123, 128, 171, 190, 201
secularism, 10, 19, 20–1, 36, 150, 151, 197
Seidel, Christian, 131, 134
sensibility, dissociation of, 85–9, 90, 95, 103, 192, 201
Sergeant, Miles, 178–9
sexual love/licence, 128, 133, 137, 149–50
Shakespeare, William, 8, 10, 95, 96, 126
Shortall, Sarah, 78, 190
Sifting Time, 133, 137, 149
sign-making, 35, 45, 49, 59–61, 67, 69
significant form, 35, 41, 42, 43
silence, 170, 173, 175–7, 180, 183–8, 192
Simpson, Canon Alan H., 177
Sinclair, May, 10, 79–80
social action, 11, 54, 78, 162, 175, 176–7, 185; *see also* practical action; spiritual action
social class, 90, 101, 172–3, 188

social context
  Eliot's *The Idea of a Christian Society*, 78, 96, 98–105, 109–11, 113, 188, 200
  Eliot's other writing, 95, 105–6, 114
  H.D., 162
  marriage and family structures, 136–7, 144, 153, 158, 160–1
  Royce, 14
  social trauma, 88
social order, 78, 98, 99–100, 190
social reform, 57, 96–7, 110
Society for Propagating the Gospel, 130, 132
Society of St John the Evangelist ('Cowley Fathers'), 170
Society of the Holy Cross, 172
Society of the Sacred Mission (SSM), 101, 170, 185
sociology
  Christian sociology, 96–7, 98, 191
  of religion, 3, 50
Soud, W. David, 36, 60
Southwell, Robert, 201
Spengler, Oswald, 50, 51, 63
spilt mysticism
  introduction to, 9–11, 12, 13, 17, 19, 21
  Eliot, 78, 98, 106, 109, 199
  Jones, 36, 45
  retreat movement, 186
  Rougemont, 127–8, 161
spilt religion, 9, 11, 78
Spirit
  Holy Spirit, 14, 35, 40, 51, 134
  Moravian church, 134–5, 138
spiritual action, 177, 189–90
spiritualism, 20
spirituality
  Eliot's *Four Quartets*, 106–7, 109–10, 112
  H.D., 123, 137, 150
  Moravian Church, 129
  mysticism definition, 1–3

retreat movement, 185, 191
Wordsworth, 11
Spurr, Barry, 76, 187
Staudt, Kathleen Henderson, 35, 36
Stead, C. K., 114
Still, Colin, 95
subconsciousness, 3, 4, 92–3, 103, 146
subliminal mind
  introduction to, 4, 5, 7, 10, 11
  Eliot, 92–5, 103, 106, 112
  Myers, 91–2
subtraction stories, 10, 22, 127, 162, 191
supraliminal self, 91, 93
Surette, Leon, 21, 128–9
symbolism, 77, 94, 95–6, 108, 133, 135
syncretism, 13, 64–8

Taille, Maurice de la, 45, 47, 50, 69
Taves, Ann, 15, 17
Taylor, Charles
  'buffered self', 3, 10, 191
  immanent frame, 10, 12, 191, 192
  A Secular Age, 3, 10, 12, 22, 42, 123, 191, 192, 199
  subtraction stories, 10, 22, 127, 162, 191
Taylor, Georgina, 151
theocracy, 99, 123, 136
theodicy, 22–3, 113
theological modernism
  Anglican modernists, 6, 38–9, 185
  neo-scholasticism, 8, 17, 47, 52, 53–4, 190, 200
  Roman Catholic modernists/Tyrrell, 51, 53
  see also Hügel, Friedrich von
Tonning, Erik, 19, 21
totalitarianism, 18, 62, 99, 155
Tuve, Rosemond, 197, 198
Tylor, Edward Burnett, 128
Tyrrell, George, 51, 53

unconscious motivations, 96–8, 100, 102–3, 146, 155, 177, 197
Underhill, Evelyn, 14, 40, 94, 169, 171, 184, 187
  Mysticism, 2–3, 4–5, 7, 92

vagina imagery, 149–50
veils, 95–6, 138–9, 154
vernacular mysticism, 79–80
vestments, 39, 40, 43, 45
Vetter, Lara, 20, 126
Victorian poetry, 198–9
Villis, Tom, 61
Virgin Mary, 95, 138, 140–1
The Vision, 171, 173, 175–9, 183–7, 189, 192
visions, 140–3, 147, 162
Viswanathan, Gauri, 140
von Harnack, Adolf, 7

Wales, 66–7
war
  H.D.'s *Helen in Egypt*, 124, 151, 158, 159, 160–1
  H.D.'s *The Mystery*, 139
  Rougemont, 25, 151, 152, 154–5
  see also First World War; Second World War
Wareham, J., 186

wavering orthodoxy
  introduction to, 12, 13, 15, 17, 21, 23
  Eliot, 109, 199
  H.D., 150
  Jones, 37
  retreat movement, 186
Welsh language, 67
West, Rebecca, 10, 125–6, 127
Williams, Raymond, 35
Wolosky, Shira, 109
women
  authors, 15, 20, 151, 158
  female body, 150
  in Moravian community, 131, 133, 147
  spirituality of, 3, 20
  see also femininity; feminism
Wood, James, 19
Woolf, Virginia
  on Eliot's baptism, 114
  To the Lighthouse, 22–3
  'Modern Fiction', 11, 18, 43, 162
  women's writing, 158
Wordsworth, William, 10, 11, 162
world religions, 18–19, 49–50, 79–80, 97, 123–4

Yealey, Fr Francis Joseph, 170

Zinzendorf, Count Nikolaus Ludwig von, 131, 136–7, 138, 148, 149, 150

EU representative:
Easy Access System Europe
Mustamäe tee 50, 10621 Tallinn, Estonia
Gpsr.requests@easproject.com

www.ingramcontent.com/pod-product-compliance
Lightning Source LLC
Chambersburg PA
CBHW070344240426
43671CB00013BA/2401